STUDIES IN IMMIGRATION AND CULTURE
Royden Loewen, Series editor

SOUNDS OF *Ethnicity*

LISTENING TO GERMAN NORTH AMERICA

1850–1914

Barbara Lorenzkowski

UNIVERSITY OF MANITOBA PRESS

University of Manitoba Press
Winnipeg, Manitoba
Canada R3T 2M5
www.umanitoba.ca/uofmpress

Printed in Canada.
Text printed on Chlorine-free, 100% post-consumer recycled paper.

Cover illustration: Josée Bisaillon
Cover design: Jessica Koroscil
Interior design: Sharon Caseburg

Library and Archives Canada Cataloguing in Publication

Lorenzkowski, Barbara, 1969–
    Sounds of ethnicity : listening to German North America, 1850–1914 / Barbara Lorenzkowski.

(Studies in immigration and culture series, 1914-1459 ; 3)
Includes bibliographical references and index.
ISBN 978-0-88755-716-3 (pbk.).—ISBN 978-0-88755-188-8 (bound)

    1. German Canadians—North America—Great Lakes Region—Languages. 2. German Americans—North America—Great Lakes Region—Languages. 3. German Canadians—North America—Great Lakes Region—Music. 4. German Americans—North America—Great Lakes Region—Music. 5. German Canadians—North America—Great Lakes Region—Social life and customs. 6. German Americans—North America—Great Lakes Region—Social life and customs. I. Title. II. Series: Studies in immigration and culture 3

FC3100.G3L67 2010   971.3'00431   C2009-906719-6

The University of Manitoba Press gratefully acknowledges the financial support for its publication program provided by the Government of Canada through the Book Publishing Industry Development Program (BPIDP) and the Canada Council for the Arts, and the support of the Province of Manitoba through the Book Publishing Tax Credit, the Book Publisher Marketing Assistance Program, and the Manitoba Arts Council.

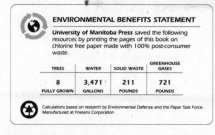

ENVIRONMENTAL BENEFITS STATEMENT

University of Manitoba Press saved the following resources by printing the pages of this book on chlorine free paper made with 100% post-consumer waste.

TREES	WATER	SOLID WASTE	GREENHOUSE GASES
8	3,471	211	721
FULLY GROWN	GALLONS	POUNDS	POUNDS

Calculations based on research by Environmental Defense and the Paper Task Force.
Manufactured at Friesens Corporation

FSC
Mixed Sources
Cert no. SW-COC-001271
© 1996 FSC

Für Steven, Sebastian und Leanna

Contents

Illustrations

The author and publisher wish to thank the following institutions and individuals for permission to reprint the illustrations and photographs in this book: Brenda Battleson, Buffalo and Erie County Public Library, Waterloo Region Museum, Library and Archives Canada, Kitchener Public Library, University of Waterloo Special Collections, and Waterloo Public Library.

Credits and Permissions

Figures 1, 6, 13–14, courtesy of University of Waterloo Special Collections. Figures 2, 5, 16–17, courtesy of Library and Archives Canada. Figure 3, from Alex Keith Johnston, *Handy Royal Atlas of Modern Geography* (Edinburgh: W. and A.K. Johnston, 1883). Figures 4, 7–12, 21–22, courtesy of Kitchener Public Library. Figures 15, 18–20, courtesy of Waterloo Public Library. Figures 23–26, Waterloo Region Museum, Waterloo, Ontario. Figures 27–28, 30, courtesy of Buffalo and Erie County Public Library. Figure 29, courtesy of Brenda Battleson.

Acknowledgements

At my grandparents' sixtieth wedding anniversary in October 1998, chairs were being pushed aside in the living room for an impromptu afternoon dance. My grandfather took out his violin—bought at the Münster flea market where he liked to hunt for instruments and used books—to play the duo for violin and piano that rang with memories of his late daughter. As I accompanied him on the piano, Steven High, who had encountered my entire German family in the past twenty-four hours and gamely conversed with them in nods and smiles, listened to a rendition more heartfelt than polished. Over the next few days, he would overhear many domestic "folk music jam sessions," as he called them. He has had to live with the sounds of ethnicity ever since.

When Chad Gaffield, my doctoral supervisor at the University of Ottawa, casually suggested looking into the history of German language schooling in Ontario, he set me onto a project that has occupied the better part of the past decade. It was Chad Gaffield who taught me to read primary sources all over again and it is a pleasure to acknowledge his influence on both my writing and my teaching. Donald Davis (University of Ottawa), Jeff Keshen (University of Ottawa), and Wolfgang Helbich (Ruhr-Universität Bochum) also acted as mentors, freely giving of their time, wit and wisdom. Colin Coates (York University), who played host to a novice instructor at the Centre of Canadian Studies at the University of Edinburgh many years ago, has always been a supportive presence, as has Royden Loewen (University of Winnipeg), whose engaging comments on my doctoral dissertation echo in the present work.

Several scholarships have aided in the completion of this work. The research and writing of this study was supported by the Ontario Graduate Scholarship Program, the Government of Canada Awards Program, a research scholarship by the Chair of German Canadian Studies at the University of Winnipeg, excellence scholarships of the University of Ottawa, and a research stipend from the Joseph Schneider Haus in Kitchener. Dedicated reference librarians at the Kitchener Public Library, the Waterloo Region Museum, the University of Waterloo Archives, the Buffalo and Erie County Public Library, to name just a few, helped locate primary sources and illustrations and guided me through the maze of finding aids. At the University of Manitoba Press, David Carr and his editorial team gently steered this project to completion. I would like to thank the two anonymous readers for their insightful critiques, and Maureen Epp for her exemplary copyediting that helped catch many inconsistencies.

As I was thinking about meanings of "home" for the nineteenth-century migrants whose stories I try to capture in these pages, I knew that my own sense of home was bound up not with places, but with people. Friends and family made Canada home, and made me feel at home once more whenever I traveled back to Germany. For this (and so much more) I am grateful to Elisabeth Bade-Lorenzkowski, Kimberly Bezaire, Carolyn Bouffard, Peter Busch, Bernd Ewers, Teresa Ewers, Diane Foltinek, Carolyn and Gerry High, Lauren Jeffs, Sonja Kretzschmar, Stefan Lorenzkowski, Petra Manzke, Jo-Anne McCutcheon, Hanna Mühlenhoff, and Garth Williams.

Just as the songs I hum to my children carry memories of my own grandparents, so too have meanings of language assumed a poignancy I could not have predicted when I first embarked upon this work. My parents, Bärbel and Josef Lorenzkowski, found themselves prevented from reading this work-in-the-making, for it was written in English, not German. Yet, they lovingly requested oral updates, and treated the distance between Germany and Canada as if it was a train-ride long only, flying across the Atlantic year after year.

Our son Sebastian was born when the dissertation, from which this book is derived, had just been completed. The adventure of parenthood delayed the revision of the manuscript (of course, I would not have had it any other way). Listening to Sebastian mixing German and English words and phrases, and catching myself immersing him in the world of German books, music and stories, made me understand a bit better the efforts of nineteenth-century ethnic gatekeepers to attain "language purity." Our daughter Leanna speaks with her eyes and her smiles. Her musical tastes run towards nursery songs and the Wiggles, and her sunrise smiles are the "best ever," to quote her older brother.

Steven High has lived with this book in its various incarnations for almost as long as I have. To see this study, finally, in print will be a source of great relief to him (he threatened to march the manuscript to the post office himself and I barely beat him to it). Here is to past and future journeys, Steven. Thanks for being you.

SOUNDS OF ETHNICITY

Introduction

*I*f we want to understand what language meant to the men and women who inhabited the worlds of German North America, we can turn to the diary of young Louis Jacob Breithaupt, who lived in the town of Berlin, Waterloo County, the heartland of German settlement in nineteenth-century Ontario. The letters on the page are fading, yet still convey a boyish exuberance. "Today," Louis scribbled into his diary on 21 March 1867, "I received a beautiful picture from Mr. Wittig [the German teacher at school] because I read from page 120 to 215 in the German reader. I'm good."[1] In being able to decipher the Gothic print of his German reader, the twelve-year-old boy enjoyed a distinct advantage. His family cultivated German as the language of the home, corresponded with friends in the old homeland, and treasured family heirlooms from Germany.[2] To the classroom, Louis brought not only a ready command of oral and written German but also a familiarity with German culture and lore that helped him unravel the cultural connotations of the lessons. For the young boy who penned his childhood diaries in German—even if his style was, at times, uneven and the grammar faulty—the school lessons in German must have presented little of a challenge.[3] Louis and his younger siblings regularly headed the honour roll of the German Department of Berlin's public school.[4]

Louis Breithaupt, childhood photograph. COURTESY OF UNIVERSITY OF WATERLOO SPECIAL COLLECTIONS, DORIS LEWIS RARE BOOK ROOM, BREITHAUPT HEWETSON CLARK COLLECTION, BHC 53.

"By the grace of God I turned 14 today," young Louis Breithaupt wrote in 1869. "I got a cup, a small book, a scarf, a horn book made with 6 pages for the 6 afternoons (Sunday excluded), ½ a dozen neck ties, a ruler, nuts from C&C, 24 cents from Grandmother (H.)."

Like his diary, Louis's world encompassed both the German and the English. In January 1872, the seventeen-year-old began to write in his diary in English, only to switch back to his mother tongue between August 1875 and August 1876. Henceforth, he alternated between the German and the English languages, but found the latter wanting in times of despair. When his father died prematurely in the summer of 1880, Louis expressed his devastation in German. He wrote the remainder of his diary that year in his mother tongue, as if to preserve a tangible bond with his late father.[5] If the German language had hitherto represented a world of childhood, it now transformed into an emotive bridge to the past. Two decades later, Louis Breithaupt would imbue the German language with yet another meaning as he spearheaded a successful renaissance of German language teaching in Berlin's public schools, in the process upholding his mother tongue as a symbol of ethnic and cultural values. As the nineteenth century drew to a close, he ever more self-consciously spoke in the language of nationalism, paying tribute to German Emperor Wilhelm I in both word and deed and infusing his accounts of the county's popular singers' festivals with nationalist overtones.

The meanings of language that resonate in Louis's diary point to the intricate ways in which a sense of cultural identity was embedded and expressed in practices of language use. They remind us of the ease with which Waterloo County residents switched from one local idiom to the other, the richness of emotions invested in the mother tongue, and the creativity with which German Canadians embraced "their" German language—be it the High German that the grown Louis Breithaupt would champion or the "local German" that many Waterloo County residents spoke. Entering the mental worlds evoked in his diary, we encounter the sounds of spoken language—as echoed in the childhood diction of young Louis— and the language of music that drew together German celebrants and Anglo-Saxon audiences at the county's festivals of German song.

This book is an account of the sounds of German ethnicity in the borderland region of the Great Lakes. It listens to the popular musical life that flourished in both Canada and the United States between 1850 and 1914, and strains to hear the languages spoken in German North America. To listen to the "heard worlds" of German North America means probing beneath the common refrain of language as a cultural bond that an ethnic group abandons at its own peril, to become attuned to language experiments and linguistic interactions that unfolded in a myriad of daily interactions.[6] It means paying as much attention to the rhythms of informal, spontaneous, spoken language and the meanings that resonated in popular music-making as to the words intoned by a self-styled ethnic leadership that linked language so closely to ethnic identity that one seemed to rise and fall with the other. It means examining musical performances not as an "echo" of ethnicity (as ethnic gatekeepers were fond of proclaiming) but as an occasion to sound out the shape of this ethnicity.

In a seminal essay, the anthropologist Frederick Barth directed attention to the *boundary* as the defining characteristic of ethnic groups. What gave meaning to an ethnic identity, he wrote over five decades ago, was not "the cultural stuff" enclosed by ethnic boundaries, but the fact of "ethnic boundary maintenance" itself. While the cultural meanings of ethnicity were subject to historical change, ethnic groups would continue to exist as such as long as they maintained markers of cultural difference, namely, a boundary between "us" and "them."[7] The concept of ethnic group boundaries appealed to historians for several reasons: it supplanted earlier notions of ethnicity as primordial; it cast migrants as dynamic actors who negotiated ethnic boundaries with the "dominant ethnoculture" rather than acquiescing to forces of assimilation; and it allowed for conflict and cooperation, invention and adaptation, thus according nicely with an understanding of ethnicity as a social and cultural construction.[8] As more and more historians donned "constructivist" lenses, they discovered anew the "cultural stuff" of ethnicity—not, as Kathleen Neils Conzen points out, as an essentialized or homogenized cultural "baggage" that migrants carried with them from the Old World to the New, but rather as understood "in a Geertzian sense as the socially produced structures of meanings engendered by and expressed in public behaviors, languages, images, institutions."[9]

This work examines the webs of meaning out of which German migrants in North America spun an ethnic consciousness. But it is interested less in a study of migrants as a bounded social entity—the ethnic *group*—as it is in the *practice* of enacting ethnicity.[10] As Rogers Brubaker writes with characteristic verve, we should dare to study "ethnicity without groups." Instead of conceiving of ethnicity in terms of belonging (which presupposes a bounded social group) we should treat ethnicity "as an *event*, as something that 'happens.'" Just as music comes alive in the moment of performance, so, too, is ethnicity expressed in the performance of "everyday encounters, practical categories, commonsense knowledge, cultural idioms, cognitive schemas, interactional cues, discursive frames, organizational routines, social networks, and institutional forms."[11]

In asking why—and how and when—people "do" ethnicity (or refrain from enacting it), Brubaker offers a fresh take on ethnicity as a category of historical analysis. Most importantly, perhaps, for the present work, he invites us to study "the politics of categories, both from above and from below." By analyzing how a certain category—such as German ethnicity—becomes invested with meaning, we can arrive at a greater appreciation of the actions of both "ethnopolitical entrepreneurs," who filled reams of newsprint with their often eloquent, sometimes biting calls for "ethnic loyalty," and the rank and file "German" migrants who either listened or turned a deaf ear to their appeals. As this book contends, the sounds of German ethnicity arose both from the speechifying of ethnic elites (who, "by *invoking* groups," sought "to *evoke* them") and those labelled "German" who, more quietly so, did "appropriate, internalize, subvert, evade or transform the categories imposed on them."[12] Theirs was a story not of loss and ethnic decline where "ethnic boundaries" gradually eroded, but a story of cultural creativity that was written by both words and actions.[13] This story did not necessarily unfold in linear terms. As Brubaker notes, "'groupness' can 'crystallize' in some situations while remaining latent and merely potential in others." At other times still, even large-scale performances of "groupness" held very different meanings for ethnic gatekeepers who—as editors of German-language newspapers, as founders and guardians of German-language schools, and organizers of singing festivals—had a vested interest in "group-making," and those whose actions left a far fainter echo in the historical record.[14]

To uncover the workings of everyday ethnicity, this book turns to the history of sound, a field of historical inquiry that has only recently come of age. It explores the meanings contemporaries attached to the "keynote" sounds of German ethnicity and asks, as Mark Smith, a social historian at the vanguard of aural history puts it, why historical actors "listened to actual and represented sounds in particular ways, and how listening shaped their understanding of themselves and their societies."[15] "Hearing is a way of touching at a distance," the Canadian composer and theorist R. Murray Schafer writes, and there is, indeed, an immediacy about sound—both the sound that delights and the sound that affronts—that resonated with contemporaries who listened to the "keynotes" of German ethnicity in the six decades prior to World War I.[16]

Before the war silenced German speech and music in the public realm, a self-declared ethnic leadership had raised its voice to extol the beauty and importance of the German mother tongue and introduce German-language instruction into the school curriculum of public Canadian and American schools. Meanwhile, the sounds of German folk music that emanated from the popular "singers' festivals"

(*Sängerfeste*) rang through towns and cities across the American Midwest, along the northeastern seaboards, and throughout the Great Lakes Region. As English-language commentators noted bemusedly at the 1860 singers' festival in Buffalo, the "snatches of song" that tumbled into the streets from private homes and the melodies that "floated far and sweetly" into the night infused the urban sound-scape, making it "thoroughly ... Germanized."[17] Sound demarcated space, but also transformed it. While marking difference, it allowed for a wide range of cultural exchanges. And despite its fleeting nature, it helped create an ethnic conscious-ness—forged in the acts of speaking and music-making—that would alter the soundtrack of public culture itself.

As an exercise in historical eavesdropping, this study charts new social spaces—created in the moment of musical performance or in the fleeting act of speaking a hybrid German-English tongue—in which to explore how ethnicity "happens." While this study is more closely attuned to acts of speaking and prac-tices of music-making than to the role of non-vocal sounds (the preferred domain of aural historians), it has been inspired by the questions aural historians pose and the methodologies they employ.[18] Accordingly, this book examines the cul-tural exchanges through which sounds were being produced and heard, the role of aural metaphors in the soundscapes of German North America, the meanings of historical silences, and the sounds of dissonance.

To argue the power of the aural is not to deny the importance of the visual.[19] In 1871, when German migrants in both Canada and the United States celebrated Germany's unification in lavish parades that wound their way through city streets and market squares, it was the sight of the colourful floats—not the sound of nationalist oratory or German song—that dazzled contemporary observers. The festivals of German song also provided an opportunity to record both the sounds and sights of German ethnicity. While marvelling at the "majestic" perfor-mances of the male mass choruses, which blended the voices of singing societies in an audible symbol of German unity, English-language commentators described "stout" and "sturdy" German singers whose faces were graced by "black, sandy and bushy moustaches," or waxed eloquent about the local "Teutons" who hosted the festivities: "the women strong and domestic looking, the men with their rosy faces and light clothing looking as though they had stepped out of one of the pictures of German artists."[20]

But while moustaches could be shaved and traditional costume exchanged for more fashionable clothing, accents were far harder to mask. "Your accent carries

Singers' festival in Berlin, Waterloo County, 1875. *Canadian Illustrated News*, September 1875. COURTESY OF LIBRARY AND ARCHIVES CANADA, C-062855.

the story of who you are," literary scholar Doris Sommer notes, and it was their distinctive accent, their use of German syntactic structures that carried over into English, their unfamiliarity with English idioms, or even just a slightly different rhythm of speech or intonation that marked German migrants as different, at times to their great dismay.[21] To be identified as German, migrants did not have to speak the German language. It was enough if they sounded German in their accents, their sentiments, and their sensibilities.[22] The sounds of ethnicity carried a story that revealed itself in daily, casual interactions, fleeting perhaps, but also inescapable.[23]

The sounds of ethnicity that reverberated in the Great Lakes Region acted as both site and symbol. As a symbol, sound produced stories about ethnicity. What was deemed noteworthy by the self-declared guardians of the German language was the word that affronted. To grasp the emotions—and indeed, the real anguish—that imbued their writings, we have to understand how deeply ethnic gatekeepers felt the connection between language, culture, and identity. Language to them was not simply a tool of communication, but—in a tradition of thought pioneered by the German philosopher Johann Gottfried von Herder—was seen as playing a constitutive role in the formation of cultural identities.[24] To acquire a language meant "becoming incorporated into a linguistic and cultural community."[25] To speak it revealed a consciousness of community. To ethnic leaders, the act of speaking (or singing) the German mother tongue anchored fellow migrants reassuringly in a soundscape of German ethnicity. The spoken word assumed even greater importance if language was construed as a tangible, audible homeland—a space liberated from place and translated into sound.[26]

If sound was a symbol, it was also a site of historical experiences. Throughout the late nineteenth and early twentieth centuries, German ethnic leaders bemoaned the noise of popular culture that threatened to drown out German folk melodies and complained of the alien sounds that had crept into the speech patterns of German migrants. But in these hybrid sounds echoed an alternative conceptualization of German North America—one where German migrants made a home for themselves in the two languages in which they lived their lives. The duality of their worlds resonated in the hybrid tongue they spoke. Their speech acts told of lives that were shaped in a series of exchanges and, for the most part, deaf to the calls for language purity that ethnic gatekeepers sounded.

In their roles as educators, ministers, and journalists, ethnic gatekeepers had, of course, a vested interest in making a home for the German language in North America. But it was precisely their indictment of what they heard as ominous cacophony that helped preserve an oral culture in print. It was because they cared so passionately about matters of both language and sound that they admonished, berated, and scolded their fellow ethnics—and in the process, brought to the fore acts of speaking and practices of music-making that otherwise would have remained inaudible. The sounds of German North America thus reach us through the "elite ears" of ethnic gatekeepers who sought to invest the aural markers of ethnic identity with meanings of respectability and modernity.[27]

The sounds of German ethnicity that carried meanings of refinement and respectability resonated with middle-class Canada and America.[28] At the singers' festivals, the heard worlds of German North America were warmly applauded by Anglo-Saxon audiences, who listened to the keynotes of German ethnicity in concert halls, city streets, and market squares, and vicariously through the medium of print, and commented approvingly on the appealing sounds of leisure and orderly amusement. Some joined in the chorus of German voices either as musicians on stage or as celebrants in picnic groves. Others listened bemusedly, enthusiastically, or indifferently, but rarely with hostility, for the sounds of music softened the bluntness of German nationalist oratory. It was in the sounds of shared music-making that German and Anglo-Saxon musicians and audiences began to forge a musical public that bridged cultural difference rather than accentuating it. German conductors crafted an identity as professional musicians equally at home in the worlds of exuberant German festivity and public musical life. Meanwhile, German singers and celebrants fashioned their own areas of cultural exchange by crossing the border to visit each other's festivals in the Great Lakes Region. If making music helped build bridges across the border, national discourses echoed in the aural stereotypes of the brash (German) American and the friendly (German) Canadian. The loud, confident "Yankees," who sought to excel in everything, as a German-Canadian newspaper described visiting German-American singers tongue-in-cheek in 1874, contrasted markedly with "Canada's Germans," who were cheerful and polite.[29]

To hear German ethnicity in the making, I have turned to two German communities whose soundscapes provide a study in contrasts: the rural quietude of nineteenth-century Waterloo County, Ontario, versus the hum and bustle of industrializing Buffalo, New York. But both communities formed part of a larger, interacting region in which ties of family, ethnicity, and religion spanned

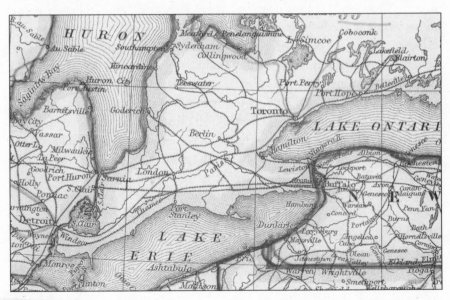

Map of Southern Ontario, 1883. FROM ALEX KEITH JOHNSTON, *HANDY ROYAL ATLAS OF MODERN GEOGRAPHY* (EDINBURGH: W. AND A.K. JOHNSTON, 1883).

the border, and border crossings represented the rule, not the exception. If we turn once more to the pages of Louis Breithaupt's diary we encounter a border transcended by the networks of family and community. Regularly, Louis and his family visited family and friends in Buffalo. They in turn hosted relatives from Buffalo and Detroit for weeks at a time. In search of education, Louis's siblings crossed the border to study in Buffalo, Chicago, and Naperville, Illinois. Business trips brought Liborious Breithaupt and later his sons to Buffalo, New York City, Rochester, and Chicago. Louis's brother William remained in the United States for almost two decades, during which he worked as a civil engineer in Pittsburgh, Chicago, St. Louis, Kansas City, and New York City before returning to Waterloo County in 1910. In the realm of religion, as well, ethnic ties reached across the border. The Zion Evangelical Church of Berlin—the spiritual home of the Breithaupt family—established close ties with the New York Conference of the Evangelical Association and frequently welcomed itinerant preachers from Buffalo.[30]

The Canadian-American borderland in which the lives of Louis Breithaupt and his family unfolded has attracted far less scholarly attention than its American-Mexican counterpart.[31] Scholars have conducted innovative cross-cultural work by tracing the historical trajectories of Mennonite and German-speaking migrants in both Canada and the United States.[32] They have also examined the cross-border movements of Canadians into the United States.[33] Only rarely, though, have they explored the making of transnational spaces in the Canadian-American borderland.[34] This book stakes out a middle ground and listens to the "heard worlds" of German North America at two different scales.[35] At one level, it offers a comparative study of two localities; for a sense of place did matter in the construction of German cultural identities, as did the national contexts in which stories of ethnicity were being told. But this study also lingers in transnational spaces in order to hear the sounds of German ethnicity.[36] In the medium of print and through the more immediate social encounters at singers' festivals, actors and audiences were lifted out of local and national worlds to listen to sounds of self and other. These sounds drew German migrants into shared "social fields" in which they debated and enacted what it meant to be "German," "Canadian," and "American."[37] From their transnational ties and social and cultural transactions arose the soundscapes of German North America that were inflected but not bounded by national borders.[38]

Located in the gently rolling hills of southern Ontario, the German settlements of Waterloo County shared many characteristics with the surrounding British

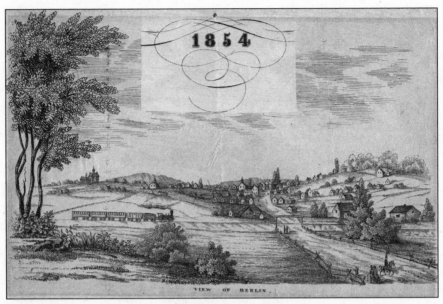

Black and white engraving of view of Berlin, Ontario, 1854. COURTESY OF KITCHENER
PUBLIC LIBRARY, WATERLOO HISTORICAL SOCIETY, P-006054.

counties in the later decades of the nineteenth century. Theirs was a rural world
whose residents pursued agricultural activities or worked in the modestly sized
factories of the county seat, Berlin, or in the emerging factory villages and towns
of Hespeler and Preston. But the rhythms of everyday life had a distinctly German
twist. Settled by Pennsylvania Mennonites in the early nineteenth century, the area
later attracted Catholics from Germany and Alsace, who worked as day labourers
on Mennonite farms until they could afford their own parcels of land.[39] Drawn to
this centre of German language and culture, and swayed by the availability of land
that was of a better quality than that of the American Midwest, migrants from central and northern Germany arrived in the 1850s. As land became scarce, German
migration spilled over into the neighbouring counties: Perth and Huron Counties
toward the east, Grey and Bruce Counties toward the north, and Renfrew County
in the Ottawa Valley. But it was Waterloo County that remained synonymous with
"German" in the public mind.[40] Here, marvelled a young Scottish Presbyterian
minister who wandered the streets of Berlin in 1871, "you heard scarcely anything
spoken in the streets but German. It was necessary for anyone living here to speak
both languages."[41] In 1871, 55 percent of Waterloo County's 40,252 residents were
of German cultural origin. This figure climbed to 73 percent in the county seat,

Berlin.[42] Waterloo County thus represented a prime example of what historian Kathleen Neils Conzen calls "the localization of an immigrant culture." Rather than assimilating into the host society, German settlers moulded "the institutions and culture of the local world itself," embedding German language and culture into the very structures of local community.[43]

If Waterloo County's local world was German, the city of Buffalo across the border constituted "an American pluralism."[44] In the 1840s, Buffalo's East Side, a flat meadowland bounded by thick forests, became the nucleus of the city's *Deutschendörfchen* (German village). Located far from the docks but within walking distance from the central business district, the area allowed for urban farming

View of Buffalo, New York, 1853. COURTESY OF LIBRARY AND ARCHIVES CANADA, C-046096.

while the nearby forest provided for building material, fuel, and employment in the lumber industry. As such, the East Side attracted migrants from the southern German states, most of whom were farmers and peasants.[45] Crop failures and the famine of 1817 had triggered a wave of emigration from southern Germany that was further fuelled by population growth and the custom of dividing landholdings equally among inheriting children, thereby breaking up land into ever-smaller parcels. The decline of cottage industries, which crumbled in the face of mechanized competition, also contributed to the intensity of emigration.[46] In 1839, migrants from southern Germany were joined by eight hundred "Old Lutherans"—orthodox Protestants from the northern states of Saxony, Silesia,

Brandenburg, and Pomerania who had endured harassment for their religious beliefs. They too settled in Buffalo's vast East Side where land was comparatively cheap and pigs and cattle could graze on nearby fields.[47]

The presence of Lutherans, southern German Catholics, and Alsatians in Buffalo led to the establishment of migration chains that contributed to a radical population change. In 1855, Americans found themselves reduced to 25 percent of the population. Among the city's 70,000 residents, 39 percent of household heads had been born in the German states, 5 percent in France (the majority of them German-speaking Alsatians), 18 percent in Ireland and 12 percent in Canada or the British Isles.[48] Within the stream of German migration, the rough balance between German Protestants and Catholics had toppled in favour of the latter. In 1855, migrants from the southern and Rhenish provinces constituted the majority of Buffalo's Germans. As historian David Gerber remarks, the city "had more Bavarians than any other American city, and more southern Germans than such equally significant centres as St. Louis, Chicago and New York." Deeply divided along denominational lines, German-speaking migrants tended to marry within their own religion and region of origin.[49]

Clustered in wards 4, 5, 6, and 7, German migrants exhibited a high degree of institutional completeness. They populated a "village" complete with several German-language newspapers, churches, social organizations, cultural clubs, three militia companies, and six volunteer fire brigades. Although largely absent from the white-collar and professional occupations, by 1855 they dominated the crafts, comprising 70 percent of brick masons, coopers, and shoemakers, and 60 percent of cabinetmakers, tailors, butchers, and ironworkers. Levels of property ownership also reflected the sound material foundations of Buffalo's German-speaking population. In 1855, 40 percent of the Germans owned real estate, compared to 43 percent of Anglo-Americans and 23 percent of the Irish.[50] Duly impressed by German respectability, one of the city's short-lived English-language journals, *Democracy*, found among them "cultivated, intellectual minds, scientific and philosophical geniuses" and foretold rich rewards to anyone "fortunate enough to break through the barriers which surround them."[51] Only five years later, on the eve of the Civil War, the sounds of German leisure and musical life would break through the barriers surrounding ethnicity as awed English-language commentators heard the city's inaugural singers' festival of 1860 as a "musical earthquake" that would permanently transform the urban soundscape.[52]

The opening chapter examines the "unbounded" German language spoken in German North America—a language that borrowed freely from both English and German and defied dictates of linguistic purity.[53] Echoes of the spoken word reach us through the caustic writings of ethnic gatekeepers on both sides of the Canadian-American border, but also through the annual reports of school inspectors who listened closely to the reading and literacy skills of local children and youth. Located at the intersection of the local and the national, the German-language classroom in public schools thrust Waterloo County's localized ethnicity into the public eye and provoked public conversations on the meanings of the German language. The local drama that unfolded—with an unexpected twist in the early twentieth century—is captured in Chapter 2. Chapter 3 listens to the writings and aspirations of German-American pedagogues whose efforts to introduce German language instruction into the public school curriculum were transformed into a quest to reform the language of pedagogy itself. The "grammar translation" method that had been pioneered in the teaching of Latin and Greek was to be replaced by the child-centred, "direct" method of modern language teaching that immersed children in the sounds of the German language.

In turning from "Language Matters" to "Sound Matters," the next four chapters listen to practices of music-making as they revolved around tunes of community, soundscapes of identity, and eventually, the making of a musical public. Chapter 4 revisits the Buffalo singers' festival of 1860 that brought together singers from a far-flung network of German singing societies. The festival of German song and sound served as a forum of communication from which community could arise. The German-language press then carried tales from the singers' festival to German North America, where audiences listened vicariously to the keynotes of a German ethnicity that rang with song and sociability, community and *Gemütlichkeit*, but did not yet self-consciously intend to alter the soundtrack of American culture itself.

It was in the jubilant celebrations of Germany's victory over France in 1871— euphemistically called "peace jubilees"—that German cultural leaders embraced the language of nationalism. But the border did matter in the construction of ethnic identities, as Chapter 5 reveals. Even in their festive exuberance, German-American leaders could never quite shed their defensive tone and felt it necessary to justify the validity of cultural difference. In Canada, a self-confidence permeated the oratory of German-Canadian leaders. Never did they seem to feel threatened by the cult of Anglo-Saxon superiority that enveloped Ontario in the closing decades of the nineteenth-century, for were they not the proud descendants of the "Saxon" who formed the other half of the "Anglo" soul?

The peace jubilees of 1871 provided the spark for the eight singers' festivals that Waterloo County's German residents would celebrate between 1874 and 1912. Chapter 6 identifies four keynotes of German ethnicity that were woven into the aural fabric of the singers' festivals. Lovers of classical music heard in the singers' festivals the tantalizing possibility of a home-grown musical culture that would bring the art of music "which is said to be so characteristic of the Germans in Germany" to Canada.[54] Ethnic gatekeepers, in turn, imbued the musical celebrations with a romantic nationalism that culminated in the erection of a monument of Emperor Wilhelm I at the 1897 festival. But just as the cadences of everyday speech bore little resemblance to the "glorious" German mother tongue that ethnic gatekeepers liked to conjure, so too did the keynote of German ethnicity that resonated most clearly at the popular singers' festivals evoke an earthy melody that spoke of frolic and fun rather than ethnic aspirations. A transnational soundscape—cast in a continental, not transatlantic mould—represented the fourth keynote of the singers' festivals.

Across the border in Buffalo, German-American leaders sounded a ringing call for ethnic regeneration in the late nineteenth century, admonishing German migrants to embrace German values and traditions as they resonated in the mystic world of German folk music. Notwithstanding the invocation of "the folk," sounds of dissonance reverberated through German Buffalo, coalescing around conflicts of class, age, and musical taste. When the singers' festival of 1901 coincided with Buffalo's Pan-American Exposition, German singers and visitors from out of town escaped the stilted atmosphere of the concert hall—with its expectation of "polite" listening—to congregate at the more convivial venue of "Alt-Nürnberg," a "medieval" village on the exhibition grounds. Here, they listened to the drum of popular culture whose melodies, more often than not, had been crafted by second-generation German-American musicians.[55] Meanwhile, Buffalo's "wealthy and fashionable people" headed to the concerts in the armoury, where a formerly "ethnic" celebration had transformed into a cultural, "public" event.[56]

Simply put, to listen to the sounds of ethnicity in German North America allows us to eavesdrop on public conversations on ethnicity and modernity, community and nation, public culture and transnationalism. In sound, the worlds of "German North America" and "North America" mingled. The story German migrants intoned was one not of cultural purity, but of cultural fusion—a symphony of overlapping, harmonious, cacophonous sounds and melodies that gave meaning to the epic story of migration and the way German migrants made a home for themselves in North America.

Part 1

Language Matters

1.

Territories of Translation
Language and Identity in the Popular Press

*G*iven the ephemeral nature of sound, how can we hope to uncover its history? In her study of the meanings and politics of speech in early New England, historian Jane Kamensky writes how "spoken utterances from the seventeenth century survive only in written form," reaching our ears through the dual filters of memory and writing. When "white, literate, enfranchised, Puritan men" commented on acts of speaking, Kamensky writes, their own voices inflected the words of those whom they had overheard. Recorded by pen and paper, these speech acts were further stripped bare of the "use of interruptions, angry tones, or supplicant inflections" and indeed, of the speaker's body language, thus being silenced even in the act of preservation. Many conversations never entered the written record, since New England's guardians of proper speech were prone to turn their ear to "spoken exchanges that stood out in some way from the seamless fabric of daily talk." It was the "deviant or 'heated' word," not the casual remark that prompted contemporary commentary. Historians of speech thus have to sift through and make sense of what Kamensky wryly calls "a rather motley assortment of thirdhand conversational fragments."[1] Although an oral culture did survive in print, it did so in fragmented, silenced form.

This chapter listens to the rich oral culture of German North America, as it has been preserved in the pages of Waterloo County's premier German newspaper, the *Berliner Journal*. The first issue of the *Berliner Journal* was not much to look at. Published on 29 December 1859, it was twenty-six inches high by twenty inches wide and offered four pages of small and fuzzy print. It promised, in ever-widening circles, coverage of Waterloo County, the Province of Ontario, Canada ("our adopted Fatherland"), and the United States, but also dedicated itself to chronicling events in "our old homeland." Its weekly fare found ready takers; the paper's circulation rose from a modest 1,000 in 1863 to 2,200 in 1893. Hereafter, the editors blithely claimed to have the largest number of readers of any German newspaper in Canada.[2] Yet if the *Journal*'s scope expanded, making it the sole German-language newspaper in southwestern Ontario by the early twentieth century, its goal remained the same—to make a home for the German language in Canada.[3]

For close to six decades, the battle cry to preserve, protect, and maintain the German mother tongue rang throughout the pages of the *Berliner Journal*. The tone of its appeals was unabashedly didactic, celebratory, and conservative. The cultural project, however, that the paper embraced was an explicitly modern one. In its readers' minds, it generated a transnational space that defied political boundaries.[4] The German homeland of language and culture, as evoked in the paper's columns, transcended the Canadian-American border and stretched as far as Germany itself. In navigating two languages and three cultures, the *Berliner Journal* assumed the role of a translator so typical of North America's immigrant press.[5] The paper attempted to locate its readers firmly in a German universe by exposing them to the grandeur of German rivers and forests, the beauty of German culture and folk customs, and the ascent of the powerful German Empire. To this end, the editors reprinted news items verbatim from German sources and filled the paper's columns with texts imported from Germany. The *Journal*'s ornamental Gothic script and German language also marked it as "German," representing a visual and linguistic link with the German homelands across the Atlantic.[6] Other materials that filled the paper's columns were culled from the English-Canadian press. Before the completion of the transatlantic cable in 1866, the paper's founders, John Motz and Friedrich Rittinger, pored over English-language newspapers to garner information on provincial, national, and international events to be translated into the German. The act of translation—facilitated by the absence of copyright laws—also entailed eliminating the "sensationalism" of the English-language press (which, according to the editors, "the average German could only poorly digest"), expanding coverage on German affairs, and making meaningful the workings and nuances of Canadian politics and government.[7]

Berliner Journal, 26 December 1981. COURTESY OF UNIVERSITY OF WATERLOO SPECIAL COLLECTIONS, DORIS LEWIS RARE BOOK ROOM.

The most popular textual source, however, from which the *Berliner Journal* liberally drew was the rich print culture of German America. Even after he had withdrawn from his position as editor, the elderly John Motz regularly stopped by the office to mine the German-American dailies—the so-called exchange papers (*Wechselblätter*)—for the telling anecdote or colourful report that German-Canadian readers might enjoy. It was not unusual to encounter a long reprint from the *Texas Vorwärts* that was "Canadianized" only by the laconic comment that "the article above also applies to Canada."[8] More typically, the editors merely acknowledged an article's provenance or left readers to deduce from the copious references to "Amerika" that the author of this particular piece resided in the nation south to the border. Close to two-thirds of the "language lessons" that the *Berliner Journal* published between 1860 and 1914 in order to generate pride in the German mother tongue had previously been published in German-American newspapers, thus making Waterloo County part of a discursive universe that spanned the eastern seaboards and the American Midwest.[9]

The well-honed rhetoric of "language loss" and "ethnic decline" that permeated the columns of the *Berliner Journal* is revealing for the glimpses it provides into the dynamics of language and identity. The paper commented on practices of language use and provided incisive, if scathing, observations on the linguistic interactions that seemed to threaten the very integrity of the German mother tongue. Finely attuned to instances of code-switching and to the emergence of a mixed German-English language, writers documented language change at the grassroots level, and pointed—with barely concealed disgust—to phonetic, lexical, and grammatical language experiments. Impartial observers, evidently, they were not. Deeply involved in ethnic politics, campaigns for German-language schooling, and celebrations of ethnicity, ethnic leaders possessed a vested interest in making the German language (and by extension, they reasoned, German culture) a permanent feature in Canadian and American life. Where scholars today can rely on written memoirs, oral history interviews, and census data in examining patterns of language change, the language dynamics of generations past reach us fractured through the lenses of ethnic leaders who feared for the "survival" of the ethnic group.[10] Yet if we peel away the thick layers of mockery that characterized their writings, we encounter astute observers of language change who intuitively arrived at many of the conclusions that socio-linguists and literary scholars would formulate over a century later.

In their writings, German editors and journalists sought to transform the family into a bastion of the German mother tongue from which all other languages were strictly barred, thereby advocating what socio-linguists call "domain separation" as the key to successful bilingualism.[11] Ethnic leaders also aspired to nurture children's German reading and writing skills in order to permit "intellectual growth" in the mother tongue and further the participation of youth in the ethnic community.[12] Finally, they recorded—with much indignation—the linguistic transactions between the German mother tongue and the English language out of which sprang, they argued, an "impure" and defective language. Recent migrants from Germany, in particular, who assumed editorial positions in North America "were shocked by the strange mixtures of German and English vocabulary which they encountered in the newspaper vernacular of the German-American press" and attempted "to stem the practice of introducing more and more 'German-Americanisms,'" as Carl Wittke notes in his account, *The German-Language Press in America*.[13]

Literary scholars have similarly pointed to the emergence of a "Germerican" in the late nineteenth century. But they cast the hybrid tongues that resulted from such linguistic and cultural negotiations in a positive light, namely as an expression of cultural creativity that embodied the "double consciousness" of migrants who navigated two cultural worlds.[14] As socio-linguist Joshua Fishman contends, to separate the ethnic mother tongue from the linguistic and cultural streams that swirl around it runs counter to "the fluidity of modern democratic speech communities in which there is such frequent change from one role to the other."[15] In exploring the close affinities of ethnicity and modernity, Werner Sollors as well celebrates the "'impure' language elements of code-switching and the bilingual pun" as expressions of cultural innovation that "foreshadow aspects of our own transnational period" in their disregard for cultural and national boundaries.[16] To listen to the musings on language in the pages of the *Berliner Journal*, then, means taking seriously the linguistic visions and values that German community leaders harboured on both sides of the Canadian-American border. Although their dreams of ethnic unity and linguistic purity would prove elusive, more often than not, their attempts to make the German language an integral part of the aural, literary, and intellectual fabric of mainstream society rescued the very language practices they criticized from historical oblivion. It is ironic that these advocates of language purity documented, albeit inadvertently, the cultural creativity with which German-speaking migrants forged new languages out of the German and English texture of their lives.

SOUNDS OF HOME

In the mid-nineteenth century, language theory advanced a new conception of language. No longer did philologists consider language to be a human construct that could be moulded to serve political principles. Instead, they emphasized the primordial nature of national languages, which they regarded as the very essence of human identity."[17] Such mystical notions of language and identity flowed directly from German Romanticism—of which Johann Gottfried von Herder (1744–1803) was the prophet—which located a nation's soul or character (*Volksgeist*) not in the high cultures of the elites but in a multitude of folk traditions: worship and poetry, dances and hunts, rituals and folk songs, myths and memories, and, foremost among these, language. In 1772, Herder had published his first major philosophical work, the *Treatise On the Origin of Language*, for which he was awarded the coveted prize of the Berlin Academy of Science. In his book, Herder rejected prevailing views of language as the creation of God or the product of human reason and argued that human beings were "fundamentally social and linguistic beings." It was through language, he wrote, that people made sense of the world around them. It was in language that they ordered their thoughts and expressed their views.[18] As a result, language shaped its speakers as much as it was shaped by them: "Whoever was educated in the same language, whoever poured his heart in it and learned to express his soul in it, he belongs to the *Volk* of this language."[19] For Herder, language existed at two levels. At an individual level, it was a shared social practice that fostered a sense of community among its speakers. At a collective level, it embodied a nation's soul, a pattern of communal life deeply embedded in history and folk traditions. It followed that to forego one's language was to lose one's identity, for language and collective consciousness were inseparably joined.[20] Although Herder saw the world divided into linguistic communities that might later evolve into political states, the philosopher offered no rationale for a hierarchy of nations. In principle, at least, each nation was considered to be of equal value, contributing its own unique way of being to the greater development of humanity.[21]

As the nineteenth century unfolded, Herder's principles of cultural diversity and respect came to be supplanted by claims of national superiority. In 1807, the German philosopher Johann Gottlieb von Fichte delivered his *Addresses to the German Nation* under the dome-shaped roof of the auditorium of the Berlin Academy (Germany). In French-occupied Berlin, Fichte had to tread gingerly when advancing his theory of the German *Ursprache*, but the thrust of his argument was unmistakable. Only the Germans, he claimed, had "remained in the original dwelling places of the ancestral stock" and thus "retained and developed the original language of the ancestral stock," whereas "the other Teutonic races speak a language which has movement on the surface only but is dead at the root."[22] For Fichte, the richness of the German language derived from the intimate link between language and place. Nurtured on German soil, the German language had remained pure and unpolluted, forever resisting the temptation to borrow from other languages.[23] Although ludicrous from a linguistic standpoint, Fichte's inflamed rhetoric inspired national movements across Europe that seized upon language as the cornerstone of national identity.[24]

In the spring of 1865, the *Berliner Journal* in Waterloo County celebrated the exalted position of the German language in a series of articles that were heavily indebted to Fichte's writings. The German nation alone, "Professor J.W. Revin" wrote, had conserved its primordial language (*Ursprache*) by resisting any attempts to adopt foreign elements into its speech. The French, by contrast, had incorporated Latin into their speech patterns, thus severing their linguistic connection to the *Volksgeist*. As a result of its bastardized language, the French nation was stagnating and poor, inferior on all accounts, whereas the German nation was "original, strong, great and free; imbued with life; sentimental, serious, and deep; ingenious in heart and soul"—constantly invigorated by the spirit that flowed freely through the *Ursprache*.[25]

If claims of German cultural superiority reverberated in the columns of the *Berliner Journal*, they did so only fleetingly.[26] Ethnic wordsmiths in North America who lived their lives in both German and English could not easily reconcile Fichte's aggressively nationalist agenda (if they were, indeed, aware of it) with their hope of entering the host society with confidence and dignity. Although they might occasionally indulge in language stereotyping, contrasting the pleasant and home-like sound of the German language with the "cold, stifled and superficial character" of the English one, they typically expressed the desire to cultivate the German mother tongue alongside English.[27]

"German and English" was the battle cry sounded by the *Weltbote* of Pennsylvania, elevating both languages to the status of "Germanic sisters," ready to "rule the world." Reprinted in the *Berliner Journal* in December 1869, the article amounted to nothing less than a celebration of the triumphal march of the German and English languages around the globe. While the German language remained "the guardian and prophet of science, the more abstract arts," the English language

had "spread its wings like a young eagle flying victoriously across whole conti-
nents." Shaped by the forces of industrial life, English was a symbol of modernity,
its sounds faintly echoing "the howling of steam engines and the deafening roar
of the iron hammers; the rapidly rotating spindles of weaving machines."[28] Here,
language was transformed into a historical actor in its own right, imbued with a
soul, a mission, and a will.[29] Following the script written by the *Volksgeist*, language
personified the perceived differences between the German and American national
characters. Where English represented the energetic and confident nature of a
young industrializing country, bustling with business transactions and techno-
logical innovations, German was the language of art, abstract reasoning, and intellectual rigour. This, importantly, was not a vision of the United States as a multilingual country where all ethnic languages were held in equal esteem, but a plea for
the privileged position of German in American affairs. The article celebrated the
unique claim of the German mother tongue—and by implication, its speakers—to
be the equal of English, and thus of the dominant Anglo-Saxon mainstream.[30]

　　With equal vigour, German journalists reminded their readers that each
nation "left its indelible imprint on its language." Ever concerned about the erosion of ethnic pride, they pointed to the intimate connection between language
and a people's soul; for was not "the shared language the first and firmest bond
that unites a people"?[31] As the German-American poet L. Castelhoun wrote in the
late nineteenth century, it was in the German mother tongue that the community
of the present joined hands with the communities of the past and the future.

>　　Tend the German language, tend the German word,
>　　　　For the Father's spirit, in them, lives on
>　　　　Whose gifts to the world are great indeed,
>　　Who planted beauty, in abundance, into her heart.
>
>　　What a Lessing thought, what a Goethe sang
>　　　　Will forever retain its beautiful sound.
>　　And if I think of Schiller, my heart is set aglow,
>　　　　Schiller to replace the world cannot allow.
>
>　　Precious, my children, for us this land shall be.
>　　Yet the ties of language link us with Germany.
>
>　　Preserve the homeland's soil, preserve it for your good,
>　　　　That the grandchildren, still, may share in it.[32]

Steeped in the rhetoric of German Romanticism, the poem offered to alleviate feelings of uprootedness that migrants might have harboured. Language, it suggested, connects us to the future by reaching out to our children and grandchildren. It also ties us to the past by revealing the feelings of our forebears and thoughts of our national visionaries. Through the bonds of language, then, German speakers could find a sense of historical continuity. Not incidentally, the metaphors with which the author sought to capture the essence of the German mother tongue were gleaned from the natural world. The German language—like the community it represented—appeared as an organic entity that needed to be tended, preserved, and cultivated. Once nurtured on the "homeland's soil," language itself became a symbol of the German homeland, evoking an enchanted world of childhood, a symbol of unity and togetherness, a sense of place and belonging.[33]

In the soundscapes that German migrants recreated in the New World, they could touch the homeland's soil. This was the promise held out by the ethnic press that told, in sentimental prose, the story of a German artisan who gathered his American-born children each night to teach them "the sounds of the old homeland." German journalists also evoked "the terms of endearment that flowed from a mother's lips" in the "sweet mother tongue."[34] Just as the German poet Ernst Moritz Arndt had once described a Fatherland that reached "as far as the German tongue resounds," a homeland was now located in the words of "a Goethe song" and the mother tongue's "beautiful sound."[35] Oblivious to political borders, this homeland of German song and sound offered solace, community, and the promise of ethnic solidarity. Yet as we shall see, in the eyes—and ears—of ethnic leaders, this aural homeland was also ever vulnerable to linguistic intrusions and sounds of dissonance so loud they threatened to dissolve the very fabric of the German language.

LANGUAGE IN THE BORDERLANDS

As the self-appointed ethnic leadership quickly discovered, not even the most intimate realm of German life—the home—offered a bulwark against the English language. In minute detail, journalists noted how the English tongue crept into the domestic domain until it had displaced German as the principal means of communication. The sarcastic tone of their observations was palpable indeed. One article, entitled "The Art of Unlearning the German Language," provided a six-step guide on how parents could raise monolingual children who would be "fortunate enough never to insult Americans by speaking German."

(1) With her first-born, the mother speaks German only, as she does not yet know the English language.

(2) With their second child, both mother and father speak German, mingled with a few English words that, of course, are poorly pronounced.

(3) With their third child, the parents and their first-born converse in German, while also using a few English phrases, still poorly pronounced.

(4) With the fourth child, both parents and the three eldest talk half in German, half in English.

(5) With the fifth child, the parents and the four eldest speak English, mingled with a few German words.

(6) In this latest stage, parents and children speak the English language only, and have thus mastered the art [of unlearning the German language].[36]

By losing their maternal tongue, ethnic leaders maintained, German youth forfeited their right to membership in the ethnic community, for only those who spoke the mother tongue with fluency and ease could claim the homeland of the German language as their own. "He who from his early days onwards is used to speaking English only is English himself, even though he may still speak some German," thundered a visitor to Waterloo County in June 1861.[37] In a similar vein, readers encountered young Lutheran ministers in Pennsylvania who "read and think" in English only. "They write their homilies in English and then translate them into the German," one writer complained. "What these homilies are like, I leave to your imagination."[38] What the guardians of the German language found so troublesome was the readiness with which the young embraced the English language, seemingly unaware, as one author chided, that the "language of a people is not a bland piece of clothing; it is the very soul of a people and intimately tied to its character."[39] To "think" in English, not in German, amounted to a betrayal of ethnic values, they suggested. To lose command of the German language was to leave the ethnic fold.

Journalists heaped scorn upon German parents who acquiesced to the "deviance" of their offspring by preferring broken English to pure, idiomatic German. Throughout the nineteenth century, a profound unease about the future of the German family permeated articles in the *Berliner Journal*. Writers described children smiling condescendingly at each other as their parents conversed with them in broken English.[40] They berated parents for allowing their children to address them in English. They doubted the loyalty and patriotism of a veteran of the Franco-

Prussian War who spoke with his children in poor English only. They observed how the bonds of the family dissolved, as children felt ashamed of their parents' poor command of the English language and ridiculed their "foreign" accent.[41] From the streets, one journalist claimed in 1901, children brought home a "disgusting gutter English" that delighted their ignorant parents. In those families, the "cosy warmth of German family life" was replaced by the "fickle spirit of the boarding house, chilling the rooms" wherein the "children commanded the mothers and, through them, the fathers."[42] Just as families were supposed to nurture the German language, so too was language supposed to ward off the contaminating influences of American family life, namely the easy relationship between American fathers and their children, and the "unwomanly" behaviour of American women.[43] To these observers, language retention and family unity seemed inseparably linked.

As German journalists reiterated time and again, children needed to learn their parents' mother tongue in order to assimilate cultural norms and traditions which, in turn, would allow them to become part of a larger linguistic and cultural community. Their appeals served a single purpose: to make the family the one domain upon which the English language would not encroach.[44] As socio-linguists tell us, this was sound advice; bilingualism can be a stable condition if the ethnic mother tongue is associated with a domain of everyday life (such as the family) from which all other languages are strictly barred. But to impose such a "strict domain separation" demanded an investment of time, energy, and determination that most families would have found daunting indeed.[45]

In 1899, over the length of two newspaper columns, Reverend Georg von Basse from Harrisburg, Pennsylvania, recounted how he had transplanted the ideal of a "cosy German family circle" onto American soil. His cultural mission began after he married an American-born woman who, despite her German heritage, had never learned the mother tongue. "As a German, I wanted to set up a German home," he recalled, and consequently conversed only in German with his young wife. Soon, she was speaking German fluently and had also learned how to bake bread ("nourishing rye bread, of course"), cook German meals, knit socks, and make her children's clothes. In sharing his devotion to German traditions and culture, Reverend Basse recalled his memories of the "dear Fatherland," bought German books, subscribed to German family papers, and travelled with his wife to Germany: "I successfully tried to show her the most beautiful and pleasant aspects of German life, introduced her to dear German families where she encountered German hospitality and heartiness, took her for long walks, ...

showed her glorious German cities, museums, etc. and to my great pleasure, she was delighted with my Fatherland."[46] Having thus established a solid foundation, both parents raised their children in the German language: "My boy speaks only German at home, even though he has learned English wonderfully fast at school and is one of the best pupils in his class. Indeed, it is touching to see how he teaches his younger sister our language by telling her: 'It is not 'yes,' it is 'ja.'" Raised on a healthy German diet, both physically and spiritually, his children would never dream of disobeying their parents. Reverend Basse concluded that "the secret of preserving the German tongue for generations to come can be found in the bosom of the family."[47]

Despite Herder's claim that a people's culture and heritage are embedded in the very fabric of their language, Reverend Basse had to recreate painstakingly a German cultural environment in which the mother tongue could thrive. His effort to construct "a viable personal ethnic linguistic system" coloured every aspect of his family life—from its diet to the German books and family papers on the shelves to ways of disciplining the children.[48] To ensure that his wife acquired an emotional attachment to the German language, he took her to the German *Heimat* itself, thereby associating the language with pleasant memories of the "hospitality and heartiness" of their German hosts, the serenity of the countryside, and the splendour of Germany's cities. In seeking to transplant his mother tongue to the United States and transmit it to his children, Georg von Basse reasoned that success depended on a family unit where both parents spoke and read the German language. But his "secret" also depended on considerable financial resources and a high socio-economic status that allowed both for travel to Germany and for the mother to stay at home, where she could reinforce both German language and customs. We are left to wonder whether or not his children would continue to speak German as they grew into adult- and parenthood. The innocuous "yes" uttered by the Reverend's youngest child certainly suggests the vitality of the English language that constituted the dominant tongue at both school and workplace and entered ethnic speech patterns in the form of frequent interjections and loanwords.[49]

Even ardent advocates of the German language realized that most German migrants were unlikely to embark on the rigorous journey of language maintenance that Reverend Basse had mapped out. Their advice was more modest in character. The best way to hone language skills, journalists (not entirely selflessly) suggested, was to subscribe to German newspapers and family magazines. Besides familiarizing young readers with a broad range of cultural and social issues, these papers would help the young to improve their reading and writing skills. Displaying a confidence that stood in marked contrast to the generally defensive tone, one article declared: "It is evident that the German press is the most powerful means of preserving the mother tongue. German newspapers reach homes and families where seldom or never does a German book go astray, and they are being read ten times, whereas a book is read but once."[50] Yet commentators also reported that many parents decided against subscribing to a German publication, since "our children prefer reading the English papers," and encountered ethnic youth unable or unwilling to read in German. Even in families that conversed mostly in German, the "young folks" reached for an English book or paper in six out of seven times.[51]

Wooing young readers was a difficult endeavour, as the *Berliner Journal* discovered at the turn of the century. In an ill-fated experiment, the paper announced a new feature—the *Kinder-Journal* (Children's Journal)—based on the conviction that "children only need to hear that this part of the newspaper is written for them, and they will shortly take interest in it." The editors voiced their "delight in publishing letters from the little folks, on only one condition: the children must have written them on their own."[52] No such letter ever arrived and, after only four editions, the *Kinder-Journal* was allowed to fade quietly into oblivion. Many editors of German-language newspapers shared similar experiences. The "youngsters of the second generation generally refuse to read the papers of their parents, and will not even read even the English sections which enterprising publishers, with shrinking circulation lists, include in a vain hope to hold the support of the American born," Carl Wittke remarks in his study of German-American newspapers.[53] And yet, in their insistence on nurturing reading and writing skills, the editors of the German language press intuitively sensed what socio-linguists have since confirmed. The higher the level of language proficiency and the broader the "range of social and cultural issues" explored in the mother tongue, the more likely the young were to become truly literate in German and unlock the rich heritage of German literature and culture.[54]

While offering models of language retention, German editors also revealed their exasperation over the lack of collective pride and "patriotism" among their fellow ethnics.[55] As one resident of Waterloo County argued in colourful language, the "silly indifference" (*Gleichgültigkeitsdusel*) of "my fellow German brethren" was to blame for the decline and mutilation of "our beautiful German language."[56] German-American leaders, too, considered pride "essential to the creation of a strong group identity" and bemoaned the "lack of self-esteem" among German migrants.[57] They had nothing but contempt for those "thousands of Germans" who had exchanged their native surnames for English ones. Surely it was a disgrace, one commentator wrote, that the brothers "Little" (*Klein*), "Small" (*Klein*) and "Klein" no longer shared a family name.[58] With equal disdain, this writer related the story of a young migrant who denied his German background:

> I still recall how I met a young man while travelling in the state of Indiana in 1855. His broken English betrayed his German origin. I said to him: "Should we not continue our conversation in German? As I hear, you are from Germany as well." He responded: "No Sir, I am a Yankee." Only after I explained to this fool in great detail that he did not truly understand the English language—his English was a mishmash of English and German words—did he confess to his German roots.[59]

The encounter can be read in a different manner. This young man, like many German newcomers to the United States in the mid-nineteenth century, enthusiastically "absorbed the English language and culture," keen to fit in and assimilate the language and customs of the new country. His ethnic speech style reflected the transformation he was undergoing. His English pronunciation was heavily inflected by the German mother tongue, his speech patterns blended English and German words and syntactic constructions, while English loanwords denoted the "objects and ideas of the new environment."[60] Yet this "linguistic inventiveness" was dismissed by his fellow traveller as foolish and misguided, since it was deemed to violate the integrity of both languages.[61] While endorsing the English language, which "our children should learn very well indeed," the German-language press insisted on keeping the mother tongue "pure" and unadulterated.[62]

In a series of satirical poems, German journalists penned the story of a "Yankee tax collector" (alternately, a newspaper agent or census enumerator) who visited a German household where he was addressed in a mixture of English and German.[63] The agent responded in beautifully crafted German sentences and then heaped ridicule on the residents who had tried to deny both their mother tongue ("Dear Sir! Me not dutch sprechen mag!") and their German ethnicity ("Me not dutch bin, me Yankee sein."). The moral of the story could not be more straightforward. Cultivated Americans—personified by the figure of the tax collector—embraced German as the language of culture and science and had little respect for newcomers who felt ashamed of their mother tongue.[64] In throwing away their "beautiful inheritance," these fools had entered a cultural wasteland. Their butchered

"English" would forever bar them from American society, just as their anglicized "German" marked them as renegades among German migrants.

Less overtly, but more interestingly perhaps, the poem captures a drama of language change. Some migrants seemed to associate the use of German with ethnic backwardness and cultural inferiority. At the very least, they regarded the German mother tongue as a disadvantage, both socially and economically.[65] As we know from letters that migrants wrote home, adaptation to life in the New World did not necessarily involve participation in, or even an emotional attachment to, German America or German Canada. Many migrants desired to conform to Anglo-Saxon values by speaking English in the home, anglicizing their names, and participating in non-ethnic politics. Not for them was the exalted pride in German culture or the continuing interest in German affairs that characterized the German-language press.[66] Their life choices, however, met with little understanding by German cultural leaders, who saw in the mother tongue a homeland that migrants could abandon only at the risk of losing their very identity.

In mimicking Anglo customs, German editorialists wrote derisively, these migrants were neither English nor German ("Englisch halb und deutsch nicht recht"), their only concession to their proud German heritage the sauerkraut they served at their dining tables ("Doetsch mit Sauerkraut").[67] While the gatekeepers of the German language liked to pit the ignorant against the enlightened, we may in fact be observing the clash between two waves of immigrants, with German journalists representing the more recent arrivals. Paradoxically, instead of invigorating ethnic community life, new waves of migrants sometimes undermined it by preventing "the settled Germans from ... developing pride in their uniquely German-American way of life" and "reminding them of how un-German they had become and how defective and corrupted their language had become."[68]

The playfulness with which migrants blended the German and the English languages in the mid-nineteenth century—a linguistic encounter that Glenn Gilbert describes as an "adventure" akin to settling the land—was deemed a problem in the closing decades of the nineteenth century, when ethnic leaders noted the stubborn presence of a "new language" that seemed a mutilated version of the mother tongue.[69] "Henceforth," Gilbert notes in his examination of Texas-German, "most writings in German became the product of strenuous, even desperate, efforts to exclude any trace of English influence. In handwriting and printing, the German *Fraktur* script was used exclusively; syntax became very heavy and pedantic. One could almost say that the colonies outdid the fatherland in their zeal for linguistic purity."[70] In mounting a defence of standard German, German editors and writers sought to protect what Brent O. Peterson calls the "unconscious brotherhood" of readers. Although German migrants in North America spoke in a variety of regional dialects such as Bavarian, Low German, Swabian, and Palatine (some of which even other Germans understood only with difficulty), they were united in the shared act of reading German-language publications.[71] Standard German served as a lingua franca that allowed readers to imagine themselves part of a greater community, linked as they were with "thousands and thousands like themselves through print-language."[72] As an article in the *Berliner Journal* noted in 1882, "For all practical purposes, we have not a shared colloquial tongue, but a written language."[73] To accept the intrusion of English loanwords and syntactic structures into standard German meant losing a bond of community, ethnic leaders contended.

In the mid-1880s, a resident of Waterloo County made a vocal case for preserving the purity of the mother tongue. In eight lengthy contributions, published between September 1885 and February 1886, the anonymous author wove together personal observations and anecdotes from German-American newspapers and journals in order to discern the direction in which "our local German community is drifting."[74] His was a tale of righteous indignation. In familiar fashion, he criticized the saturation and alteration of the German language with English idioms and loanwords, thus providing glimpses into local patterns of language use. In order to castigate the language that the county's residents had "patched together," the author listed infractions in which English words and syntax blended with the ethnic tongue: "Ist plenty Room in Deinem Shop?" (Is there plenty of room in your shop?); "Der Butscher hat das Bief geschickt" (The butcher sent the beef); "Mein Freddy is gehn fischen" (My Freddy is going fishing); "Die Horses ziehen steddy." (The horses are pulling steadily); "Er hat die Sach' neglektet" (He neglected this task); "Sind das die ganzen Kinder?" (Are these all the children?).[75] In the language of everyday life, rules of spelling and grammar were suspended and a new local idiom was created that reflected the German-English world that was Waterloo County. The author's greatest scorn was reserved for instances in which the "mixture" (*Gemengsel*) of English and German phrases spilled over into the public sphere. Since the early 1880s, the residents of Waterloo County had enjoyed the privilege of having council resolutions published in their native tongue. In 1885, employing the services of an English printing office, one township council issued a translation that hardly deserved this name. It was "a dishonour and disgrace," the author fumed, "to see the language of

Schiller and Göthe [sic] dragged into the mud with such insolence," in a county, no less, that possessed an abundance of German printers, learned editors, and highly educated citizens who could have easily produced "a pure, grammatically correct" work. The alleged "translation" constituted but "utter nonsense" and a "shameful adulteration of our noble German tongue."[76]

In a more lighthearted tone, a German-American observer recorded "the richness and pleasant sound of the German tongue" in the classified advertisements of a New York newspaper where readers searched for young male apprentices ("Zehn Knaben, um das Painten zu erlernen"; "Ein Bottelfiller, muss Bottlen und Labeln koennen"), barbers ("Acht Barber in's Land; müssen Schampooen können"), housekeepers ("Ein Housekeeper für den 2. Floor; muß einen Flat übernehmen."), female textile workers ("Mädchen an Cloaks im Shop") and sewage workers ("Mehrere Laborer beim Sewer-Contraktor verlangt"). It was reassuring, the author claimed ironically, to witness a language "so purely preserved, so carefully cultivated," thanks to the concerted efforts of the German populace: "der Carpenter hobelt sie, der Painter giebt ihr einen neuen Anstrich, der Plumber löthet sie zusammen, der Laundrymann wäscht sie." (the "carpenter" is shaping it [the mother tongue], the "painter" adding a fresh coat of paint, the "plumber" soldering it, the "laundryman" washing it).[77]

In documenting the anglicized speech patterns of German migrants, these astute observers of language change arrived at much the same conclusions that Carl Wittke would offer in his analysis of the German-American press in 1957. As German editors and journalists "stepped into the homes of German families" and "listened closely to their language of everyday life," they encountered "our magnificent German language, clothed in English rags." Was it any wonder, they asked, that children rejected their ethnic heritage and showed contempt for their parents, who had allowed their "vigorous German" to devolve into a "pidgin language" (*Kauderwelsch*)? This article, as did many others, ended with the heartfelt appeal to "teach your little ones the dear, familiar tongue your mother spoke to you when she cradled you in your arms: the mother tongue. There is no other whose familiar sound reaches the heart so sweetly and mildly."[78] If a German homeland was located in the sounds of the mother tongue, its very essence seemed threatened by the emergence of an anglicized German that blended English and German words, idioms, and sentence structures.

In May 1914, the *Berliner Journal* published an editorial on "The German Language in Canada" that neatly summarized the paper's musings on language and identity. "It is ridiculous," the author wrote, "how Germans living in English-speaking countries translate English words into the German and incorporate them into their speech (which would never have occurred to them in Germany), just as they borrow English phrases. It is an even bigger, and more common, folly to weave English terms into a German conversation." If only parents spoke proper German at home, their children would learn how to converse in the mother tongue. If only they raised their children "in the German spirit, the German language, and the faith of our fathers," our "young German-Canadians" would be granted the key to unlock "the treasures of German poetry and prose."[79] The repeated appeals to keep speech domains strictly separate and to refrain from blending German and English in vocabulary, grammar, and syntax leads us to suspect that Waterloo County residents were guilty of both offences, for the greater the perceived transgression, the more fervent the preaching.

MOTHER TONGUE IN THE MAKING

Some writers, however, embraced the German language spoken in the New World. There had always been voices that rejected pleas for "High German" or "pure German" as unrealistic in the North American context and instead invited families to speak "as you like" ("wie ihnen der Schnabel gewachsen ist") or use the old German dialects, "for what more can we expect under the present circumstances?"[80] Yet there were others who claimed that the German language spoken in the United States was the true mother tongue that alone had remained faithful to its roots. As an editor of the *Illinois Staats-Zeitung* complained in 1876, upon receiving newspapers from Germany he had to translate the "revolting language filth" of his colleagues across the ocean into a language accessible to German-American readers. In ridding the exchange papers from the "despicable French-Latin mixture" that was distorting the German language in the Fatherland, German-American journalists helped the mother tongue regain its original vigour. Implied in the editorial was a class critique. The "noble" writers in Germany, the author claimed, wrote for a class of readers that rarely, if ever, migrated to North America. Unlike the German-American farmers and citizens, who cherished the clarity of their mother tongue, middle-class readers in Germany embraced the profusion of French and Latin loanwords in the German-language press, mistaking it as a sign of learning and prestige.[81]

Thirteen years later, another commentator suggested that German-American writers had transformed the German language into a more poignant tongue.

Inspired by the "precise and powerful" style of English-language newspapers, which they regularly translated into the German, they had learned how "to render home, in the German language, the robust brevity of the closely related English tongue." Instead of altering the German language they were tracing it back to its very roots, thereby restoring its earthy quality and strength that had suffered in the "oppressive, unfree air" in Germany. In rejecting the "language of bureaucrats and underlings that still permeates books and newspapers" in the old homeland, this commentator celebrated "the frankness of our republican spirit" that assisted German-American editors in eliminating Latin, Greek, and French loanwords from their writings. The article conceded that some migrants such as Pennsylvanian Germans had infused their language with English phrases. But "the more recent and educated immigrants, who know both languages intimately, are capable of keeping them separate—both orally and in writing—while also avoiding all foreign loanwords." Thus, the author argued, German Americans had helped keep their mother tongue pure.[82]

What this argument demonstrated was, of course, not the alleged purification of the German language (which in Germany, as in North America, was in a state of flux) but a yearning of a different kind, namely the desire to make a home for the German mother tongue in the New World. "We simply deny that English is the language of the country," the *Illinois-Staatszeitung* declared in 1887.[83] Three years later, the *Indiana Telegraph* chimed in: "How could a language that is spoken by ten million citizens—in a country which is settled by foreigners alone—be un-American?"[84] Implied in these statements was a conviction that the German-American linguist H.L. Mencken put into words in his pioneering study, *The American Language: An Inquiry into the Development of English in the United States,* first published in 1919. Immigrant languages, Mencken argued, were not "foreign" tongues but "dialects in American." His own mother tongue, for one, could no longer be described as "German," as this would obscure the dramatic cultural transformation the German language had undergone since the arrival of the first German-speaking settlers in the American colonies. Written during the difficult years of World War I, "Mencken's classification ... may have been historically understandable rather than linguistically sound," as literary scholar Orm Øverland remarks, but it does attest to a multilingual vision of the United States where loyalty to the nation-state could be expressed in many tongues, and "Germerican" was as American as "American English."[85]

The elastic nature of the term "mother tongue" belies the images that German journalists liked to evoke in their writings. Although the figure of the German mother, cradling her children and humming to them in the mother tongue, represented a perennial favourite in the rhetoric of cultural leaders—as did the earnest appeal to preserve the German language as an expression of one's cultural roots—the mother tongue thus celebrated was not the existential and timeless language conjured by Herder and Fichte. Instead, it demonstrated a remarkable capability to change with the times. Some writers, as we have seen, located the "true" home of the German language in German America itself, while others—like Reverend Georg von Basse—recreated patterns of family life and language as a mirror image of an idealized and mythical Germany.

By the close of the nineteenth century, ethnic cultural leaders had begun to reinvent the German language once again as a language of culture and learning. In urging "all parents to send their old dialects—Low German, Hessian, Palatine, Swabian, and others—into retirement and devote more time to cultivating High German," one German-American writer removed the mother tongue from the spheres of the family and everyday life to the seemingly higher planes of literature, culture, and science. "Here, we do not live in *Plattdeutschland* [Low German Country]," he admonished his readers. "In this country, we should be content to preserve High German and make it respectable."[86] His sentiment was echoed in numerous writings in the 1880s and 1890s that celebrated the German language as a symbol of an educated and cultivated mind, as the idiom of "a people of poets and thinkers" (*Volk der Dichter und Denker*), as the language of "abstract thought and pure science" spoken by an international community of scholars, as the medium of international trade and business, as the favoured language of art and literature—in short, as a "language of the world" (*Weltsprache*).[87] None of these articles made any mention of ethnic community life, nor was it necessarily the mother tongue that the writers championed. Theirs was the language of Goethe and Schiller, a language of cultural significance and practical merits, a language symbolic of High Culture, learning, and national glory.

Ethnic spokespersons liked to bask in the recognition accorded to them by their host societies. They pointed to the high regard in which American elites held the German language, and contrasted the indifference of German Americans with the prudence of American families who sent their sons and daughters abroad to learn the German language and benefit from the "excellent classic German education" offered at Germany's leading universities.[88] At the beginning of the twentieth century, as the socio-linguist Heinz Kloss remarks, "German in the United States enjoyed unequalled prestige as *the* language of education and learning."[89]

Journalists felt confident in their assertion that bilingualism was a cultural and intellectual resource beyond any role it might play in ethnic life. As early as 1886, one commentator marshalled an argument for language maintenance that discarded any notions of ethnic belonging and togetherness. In quoting the president of Cornell University, Professor A.D. White, the author suggested that the German language should be studied at the nation's public schools for three compelling reasons: it was the language of the "greatest nation of our time"; it represented the key to the "richest and most powerful literature" in the world; and it offered "the best remedy against a certain inflexibility of the mind."[90] Although romantic representations of the German mother tongue persisted into the late nineteenth century, rationality and logic emerged as the preferred rhetorical weapons of German-language journalists.

In the early twentieth century, articles published in the *Berliner Journal* measured the qualities of the German language by how it compared to English. "Gone are the times when German was regarded as a peasant language," one editorial proclaimed. "A new age" had dawned in which the German language dominated the globe alongside English. German and English represented the leading languages in the arts and sciences. German and English were the cultural languages (*Kultursprachen*) of the world, with English being spoken by 125 million people, followed by German, spoken by 87 million. German and English sprang from the same linguistic roots that had given birth to a "grand German-American literature."[91] What emanates from these writings on language is "a colonizing vision" of the German language, writ large as a global tongue and celebrated nationally as a language of learning.[92] At the same time, the sense of defiance that permeates so much of German-American writing does linger—in the indignant rejection of the humble roots of the German mother tongue and the repeated reference to the more influential English language.[93]

In the age of empire, even the usually moderate *Berliner Journal* could be found indulging in nationalist sentiment. In 1912, the *Journal* published "A National Catechism for Germans in Canada," whose patriotic fervour contrasted with the paper's normally restrained tone.

> Let your home become a German castle! Allow only German to be spoken therein! ... Speak only in German with your fellow-country men! Otherwise, you treat your homeland with contempt ... Speak the German language as purely as possible ... Do not speak of Mr. or Mrs. when referring to your

husband and wife. This is not a German thing to do. German husband, German wife! Is this not the strongest foundation for a shared life?[94]

This "national catechism" carried more than a hint of anxiety. Once again, a local guardian of language purity and preservation advised his "fellow country-men" how to fence off any intrusions of the English language into the private realms of family and ethnic sociability. Once again, he outlined how to trans-form home and hearth into a bastion of the German language and how to keep the German language "pure." The author demanded, in effect, to use the mother tongue exclusively in some speech domains and reserve use of the English lan-guage for others.[95] The editorial's stern tone softened only in its closing plea to pass on the German folk songs to the next generation: "We Germans are said to love singing our songs more than any other people in the world. Oh, do sing them all in your home, in the circle of your family, and your Canadian-born children will learn to love our Germandom from the bottom of their heart … If you do all this, you are keeping faith."[96] In the sound of folk tunes, the memory and love of the German homeland would be preserved, and with it, the *Berliner Journal* implied, an echo of the German language.

CONCLUSION

People belonging to "cultures of hybridity," Stuart Hall argues, "must learn to inhabit at least two identities, to speak two cultural languages, to translate and negotiate between them."[97] While usually associated with the era of late modernity, this was an experience intimately familiar to migrants of the late nineteenth and early twentieth centuries, as it was for the authors of the German ethnic press.[98] For them, the task of translation assumed a literal meaning as they scoured the English-language press for articles to be translated into the German. Translation also meant conveying the convoluted German that prevailed in the Fatherland (or so indignant editors would have us believe) in a more direct and simple language, devoid of French and Latin loanwords. The business of translation, finally, carried the editors of the *Berliner Journal*—and, subsequently, their readers—into a trans-national space as they liberally "borrowed" musings on language and identity from their colleagues south of the border. In the shared concern over the future of the German language in the New World, the international border between Canada and the United States was momentarily suspended.

In both countries, German journalists pointed to the emergence of a hybrid language that blended German and English linguistic sensibilities and exhibited a remarkable longevity. Indeed, it appears that the German language was not so much "lost" in German immigrant communities in the late nineteenth century as it was transformed into a local idiom in which German and English mingled merrily in vocabulary, syntax, and idiomatic speech. In scorning this "language mishmash" and advocating language purity, the editors of German-language publications in Canada and the United States proposed a language of their own. Their mother tongue was an exalted High German that promised entrance to the world of higher learning, the arts and the sciences, and offered practical benefits as a language of trade and commerce. This cultural construct donned the gown of rationality and joined earlier notions of the German language that had offered a more emotional rationale for preserving the native tongue in the soundscapes of a mother's (German) voice and the endearing folk tunes from the old homeland.

World War I cut short a language odyssey that had spanned over half a century. On 9 October 1918, the *Berliner Journal* appeared under a new name—*The Ontario Journal*—and, in compliance with an Order-in-Council by the Union Government, was published in English.[99] The war, however, only hastened the transformation of an ethnic identity that, as scholars agree, had begun long before. Already by the closing decades of the nineteenth century, the map of the world that the *Berliner Journal* evoked in its writings had become firmly centred on Canada and the United States. To borrow a metaphor from novelist Salman Rushdie, in the act of translation, the self-declared guardians of the German language had themselves been translated.[100]

2.

Languages of Ethnicity
Teaching German at Waterloo County's Schools

To argue that language held special meaning for ethnic leaders in North America who regarded their mother tongue as a signifier of cultural identity is hardly a surprising notion to scholars of migration. The historian April Schultz writes movingly of the "poignant struggle between children and immigrant parents" who regarded language as the very essence of their cultural identity and keenly felt the gap that separated them from their English-speaking children. The bitterness that infused private and public conversations over language, Schultz holds, stemmed from the conviction that "endemic in language was an immutable national personality" without which both ethnic and familial bonds would dissolve.[1] It was a conviction that leaders of Swedish, Spanish, Irish, Polish, Bohemian, Jewish, and German communities across the continent shared as they bemoaned the indifference of their fellow migrants to preserving their mother tongues—in strikingly similar terms and with equally dismal results.[2] As literary scholar Orm Øverland has found, no matter how loud the gatekeepers of the ethnic language sounded their warning, they seemed to speak "to ears that were so attuned to the more enticing tunes of Anglo-America that they could hardly hear those who admonished them to stay away from the very culture they had come to be part of."[3]

The inherently conservative tone that permeated the intellectual conversations of ethnic leaders is echoed in the historical scholarship on language and ethnicity.[4] Threats from without, historians have contended, eroded foreign-language programs in North America in the late nineteenth and early twentieth centuries, for the latter were ill-equipped to withstand the cumulative pressures of coercive assimilation, restrictive language laws, and the impact of World War I.[5] In a local variant of such external threats, historians of Waterloo County—the heartland of German settlement in nineteenth-century Ontario—have found in the county's school inspector, Thomas Pearce, a formidable adversary who "deliberately discouraged" the teaching of German from the time he was first appointed in 1871. The story of a government bureaucrat who single-handedly strangled German-language instruction at the county's public schools lent dramatic flair to the waxing and waning fortunes of German-language schooling and seemed to promise an answer to the vexing question as to why instruction in the mother tongue failed to thrive even in the centre of German culture that was Waterloo County.[6] Threats from within have also been held responsible for processes of language loss, most prominently the failure of immigrant families to cultivate German as the language of the home, the readiness with which immigrants assimilated into mainstream society, and the striking indifference of immigrants to enrolling their children in German-language programs at public schools.[7]

In his innovative rebuttal of these earlier interpretations, historian Jonathan Zimmerman rejects the rigidity of notions of language that make no room for the many tongues in which immigrants expressed their ethnic identity. "The same immigrants," Zimmerman holds, "who proudly embraced ethnic heroes, holidays, foods, and dances eschewed a single ethnic tongue, preferring to communicate in 'a Babel of dialects'—as one caustic observer complained—or in English."[8] Language, in other words, did not necessarily act as a marker of ethnic identity, nor did the sound and texture of ethnic languages need to conform to the aspirations of cultural leaders who championed a "pure" ancestral mother tongue.[9] In their daily speech patterns, nineteenth-century migrants in North America infused their German dialects with English phonology and syntax, just as Polish and Norwegian migrants incorporated English vocabulary into their spoken and written language.[10] In a similar vein, historian David Gerber finds tantalizing evidence of the "extraordinary word-play by which some German immigrants sought to combine English and German in the daily use of written and spoken language," thereby expressing their symbolic mastery of the two cultures they called home.[11]

Then as now, ethnicity spoke in many languages. Just as Mennonites in Western Canada celebrated their ethnic consciousness in both the English and Low German languages in the decades following World War II, so too did the speech patterns of German-speaking migrants in mid-twentieth-century Waterloo County reveal traces of the same cultural and linguistic interactions that had shaped the lives of their predecessors in an earlier century. Instances of code switching abound, as do deviations from standard German.[12] These migrants, much like Waterloo County residents between 1850 and 1915, defined their ethnicity on their own terms and in a multitude of tongues, be it High German, Pennyslvanian Dutch, a local German-English hybrid, or the English language itself.

This chapter examines the fluid meanings of the languages of ethnicity by turning to a public site that brought together—though not necessarily on equal terms—children, parents, ethnic leaders, and government officials. Ethnic leaders sought to preserve the German mother tongue in its ancestral "purity" and bolster enrolment figures in German-language programs. In pursuing this inherently conservative goal, however, they demonstrated much creativity in lobbying government officials and developing methods of modern language instruction that would render the German language classroom into an effective and attractive learning environment. Waterloo County families, in turn, participated in the public debates over language and ethnicity mostly through their telling silence. Although they continued to use the mother tongue as a language of the home, they refused to elevate it to an emblem of ethnic identity that was to be cultivated in the formal setting of the school. To them, the German language was a medium of common parlance, not a symbol of ethnicity, and if their children resented the additional school hours spent in the German language classroom, they would not force them to enrol.

More quietly still, the public conversations over language and ethnicity resonated with the sounds of the spoken word that blended the German and English languages into a new local idiom. The history of spoken language easily eludes the keen eye (and ear) of the historian. And yet, it proves an important corrective to the language jeremiad that could be heard echoing in ethnic newspapers across North America. As this chapter posits, languages of ethnicity in Waterloo County were not bound by the standard German that ethnic leaders sought to propagate as the only legitimate expression of German identity. Rather, a "local German" that infused the German language with English phrases, syntax, words, and idioms remained a medium of communication well into the twentieth century—much to the chagrin of the self-declared guardians of the German language, who were loath to recognize the German-English hybrid as equal to the "authentic" German mother tongue they envisioned. In its local incarnation, the German language remained a medium of communication long after the immigrant leadership— journalists, clergy, professionals, manufacturers, merchants, and small business-men—had declared its demise. At the heart of this chapter, then, lies a tale not of language decline and language loss—two storylines that have hitherto dominated much of the literature—but of migrants who straddled two cultural worlds and, in so doing carved out the contours of an ethnic identity that was most certainly not "pure," but infinitely more interesting because of it. The fluidity of the new idiom—pidgin German, as ethnic leaders called it derisively—reflected the cultural hybrid that was Waterloo County.

STATE, COMMUNITY, AND THE CLASSROOM

As the local charter group, German settlers established German schools. "A large proportion of the inhabitants of Wilmot are Germans, and more than half of the schools are so exclusively," reported local superintendent John Finlayson in 1851. "These schools are very inferior in every respect. The books used are the German New Testament, a Roman Catholic catechism, and a Bible history."[13] Other superintendents, as well, pointed to the peculiar burden under which teachers in Waterloo County laboured. "An English teacher who is not acquainted with the German language," Superintendent Martin Rudolph wrote in 1854, "will meet here with a great many difficulties; as most of our children speak the German language in their families, and he is not able to make familiar explanations to them."[14] In a subversion of widespread notions that acculturation meant anglicization, in Waterloo County it was the English-speaking newcomers who had to adapt to the local German mainstream. "The talking or explaining ... was all done in German, So we were kept Pensylvania [sic] Dutch," Isaac Moyer recalled of his early schooldays. "If an English family moved in, there [sic] children soon learn [sic] to speak our language."[15]

Even in this Germanized local world, however, settlers held the English language in high esteem. Young Isaac was painfully aware that he never acquired facility in English, since his labour was needed on the family farm and his school attendance only sporadic. Unlike his younger brothers who became schoolteachers, Isaac "was trained to Farm [sic]." And, as he added somewhat defiantly, "I made a success of it, so that I came out at the end About [sic] as well as the rest. But I do miss very much good common English language."[16] By all accounts, Isaac Moyer's feelings were shared by many German-origin settlers who desired their children "to be instructed in both languages."[17] Convinced of the necessity of "obtaining knowledge of the language of the country," they embraced English as both the language of instruction and a school subject as early as the mid-1850s, much to the satisfaction of John Finlayson: "The Germans in the township of Waterloo, Wilmot and Wellesley, are becoming alive to the uselessness of teaching German only, in their schools;—so much so, that in some school sections among them, the German is excluded, and all the ordinary branches of a common English education is taught."[18]

The skill with which migrants conversed in two cultural languages is reflected in the story of Otto Klotz, who left his hometown Kiel in Germany at the age of twenty in 1837, drawn to the New World out of a sense of adventure. The young man dabbled in agriculture and the brewing business before building a hotel in Preston, Waterloo County.[19] Without delay, he immersed himself in local affairs. In 1838, he was elected trustee of the Preston School Board, an office he held for fifty-four years. In 1853, he was appointed local superintendent and as such entitled to a seat on the Board of Examiners for the County of Waterloo. During a tenure as County Examiner that spanned almost two decades, Klotz dispelled any notions that mass schooling was a process imposed solely from above. Professing "great love and enthusiasm for the cause of education," he frequently deplored the incompetence of fellow superintendents who "were not capable of answering one half of the questions required to be answered by Candidates applying only for a third class certificate." When the School Act of 1871 rendered the office of local superintendents superfluous, Klotz welcomed the innovation.[20] This local school supporter, for one, was averse to neither regulation nor professionalization, if only they helped to raise the quality of instruction. At the same time, however, Klotz did not hesitate to tailor provincial regulations to local needs.

Since the early 1840s, the status of German-born teachers had been somewhat ambiguous. The schools acts of 1841 and 1843 had stipulated that teachers be British subjects by either birth or naturalization. But to enforce this rule rigidly would have meant depriving the townships of Waterloo, Wilmot, Wellesley, and Woolwich of many instructors. In heeding local concerns, Egerton Ryerson, the Chief Superintendent of Education, exempted European-born teachers from the regulation, provided they applied for a special teaching licence.[21] In 1851, the Council of Public Instruction further sought to clarify language requirements for aspirant teachers by ruling that "in regard to teachers of French or German … a knowledge of French or German Grammar can be substituted for a knowledge of English Grammar, and that certificates to the teacher be expressly limited accordingly."[22] In the eyes of Otto Klotz, this concession did not reach far enough. In demonstrating the confidence and creativity with which historians D.A. Lawr and R.D. Gidney have credited many local leaders, he devised German examination papers for all branches of instruction, rather than for grammar alone, when he sat on the Board of Examiners for the County of Waterloo.[23] This liberal interpretation of provincial law, Klotz held, would allow for a gradual transition from German to English, for it "was only a matter of time and of short duration when the people would come to the conviction that the teaching of English to their children is of paramount importance and that instead of teaching German exclusively, it should be taught as an auxiliary."[24] With only one dissenting voice, the Waterloo County Board of Examiners consented to Klotz's decision to skirt the letter of the law.[25] Even the English-speaking chairman of the Waterloo County Board of Examiners, who vocally opposed the German certificates, had to bow to the authority that Klotz quietly wielded among board and community members.[26]

Notwithstanding his personal attachment to the German mother tongue, Klotz embraced English as "the language of this country." He encouraged German-born applicants "to study English, so as to qualify them to obtain a certificate to teach English." Similarly, he advised Canadian-born candidates to obtain additional German certificates to "be able to command higher salary." "A number of them followed my advise [sic]," the aging Otto Klotz wrote in his school chronicle, "and it was pleasant to note that after a lapse of some years there was quite a number of Germans who had obtained certificates in English and could teach both languages."[27] The cultural duality, which Klotz envisaged for the county as a whole, had long become embedded in the structures of schooling in his local Preston.

Schools where only German was taught "belonged to the past," declared Klotz. As early as 1852, the Preston public school had made English the language of instruction.[28] This, however, did not prevent the trustees from lavishing time, care, and energy on German as a special branch of education. The minute books of

the Preston Public School Board reveal how many a meeting was devoted to finding competent candidates, expanding the hours of German-language instruction,
selecting appropriate German readers, and making German lessons mandatory for
all pupils.[29] As a special branch of instruction, the German-language department
was to ensure the purity and preservation of the German mother tongue, while
English-language instruction in all other school subjects would allow Preston's
Germans to navigate Ontario's cultural mainstream. Long before the School Act of
1871 came into force, the status of German had thus changed from a medium of

Studio portrait of Otto Klotz. COURTESY OF KITCHENER PUBLIC LIBRARY,
WATERLOO HISTORICAL SOCIETY, P-006048.

communication to a subject of instruction. Preston's residents, quite evidently, did not seek to remain an ethnic world apart.

As the historian Neil Sutherland wryly notes, "schooling is more a matter of learning than it is of teaching," and learning depends more on a child's personality, family, ethnicity, and class than it does on textbooks, teachers, and curricula.[30] This certainly held true for Louis Breithaupt, heir of one of Waterloo County's leading families, whose members wielded their influence as mayors, school trustees, wardens, church patrons, benefactors, and members of the provincial legislture.[31] Theirs was a world of class privilege: an affluent home with a servant girl; a close and caring family environment; a social world that encompassed prayer meetings, Sunday school, singing and piano lessons. Yet although the Breithaupt family was affluent in its ownership of a leather tannery and real estate, its outlook was essentially middle class. Family routines evolved around domestic life, with child-rearing practices seeking to inculcate character, instill ambition, and nurture habits of thrift, hard work, and piety.[32] Louis's parents expected their children to excel at school and to internalize proper notions of conscience and responsibility. In eschewing corporal punishment, they relied on the power of emotional rewards, financial incentives, and mild reprimands.[33] When Louis and William arrived home late one evening, their mother's agitation was punishment enough.[34] Frequently ill, Katharina Breithaupt encouraged her children to keep extensive journals, attend church, and read the Bible. Louis followed her example, and soon the pages of his diary recorded his efforts at character refinement. In attending prayer meetings of the Evangelical Congregation and visiting the Sunday school of the English Methodist Church, his religion was bounded by neither denomination nor language but by the number of verses memorized, the Bible chapters read, and the money donated to charity, which he paid out of his own pocket money.[35]

Louis himself did not let school interfere too much with the pursuits of his boyhood. When he remarked upon his schoolwork, his comments were brief and perfunctory: "Lessons good," "Lessons not so good," "Lessons fairly good," "Lessons good today," "Lessons not good."[36] By contrast, he meticulously chronicled his father's business trips, negotiations, and investments, thus growing into a world of work that gradually began to overshadow his life as a student. "We had exams at school today," the twelve-year-old heir of one of Berlin's most prominent families wrote on 12 July 1867. "August Werner and I were the best pupils in German class. After the exams, Father and I went to Mannheim and Williamsburg to buy building timber."[37] Liborious and Katharina Breithaupt readily pulled their eldest sons out of school to work at the store, run errands, buy staples, help on the farm and tend to pigs, cows, and horses, thereby tempering the demands of school with the requirements of a family economy that valued children's labour over regular school attendance.[38] In the fabric of Louis's childhood, schooling represented but one thread that was tightly interwoven with many others, and whose pattern was shaped more by the rhythms of family life than by government policies or local language politics, no matter how far-reaching the latter's scope.[39]

The School Act of 1871 enacted sweeping changes. It made common schools, now renamed public schools, free and school attendance mandatory for all Ontario children between the ages of seven and twelve. Teaching was recognized as a profession, with teachers' examinations becoming standardized and centralized. Where formerly each County Board had prepared its own examination papers and awarded certificates according to its own discretion, the new Board of Examiners under the direction of County School Inspectors administered centrally prepared questions simultaneously across the province. Although examination papers for Third and Second Class Certificates continued to be evaluated locally, the Education Department in Toronto reserved the right to decide on the merits of candidates for First Class Certificates. The School Act also established a new agency that was to enforce these regulations. Professional school inspectors, appointed by the County Council yet responsible to the Department of Public Instruction, replaced the more locally controlled lay superintendents. Unlike their local predecessors, the new corps of school inspectors had to hold a First Class Provincial Certificate and furnish proof of five years of teaching experience.[40]

When the County Council prepared to appoint a school inspector in June 1871, the *Berliner Journal* became the platform upon which a vocal campaign for a German-speaking inspector was waged. In a letter to the editor, one reader stated emphatically that Waterloo County, with its German settlements and German schools, needed the services of a school inspector who understood "our language." In appealing to the "German members of the esteemed council," the writer lobbied for the appointment of a qualified candidate who possessed an intimate knowledge of both languages.[41] This plea was to the liking of the *Berliner Journal,* which endorsed the candidacy of John Moran, a man it considered sufficiently qualified to examine students in German language classes, since his knowledge of the language was "quite good."[42] Despite the *Journal*'s efforts, the Council appointed Thomas Pearce, whose command of German was perfunctory at best. Slightly outnumbered by their anglophone colleagues, the German members of the Council might have been frustrated in their effort to elect a German-speaking school inspector. More likely, however, they viewed the choice of county inspector through the prism of professional credentials, not ethnicity. Rather than selecting a German-speaking candidate of unproven abilities, they were willing to entrust the office of school inspector to the Irish principal of Berlin's Central School, a man of experience and prestige who also possessed the necessary qualifications.[43]

In both Canada and the United States, a particular class of men was recruited for the business of school promotion.[44] Middle-aged, middle-class, native-born, white, Protestant, and Anglo-Saxon married men came to oversee a teaching force that increasingly comprised young and single women teachers.[45] Thomas Pearce fit this profile. Having migrated from Ireland in 1857 at the age of twenty-two, he attended the Normal School in Toronto upon the suggestion of his old teacher, "who knew something of his former pupil's ability and scholarship," as Pearce proudly recalled.[46] As for many superintendents in the United States, encouragement and sponsorship by older male administrators and professors played an important role in his career. After a Normal School instructor had recommended the young man to the Central School in Berlin, Pearce became "the first Normal trained teacher, not only in Berlin, but for several miles around."[47] It was in this overwhelmingly German community that his "occupational socialization" began.[48] First as a teacher, whom colleague Elizabeth Shoemaker remembered as "a very nice, young man much more sociable than Mr. Strong," and then as principal (1864–71), Thomas Pearce internalized role prescriptions for good teaching that he would later spell out to novice teachers.[49] A familiar figure in the educational landscape of Waterloo County, schoolchildren like M.G. Sherk watched "in awe" when they saw him "arriving and tying his horse near the gate ... for he was very dignified looking. We found, however, unless we deserved it, we had nothing to fear, for he was a very kindly disposed man. I think perhaps the teacher feared him as much as we did."[50] Teachers might indeed have noted Pearce's arrival with great apprehension, as the school inspector was not one to mince words. Generous in his praise where he perceived "splendid ability," and acutely aware of intolerable overcrowding that often made it impossible for him to offer a fair assessment of a teacher's merits, he refused to issue teaching permits to instructors he deemed unfit.[51] The trustees, in turn, were publicly admonished for employing "cheap incompetent teachers," seating the children at "miserable desks," tolerating "very dirty" rooms, and "throwing obstacles" in the way of earnest, diligent teachers.[52]

Thomas Pearce was keenly aware of the fact that 50 to 75 percent of all children in Waterloo County—"yes, in some sections, even 100 percent"—made their first attempts to speak English when they entered school. But for the freshly minted school inspector, rudimentary language skills were just one among many educational challenges. His was a crusade to boost rates of school attendance, build solid schoolhouses, raise standards of scholarship, and attract highly qualified teachers. As long as German language instruction did not interfere with these goals, it presented but a curious feature of the local fabric of schooling which Pearce faithfully sought to convey in his annual reports.[53] Throughout Waterloo County, he wrote, teachers faced a peculiar challenge: "Until the pupils become tolerably familiar with the English language, a very great part of the teacher's explanation and instruction is entirely lost."[54] As many schools devoted "a considerable portion of each day" to the study of German, they could not be reasonably expected to have as "high a standing in the classes of the programme, as in schools where instruction is given exclusively in English and the whole school-time devoted to the prescribed subjects."[55] The inspector, however, did not seem particularly unsettled by his findings. Given his familiarity with local conditions, it might rather have come as a pleasant surprise that "there are at present very few pupils in the County studying German exclusively," the sole exception being New Hamburg, where 120 to 150 pupils received German instruction only.[56]

Schoolchildren and teacher, Noah Martin, at Rummelhart School S.S. # 9, Waterloo Township in September 1897. COURTESY OF KITCHENER PUBLIC LIBRARY, WATERLOO HISTORICAL SOCIETY, P-00789.

The annual reports of Thomas Pearce provide glimpses into practices of language use at Waterloo County public schools. Finding "reading and spelling ... very much neglected" in the county's rural township schools when he began his annual rounds in 1872, he soon noted improvements "beyond my expectations."[57] And yet, the County School Inspector encountered a source of constant frustration in that the children's English, although competent, was heavily accented. With more than a hint of exasperation, Pearce remarked upon a visit to St. Jacobs in March 1880 that the "pupils did fairly in the subjects in which I examined them, except in reading, which is, apparently, very difficult to teach in this place." When visiting the county's Roman Catholic Separate School in 1876, he found "room for improvement, perhaps, in the subjects of reading and arithmetic" in an otherwise glowing report. Two years later, having paid a courtesy visit to the school once again, he declared, "Reading on the whole good—making allowance of course for the strong German accent of many of the pupils." In 1894, he reported rather regretfully that still, "distinct articulation, good inflection and naturalness of expression are heard in few schools."[58] The repeated references to the children's German-accented English reveal Inspector Pearce's deep-seated reservations against enrolling "very young children" in German language classes. This practice, he charged, led "to such confusion of sounds of letters and pronunciation of words in the minds of the little ones as greatly to retard their progress in both languages." In attributing the low standing of several rural schools to the attempt "to lead children to this bewildering maze," Pearce recommended reserving German-language instruction exclusively for the higher grades.[59] Seemingly unaware of the success of bilingual school programs in the United States that enrolled elementary schoolchildren as young as five years, Pearce reasoned that children could not simultaneously assimilate the sounds and structures of two different languages.[60] His criticism, importantly, was not of German language instruction per se, but of bilingual instruction in a child's early years. When his suggestions went unheeded, he did not press the matter further.

In fact, Thomas Pearce advised Chief Superintendent Egerton Ryerson to tread carefully on issues of language. "The Germans in this county," he wrote, "are a brave and highly intelligent people, but exceedingly sensitive on the question whether their language is to be continued in the schools."[61] Pearce's letter revealed an apparent fondness for the people in his inspectorate who supported the project of mass schooling by constructing decent schoolhouses and hiring qualified teachers.[62] As early as 1872, he praised the school trustees of Waterloo Village, Preston, and Hespeler, who had met all his suggestions "with the heartiest response."[63] Five years later, he detected "general improvement in almost every department of school work" and commended trustees and ratepayers for "taking a more lively interest in school matters."[64] Surely, in a county whose people embraced public education and English-language instruction in such a manner, educational authorities could indulge local desires for German language lessons.

It is, perhaps, not surprising that neither Pearce nor Ryerson perceived German language instruction as a threat to the project of mass schooling. Between 1874 and 1880, the percentage of schoolchildren studying German in Waterloo County fell almost by half, from 16 to 9 percent. During the same decade, the county's German-origin population slightly increased, from 55 percent in 1871 to 57 percent in 1881. The data that Thomas Pearce so painstakingly compiled reveals that the strongholds of German language instruction were located not in rural areas but in towns and incorporated villages—Berlin, Preston, New Hamburg, and Waterloo Village—which enrolled roughly equal percentages of "German" and "English" children by the late 1880s.[65]

Table 1 Enrolment in German Language Classes by Ethnic Origin, Waterloo County, 1889

	German Pupils	German Pupils Studying German	English Pupils	English Pupils Studying German
	N	%	N	%
Berlin	745	9	202	6
Preston	173	29	76	22
New Hamburg	201	17	37	14
Waterloo Village	371	9	76	9

SOURCE: *REGULATIONS AND CORRESPONDENCE*, 114.

By 1889, only six schools in the townships of Waterloo, Wilmot, Woolwich, and Wellesley offered German language classes that, taken together, enrolled a quarter of the local school population.[66] Teachers at Waterloo County's rural schools seemed content to instruct their flock in reading and writing only, with many limiting their lessons to reading exercises. Public schools in urbanized areas offered a more comprehensive German-language curriculum that included ten to twelve hours of weekly instruction in reading, writing, and grammar.[67] It was here that the transformation of German from the language of the classroom to a special subject of instruction had been completed. Failing to win the unequivocal support of German-origin settlers, German had become an elective subject for the general school population.

Graph 1 Schoolchildren Enrolled in German Language Classes at Public Schools, Waterloo County, 1874–1889 (in percentages)

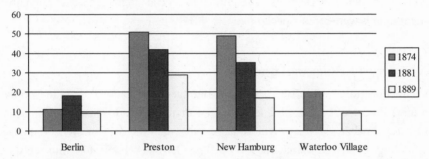

SOURCE: *REGULATIONS AND CORRESPONDENCE,* 114; KPL, WHS, WAT C-87, MANUSCRIPT ANNUAL SCHOOL REPORTS FOR 1874 AND 1881.

This finding was greeted with delight by the Commission of 1889 that had been charged with inquiring into the conditions of minority-language schooling in the province of Ontario. Authorized "to consider and report in what way the study of English may be most successfully promoted among those accustomed to the use of the German language as their mother tongue," the commissioners noted that German language instruction did not impede the children's overall progress: "The German pupils who were learning German were quite as well advanced in their studies as those who were not learning German."[68] Indeed, the German language itself seemed to be in retreat. As the commissioners stated, the sustained interaction between German and English settlements had resulted in English schools that were attended by German children: "The German language is no longer used as the medium of instruction in any of them, except so far as may be necessary to give explanation to those pupils who, on coming to school, know but little English."[69] While preserving "their attachment to their mother tongue," German parents had recognized "the necessity of an English education in this country." This reasonable attitude, the commissioners held, accounted for the smooth, if gradual, "transition from German to English."[70]

The report pointed to a marked drop in enrolments in the county's German departments. Except for fluctuating enrolment figures in Berlin—which in any case had always been substantially lower than in either Preston or New Hamburg—the percentage of children studying German had been cut in half between 1874 and 1889. Even in the province's German heartland, English now represented the language of instruction, German was confined to special language lessons, and enrolment figures were rapidly declining.

A LAMENT FOR LANGUAGE LOSS

What educational authorities praised as voluntary assimilation, Waterloo County's leaders lamented as ethnic decline. With keen attention, the *Berliner Journal* followed the heated debates in the provincial legislature when the issue of French-language schooling erupted in March 1889, propelling German schools, too, into the spotlight.[71] The editors need not have worried. Providing a convenient rhetorical counterfoil to French Canadians, the German settlers of Waterloo County were lauded for learning the English language, while Franco-Ontarians were berated for stubbornly clinging to their mother tongue.[72] In an interesting twist, the *Berliner Journal* heartily sympathized with Franco-Ontarians' rights to conduct schools according to "the language and customs of their forefathers." Did not French-Canadians resemble the early German pioneers who had eked out a living with meagre resources and channelled their energy into working the land? Forty years ago in Waterloo County, the *Journal* wrote, there had been "many sections where both children and teachers understood little English, or none at all; and it would have been foolish to suggest the appointment of English teachers or the introduction of English school readers."[73] The *Journal*'s editors professed little patience for the "linguistic fanatics" who saw their country's salvation in "anglicization" and who betrayed an "ignorant arrogance" (*dummen Dünkel*) by treating all non-English speakers with contempt.[74]

The colourful rhetoric notwithstanding, ethnic leaders in Waterloo County blamed the waning fortune of the German-language classroom not on "linguistic fanatics" but on the seeming indifference of the county's German residents. "I am afraid," mused the chairman of the Berlin School Board, L. Janzen, in September 1889, "that parents let children have their own way in this important matter far too often" by failing to take advantage of the town's fine German Department. "Once those children will have grown into men and women, they will realize their great mistake and rebuke their parents for having been so indulgent."[75] Old and faded as they are, the pages of the *Berliner Journal* still exude a righteous indignation that comparatively few German families took advantage of the Central School's German Department or showed an interest in its semi-annual examinations.[76] In 1874, the audience at the public examination comprised a single observer who praised the children's progress and commended the English children who "diligently applied themselves to the study of the German language."[77]

Seven years later, the German teacher at Berlin's public school was so exasperated over the general levels of apathy that he resorted to an unusual step. In a letter to the editors of the *Berliner Journal*, Louis von Neubronn publicly reprimanded the "many Germans in Berlin" who "care little, or none at all, whether or not we have a good German school in our midst; otherwise they would behave differently and let their children enjoy the privilege of which even many English-speaking pupils take advantage ... those people show no interest in their beautiful and noble mother tongue."[78] Neubronn distinguished between two classes of parents, those who completely deprived their children of German-language instruction — "which is shameful enough for a German family" — and those who sent their child to the German Department for less than a year, falsely assuming that a term or two in the German classroom would suffice to acquire fluency in German reading, writing, and grammar. The latter group, Neubronn wrote, seemed unaware that progress only occurred after months of study. "Yet instead of obliging and encouraging such a child to attend the German classroom regularly, it suddenly occurs to those people that 'My son or my daughter has to learn too much in the English subjects; thus, away with the German.'"[79] Robbed of the fruits of his labour, Neubronn saw the German classroom becoming the poor cousin of Berlin's public school system. Sternly, he told the residents of Berlin to "send your children to the German classroom regularly and for an extended period of time; and do not act as if you were ashamed of the German language."[80] But his heartfelt plea went unheard. Enrolment figures in the German Department continued to decline over the next two decades.

Anxious to shore up institutional support for the German language, Otto Klotz convened with like-minded activists in January 1877 to discuss prospects of German-language schooling and urge the newly appointed Minister of Education, Adam Crooks, to institute a "German School Inspector for the German Schools of the Province." Confronted with the fact that over 90 percent of the county's teachers had been born in Canada, the petitioners also deemed it necessary "to grant German-Canadian teachers the opportunity to learn proper German" by hiring a professor of German at the Toronto Normal School.[81] The passing reference to "proper German" indicates an important shift in the thinking of language advocates. To preserve German as the language of home and hearth no longer sufficed, for the German mother tongue seemed hardly recognizable in the idiom spoken in Waterloo County homes. Language purity was the new battle cry.

Crooks refused to hire a German professor at the Toronto Normal School and also rejected the demand for a provincial German school inspector. He did, however, assure the petitioners that German could be taught at public schools wherever parents and trustees so desired. The Minister of Education's simple formula, combining provincial protection with local initiative, accorded well with the world view of community leaders and was reiterated at public meetings on language matters throughout the late nineteenth and early twentieth centuries.[82]

In the years to come, the county's German-language newspapers would increasingly deride the "gibberish" (*Kauderwelsch*) spoken on streets and homes. German syntax, they alleged, had fallen victim to literal translations from English, as children complained, "Es ist kein mehr Brod da" (There is no more bread here), rather than using the grammatically correct "Es ist kein Brod mehr da." English fillers such as "well," "yes," "no," and "certainly" peppered the talk of German settlers. In the patterns of everyday speech, German and English words and phrases readily intermingled, as doctors "fixt" the medication and Johann earned praise for being a "schmärter" (smart) boy. In the eyes of ethnic leaders, the local German-English hybrid foreshadowed language loss and ethnic decline, since only a "pure, cultivated language" could act as a bulwark of "the German way of life, the German song, and even the German *Gemütlichkeit*" (a term for which "cosiness" is but a poor approximation).[83] As early as 1876, Reverend Ludwig mused in the pages of the *Berliner Journal* that "an oral acquaintance of the mother tongue may outlast, for over a century, a true knowledge thereof," only to add that "such a way of speaking will gradually become so hideous as to defy description." While his fellow migrants still *spoke* the German mother tongue, Ludwig no longer felt they *knew* it.[84] To preserve the German language in Waterloo County, Ludwig and others reasoned, the casual use of the local German idiom needed to be complemented with formal school lessons that would nurture reading and writing skills and provide instruction in proper grammatical speech, as only a high level of language proficiency would grant access to the rich heritage of German literature and culture.[85]

Unlike ethnic leaders, few parents publicly commented upon German-language schooling. Their attitudes have to be read through their behaviour, namely their willingness—or lack thereof—to enrol their children in the German-language classroom. It is difficult to escape the conclusion that by the late 1880s, German-language classes reflected the desire of some, but not the need of many. By all accounts, German parents and children did not consider it necessary to cultivate a medium of common parlance in the formal setting of the classroom. Their reluctance to provide their children with formal instruction in the mother tongue, however, did not prevent them from identifying with the German language or speaking it at home. In the 1890s, a sizeable proportion of Berlin's schoolchildren still spoke a German-accented English that was modelled after the linguistic structures of the German mother tongue, thus prompting Berlin's teachers to develop grassroots programs of English-language immersion.

At a meeting of the Berlin Teachers' Association in May 1895, Miss Scully presented a step-by-step guide on how to teach composition to "Junior Pupils, especially German Children." Rather than relying on the rehearsal of grammatical rules, she regarded oral lessons—the hearing and speaking of English—as the key to learning. She granted her pupils the time to assimilate the structures of the English language inductively before moving on to written exercises. Gentle coercion, as well, played an important role in Miss Scully's teaching arsenal. She confined the use of German to the German-language classroom and insisted that children spoke English even on the playground. In practising the children's writing skills, she favoured the writing of simple stories ("Going to School," or "What I would do if I had $10") over having the children copy English-language lessons at their desks.[86] Intuitively—by drawing on her experiences in the classroom—Miss Scully had arrived at much the same pedagogical principles advocated by the National German-American Teachers' Association south of the border.[87] In her classroom, the textbook constituted just one teaching tool among many, while active language skills were nurtured in conversational exercises.

Indeed, as the Canadian Census of 1901 reveals, English was a foreign language only for the very young and the elderly in Berlin, Ontario. Only 9 percent of Berlin's five- to six-year-old children of German origin did not speak English at the turn of the century. Yet even children like Walter Hauser, Neillie Decker, and Olivia Koebel, whose parents upheld German as the language of the home, would soon learn English in the classroom, much as their older siblings Emma, Norman, Matilda, and Edgar had done. Familiarity with English represented the rule among Berlin's school-aged children and youth; a negligible 0.3 percent of the town's seven- to nineteen-year-olds was unable to speak English.[88] For German migrants more advanced in years, social mobility provided a powerful impetus for learning English. This, in fact, was the experience of Karl Müller. Upon migrating to Canada in 1872, the twenty-four-year-old heeded his brother's advice and attended the local high school. After his language immersion, which lasted six months and included tutorial lessons by brother Adolf in the evening, Karl began an apprenticeship as a telegraph operator for the railway. Later, he operated a successful painting business in which he comfortably interacted with both German- and English-speaking patrons.[89] Like earlier migrants to Waterloo County, Karl Müller relished the region's German culture and character but embraced the occupational mobility that mastery of the English language promised.

But the census also illustrates the remarkable persistence of the German language in Waterloo County. In 1901, close to 90 percent of Berlin's German-origin residents identified German as their mother tongue.[90] As census enumerators were explicitly instructed not to inquire into language proficiency, we are left to wonder to which extent English syntax, idioms, and vocabulary carried over into German. As socio-linguist Joshua Fishman points out, census data on language practices are notoriously "suspect not only because they are based upon claims rather than upon actual proof of language use, but also because they relate to mother tongues rather than to current facilities."[91] Yet although German might have been spoken with varying degrees of ease and fluency, its mere mention on census forms reflected an emotional attachment to the mother tongue that was significant in itself.[92] The census returns also suggested, albeit tentatively, that ethnic leaders may have exaggerated the spectre of "language loss" in Canada's German capital at the turn of the century, since they were prone to measure language skills in terms of linguistic purity and enrolment figures in the German classroom. By contrast, most of Berlin's residents seemed content to use the mother tongue as a conversational tool, just as they seemed to be unperturbed by the prominence of the "local German" in which the German and the English languages mingled merrily.

LANGUAGE RENAISSANCE

It would take a moment of crisis to publicize the "plight" of the German language in the public mind and lend momentum to the aspirations of ethnic leaders. The trigger of the Berlin school crisis was innocuous enough. In February 1900, School Inspector Seath had criticized the reading at the local high school "rather adversely."[93] Always striving for excellence in schooling, the Berlin Public

School Board instructed Inspector Pearce to submit a report on the situation, which the latter promptly delivered. "I was more than surprised to find children of British parentage reading and speaking fully as 'broken' as those of German parentage," Pearce wrote in his submission to the school board. By allowing young children to study two languages simultaneously, their minds became "confused with the sounds of letters and the pronunciation of words of two languages in many respects so very different ... the result is they read and speak English with a German accent and pronunciation and vice versa."[94] Pearce's thinking seems to have been informed by academic studies of his time that held that "bilingualism created failure and mental confusion and damaged the psychological well-being of immigrant children."[95] Was it not a matter of common sense, Pearce asked, to limit German-language instruction to the upper grades, where pupils were not quite as easily confused by the "bewildering maze" of two languages?[96]

Little was Inspector Pearce aware that he had stirred up a hornets' nest. The outcry in the community was almost immediate. Painter Karl Müller called upon Berlin's "Germandom" (*Deutschthum*) to fight for "our language" and professed himself incensed that "a school inspector who has held office in this German County for forty years and has yet not mastered the German tongue ... is incapable of judging either the strengths or weaknesses of German-language instruction."[97] On a more moderate note, Reverend Teufel refuted the inspector's claim that bilingual instruction impeded the progress of young children: "We have always found that pupils who learn more than one language are superior to those who deal only with one."[98] It was the craftsmen of the Concordia singing society, supported by the *Berliner Journal*, who organized an indignation meeting on 22 June 1900 to discuss "the better development of German instruction in our public schools."[99] In attendance were prominent local citizens, including "some of our English fellow-citizens who recognize the use and desirability of a broader education for our children."[100]

Unanimously, the assembly rejected the assumption that German-language schooling accounted for low reading standards. Instead, it held that "the thorough study of German, as both a written language and a colloquial one, will benefit the pupils most highly."[101] The passage of time had woven changes into the rhetoric of language advocates. No longer did ethnic spokespersons seek to transform the family into a bastion of the German language. Instead, they presented German-language instruction as a political entitlement and eloquently evoked the "twin souls" that imbued their lives, namely the German and English languages. Entrepreneur Louis Breithaupt portrayed German as a language of "modernity

Studio portrait of Thomas Pearce. COURTESY OF KITCHENER PUBLIC
LIBRARY, WATERLOO HISTORICAL SOCIETY, P-000159.

and progress" that children should learn for their own benefit.[102] In Breithaupt's
sweeping redefinition, the social setting of the family that had hitherto provided
a metaphorical home for the German language was supplanted by political principles, cultural abstractions, and material advantages.

The birth of the German School Association (Deutscher Schulverein), formally founded in August 1900, allows us to probe the social profile of the groups
that rose to the defence of German language and culture between 1900 and 1914.[103]
It was men of the middle and upper classes, distinguished by either their education or their wealth, who led the campaign of language renaissance. Lawyers, physicians, newspaper editors, and, most prominently, clergymen accounted for 25

percent of the association's members, thus emerging as "custodians of culture." Their education and professional training singled them out as men of value and virtue who sought to translate their "cultural capital" into political leverage.[104] They were joined by Berlin's leading property owners—manufacturers, merchants, hotel keepers, and landowners—who represented 20 percent of the membership and whose economic power enhanced the prestige of the young association. The remaining members who can be identified were tradesmen (21 percent), shop-keepers (11 percent), and white-collar workers, among them two store clerks, the town clerk and treasurer, and the manager of an insurance company (8 percent).[105] Teachers, by contrast, were conspicuously absent. Clearly, support for German-language schooling was generated outside the school system, not within it.

To appreciate the extent to which Berlin's elites rallied behind the cause of German-language schooling, we only have to turn to the local assessment rolls of 1897.[106] Among Berlin's top forty-six property owners, we find no fewer than eleven members of the German School Association.[107] The ranks of the German School Association also included eight past and two future mayors, seven members of the county council, ten members of the municipal council, and twelve members of the Board of Trade.[108] The founding meeting of the association was graced by the presence of Hugo Kranz, who as a member of the Conservative Party had represented North Waterloo in the House of Commons between 1878 and 1887. Also in attendance were two members of the provincial legislature, Dr. G.H. Lackner (South Waterloo) for the Conservatives, and Louis Breithaupt (North Waterloo) for the Liberals. The Schulverein's ranks were further bolstered by seven school trustees, whose long-standing or present service on the Berlin School Board helped to ensure that the Verein's suggestions would be granted a hearing at future board meetings. Notwithstanding the repeated praise for the class-transcending power of language, the leadership structure of the German School Association was strictly hierarchical, with clergymen, manufacturers, journalists, physicians, and lawyers occupying the positions of president, vice-president, German school inspector, and treasurer, respectively.[109] Yet although tradesmen rarely spoke up during meetings and only once joined a delegation to the Berlin Public School Board, their presence illustrated the association's ability to draw upon the support of many classes, encompassing artisans and entre-preneurs, labourers and professionals.[110] It was Karl Müller, in particular, whose quiet work behind the scenes would keep the association afloat during the coming decade.[111]

The Schulverein's public face was constituted by its eleven clergymen, who performed the time-consuming task of visiting the town's German-language programs and submitting detailed reports to the Berlin Public School Board. Their close cooperation symbolized the common meeting ground that language could provide. Clergy from six denominations joined forces in the association.[112] To the men of the cloth who had witnessed the gradual shift from German to English as a language of worship, the German School Association might have appeared as a bulwark against language change.[113] That linguistic loyalties reached across denominational boundaries is also suggested by the religious profile of the German School Association. The forty-three members whose religious affiliation can be traced belonged to eight denominations, most prominently the Lutheran Church (46 percent) and the Evangelical Association (15 percent). For both denominations, the use of German as a language of worship was an "article of faith," with ethnic and religious identities complementing and reinforcing each other.[114]

Confronted with the determined campaign for German-language schooling that united Berlin's political, economic, religious, and intellectual elites, School Inspector Thomas Pearce made one feeble attempt to clear up the matter, and then fell silent.[115] In future years, he seemed determined to avoid any further controversies by describing the reading ability of Berlin's pupils as "generally speaking, good."[116] For a man used to having his suggestions followed to the letter, the "agitation in town to resume German in the schools"—as he would indignantly describe it in his local school history many years later—must have been injurious to his professional pride.[117] Pearce also felt woefully misunderstood. Had he not enrolled his very own daughter Harriet in the German Department of Berlin's Central School?[118] It did not help that the *Berliner Journal* gloated over its victory.[119]

It took a good deal of creativity to provide German-language teachers with a room of their own. In March 1903, the school board redrew the school boundaries and approved schoolhouse additions, thereby providing for a German-language classroom in each of Berlin's four elementary schools. One and a half years later, the Schulverein could credit itself with yet another major success. After four years of lobbying, German-language lessons were integrated into the regular curriculum and taught by two full-time German teachers who divided their time between Berlin's four public schools.[120] The official recognition for German-language instruction was also reflected in the marks that pupils now received for their efforts.[121] From a special branch of education, German had been transformed into

Courtland Avenue School in Berlin, Ontario. COURTESY OF KITCHENER PUBLIC LIBRARY, WATERLOO HISTORICAL SOCIETY, P-000306.

a regular, if optional, subject of instruction, taught in regular classrooms at regular times and equal to all other subjects.[122]

In establishing the German-language classroom as a prominent feature of Berlin's schools, the members of the German School Association emulated the methods of educational authorities. The first step was to institute the appointment of honorary German School Inspectors who would help develop a curriculum of German-language instruction, group pupils according to their abilities, assess the children's progress, examine the language and teaching abilities of German-language teachers, alert school trustees to weaknesses in the present system of instruction, and submit biannual reports to the Berlin Public School Board.[123] In January 1901, the School Board officially appointed Reverends R. von Pirch

(Lutheran), W. Friedrich (Baptist), and M. Boese (Lutheran) as "Inspectors for the German Classes for 1901."[124] In later years, this team of inspectors would be succeeded by Reverends Henry Wagner (Evangelical), E. Hoffman (Lutheran), and A. Mihm (Baptist).[125]

The Department of Education in Toronto was contacted only when the trustees requested exemptions from school regulations on behalf of the German School Association. In June 1903, the Department declared that the German language could be added to the entrance exam for the local high school, provided that all other subjects would be retained.[126] The Schulverein's suggestion to substitute the provincially authorized German readers with a new series of textbooks also met with success, despite some initial difficulties.[127] In January 1904, children in Berlin's German-language classrooms opened their new German readers, sanctioned by the Schulverein, the trustees, and provincial authorities alike.[128]

Having decided what was taught in the town's German classrooms, the members of the German School Association now sought to determine who would teach the German mother tongue. At the turn of the century, it had become increasingly difficult to secure qualified teachers for German-language instruction. With Louis von Neubronn heading for retirement in 1893 and William Euler leaving the profession in 1899 , an era of revolving doors began during which inexperienced teachers followed each other in quick succession.[129] In August 1900, John C. Buchhaupt, chairman of the Berlin Public School Board, offered to top up the salary of Miss Bornhold of Waterloo out of his own pocket.[130] Following his lead, the board decided to offer an annual stipend of $100 to teachers of German-language classes. The extra money allowed female teachers to break through the local salary ceiling. Between 1901 and 1905, the only years for which such data are available, Berlin's German-language instructors were among the highest paid women teachers in Waterloo County.[131] Given the added prestige and value of German teaching positions, it is hardly surprising that the number of applicants soared. In June 1906 alone, teachers from Goderich, Kingston, Penetang, Greenzolle, Sargenoon, Branchton, and Berlin applied for a vacant position.[132]

Preceding this hiring process, a heated controversy had erupted regarding the competence of Simon Reid, a Canadian-born German instructor. While conceding that Reid might be an excellent English teacher, the Schulverein questioned his German language abilities: "Our Mr. Teacher may well have mastered our local German. But between our local German and written and High German there is a difference so vast that a teacher can not possibly bridge. Mr. Reid does not live in the German-language. He thinks in English."[133] The Berlin Public School Board did not take kindly to this pointed criticism. Insisting on its prerogative to hire teachers, it faulted the association for not having voiced its objections sooner.[134] Simon Reid then rose to his own defence. In a letter submitted to the editors of the *Berliner Journal*, he insisted that Canadian-born teachers were as capable of teaching their young wards as were German-born instructors.[135] Reid's letter helped resolve the issue, albeit hardly in the way he had envisioned. His shaky construction of German sentences, compounded by no fewer than fifty mistakes in fifty-five newspaper lines, swayed the opinion of the trustees.[136] On 26 June 1906, a "joint committee composed of three members of the School Board and three members of the German School Association" was appointed to recommend "no less than two applicants whom they consider capable of filling the vacancy on our staff of German language teachers."[137] When teacher Theo Schultz of Berlin received his job offer two weeks later, the German School Association had not only rectified a "scandalous" situation, but also asserted its right to shape the German language curriculum.[138] As a language of modernity and culture, German had won the acclaim of local elites while becoming ever further removed from the local idiom of Waterloo County's German residents. The number of schoolchildren enrolled in the program increased from 12 percent in 1900 to 67 percent in 1912, among them many British-origin children who garnered praise from the German school inspectors.[139] The German School Association subsidized the children's school readers, organized school picnics, awarded prizes to outstanding students, and continued to lobby the school board.[140] Once the infrastructure of German-language instruction had been established, the association turned to Berlin's parents, appealing to their sense of duty to preserve "our dear mother tongue" and urging them to send their children to German classes.[141] With enrolment figures still rising in 1908, the membership of the Schulverein began to decline.[142] The sense of urgency that had led to its birth was fading.

But the search for ever better methods of German language instruction continued, now spearheaded by the Berlin Public School Board itself. Given the scarcity of qualified German language teachers, the School Board arranged for the granting of "special permits" by the Education Department that allowed uncertified teachers to work in the German classroom.[143] Abandoning the hitherto strictly voluntary nature of German language studies, it resolved "that the pupils who commence taking German be requested to continue until the end of the term unless the Parents furnish to this Board satisfactory reasons for wanting their child to drop that subject."[144] The board also introduced German lessons into all kindergartens and lower grades.[145] Tacitly acknowledging the fact that German had become a foreign language to many, if not most, schoolchildren who were likely to use either English or the "local German" at home, the Berlin School Board instructed the teachers in its employ "to make more use of conversational exercises and not lay so much stress as heretofore on reading and writing."[146] The German-language classroom that emerged from these measures was an innovative, flexible teaching space that County School Inspector F. W. Sheppard described to the Superintendent of Education in 1913 as follows:

> In Berlin an average of ½ hours per lesson is given twice and three times per week respectively to lower and higher classes, beginning with the Kindergarten and ending with Junior Third classes ... Teachers are well educated Germans and speak the language fluently, but none of them at present engaged has any professional standing as teacher in Ontario ... The teachers of German pass from room to room and from school to school ... The regular teacher in charge of the room remains in the room during the German lessons and is responsible for discipline ... The lessons consist of Reading, Writing, Spelling, and Translation; but most of the time is given to oral composition of conversation.[147]

While German-language instruction had become embedded in local structures of schooling, it never quite lost its transitory character. It was a part within the system but not of the system. Teachers were special instructors who did not possess provincial teaching certificates; German-language classrooms had been abolished in favour of a system of itinerant teachers; German-language instruction was optional, not mandatory.

In a local context where the German current intermingled comfortably with the Canadian mainstream, the ripples of World War I were felt keenly. To counteract any allegations of German-Canadian disloyalty, the city's political and economic elites rushed to found the Berlin branch of the Canadian Patriotic Fund Association—headed, among others, by two members of the German School Association, W.H. Schmalz and Louis Breithaupt—which collected $95,000 in support of families of Canadian soldiers. Meanwhile, local businesses were able to secure government orders for the production of war-related goods. By the fall of 1914, Berlin's shoe factories had churned out 20,000 military boots, while local textile factories produced 10,000 military shirts and Berlin's button factories manufactured 420,000 dozen buttons for uniforms.[148] Nonetheless, in 1915 the city's innovative German language program was dismantled and a year later, the city's name was changed from "Berlin" to "Kitchener" after a long and divisive debate.[149]

The school trustees who voted for disbanding German-language classes in· March 1915 advanced a pedagogical rationale for their decision. Unsettled by the fact that two-thirds of the city's schoolchildren did not complete the highest grade of the elementary school course before reaching the legal school-leaving age of fourteen, the trustees searched for ways to condense the curriculum in the earlier grades. By abolishing the teaching of German, they proposed, time would be freed up to teach the core subjects of "the highest grade, the senior fourth, in which a pupil acquires the greatest knowledge of the practical affairs of the world in which he is to spend the rest of his natural life."[150] The earnest arguments exchanged by supporters and critics of this measure at a meeting of the school board, which welcomed forty members of the German School Association to its deliberations, belie the assumption that World War I demolished a thriving, confident German-Canadian identity in Waterloo County.[151] Rather, in the uneasy mood of the war, different strands of criticism concerning German-language instruction were bundled together into an argument that swayed a board of trustees whose election the *Berliner Journal* had welcomed only a year earlier as an endorsement of the "friends of German language teaching."[152] Trustee Louis Sattler, one of the three dissenting voices on the board, stated that "there is no school in Ontario that has the standing that our schools have, even if they do not take up the study of German."[153] Indeed, as the local *Daily Telegraph* admitted, "the one weak feature in the school board's case" was its inability to prove that the teaching of German constituted "a detriment to the progress of the pupil."[154] Yet neither the admirable record of Berlin's public schools nor Mayor Hett's impassioned statement that bilingualism represented a "decided advantage" persuaded the majority of the trustees, who for various reasons had arrived at the conclusion that "we are not pledged to look after the teaching of one single subject but rather to see to the welfare and the highest education of the masses of children in our care," as board chairman, Arthur Pequegnat, put it.[155]

In his comments, Pequegnat—a long-time supporter of German-language instruction—recalled how he had kept alive his own mother tongue, French, by speaking "nothing else at home but French—the result is that today none of my children will attempt to address me in another language excepting in the presence of company."[156] In order to learn German, Pequegnat had attended church services of Berlin's many German-speaking congregations. Later, he offered a "helping hand" in introducing German lessons into the local school curriculum:

> My main expectations were that by giving the children German lessons, they would learn to love the language and that at least those who attend German churches would help to preserve the language there, but what do we see today? The scheme is a failure; it has been killed—not at school—please don't blame the school—but in most of the German homes and in the churches.[157]

Group of children in front of the Berlin Public Library, Berlin, Ontario, 1912.
COURTESY OF KITCHENER PUBLIC LIBRARY, P-010261.

The thrust of Pequegnat's argument was taken up by other board members and by the English-language press, who reasoned in unison that English had supplanted German as the medium of local communication. "While ten or fifteen years ago the ability to speak German was looked upon as one of the necessary qualifications of salesmen in Berlin stores, this is no longer the case," the *Daily Telegraph* wrote. "English ... has become the language of business even in places like Berlin."[158] Trustee E.D. Lang pointed to "our Public Library, where only the older folks and those of more recent arrival from Germany are taking German books. The young people who have in the past 10 or 15 years had German instruction in our schools are not reading German books."[159]

Detached from the fabric of everyday life, standard German had become yet another school subject, albeit one with local "sentimental" value.[160] But sentiment alone, as the trustees held, was not enough to justify the continuation of German-language classes if the time could be spent much more fruitfully on teaching "the practical affairs of the world."[161] Other trustees voiced misgivings over the presence of a language other than English in the public school system which, after all, was to serve the goal of "a thorough English education."[162] They stated that bilingual instruction represented "a hindrance in the lower grade," where it led to confusion in the pupils' minds and questioned the merely conversational character of German-language teaching, concluding that the "cultural study" of modern languages was best served by high schools and universities, where "those students of German who have not studied the language in the Public Schools make just as much progress as those that have."[163]

In earlier decades, the *Berliner Journal* had been quick to refute objections against bilingual school instruction (which in any case enjoyed far greater currency in the United States than in Waterloo County) and again, the *Journal* interjected that the ability to speak the German language was sadly ignored in high schools and universities.[164] But to no avail. In the fall of 1915, German-language instruction was removed from the public school curriculum in Berlin. The creative classroom experiment in Waterloo County's public schools that emphasized conversation and oral mastery of the language over grammar and literature thus ended one year into World War I. By then, English had supplanted standard German as the medium of everyday communication, although a local German-English hybrid proved remarkably persistent well into the twentieth century, much to the irritation of ethnic leaders who had publicly ridiculed teacher Simon Reid for his "local German" and declared him unfit to teach in Berlin's German-language classes.

Significantly, the extensive German -anguage program offered at Berlin's public schools came to an end not because of external intervention or threats, but because the local rules of the language game had changed—rules devised by German community leaders who continued to remain in control of the county's economy and its civic institutions. For them, it had become less pressing to express their ethnic heritage in the German mother tongue. The elderly Louis Breithaupt, who had acted as the president of the German School Association for many years, serves as a case in point. Although German was still his language—and one whose value and importance he eloquently defended in 1915—it no longer was the language he used in his family correspondence. When writing to his daughter Catherine in September 1913, only the heartfelt "God Bless" with which he opened his letter was written in German: "Ich wünsche Dir den Segen Gottes zum Gruß."[165] Even

Colour postcard of Berlin, Ontario, 1914. COURTESY OF KITCHENER PUBLIC LIBRARY, P-000246.

in this most German of families, language had become dissociated from ethnicity. And yet, the German mother tongue continued to resonate with emotions, just as it continued to serve as a signifier of an ethnic heritage. That the latter was, by now, mostly symbolic in nature did not make it any less real.

CONCLUSION

The self-declared guardians of the German language in Waterloo County championed a pure and proper German which, particularly after Germany's 1871 victory over France, was thought to echo the glory of the German empire—a language of learning, literature, and cultural refinement. At a time when enrolment figures in the county's German departments were steadily declining, ethnic leaders in Waterloo County identified the German language as a badge of ethnicity that had to be sheltered, nurtured, and protected.[166] Yet such grand ambitions rarely resonated in the lives of migrants, whose transcultural experiences defied neatly drawn national or linguistic boundaries.[167] They regarded language as a conversational tool and saw no need to study the mother tongue at school; for was it not spoken daily at home? The telling refusal of many families to enrol their children in German-language classes suggests that they were eager for their youngsters to move comfortably in Waterloo County's German-English world. To do so, the children needed to learn English at school in addition to the German they already spoke, albeit not with the "purity" that ethnic leaders desired.

Even in Waterloo County, where German culture was embedded in the very structures of local community, the notion of language as a symbol of ethnicity thus failed to capture the hearts of German settlers and their descendants. While embracing the stereotypical compliments paid to the county's "good Germans," Waterloo County's German residents expressed their ethnic consciousness in the many languages of ethnicity—in a "local" German that captured the dual sensibilities of their lives; in the popular Pennsylvanian-Dutch dialect that was regularly (if gently) ridiculed in the county's German-language press, although it remained inaudible in the public debates surrounding German-language schooling;[168] in High German; and increasingly in the English language. An emotional attachment to their linguistic heritage lingered, as reflected in the 1901 census that saw close to 90 percent of Berlin's German Canadians identify German as their mother tongue. And yet by the turn of the century, most parents had begun to converse in English with their children, just as they ignored the German-language offerings at Berlin's public library.

These casual attitudes toward the German language clearly exasperated cultural leaders, who had begun to complain of the misuse of their mother tongue in the mid-1870s. They advocated the German language classroom as a means to instill proper norms of language use, respect for grammatical rules, and facility in reading and writing standard German, thereby seizing upon language as a symbol of ethnic values and cultural continuity during the very decades in which Western nation-states sought to achieve national cohesion through linguistic homogenization.[169] Their efforts culminated in an elaborate ethnic revival at the turn of the century that was prompted by a perceived external threat and resulted in a fairly comprehensive German-language program. Indeed, what gives this tale of languages of ethnicity an intriguing local twist is the turn-of-the-century flowering of German-language instruction that saw enrolment figures in Berlin's German-language programs increase from 9 percent in 1889 to over two-thirds of the local school population in 1912. While conservative in their belief in language purity, these language advocates exhibited much ingenuity in their attempts to teach the German mother tongue to local schoolchildren. In close cooperation, the German School Association and the Berlin School Board devised a modern-language curriculum—taught by recent German immigrants—that focussed on spoken language and conversational skills and offered instruction in theory and grammar only as a means to further the oral command of (standard) German. Devised at the grassroots level and informed by local knowledge and expertise, this curriculum represented a radical departure from German-language instruction at Canadian high schools and universities, which were preoccupied with the study of grammar and literature.

Ethnic leaders failed to make language the clay out of which to mould a public group identity, for their rigid notion of language did not allow for the many languages of ethnicity spoken in Waterloo County. Ironically, it was their very exasperation over such "ugly" practices of language use as the local German-English hybrid that rescued the history of the spoken word from the silence that so often surrounds it. In refusing to make High German the cornerstone of their ethnic consciousness, the Germans of Waterloo County embraced the more fluid currents of language practices, easily moving back and forth between the German and English streams of their lives or blending the two in a local undercurrent that fittingly expressed the cultural duality of their world.

3.

Speaking Modern

The Culture of the German-Language Classroom, Buffalo, New York

*O*n 1 August 1870, ninety-six men and twenty women gathered in Louisville, Kentucky, for the inaugural meeting of the National German-American Teachers' Association.[1] Their goal was, as the *Amerikanische Schulzeitung* reported, "to assemble and unite the guardians of the German language and spirit who have been scattered across our adoptive Fatherland."[2] By promoting German-language instruction at American schools, they sought to reform the public school system. The mindless recitation of facts, the reliance on textbooks as the source of all knowledge were to be replaced by the rational and natural methods of German pedagogy as they had been pioneered by Pestalozzi and Fröbel in the early nineteenth century.[3] The German language, in short, presented but a vehicle for the transformation of public schools into "a modern school of culture."[4]

The enthusiasm of the participants that found expression in an almost missionary zeal was fuelled by the Franco-Prussian War of 1870–71. The war, one member mused, was nurturing a new sense of national pride both in Germany and abroad. Hitherto, Germans had loved their *Heimat* (homeland) but not their nation, for the tiny German states and principalities could hardly lay claim to so proud a title. Now, Germany seemed poised to fulfill its mission as "the bearer of culture and humanist education."[5] In turn, German-American teachers were urged to cling tenaciously to German language and learning so that they, "as Americans among Americans," could introduce German pedagogy into American schools.[6]

At the Louisville convention, dominated as it was by political exiles of the failed 1848–49 revolutions, the language of educational reform was inseparably intertwined with expressions of ethnic pride and the desire to preserve the German language on American shores.[7] Like other reform movements, this one was community oriented, but its community was rooted not in place but in the emerging networks of a German America that would spring into bloom in the exuberant German peace jubilee celebrations in the spring of 1871.[8] Like other reform movements, too, its rationale was as much geared toward child-centred education as it was toward legitimizing the political agenda of its leaders.[9] And yet, precisely because its goals were couched in the language of ethnicity, historians have tended to dismiss any claims of larger societal changes. Dissatisfied with the writings of "contributionist" ethnic historiography, they have focussed instead on the ever-declining enrolment figures in public school language programs that testified to the gap between the expectations of ethnic leaders and the majority of migrants.[10]

This chapter takes a fresh look at the writings and aspirations of German-American pedagogues in the late nineteenth and early twentieth centuries. Their proposals were more firmly embedded in the American educational landscape than their proponents might have either realized or cared to admit. But in their sophisticated treatment of language instruction methods they sounded a unique note that reverberated far beyond the select circle of the National German-American Teachers' Association (Nationaler Deutsch-Amerikanischer Lehrerbund). Indeed, the Lehrerbund, as it became known, may best be understood as a social movement intent on spreading the virtues of German pedagogy and language across the continent. Each year, it convened to debate strategies for promoting the teaching of German. Its monthly journal, the *Amerikanische Schulzeitung*, came to offer a forum for animated discussions on methods of instruction and the role of the German language in the United States.[11] Equally important, the columns of the *Schulzeitung* chronicled the state of German language instruction. Under the heading "Statistics" (later "Correspondence"), members reported on the bewildering diversity of German-language programs at parochial, private, and public schools.

Classroom teachers of German were thus drawn into a professional network that derived its authority from both pedagogical innovation and ethnic ambition.[12] In a fascinating microcosm, the Lehrerbund writings reveal how ethnic and professional networks converged over time, in the process transforming German from a "mother tongue" to a "modern language."

LANGUAGE AND THE LEHRERBUND

The Nationaler Deutsch-Amerikanischer Lehrerbund was many things, but "national" it was not. The bulk of its founding members came from the so-called "German Triangle," the area defined by the cities of Cincinnati, St. Louis, and Milwaukee.[13] In 1870, delegates from Ohio, Kentucky, and Indiana represented almost three-quarters of the participants, compared to the lone representative from Buffalo, a certain W.H. Weick.[14] Until December 1918, when the last issue of the *Schulzeitung* would appear, these midwestern states constituted the stronghold of the Lehrerbund. The Lehrerbund was a self-selected group in another way as well. In its early years, it was dominated by refugees of the failed revolutions of 1848–49, among them the association's first president, E. Feldner.[15] The radical bent of the "Forty-Eighters" manifested itself in a strong resentment of religious education and a firm belief that education had the power, nay the obligation, to reform society.[16] In early nineteenth-century Germany, these reformers—many of whom were ordinary schoolteachers—had enthusiastically endorsed efforts to liberate German schools from clerical supervision and introduce child-centred methods of instruction into the classroom.[17] They had also revolted against the conservative backlash in the wake of the Congress of Vienna (1815), which pitted progressive teachers associations against repressive governments.[18] Crossing the Atlantic, these men and women brought with them both a zeal for reform and an aversion to religion, which they eloquently expressed. The "sectarian schools," one delegate held, presented "a weapon ... against German character and civilization, against modern science and progress," while another spoke of the "poison of sanctimonious stultification."[19] Only one voice of protest could be heard when the Lehrerbund's inaugural meeting voted to ban the Bible from the schools.[20] This rhetoric, of course, could not but drive a wedge between German-language teachers of secular and religious persuasions. Teachers at parochial schools tended to remain aloof from the Lehrerbund, thereby depriving the association of a large contingent of potential members.[21]

United in their rejection of religious instruction, the founding members of the German-American Teachers' Association agreed that the United States presented "a nation in the making," as one speaker put it in 1871.[22] The pervasive use of the 'melting pot' metaphor did not necessarily imply a duty to assimilate.[23] Rather, it offered a justification for the continued existence of the German language.[24] "Germans and Americans should complement each other," the editor of the *Schulzeitung*, L. Klemm, wrote in October 1870. While "the American" possessed a healthy realism, stout manliness, and practical sense, "the German" brought to the United States the treasures of German science, art, and culture, coupled with an innate humanity. It was in the mutual exchange of languages, Klemm argued, that "the student of language acquired the spirit of language and, thus, partook in the spirit of the nation."[25] In the case of German migrants, this cultural exchange entailed both a duty to learn English "as perfectly as possible" and an obligation to cultivate the German language.[26]

Importantly, although the members of the Lehrerbund saw themselves as "citizens of two tongues," they pledged their *political* loyalty to one nation-state only: the United States.[27] Coloured by an air of cultural superiority, this dual identity found expression in the association's constitution. Having announced their goal "to cultivate German language and literature alongside the English one," the writers of the constitution voiced their intention to "raise truly free American citizens" by introducing the natural methods of German pedagogy into the schools.[28] It is the subtext of these claims that is of interest here. In the homeland of republicanism, the Lehrerbund suggested, the prevalent methods of teaching fostered a blind belief in authority. The "slavish dependency" on the textbook stifled the child's natural curiosity and ought to be replaced by teaching methods that encouraged both independent thinking and true understanding.[29]

If the delegates concurred in their overall goals, they engaged in a heated debate as to the best vehicle for language maintenance. In addressing the first meeting of the Lehrerbund, President Feldner was adamant that the increase of private German-American schools was the key goal of the association.[30] Like others, he felt that these independent schools fulfilled a pioneering role in teaching their students both the German and English languages. By contrast, pupils at public schools rarely acquired more than a smattering of German.[31] Further, in the select circles of the Lehrerbund, German-American private schools enjoyed the enviable reputation of being far superior to public schools. As faithful followers of German reform pedagogy, private schools offered child-centred instruction that cultivated a lively discourse between teachers and students rather than textbook learning and memorization.[32] Finally, as delegate W. Müller argued in 1873, an independent German-American school system offered the only true bastion for the German language, for the introduction of German-language classes in American public schools was a political concession that American shrewdness could withdraw at any moment.[33]

Notwithstanding the vocal support for private schools, a new strategy for promoting German language instruction emerged in the 1870s. Buoyed by Germany's victory in the Franco-Prussian war, the *Schulzeitung*'s editor, L. Klemm, became convinced that public schools represented the future home of German language and pedagogy. "Let's change our tactics!" he proclaimed in a programmatic article. "The public schools are the proper place for cultivating true pedagogical principles among Americans."[34] At the association's third convention in 1872, he demanded that German teachers join the American mainstream. He did so in a display of rhetorical fireworks that left many of his colleagues reeling.[35] Klemm professed little patience with "German haughtiness" that preferred to remain aloof from the grand project of nation building. Instead, he aspired to apply the principles of German education to the country's public schools. "The more refined metal we cast into the pot," he concluded, alluding to the melting pot metaphor once more, "the more refined the blend will be."[36]

In the early 1870s, Klemm's optimism seemed to be well founded. Between 1864 and 1874, eight major American cities had introduced German-language instruction into their public school systems.[37] Cities like Cleveland, Indianapolis, and Baltimore established extensive bilingual programs. Others, like Chicago, Buffalo, Milwaukee, and New York were content to integrate German-language classes into the regular curriculum.[38] To the chagrin of the German-American Teachers' Association, only a few cities emulated the example of Cincinnati, "the unchallenged pioneer in nineteenth-century German-language education," as Steven L. Schlossman has remarked.[39] Here, as early as 1840, German had become part of the regular school curriculum, and by the 1870s had flowered into a sophisticated program of dual language instruction. In the first four elementary grades, two teachers—a German and an English one—were jointly responsible for teaching the class. While half the children attended the German lessons during the morning, the other half pursued their studies in the classroom of the English teacher, switching places in the afternoon. In the higher grades, children had one German language class daily.[40] Still, even though few cities matched the scope and quality of Cincinnati's bilingual curriculum, the readiness to open the doors of the public school system to the German language must have seemed encouraging.

The reasons why German gained a foothold in the public system were complex. By 1860, the massive number of Germans who had emigrated before the Civil War had settled on farms in the Midwest and in the country's burgeoning cities.[41] By the early 1870s, many of the migrants had acquired American citizenship and entered the electoral rolls, thereby increasing German political clout.[42] As a result, their lobbying efforts for German-language instruction became harder to defuse. Simultaneously, Anglo-American educators such as William Torrey Harris, the superintendent of education in St. Louis, Missouri, developed a pragmatic socio-political rationale for introducing German-language classes. If public schools offered instruction in German, Harris reasoned in 1869, German children would be drawn from the private schools into the public system, where they could be rapidly assimilated.[43]

Triggered by the economic recession that hit the country in 1873, there was indeed a noticeable shift in enrolment from private to public schools.[44] As Bettina Goldberg has demonstrated for Milwaukee, once the school board added German-language lessons to the public school curriculum in 1870, public school enrolment rose significantly, "especially in Milwaukee's heavily German wards."[45] As enrolment patterns changed, so too did the membership structure of the Lehrerbund. As early as 1876, delegates from public schools began to outnumber teachers from private schools at the annual conventions.[46] Given these developments, it is hardly surprising that public schools came to occupy a central position in the Lehrerbund's agenda.

Although tensions between public and private school supporters never completely subsided, both factions found common ground in the pedagogical principles they advocated. Long before the reform movement of modern language teaching rose to international prominence in the 1880s, the members of the Lehrerbund formulated innovative teaching strategies that treated German as a living language, not a dead one.[47] In discarding the conventional grammar-translation method, they stipulated that language lessons ought to teach children to *speak* German fluently, correctly, and clearly.[48] This goal presented a radical departure from contemporary thinking on modern language instruction. As Susan N. Bayley has shown for a British context, modern languages had "won inclusion in the liberal curriculum by capitalizing on their similarity to the classics as subjects with complex linguistic textures and rich literatures."[49] In an academic culture that regarded conversational skills as a "trifling accomplishment," modern languages were valued not as a medium of communication but as a means to sharpen the intellect. Accordingly, French and German were taught like the classics: "by memorization, recitation, parsing and translation."[50]

Understandably, this practice held little attraction for the members of the Lehrerbund. As native speakers who were deeply involved in their respective German-American communities, they could not but think of their mother tongue as a living language. As professionals, moreover, they were finely attuned to a language shift that manifested itself among their young charges as early as the 1870s. On the playground and the streets, members observed German children speaking English among themselves. Even in *Turner* (gymnastic) societies and German-American publishing houses, those bulwarks of German language and culture, young gymnasts and typesetters were overheard conversing in English.[51] In this era of transition, German had become a foreign language for many youth, a process that could be reversed only through the concerted effort of dedicated educators who sought to instill "the love of German language and German spirit into our pupils' hearts."[52]

German thus emerged as a peculiar hybrid of "mother tongue" and "foreign language." While retaining the emotive power of the former, it was its latter incarnation that called for new methods of instruction. Hearing and speaking, German-American schoolteachers urged, were the foundations of all language teaching. Instead of submitting children to a torturous course of grammatical rules, conjugations, and declensions, designed only to stifle their interest and discourage them, they were to learn grammar inductively. Conversational exercises and a systematic course in *oral* instruction were to supplant formal lessons in grammar and translation.[53] In heeding Pestalozzi's advice to see the world through the child's eyes, teachers were to proceed from the simple to the difficult, from the concrete to the abstract, from the known to the unknown. Instruction in reading and writing was to be postponed until children had immersed themselves in the sounds of the German language, able both to understand the teacher (who of course spoke in German only) and formulate simple thoughts of their own.[54]

At the heart of the new course of study was "object-teaching," or, more precisely, *Anschauungsunterricht*. In simple conversations, children were to be encouraged to observe their surroundings and describe what they saw. "The language of the teacher has to be stimulating and lively," one school instructor recommended. "Incidentally, the teacher should speak less and the pupils more."[55] The topics of conversation were many, he continued. In the first year, the school, the home, animals, and plants provided ample opportunity for building a vocabulary and nurturing a "feeling for language" (*Sprachgefühl*). In the second year, conversation might turn to fields and woods, the sky, sun, moon, and stars. By being asked to describe the names, shapes, parts, and colours of the natural world, the children would playfully learn about adjectives, adverbs, and gender. Learning by doing would thus replace the dry study of grammar.[56] At all times, children were asked to speak in complete sentences. Their pronunciation had to be correct from the very beginning, while the English language should be barred from the German classroom.[57]

In this ideal course of instruction, children proceeded to a *study* of language only after they had learned how to *speak* it. Phonetics provided a particularly useful tool, not only in teaching pronunciation but also in helping children to analyze the components of sentences and words: "The spoken sentences—or parts thereof—have to be broken into words, words into syllables and, thereafter, into sounds."[58] These exercises prepared students to learn reading and writing; for written language simply visualized the sounds of spoken language, an area with which the children were already familiar. [59] Grammar and translation, finally, should be limited to a minimum. While undoubtedly useful in helping older students understand the nuances and structure of language, they should not be taught at the cost of conversational skills. "In my many years of teaching," one teacher recalled, "I have encountered several students who had gulped down the entire grammar à la Ollendorf and yet could not express a single thought in correct German."[60] Conversational skills and oral fluency, German-American pedagogues agreed, were the stepping stones to a true mastery of the German language. Needless to say, these well-tried principles of German-language teaching were advocated for Anglo-American pupils as well. Although it might be advisable to teach Anglo-American children in separate classrooms, they also had to learn how to understand, speak, and then write and read the German language.[61]

These recommendations presented the distilled wisdom of years of classroom teaching, mostly at private German-American schools. The approach that thus emerged was remarkable for its practical suggestions. It was developed by schoolteachers who were guided not by academic aspirations but by the desire to keep the German mother tongue alive as a medium of communication. Their detailed suggestions, which drew upon their personal experiences, provide glimpses into the German-language classroom that was idealized as a place of true learning.

Their enthusiasm notwithstanding, German-American teachers were pragmatic enough to realize that the pedagogical principles they advocated were a far cry from the textbook-centred learning that characterized many an American school. To disseminate their methods, it was not enough to present them at the Lehrerbund conventions or publish them in the pages of the *Amerikanische Schulzeitung*. Rather than preaching to the converted, they had to reach out to both the German-American public and their Anglo-American colleagues.

In seeking to enlist the help of German associations and communities across the country, the German-American Teachers' Association presented itself as the guardian of German language and culture. Its proclaimed goal was to fight a "battle for the preservation of *Deutschthum* [Germanness]."[62] For this worthy endeavour it welcomed the support of gymnastic societies, singing societies, and German clubs.[63] It also encouraged the founding of German school associations that were to lobby for the "reform of public education" in general and the introduction of German into the public school curriculum in particular.[64] The daily press, in turn, was asked to publicize the Lehrerbund's agenda and mobilize the German-American population.[65] If these appeals lacked in fervour, the detailed suggestions on how to harness German political clout did not. In no uncertain terms, the Lehrerbund called upon "all German-American citizens" to "stand guard that no delegate of the people or public official will be elected ... who has not fully committed himself to the program of school reform."[66] Neither petitions nor mass meetings would ensure the success of German language instruction, L. Klemm reminded his audience. Instead, it was at the ballot box that the fate of German would be decided.[67] This strategy, of course, could not succeed without German unity. German particularism, that deplorable "enemy in our own ranks," had to be overcome, Klemm urged.[68]

But if the Lehrerbund was a German-American association whose members proudly asserted their ethnic identity and sought to mobilize ethnic organizations and newspapers, it also was a professional association that was dominated by schoolteachers and pedagogues. In this latter function, the Lehrerbund reached out to Anglo-American educators with whom it shared a common interest in school reform. As historian Daniel T. Rodgers has shown, such professional networks crossed boundaries of nationality or ethnic identity and drew upon "foreign models and imported ideas."[69] In a similar vein, the Lehrerbund was keenly aware of debates within the National Education Association (NEA), which had been founded in 1857 as an association of professional teachers.[70] It was with evident satisfaction that the *Amerikanische Schulzeitung* described the mounting support for object-teaching and the "natural method of instruction" (*die entwickelnde Methode*) that it perceived among Anglo-American educators. Little wonder, then, that the Lehrerbund sought to forge bonds with the NEA, whose political influence it admired and wished to emulate.[71]

As early as 1872, the Lehrerbund began to make overtures by inviting "renowned Anglo-American reform pedagogues" to participate in special English-language sessions at its annual conventions.[72] The dialogue thus initiated was continued by publishing conference proceedings in both German and English and by sending delegates to the twelfth annual meeting of the NEA in Boston in 1872.[73] In detecting a potential ally, the Lehrerbund delegation submitted a communication in which they assured their Anglo-American colleagues of their "desire to join their earnest efforts with yours."[74] But how far should cooperation extend?

An eloquent few enthusiastically advocated a merger with the NEA. For men like P. Stahl or L. Klemm, a "melting" of the two associations was the only sensible course. As a subsection of the NEA, the forces of reform would be united and the Lehrerbund's prestige enhanced.[75] Yet when, in 1872, delegate Schrenck proposed to hold a joint convention with the NEA (provided, of course, the selected location was reasonably close to the "centres of *Deutschthum*"), his suggestion was soundly rejected. His critics cautioned against the danger of reducing the Lehrerbund to a mere appendix of the Anglo-American association. They felt that in order to wield its influence, the Lehrerbund had to preserve its independence. In a strongly worded resolution, their argument carried the day. Until its dissolution in 1918, the German-American Teachers' Association would remain an independent organization that politely rejected any offers from the NEA to join its ranks.[76] This independent stance, however, did not prevent the Lehrerbund from forging ever-closer ties with Anglo-American educators. Eventually, in 1874, the Lehrerbund and the NEA convened simultaneously in Detroit, Michigan. And rather than being swallowed by their English-speaking counterpart, the members of the Lehrerbund revelled in the praise that was heaped upon Germany for its pioneering role in promoting rational principles of education.[77]

The accolades of Anglo-American pedagogues figured prominently in the pages of the *Amerikanische Schulzeitung*. Perhaps betraying a craving for recognition, the official organ of the Lehrerbund meticulously listed any speech that showed appreciation for "the true value of German-language instruction for the cultural development of the United States," as the Cleveland superintendent of education, Andrew Rickoff, put it in 1876.[78] For the German migrants who had

tirelessly championed the virtues of German pedagogy, Rickoff's words provided a welcome assurance that the German language had successfully entered
the American mainstream, suffusing it with a cultural sophistication hitherto
unknown. No longer did German educators work in an ethnic enclave, their grand
vision going unheard. Instead, as the smug satisfaction in the *Schulzeitung* reflected,
their contributions to American culture seemed to be recognized at last.[79]

German-American campaigns for language maintenance, by contrast, failed to
garner similar effusive praise. When it came to their fellow German migrants, the
Lehrerbund members did not hesitate to admonish and preach, scold and berate.
If only more German teachers attended the annual conventions; if only German
immigrants learned to set aside their differences; if only German Americans
shook off their infuriating apathy; then, the reasoning went, the cause of German-
language teaching would be won.[80] In trying to spur German Americans into
action, the Lehrerbund clearly preferred the proverbial whip to the carrot. No
German language program shy of a comprehensive bilingual curriculum could
hope to win its admiration

NETWORKS OF ETHNICITY

In the discursive universe of the Lehrerbund, Buffalo was one among many delinquents. It was in 1866 that the German language had first entered Buffalo's elementary schools.[81] Upon the suggestion of Aldermen Jacob Schau and Richard
Flach, Superintendent John S. Fosdick proposed to City Council "to employ two
German teachers" to be "assigned to Public Schools Nos. 12, 13, 15 and 31, which
Districts are principally inhabited by citizens of German descent."[82] Remarkably,
for a city in which the issue of German-language instruction had stirred public
debate and nativist sentiment in 1837–39 and again in 1850–51, not a negative
word was to be heard in either the council or the local newspapers.[83] It might have
helped that German migrants had enlisted in the Civil War in greater numbers
than had either Anglo-Americans or Irish-Americans, the city's two other major
nationality groups.[84] In addition, Democrats, those self-declared "protector[s] of
ethnic communalism," now dominated the city council.[85]

In the following years, the German-language program grew steadily, soon
encompassing thirteen elementary schools, 774 pupils, and seven instructors,
four of them male itinerant teachers who had been hired at the generous salary
of $1,075 each. By comparison, the three female teachers of German earned an

average of $557 per annum.[86] In the words of David Gerber, a "small, token program in German" had quickly metamorphosed into "a large, expensive, and ethnically separate program, staffed by ethnic teachers with no other obligations."[87] To the dismay of Superintendent Larned, the system of itinerant teachers proved both ineffective and expensive: rather than spending their time in the classroom, the four male instructors spent long hours walking from one school to the next, for a trolley service was available only on Main and Niagara Streets.[88] Female teaching assistants, Larned suggested, should replace the itinerant teachers. They would "teach at only one school ... and assist instruction in other subjects, but earn about half the salary."[89] The vocal resistance of German Americans prevented Larned from implementing the change. Still, he began to hire female assistants in greater numbers, examine male itinerant teachers, and standardize the course of study.[90]

Given Larned's well-known objections to the itinerant system, it could only look suspicious when he submitted a school budget for the year 1873–74 that did not include the salaries for the four male German teachers at elementary schools. Larned was adamant that the omission had been an oversight and immediately asked City Council to reinstate the funds.[91] However, the council thwarted his efforts. In a heated, often acrimonious debate, the Republicans, who now held twenty-two out of twenty-six seats, rejected any attempt by the school committee to restore the salaries.[92] Alderman Webster spoke for many when he said that the "Germans came here to be American citizens. Let them forget their old country and prejudice as soon as possible."[93]

It was the representatives of organized *Deutschthum*, mainly of secular and liberal persuasion, who spearheaded the "restoration campaign" of 1873–74: the gymnasts (*Turner*), the German Young Men's Association, the newly appointed Committee of Thirty-Five (a body of renowned professionals and businessmen), and the local German-American press.[94] As it turned out, the *Turner* had not delivered an empty threat when they warned to "use all honourable means in future to keep those holding such narrow know-nothing views out of office."[95] In the fall of 1873, the city's election results indicated the existence of "a significant German protest vote."[96] After this resounding rebuke for the Republican Party, City Council listened carefully when the German Committee of Thirty-Five delivered a petition for the continued existence of German language classes in March 1874.[97] Only three weeks later, it decided "that provision be made in the estimates for the School Department for the year 1874, for teaching the German language in the public schools of the city where the patrons of such schools desire it."[98]

The new system of instruction owed much to the recommendations of Superintendent Larned. Upon his advice, female assistant teachers of German origin replaced the male itinerant teachers. Permanently assigned to one school, they worked together with their English-language colleagues, in whose classrooms they assisted when necessary.[99] German-language instruction subsequently became a popular option within the regular school curriculum and was offered in 73 percent of the public elementary schools by 1910.

If the success of the restoration campaign was remarkable, so too was the way in which news about its trials and triumphs travelled along the East Coast and across the Midwest. German-language newspapers in New York, Chicago, Milwaukee, Evansville, and Cincinnati denounced the decision of the Buffalo City Council to withhold funds for German instruction. Their greatest wrath, however, was reserved for the four German Republicans who had sided with the "know-nothings."[100] "Four German villains," wrote the *Seebote* from Milwaukee, had joined the ranks of the enemy.[101] They had betrayed the "dearest treasure of *Deutschthum*, its beautiful language," chimed in the *Union* from Evansville, while neither the *Illinois Staatszeitung* (Chicago) nor the New York *Demokrat* hesitated to pillory in bold-letter print the "traitors"—Louis Herman, Jacob Bott, Louis P. Reichert, and Wilhelm Heinrich.[102] Historical hindsight makes it evident that these aldermen were not necessarily opposed to German language and culture. Rather, as historian Andrew P. Yox has pointed out, they represented a German constituency whose educational needs were already met by parochial schools.[103] Judging from the city council minutes for 1873, their refusal to restore the salaries of the male itinerant teachers was motivated largely by their austerity in public school matters and the wish to expedite the end-of-year budget deliberations that were nearly wrecked by the restoration debate. Yet in the aftermath of the council's controversial decision, these nuances were lost in a whirlwind of indignation.

The spirited defence of the German language was never understood as an endorsement of foreign language teaching per se. As Kathleen Neils Conzen observes, German spokespersons advanced a "Germanocentric argument, not so much for the right of all groups to coexist but for the special right of Germans to support an ethnic existence in America because of the special gifts they would ultimately bring into the melting pot."[104] While defending their own ethnic rights, Buffalo's German-language newspapers were not above ridiculing the demand of Alderman Jessemin that the Celtic language be taught at the city's schools. Did he not know, thundered the *Freie Presse* in March 1874, that Celtic no longer represented a living language? The Celtic language, the *Demokrat* seconded, was spoken only by a tiny percentage of Ireland's population, namely those most ignorant and destitute.[105]

A quarter of a century later, the *Amerikanische Schulzeitung* exhibited a similar ethnic chauvinism, this time directed against the "hordes of Slavs." In an attempt to refute demands for Polish language instruction, the *Schulzeitung* suggested that "even the roughest Germans" were preferable to the "best Slavs."[106] Another author was adamant that "no foreign language should be taught in the American public schools simply because the pupils and patrons of the schools speak the foreign language in question. If this be not recognized we should have not only German schools, but Hungarian, Polish, Italian as well." Instead, the author wrote, "only such foreign languages should be introduced as have a general cultural importance or commercial value for Americans."[107] In a nutshell, we have here the rationale for German-language instruction in public schools. The German language, ethnic spokesmen argued, represented a symbol of culture whose presence would enrich the American nation as a whole. By contrast, the ill-informed attempts to introduce Hungarian, Polish, or Italian would surely lead to the Balkanization of public schools.

When, in 1910, Buffalo's superintendent of education, Henry P. Emerson, wrote of the daunting task of shaping "this strange population into a useful, homogeneous citizenship," he meticulously described a "foreign population that included 80,000 Poles, 30,000 Italians, 8,000 Hungarians, and many thousands of Slavs, Greeks, Ruthenians, Syrians and others."[108] Markedly absent from his list were Buffalo's 43,815 German-born residents who, together with the American-born Germans, constituted 29 percent of the city's population.[109] In the eyes of Emerson, German Americans had blended into the Anglo-American mainstream. They had acquired the distinction of being "good American citizens" that still eluded the more recent arrivals.[110] Although Emerson's implicit praise did not seem to translate into a special interest in German language teaching, his long-term tenure did provide a generally supportive climate in which German-language classes could prosper.[111]

The Birth of a "Modern Language"

The graded course of instruction that Superintendent Larned had devised for the German language classroom in 1872 reflected the pervasive influence of the grammar-translation method. Conversational exercises were entirely absent from the curriculum. Instead, the course of study consisted of exercises in spelling, grammar, and translation. When reading Larned's detailed instructions, it is difficult to escape the conclusion that the "declension of nouns, declension of adjectives, auxiliary verbs, ... conjugation of regular and irregular verbs, adverbs, prepositions, conjunctions, interjection" must have proved sorely trying and tiring for schoolchildren.[112] Yet only when the National German-American Teachers' Association convened in Buffalo in July 1882 did conversational exercises find entry into the curriculum.

It was with some trepidation that the Lehrerbund had chosen Buffalo as the site of its annual convention. The city, after all, did not enjoy a reputation of being progressive in matters of education.[113] However, the hospitality of Buffalo's German population left a lasting impression on the Lehrerbund members, who met daily in the chapel of the Central School to discuss educational reforms.[114] Among their attentive audience, it seemed, was Superintendent James F. Crooker, who took to the new ideas with great enthusiasm. With the zeal of the converted, his annual report for the year 1882 announced the end of the grammar-translation method. "In studying a modern language," Crooker wrote,

> it is absolutely necessary to get acquainted with the idioms of the language to be mastered, but this cannot be done by grammatical rules alone. There is no practice better adapted to become a master of a foreign language than conversational exercises, in which the foreign language is made the only means of communication. The pupils, therefore, should gradually be led to talk about the things which surround them, and to ask (or be asked) simple questions concerning things they have before their eyes. The object of instruction in German should not be to stuff the pupils with dry grammatical rules.[115]

In his endorsement of the reform methods, Crooker paid tribute to the principles which the Lehrerbund had been promoting for over a decade. Hearing and speaking skills formed the core of the new curriculum. Phonetics was singled out for special attention. Oral instruction preceded lessons in reading and writing. Teachers were cautioned against using English in the German-language classroom.

Object-teaching, finally, was hailed for its success in awakening the students' interest while honing their language skills.

Importantly, Crooker was not alone in recommending the natural method of instruction for the city's German-language classrooms. When Buffalo's newly appointed superintendent of German, Adolf Fink, took over the portfolio in 1887, he too instructed teachers "to use the 'natural method' almost exclusively."[116] The natural method, Fink elaborated in 1890, was modelled after the way in which children learned their mother tongue; for even in the foreign-language classroom, he continued, "the main end to be kept continually in view is to teach the pupil, to whatever nationality he may belong, to speak German."[117] In the years to come, Fink's successor, Matthew J. Chemnitz, would engage in a similar unending quest for the best methods of teaching the German language. His goals were modest: "a good pronunciation, an ability to understand easy German when spoken, an ability to read simple German stories without painful efforts, and an ability to construct short German sentences by applying the elementary rules of grammar."[118] But in order to achieve these goals, Chemnitz realized, the so-called "natural method" would have to be modified to the less-than-ideal learning conditions in the city's overcrowded German language classrooms.[119]

Where the Lehrerbund endorsed the natural method unhesitatingly, Chemnitz cautioned against discarding translation and grammar altogether. "Much damage has been done in this country by following too closely the natural method and despising the scientific one of our ancestors who carried it too far," he wrote in his 1897–98 report on German education.[120] Although Chemnitz did seek to hone the conversational skills of Buffalo's schoolchildren attending the German language program, he was not prepared to relinquish the mental and intellectual benefits offered by exercises in grammar and translation. His hesitation may have stemmed from his frustration with the German Department. In overcrowded classrooms that featured "benches instead of desks, desks without ink," book-centred learning provided an invaluable aid for teachers who were frequently unprepared for the exigencies of modern-language instruction.[121]

In sifting through the city's *Annual Reports of Education*, it is easy to forget that the focus on educational methods was in itself remarkable. In Buffalo, the energies of local educators were no longer bound up in the question of *whether* the German language was to be taught at public schools. Instead, successive superintendents of education were occupied with the question of *how* to attain "progress in methods and achievements."[122] At a time when German communities across the United States reported hostile attacks against German-language instruction, Buffalo seemed to be shielded from the nativist resurgence of the early 1890s.

The comparatively low enrolment figures in Buffalo's German language program may help explain why German received scant criticism. In a city where 40 percent of the population was of German origin, only 17 percent of the schoolchildren studied German in 1896, nearly half of them at parochial schools. Among the large American cities offering German language instruction, only Chicago and Toledo showed similar disproportional numbers. The political influence of Buffalo's *Deutschthum* seemed to provide protection against nativist attacks. With the vast majority of Irish Catholics voting for the Democrats and Anglo-American wards leaning heavily toward the Republicans, the German East Side cast the deciding vote in election after election. Two German Democrats, Charles Bishop and Conrad Diehl, rose to the mayoralty in the 1890s, visible symbols that Buffalo's German population had come of age.[123]

It might have helped that the local educational hierarchy was outspoken in its support for German language teaching. In 1895, Matthew J. Chemnitz, whose long tenure as German superintendent coincided with Superintendent Emerson's reign, voiced his hope "never again to hear the preposterous assertion that teaching a foreign language will tend to make the children less patriotic."[124] The study of German, he said, was based

> upon the weighty fact that German, next to English, is the commercial, as well as scientific and educational language of the world; that it is the language of the greater part of our foreign-born population, and is used extensively in trade and business; that it is the Saxon relative to English, therefore easier and more comprehensive to us; and last, but not least, that nothing is as essential to the training of the minds as the study of a foreign language.[125]

In formulating his "vigorous encouragement of our German instruction," Chemnitz drew upon the writings of Anglo-American educators who had endorsed the study of foreign languages.[126] Like his predecessors, he pointed to the experiences of his colleagues in Cincinnati, St. Louis, Chicago, Cleveland, and New York who had encouraged German language teaching in the strongest possible terms.[127] Reassured by contemporary pedagogical wisdom, Buffalo's German superintendents praised the intellectual and cultural benefits of German language classes that were taught by fifty-three teachers at thirty-eight elementary schools in 1896.[128]

The Lehrerbund also found comfort in the speeches of Anglo-American pedagogues who considered German not an "ethnic" subject of instruction but a "cultural" one.[129] Disenchanted because of its failure to mobilize German-American communities against nativist attacks, the association changed its tactics. If the American educational system could not be reformed from the bottom up, perhaps it could be changed by adopting a top-down approach, namely by convincing "our colleagues at the universities" and in the National Education Association of the values of German language instruction.[130]

While it is difficult to gauge the success of the Lehrerbund's strategy, three decades of educational reform had prepared the ground for a hospitable reception of its ideas. By the turn of the century, the idea of child-centred instruction had gained wide currency among American educators.[131] Popularized by Joseph Mayer Rice's attacks on the blight of textbook-centred schooling and mindless memorization in a magazine series in 1892, the tenets of the "new education" were carried by reformers into the nation's public school system. As much as German Americans would have liked to claim exclusive authorship, the new education constituted a transnational amalgam shaped by American educators' long-standing familiarity with Pestalozzian and Froebelian ideas, the visits of scholars to Germany, and the multitude of educational experiments carried out in settlement houses and independent schools.[132] Partaking in the reform spirit were leading Anglo-American educators who looked favourably upon foreign-language teaching. In the U.S. Commissioner of Education, Professor William Torrey Harris (the former superintendent of education in St. Louis), the Lehrerbund could appeal to a man whose intimate familiarity with and positive attitude toward German-language instruction were well known.[133] In a similar vein, in 1894 the National Education Association lauded the "immense benefit" of studying modern languages, which it viewed in purely educational terms:

> It will train their [the children's] memory and develop their sense of accuracy; it will quicken and strengthen their reasoning powers by offering them at every step problems that must be immediately solved by the correct application of the results of their own observations; it will help them to understand the structure of the English sentence and the real meaning of English worlds; it will broaden their minds by revealing to them modes of thought and expression different from those to which they have been accustomed.[134]

Three years later, the Modern Language Association of America commissioned a nation-wide survey on the status of French- and German-language instruction at secondary schools that explicitly endorsed the teaching of German in the primary grades. The survey findings and recommendations were presented at the 1898 annual meeting of the National Education Association in Los Angeles, where they met with "extraordinary approval."[135] Clearly, in its new guise as a "modern language," German-language instruction could rely on the approval of professional networks of education, just as it hitherto had relied on networks of ethnicity.

THE CULTURE OF THE CLASSROOM

As much as the prescriptional literature in the *Amerikanische Schulzeitung* can teach us about changing meanings of language, it reveals little about the culture of the local German classroom. Who enrolled in the German language program? Who taught it? How effective were the lessons? The contrast between the Lehrerbund's high hopes for the German language classroom and the practice of German-language teaching at the grassroots level was striking indeed.

Tired of lamenting its shortcomings year after year, Superintendent Matthew J. Chemnitz pictured an "ideal German Department" instead. His 1895 utopia offered a counterpoint to the very real challenges that faced Buffalo's German-language teachers.[136] Where Chemnitz dreamed of "a separate German room" in which twenty to thirty pupils received "fully thirty minutes" of instruction daily, German teachers laboured in overcrowded makeshift rooms where students arrived late and left early.[137] Where Chemnitz pictured a supportive staff of English-language colleagues who did not "let the pupil suffer for his attention to the German lesson, but ... instruct[ed] him in the missed subject willingly," German teachers worked in isolation, unable to draw upon "the constant help of principal and associate teachers, as is the case in the English branches."[138] Where Chemnitz envisioned an enhanced prestige for the German-language program, with "proficiency in German to be mentioned at graduating and other exercises," German teachers faced "a marked drop in registration from first to second grade" and parents all too willing to let their children abandon the study of German.[139]

These "negligent" parents were mostly of German origin. Although the city of Buffalo kept meticulous records of the "nationality" of its pupils, it tended to under-enumerate the percentage of German-origin children. Rather than asking for the children's ethnicity, the school statistics recorded their parents' birthplace.

With increasing numbers of German Americans born in the United States, the number of "German" children in the German Department declined rapidly, to be superseded by "American" children as early as in 1900.[140] Still, it is possible to discern two general trends. German names dominated the school register of the German Department as late as in 1915.[141] In addition, while retaining its ethnic "flair," the German language classroom attracted increasing numbers of Anglo-American pupils, particularly after German was recognized as "one of the studies entitling to entrance into the high school" in 1896.[142] Almost imperceptibly, it seems, German was being transformed from an "ethnic" language into a "modern" one whose study promised cultural and material benefits to pupils beyond Buffalo's German-American community.

The children who flocked to German-language classes encountered a teaching force that comprised German-born and German-American teachers.[143] According to an observer sent by the New York State Education Department in 1915, the teachers' "knowledge of the subject is adequate, although nearly all have traces of dialect in their speech." In fact, he continued, one "may hear as many different pronunciations, in some respects, as there are teachers."[144] When it came to their teaching ability, however, the visitor delivered a devastating judgement. He declared the extensive German-language program to be "a non-productive investment," "largely a waste," and recommended "that the study of German be deferred until the high school is reached."[145] Under present conditions, he elaborated, "nearly ten thousand pupils are taught by 67 teachers in 43 schools in order that approximately 400 may get what they would have been able to obtain under two or three teachers in one year of the high school course."[146]

The ailments of Buffalo's German-language program were many, and dissected with professional detachment by the New York State inspector. Most importantly, he argued, Buffalo's German-language teachers were insufficiently trained and supervised. Lacking "adequate teaching ability," they perfunctorily "went over" the assigned pages in the German reader, without demonstrating any understanding of general "aims of instruction." The archaic classroom vocabulary had little relation "to the sphere of activities of the pupils in his home and school life," nor did it enable them to read German-language newspapers or literature. Conversational exercises were rare. The poor reading skills of the pupils were matched only by their poor pronunciation, which proved difficult to eradicate in the ensuing high school course. Given the dismal results of the German-language program, the visitor found it impossible to escape the conclusion that German was taught "for purely sentimental reasons."[147]Instead of presiding over an interactive classroom in which children honed their conversational skills and engaged in active learning, teachers clung to textbook lessons which they taught with little imagination. A more glaring contrast to the idealized German language classroom that the Lehrerbund had promoted since its inception is hard to imagine.

CONCLUSION

"The language of education," wrote Lawrence A. Cremin, "probably changed more rapidly than the practice of education."[148] This statement certainly holds true for the imaginative attempts of German pedagogues to carry into American schools not only the German language but also the tenets of child-centred education. Promoting German as a language of modernity, the Lehrerbund found allies in the Modern Language Association of America, the National Education Association, and Buffalo's superintendents of the German Department. In so doing, the association wisely toned down its agenda. By the late nineteenth century, it was content to advocate natural methods of foreign-language teaching rather than trumpeting a sweeping reform of the American public school system. Rather than seeking to mobilize German-American communities in an effort to introduce German-language classes into the public school curriculum, it cherished the more modest accomplishment of having forged close contacts with Anglo-American educators with whom it shared a common interest in the educational values of foreign-language instruction.

If the Lehrerbund had found a comfortable niche in the mainstream of educational thought, this did not mean that its prescriptions were translated into practice in the local German-language classroom. Far from it. With a few exceptions, like Milwaukee, where the National German-American Teachers' College offered a comprehensive curriculum complete with practice lessons at the local German-English school, the training of German-language teachers was woefully inadequate. In Buffalo, the German superintendent, who also occupied the position of clerk to the superintendent of education, was too overworked to offer more than monthly workshops on German-language instruction. Similarly, his annual foray into German-language classrooms was hardly enough to give teachers proper guidance as to the intricacies of teaching modern languages.

But before dismissing the Lehrerbund's impassioned writings as inconsequential, we need to recall that the high hopes of educational reformers all too often clashed with the harsh realities of schooling. Teaching strategies nurtured in private, independent schools did not necessarily translate into the public school system.[149] And yet, they served as an important stimulus for rethinking the very underpinnings of public education. In reformulating the goals and methods of modern language teaching, the Lehrerbund left its legacy, even as the German language in Buffalo's elementary schools was washed away by the currents of World War I.[150]

Part 2

Music Matters

4.

Tunes of Community, Melodies of Race
The Buffalo Singers' Festival, 1860

*I*n the early evening hours of 24 July 1860, ten thousand people began to pour into the railroad depot at Exchange Street that provided the stage for the "monster concert" of the Buffalo singers' festival. At the west end of the hall, six hundred feet long and one hundred feet wide, five hundred singers were seated in ascending tiers, surrounded by the flags and banners of twenty-four singing societies.[1] Gas lamps illuminated the platform, where an orchestra of sixty-five musicians awaited the signal of conductor Carl Adam. The first low notes of *Tannhäuser* "hushed the audience to entire stillness," marvelled the reporter of the *Commercial Advertiser*.[2] Yet more than the music, it was the grandeur of the event that captivated the local press:

> We, who were not at the Handel celebration in London; who have never heard the Orpheonists in the Crystal Palace; who have been accustomed to think that a hundred voices pealing over a St. James Hall full of people is a

great exhibition,—to us, we say, the monster concert last night was simply a musical earthquake, or deluge, or anything else that conveys ideas of vastness and sublimity.[3]

For one evening, the "sublime" sound of music—displayed on a scale grander than what most American cities had ever seen—lent the city an air of sophistication that many contemporaries found sadly missing in Buffalo's barren urban landscape.[4] The sonorous voices of the male mass chorus also made audible the contours of a German community that, like its music, reached out across boundaries of ethnicity.

In song and sound, the singers at the Buffalo festival celebrated the German language, which in its musical incarnation would far outlast the spoken language. Intimately intertwined with a festive popular culture, the musical gathering allowed both singers and audiences to locate a German cultural identity in the chorus of German voices and to imbue the vocal harmonies with cultural, social, and political meanings. Looking inwardly, the festival nurtured bonds between Buffalo's German-speaking residents while also providing a meeting ground for German singing societies from Ohio, New York State, Pennsylvania, Michigan, Massachusetts, New Jersey, and southern Ontario.[5] Looking outwardly, it acted as a prominent expression of German culture that attracted a vast non-German audience that enthusiastically embraced the universal language of music.[6] The ready praise was all the more remarkable if viewed before the backdrop of anti-foreign nativism that had gathered force in preceding years and led to denouncements of both Sabbath recreation and alcohol consumption, two key ingredients of German popular culture.[7]

The "ocean of music which rolled its harmonies down the vast length" of the railroad depot is as lost to the historian's keen ear as are the melodies that floated from taverns and homes onto Buffalo's streets, a faint echo preserved only in the city's newspapers that faithfully chronicled the musical extravaganza.[8] Yet if we seek to unravel the meanings that resonated in this music, the local press allows us to eavesdrop on musical experiences that were not limited to the stage alone. Music resounded at railroad stations, where visiting singers were welcomed by their Buffalo hosts and ceremoniously guided to the festive headquarters, the air punctuated by the marching tunes of the Union Cornet Band.[9] Music flowed in the city's taverns as liberally as lager beer, long after the railroad depot at Exchange Street had been reclaimed by the "music of the locomotive."[10] Music infused the local landscape with sounds of "jollity" as hosts and visitors made the city "vocal with mirth."[11] Music echoed back and forth in "harmonious notes" as singing societies at the grand banquet "would hail each other across the room, each rising and cheering antiphonally, after which a grand rollicking chorus would follow for a moment."[12] Music enveloped the festive revellers at the closing picnic in Moffat's Grove, where "rich snatches of song" emanated from "all parts of the grove ... caught up or re-echoed by others, until the air was alive with music."[13] So clearly, in fact, did the keynotes of German ethnicity sound through Buffalo's urban landscape that the *Daily Courier* invited its "fellow citizens to open their ears" to listen to the festive tune of a city "*saturated* with music."[14]

To listen to the sounds of an ethnicity means to be carefully attuned to the transformative power of performance. It was in the moment of performance that "singers made songs their own with vocal inflections, gestures, and the particular circumstances under which they chose to sing," thereby appropriating folk tunes and classical melodies to their own ends. Audiences, in turn, "helped to shape a song's meaning" by listening to the singers' performance either in "hushed" reverence in the concert hall or with "hearty" approval in beer halls and picnic grounds where the boundary between performers and spectators dissolved in the shared rendering of German songs.[15] The city itself served as a stage for these performances, whose theatrical flair shaped the meanings that emanated from the music. As ethnomusicologist Philip V. Bohlman has remarked, music "creates its own social contexts. Music exists not as a product, but rather as a process ... Just as music becomes independent from text, it becomes increasingly dependent on performance ... with social spaces resulting from the placing of performances on stages." Forged in the moment of performance, the new "social spaces" in 1860 Buffalo provided an arena where German Americans and Anglo-Americans could, and did, mingle.[16] Unlike the German language, the festive tunes were accessible to all, thereby allowing Anglo-American observers to join the celebration. The festival's offerings of music, mirth, and sociability thus offer glimpses into an ongoing dialogue between German-speaking migrants and Anglo-American observers, whose look into the German mirror led them to reflect out loud on the meaning of being "American."

If music became a bridge that allowed Anglo-Americans to enter, albeit momentarily, a German festive space, the shared act of making music also created a sense of community among the German singers. Here too, the aural product was invested with meaning in the process of musical production. In Buffalo, as at the earlier gatherings of the North American Sängerbund, the performance of music from the Fatherland did not so much "echo" a German ethnicity (as Anglo-American observers commonly assumed) as it helped sound out the shape of this ethnicity by bringing together singers from a far-flung network of German singing societies. Singers who arrived in the host city stayed at private homes, joined musical forces in the grand concert, greeted friends at the festival's headquarters, and forged new friendships in the casual encounters at banquets and taverns, picnics and excursions. Returning home, they carried with them not only tales and anecdotes which they shared with friends and relatives, but also a sense of belonging to a community of singers.[17] It is "*through* cultural activity," Simon Frith suggests, that social groups "get to know themselves *as groups*."[18] In a similar vein, the Buffalo singers' festival served as a forum of communication from which community could arise. Rarely, of course, did the many voices of German America speak with the "unisonality" that the mass choruses in the railroad depot required.[19] Yet the tunes of community that were enacted both on stage and in informal encounters drew the singers closer into an emergent German America and allowed them to perform a German identity in the public sphere, much like the choral movement in early-nineteenth-century Germany had done.

MUSIC AND NATIONAL IDENTITY

As early as 1778, the German philosopher Johann Gottfried von Herder had infused song with national meaning when he evoked the "voices of the people" that resounded in their folk song. Yet the Germany that was imagined into being in the late eighteenth century revolved around language, not music.[20] "Germans who actually thought of themselves as such did not think of their wholeness in musical but in linguistic and literary terms," historian Celia Applegate has argued. German literary elites turned to crafting a national literature, not a national sound, as they celebrated a nation that still existed in the cultural realm alone.[21] So closely was the search for a national syntax linked to "a culture of readers and writers for whom print had become the essential means of communication," to quote James Sheehan, that the more ephemeral language of music seemed an ambiguous vehicle for nation building. Only gradually did an emergent national consciousness, which had been honed in debates over literary taste and national style, embrace the national significance of music.[22]

In 1808, the composer Karl Friedrich Zelter linked music to the national movement by founding the Berlin Liedertafel, an exclusive singing society that he named after the famed "round table" of King Arthur. Once a month, the singers met to share a "frugal meal" and cultivate songs that "breathe German spirit, solemnity, and joy."[23] The singers' circle sounded not so much a patriotic note as it did a pride in the performance of songs (often composed by the members themselves) that were dedicated to love, friendship, women, and wine, or the more sombre motifs of nature and death. Avowedly elitist, Zelter restricted the number of singers to twenty-five men from Berlin's upper classes. The members met behind closed doors to practise artful singing, their gathering an "extension of bourgeois domesticity." In their songs, they celebrated a German nation that was bounded by language, music, and culture, but their most fervent musical tributes continued to be reserved for the Prussian Fatherland.[24]

The Liedertafel never inspired a mass choral movement. Its influence was felt in different ways, namely in its repertoire that blended the old and the new. Modelled after folk songs, many of the songs the singers performed had in fact been penned by the poets of the early romantic period, among them Goethe, Friedrich Schlegel, and Ludwig Uhland. The musical settings, too, changed from songs with just a single melody to arrangements in four-part harmony that would be eagerly embraced by the nascent choral movement, thereby transforming local songs into a national musical fare.[25] Poets, composers, and singers helped create a new genre—the German *Lied* (song)—that later generations came to regard as a particularly genuine and authentic expression of the German language.[26]

More influential in creating a national singers' movement was the Swiss music teacher, Hans Georg Nägeli (1773–1836), who wanted to transform the music movement from exclusive singing circles to a "public activity" that would create a "decent, refreshing, patriotic publicity."[27] Inspired by the teachings of Pestalozzi, who had emphasized the formative influence of music on young minds, Nägeli suggested that a national consciousness could be nurtured in male choral singing. The German language, he felt, possessed an innate declamatory quality that was best rendered in the deeper, more sonorous male voices. Nägeli's vision of a choral movement that celebrated the German nation in four-part harmony was socially inclusive. As long as a singer possessed a "pure voice" (or, at the very least, showed some self-awareness when hitting the wrong notes), he should give voice to dreams of nationhood by joining a choral association. Between 1819 and 1825, Nägeli travelled repeatedly to southern Germany to encourage the founding of singers' circles. In his tract "The Cultivation of Song for the Male Chorus," he conjured the image of male mass choruses whose performances would embody "the ennobled voice of a people."[28] His vision of a patriotic choral movement that would mobilize German patriots through song came to fruition in the 1820s, when the singers' movement achieved momentum in southern Germany and from there gradually spread to the north.

As Dieter Düding has argued, the German singers' associations of the 1820s and 1830s helped create a politicized public by carrying political aspirations into the public sphere. At the same time, the movement's cultural outlook helped to obscure its political ideals and shielded it from the ban on political associations that the German Parliament had imposed on 5 July 1832.[29] Equally important, the choral movement brought together singers from various localities in face-to-face encounters.[30] The Stuttgarter Liederkranz, for example, which had been founded in 1824, became the hub of an emerging web of regional associations that generated state-wide publicity with their performances and festivals. At first, correspondence between singing associations in Swabia centred on eminently practical matters, such as the exchange of sheet music for four-voice settings for chorus. Soon, however, singers began to organize regional festivals, hosted by both smaller and larger centres. Organizing committees placed public notes in regional newspapers to spread the word on upcoming musical gatherings and invited their fellow Swabian singers "to voice their opinions and views" on the order of festivities in formal circulars. Visiting singers also had their say by sending delegates to the host cities to help deliberate on the program. By the early 1840s, regional singers' festivals in Swabia attracted between 1,500 and 2,300 participants. Celebrating German culture in song and sociability, both singers and spectators engaged in lively conversations that, more often than not, spilled over into impromptu speeches and patriotic toasts.[31] In such acts of communication, both grand and mundane, celebrants knit together networks of community that gradually assumed a nationalistic air.

If the regional festivals of the 1820s and 1830s promoted the idea of a pan-German nation, the "national" festivals at Würzburg (1845), Cologne (1846), and Lübeck (1847) embodied it. Travelling to Würzburg in 1845 via steamships, stage-coaches, and horse-drawn wagons were 1,626 singers from Northern Germany, Saxony, Thuringia, Hesse, the Rhineland, Baden, Wuerttemberg, and Bavaria. For a moment, the city became the focal point of a burgeoning German-patriotic movement. One year later, the organizers in Cologne invited local dignitaries to join the festival's central committee. Courtesy of such prominent sponsors as the executive managers of the Bonn-Cologne Railroad Company, the Rhenish

Railroad Company, and the Steamship Company of Cologne, singers travelled to the Cologne festival with complimentary railroad and steamship billets. While modern transportation helped collapse geographical distances (one-third of the singers at Cologne had arrived from beyond the Rhineland), the shared act of music-making helped level social distinctions.[32] At the singers' festival in Lübeck in 1847 the ranks of active singers included intellectuals, artisans, civil servants, teachers, merchants, petty bourgeoisie, and a small but prominent cross-section of musicians and industrialists.[33]

The failure of the democratic revolutions of 1848 and 1849 silenced the singers' patriotic tunes and with them a movement that encompassed 1,100 singing associations in Germany with a combined membership of 100,000.[34] Although choral associations continued to meet at regional festivals throughout the 1850s, they now sang of the folk, not the nation, and carefully camouflaged any political intent. Only in 1861 would the choral movement once again call for national unity. At the singers' festival of Nürnberg, the greater nation of German was celebrated at the main concert by twelve of the sixteen performances, many of them infused with anti-French sentiment. A year later, German singers asserted themselves in the public sphere through the founding of the German Singers' League (Deutscher Sängerbund), which dedicated itself to "the promotion of German feeling [t]hrough the unifying power of German song … to preserve and enhance the German national consciousness and a feeling of solidarity among German tribes."[35] Music had joined literature as a national idiom.

CREATING A FESTIVE CULTURE

It was this symbolic vocabulary of music, festivity, and the nation that was intimately familiar to the German migrants who arrived in Buffalo in the late 1840s and early 1850s. The number of middle-class intellectuals—among them Carl Adam, the musical director of the 1860 *Sängerfest*—who had fled the German states after the failed revolutions of 1848 and found employment in Buffalo was not large.[36] Yet their ranks were joined by an indeterminate number of "radicalized artisans" whose local presence led to a brief flowering of a German labour movement and the founding of two singing associations, the Buffalo Liedertafel and the Sängerbund, whose members would organize the 1860 singers' festival.[37] What distinguished the political refugees, the "Greens," from the old settlers (the "Grays") was the outlook of exile. Theirs was not a voluntary migration, but an inherently political one. The nation left behind continued to exert a powerful hold on their imagination, even though it did not yet exist as a political entity.[38] Almost immediately, the newcomers began to attack the world their German predecessors had created. Exile Dr. Karl De Haas, for one, held the Grays' "lower and middle class" origins responsible for the parochial character of German Buffalo and promised that the newly migrated "educated and cultured strata" would strive to fill the cultural void. The charge left settlers like Dr. Francis Brunck, the editor of the *Weltbürger*, fuming. He in turn accused the Greens of elitism and arrogance. The leadership struggle between the Grays and the Greens rocked Buffalo's German village (*Deutschendörfchen*), as the two groups were sharply divided on questions of politics, slavery, capitalism, and religion.[39]

What bridged these ideological divides was "an existential commitment to a shared, daily way of life," as David Gerber, among others, has argued. In picnics and excursions, family outings in beer gardens, procession, and musical performances, German-speaking migrants came together. When the German Young Men's Association instigated the celebration of St. John's Day in 1851—a folk festival that marked the onset of summer—the annual festival became a "showcase for all of German popular and high culture" that was eagerly awaited by the city's English-language press and attracted large numbers of American attendees.[40] Conversely, when nativist "ruffians" heckled musical and social gatherings, Greens and Grays, united, rose to the German defence. "Ever ready," as an anniversary pamphlet mused in 1903, German gymnasts lined up to greet the roughnecks with their fists, pushing the latter toward the exit and throwing them down the stairs, thus fending off the forces of Sabbatarianism and temperance that threatened to rupture the unique fabric of German sociability.[41]

Under the auspices of the German Young Men's Association, the Buffalo Liedertafel was founded in May 1848 by "twenty-one gentlemen from among the German population of our then small city." Its constitution was a meticulously crafted document that stated the Liedertafel's purpose, namely, "the encouragement of music, particularly men's and mixed chorus singing, and the promotion of sociability and the love for art and beauty," and established guidelines that governed the behaviour of its members as both singers and citizens. Unlike its prestigious Berlin namesake, the Buffalo Liedertafel promoted both male and mixed-chorus singing. In 1854, a mixed chorus was formed that consisted of eighteen female and thirty-one male singers. Seven years later, the membership ranks had swelled to twenty-four female singers, forty-six male singers, and thirty-five non-participating members—the so-called "friends of art" (*Kunstfreunde*)—whose support not only helped finance four annual concerts but also broadened the association's social base. [42] From its beginnings, the Liedertafel tailored its performances to American audiences, with conductor Carl Adam explaining the meanings of songs in halting English. The musical offerings must have sufficiently enamoured some American concertgoers to make them join the society as non-participating members, thus qualifying for complimentary tickets at the 1860 Buffalo *Sängerfest*. [43]

Buffalo's second German singing society, the Sängerbund, sprang from more modest and radical roots. In May 1849, German tailors, shoemakers, and carpenters banded together as the German-American Workingmen's Union (GAWU), which not only united workers of different crafts but also sought to appeal to Irish and American workers. The association's principal goal was the abolition of the "oppressive and intolerable" system of store-pay that paid workers in signed notes rather than cash. By having to redeem notes at specific stores, workers had part of their earnings removed from their control and were at the mercy of an often corrupt system that overpriced essential goods. In July 1850, two hundred German tailors organized a rowdy procession, "on which occasion one of their principal store-pay bosses was hung in effigy in front of his store on Main Street," as Sängerbund member Ernst Besser recalled. "This led to a sundry law suits; it was however one of the means which brought about the final abandonment of the obnoxious custom." Once its major rallying point disappeared, the GAWU dissolved into trade unions, cooperative workshops, and cultural organizations, the last of which would outlast the brief attempt at multi-ethnic mobilization. [44]

In the mid-1850s, a fragment of the GAWU singing society organized a new choral association, the Sängerbund, which met for its weekly rehearsals in a private home. In the autumn of 1855, the young association entered the public stage with its inaugural concert at Gillig's Hall. [45] Buffalo's cultural scene now featured a new choral society that, alongside the Liedertafel, helped create a local musical life. Both associations combined performances of classical and sacred music with appearances at picnics and people's festivals. Both, too, courted American attendance by advertising in the English-language press and inviting Americans to join the festive sociability at Westphal's Garden, a beer garden in the north end of the city. The city's musical life, orchestrated almost single-handedly by recent German migrants, brought together Americans and Germans in the shared enjoyment of serious and popular music, performed by increasingly experienced and ambitious voices. [46]

When the Buffalo Liedertafel and Sängerbund attended a singers' festival in Cleveland, Ohio, in 1859, the young associations joined the eleventh gathering of the North American Sängerbund. Since the 1840s, German singing societies from Philadelphia, Baltimore, and Cincinnati had visited each other occasionally "to sing, to drink, to enthuse, and to amuse themselves."[47] Yet only in 1849 were their contacts formalized, as singers from Cincinnati, Louisville, and Madison, Indiana, decided to meet annually for a singers' festival to cultivate male chorus singing.[48] In 1859 in Cleveland, the Buffalo Sängerbund's soulful rendering of "Lebe wohl, mein Vaterland" (Farewell, my Fatherland) was greeted "with general applause," but it was the Liedertafel that brought home the much-coveted first prize, a silver goblet. "The honourable distinction of this [sic] two Buffalo societies was perhaps the cause of bringing to Buffalo the next Saengerfest of the North American Saengerbund," singer Ernst Besser wrote in his reminiscences.[49] In hosting twenty-two singing societies, among them famed New York associations such as the Arion and the Liederkranz, Buffalo became the stage for five hundred visiting singers who, undeterred by the rainy July weather, "hobnobbed together round beer tables" and burst into song in both informal and formal venues.[50] In recording their musical escapades, it was Buffalo's English-language press that observed with fascination this strangely appealing German festival, while the Buffalo *Demokrat* commented more dryly on the organizational efforts behind the singers' gathering.

GENDERED NOTES

Preparations for the festival had begun in early January 1860, when the organizing committee appealed to the city's German citizens "to take pride in supporting our singers, in both word and deed."[51] In the following months, the Buffalo singers proved themselves to be skilful organizers. Drawing upon the programs of previous years, they compiled a list of singing societies whom they formally invited to the *Sängerfest*. They also extended a warm welcome to any singing society that wished to join the festive gathering by publishing notices in the regional German-language press.[52] In mobilizing Buffalo's German citizens, organizers solicited financial contributions and posted "accommodation lists" in stores and taverns where local residents could indicate their willingness to open their homes to visiting singers. The committee was quick, however, to add a word of caution. Prospective hosts should consult with their wives, "who did not suffer gladly to being ignored" in this important domestic decision. Only if the women agreed to accommodate guests "will we celebrate a singers' festival in which we may take pride and which the singers will fondly remember." In their ironic nod to the power of the housewife, who could greet visiting singers with either "a friendly 'Welcome'" or cold indifference, the organizing committee recognized women as rightful "dictators of domestic and familial standards," whose support was critical to the atmosphere of the festival.[53] Just as easily, though, the committee banned women from most public forums, thus recreating the inherently male space that singers' festivals had occupied in the German states.

If custom demanded their exclusion from the beer-fuelled jollity at the singers' banquet or the performance of the male mass chorus, women revellers joined the festivities in different capacities. When the German *Männerchor* from Rochester boarded the train to Buffalo, its delegation numbered "over fifty ladies and gentlemen." For them, the musical journey began with an impromptu concert in the Rochester railway station "which drew a large crowd about them in the Depot."[54] In filling a railway compartment of its own, the Rochester choir came accompanied by "nearly the triple of passive members"—family, relatives, and friends who formed an integral (if less prominent) part of the musical networks that congregated in Buffalo.[55] Over the next week, an estimated influx of 1,700 visitors would explore the city, escorted by their Buffalo hosts in carriages, braving strong gusts of wind and clouds of "gritty dust" or seeking respite, between concerts and sights, in one of the city's principal beer halls.[56] During these excursions, women visitors at the festival likely formed networks of friendship much as the male singers did, but the sources remain mute on their social interactions. Even if they had paid attention, English-language observers would have been hard pressed to decipher the flow of conversation between women visitors, for German, as the Buffalo *Daily Republic* admitted, "by some terrible paradox was Greek to us."[57] Instead, local newspapers focused on visual signs of the singers' presence, such as the "society badge" which both active and non-participating members of singers' associations pinned to their clothes—"an ubiquitous object, discernable at every turn of the eye."[58]

In anticipation of the week-long festivities, Buffalo's residents had adorned the streets with banners and buntings, flags and festoons, with Americans "busily decorating" alongside their "German brethren."[59] Onto this stage marched the visiting singers. Delegations of both the Liedertafel and Sängerbund greeted each association at the railway depots—among them the sole Canadian representative, the Concordia society from Preston, Waterloo County—and escorted them to St.

James Hall, the festival's headquarters. Preceded by marching tunes played by "the splendid band of the New York Society," the singers moved up Main Street to St. James Hall, which had been transformed into a "temple of song," its entrance "a massive arch of evergreens."[60] After a personal welcome by Mayor Alberger, the participants were free to enjoy food and drink in the reception room and then dispersed to their various quarters, while their hosts set out, once again, to the railway depot. The marches back and forth along the city's main arteries kept Buffalo "stirring and musical throughout the day," priming the local audience for the first musical event of the singers' festival.

At the reception concert in the evening, traditionally given by the local singers and musicians, the visitors crowded early into St. James Hall, among them many "ladies whose gay dresses added largely to the beauty of the richly decorated hall." When the curtain rose, it revealed forty female singers, dressed in white, who performed alongside seventy-five "gentlemen" and an orchestra of thirty-five. Couched in Victorian gender ideology, the press lauded the female soloist, Mrs. Carl Adam, for the "tenderest expression" and "delicacy of feeling" with which she delivered the alto part of "Gypsy Mother." But more than the assured performance of a well-known local musical figure, it was the sound of the choruses that captivated a local writer: "They were rendered with a time like a drum beat, no drag, no hurrying, the orchestra and voices harmonizing to perfection, and all blending into one grand whole which realized our highest conception of what a chorus should be."[61] Such grand praise could have flown only out of the pen of an English-language observer, for in the tradition of the German choral movement, mixed choral singing was tainted with allegations of "glitter" and "artifice," and women were customarily excluded from active membership in singers' associations.[62] The reception concert at St. James Hall thus offers a musical hint of the transformations that could occur on the American stage, where women's voices joined those of men without even a note of criticism.[63]

"A MUSICAL EARTHQUAKE"

The keynote event of the festival, however, remained the joint performance of the male singing associations. To accommodate a male mass chorus that had swelled from 118 singers in Cincinnati in 1849 to 500 in Buffalo in 1860, conductor Carl Adam had persuaded the New York Central Railway Line to relinquish its railroad depot for an evening.[64] On the morning of the festival's second day, workers transformed the vast depot into a provisional concert hall while passengers had to board their trains from the tracks just outside the depot. The hall's acoustic was deplorable—but then again, to focus on sound quality would miss the point of the "monster concert" that impressed through its sheer size alone.[65] "Vast" was the audience and "mighty" the building, "majestic" the music and "grand" the singers' voices.[66] In fact, just as the melodies were amplified by five hundred voices, so too did the concert's significance seem to rest in its scale. "In such a concert," wrote the Buffalo *Commercial Advertiser,* "multitude is the great feature. It drowned out everything else, and noble as was the music, the sight of that grand gathering of humanity was the wonder of the night."[67] Nearly an hour before the concert began, the audience began to pour into the building in three "unbroken streams." Quiet, attentive, and orderly, the festive crowd included "thousands of ladies."[68] The only disturbance occurred when "Young America" tried to sneak into the depot without having paid the modest fee of twenty-five cents. Local authorities thwarted their plan, as the mayor himself quietly restored order with the help of police.[69]

The musical offerings for the evening included one instrumental and eight vocal numbers, all of which had a distinctly classical bent. Rather than regaling the audience with the familiar sound of German folk tunes, festival conductor Carl Adam had opted for an artful repertoire, including, among other pieces, Liszt's "Light, More Light," Schumann's "Hunter's Song," and the "Pilgrim's Chorus" from Wagner's opera *Tannhäuser*. Six of the vocal numbers also featured "Quartettos" that allowed the more accomplished choirs on the podium to shine individually.[70]

To listen to a choir of five-hundred voices was an experience whose novelty stunned English-language commentators in Buffalo. They called the event a "musical earthquake" and struggled to translate what they had heard into language. The result was a potpourri of superlatives that captured the sounds of music in adjective, metaphor, and hyperbole.

> The unsurpassable music of this composition seemed incarnate with the battle-spirit of the first Emperor, as it rolled its majestic vocal and orchestral cadences over the silent multitude. The massive, deep-toned chorus by all the voices, the burden and the refrain, the mighty storm of sound that gathered near the close, and the beautiful, distant "dying away" of every note thereafter, left an impression upon all that must surely abide forever.[71]

As Mark M. Smith reminds us, nineteenth-century print culture "was not necessarily a silent medium" but instead, "laden and infused with aural representation." In an innovative study of how Northerners and Southerners came to "hear" their differences in the decades leading up to the Civil War, Smith observes how "time and again the imagery of how each section sounded was recorded first in the ear, then in a print version that stripped the sounds of their nuance and replaced them with a clumsy, written representation, thus giving readers access to a captured record of sectional aurality that they in turn could repeat with their voices to other ears." In Buffalo, too, the English-language press was charged with the task of describing an aural experience with the written word.[72] But the editors' ears, so familiar with the sounds of growing sectional strife, were not necessarily attuned to the nuances of the musical repertoire performed on stage. Thus although they listened intently, they did not hear what was recorded in the German-language Buffalo *Demokrat*, whose writer called the concert merely "satisfying" and offered a nuanced, rather critical review.

The criticism that the Buffalo *Demokrat* levelled was somewhat softened by its acknowledgement that the male mass chorus performed after only a single practice session together. The paper, however, did question the director's choice of opening the concert with Wagner's orchestral Overture to *Tannhäuser*—a piece ill-suited "to the taste of a mass audience." It did not help that the orchestra played so softly (albeit with "great precision") that nearly half the audience had to strain to hear Wagner's "music of the future." Far more promising was the vocal rendition of the "Pilgrims' Chorus" from *Tannhäuser*, which the mass chorus performed with "verve, energy, and precision." In the second half of the program, the chorus began to show signs of fatigue as the amateur singers struggled to sustain a lengthy performance without intermission. The audience, in turn, seemed more enamoured by the more popular tunes on the program, such as the "Hymn to the Fatherland" by Tschirch and the "Midnight Review of Napoleon Bonaparte" by Titl, than by the compositions by Schumann and Liszt. The ease with which the local editor of the Buffalo *Demokrat* rendered these musical judgements points to an intimate knowledge of the repertoire of German choral and classical music, which he likely acquired in the repeated acts of listening to and writing about local performances. His verdict: a respectable performance with several fine moments, but hardly the earth-shattering event that most English-language papers had conjured.[73]

The concert review in the Buffalo *Demokrat* also revealed the writer's familiarity with the "forms and character of verbal descriptions of music," to quote the music historian Leon Botstein. In broadening the field of music history, Botstein has called attention to the "role of language in mediating and shaping the musical, in the formation of taste, in the vocabulary of judgement, and in the musical education of the amateur and listener." In reflecting on the music performed in the railroad depot, the Buffalo *Demokrat* had to translate the ephemeral language of music into an informed verbal judgement which, in turn, became the idiom through which its readers interpreted and heard the musical event. In the columns of Buffalo's local press, musical culture became intertwined with literary culture and language the medium that shaped ways of listening to music.[74] A critical musical ear was far less likely to revel in the "unsurpassable music" of the evening or describe a "thrillingly grand" mass chorus, as the Buffalo *Daily Courier* had done.[75] Instead, it carefully measured out praise and criticism, pointed out flat performances and the lack of musical effects, and sought to cultivate musical taste, all the while lending its support to a worthwhile venture.

What English-language commentators might have lacked in musical literacy, they made up for in awed delight.[76] The sight of the male mass chorus, which some observers in their enthusiasm pegged at "seven or eight hundred men," projected the image of an ethnic group that forged unity out of diversity and transcended individuality in a grand harmonious whole.[77] Although the chorus was German in sound and appearance, its music struck a deep emotive chord among Anglo-American observers. In the harmony of its songs—and the sheer volume emanating from five hundred men's voices—the chorus spoke to Anglo-American audiences with a more powerful immediacy than either the spoken word or the singers' colourful processions through Buffalo's main arteries could attain. In the reassuring timbre of the "massive, deep-toned chorus," the linguistic barriers that a performance in German might have posed to an English-language audience conveniently dissolved. Musical harmony spilled over into inter-ethnic harmony as Buffalo's English-language press edged closer to the stage, curious over what fuelled the secret of such "splendid music."[78]

As workers dismantled the seats in the railroad depot, singers, families, and friends retired to the Buffalo's "principal German Wein and Bier Halls," where they continued to sing "with Teutonic energy."[79] In the sounds of German folk songs, the geographical distance to the German homelands seemed to collapse. "Any one who walked the streets," wrote the Buffalo *Daily Courier*, "might have fancied that he stood in genuine Deutschland, and heard the prolonged merriment of a song-festival in some beautiful city of the Rhine." This prospect did not overly concern the *Courier*'s reporter, who rather enjoyed the musical transformation of Buffalo that had added subtlety and sentiment to a city known for neither:

> Snatches of song run forth from half shut doors and windows, fully as fine as anything to which the public are invited in the concert room. Sounds melodious and soft, of instrumental music floated far and sweetly in Buffalonian Germany, and it is not to be doubted that when at last, far in the night, the final echo died away into silence, many a stout Teutonic heart dreamed itself to the other side of the Atlantic. So thoroughly for the time being is Buffalo Germanized.[80]

Five years later, Friedrich Kapp, immigrant and chronicler of German life in the United States, would describe music and song as "bridges on which we can hasten back to Germany at any time."[81] Yet the transformative power of music was always twofold, as Kathleen Neils Conzen has argued: if music represented a tangible connection with the German homelands left behind, it also had the potential to transform the American landscape by infusing it with culture and sophistication.[82] To have such claims recognized by Anglo-American audiences in Buffalo in 1860 was for its German residents a gratifying feeling, still fondly remembered over four decades later.[83]

MELODIES OF RACE

The descriptions of the 1869 *Sängerfest* in Buffalo's English-language papers are striking for their positive tenor. The local press not only devoted long articles to the singers' festival, it also revelled in the exotic gathering that, for a moment, seemed to transform the city into "Buffalonian Germany." Rather than perceiving the "German invasion" as a threat, even the nativist *Commercial Advertiser* embraced "this splendid achievement of our Teutonic cousins," a remarkable endorsement from a paper that only three years earlier had sputtered with rage when the immigrant vote swept the Democratic Party to a decisive victory in the mayoral election.[84] Blaming the "consolidated foreign vote" for the Republican defeat, the *Commercial Advertiser* had scornfully characterized Buffalo's East Side "as little American as the duchy of Hesse Cassel; their population speaks a foreign language, reads foreign papers, isolates itself from the American element, and, steeped in ignorance of American politics, it clings to the bald name of democracy, and claims the right to subject the sons of the soil to the despotism of the brute force of numbers."[85]

To understand the *Advertiser*'s reversal of opinion, we have to look beyond the party realignment of the late 1850s that saw German-speaking citizens supporting the local Republican fusion ticket.[86] And neither should we be satisfied with the observation that the *Commercial Advertiser* indulged in violent rhetoric primarily when "foreigners" appeared as a political threat, while showing considerable tolerance for cultural manifestations of ethnicity.[87] Without dismissing either factor, the *Advertiser*'s change of heart appeared to reflect larger cultural currents that redefined the meanings of both race and recreation, to the subsequent benefit of German-speaking migrants.

As historians Theodore W. Allen and Alexander Saxton remind us, the republic's promise of the pursuit of happiness was racially exclusive; the 1790 naturalization law held out the promise of citizenship to "free white persons" only. The law, as Matthew Freye Jacobson notes, was remarkable both for its "fierce exclusivity" and "staggering inclusivity": it denied political rights to Asian Americans who were left vulnerable to white mobs or wartime hysteria, while granting successive waves of Irish, German, Scandinavian, East European, and Southern European migrants access to the civic polity.[88]

In the 1840s, the monolithic conception of whiteness began to fracture under the impact of unprecedented numbers of newcomers.[89] Concerns about the migrants' assimilability combined with ethnologic discourses on race to supplant the image of a unified "Caucasian race," a term first used by Samuel George Morton in his *Crania Americana* (1839).[90] The new thinking on race was reflected in *Types of Mankind* (1854), in which Josiah C. Nott and George R. Gliddon set out to prove that humanity was divided into different "races" that displayed discrete physical, moral, and intellectual capabilities. The virtuous Anglo-Saxon, for instance, differed sharply from the "dirty," "ragged," "dark," and "choleric" Celt.[91] The idea of a hierarchy of races soon came to suffuse medical journals, school readers, and newspapers. In 1854, the *Buffalo Medical Journal* reported that the local "Teutonic races" had the highest "cranial capacity" (92 cubic inches), compared to the Celts (87 cubic inches), Aboriginals (84 cubic inches), and African Americans (83 cubic inches).[92] Three years later, the Buffalo *Commercial Advertiser* evoked a kinship between the "Teutonic" and "Anglo-Saxon" races in an unabashed attempt to lure German Protestants into the Republican fold.[93]

By 1860, scientific discourses on race had become part of "the shared currency of cultural imagery."[94] In fact, so deeply embedded was the new racialism that it surfaced in the "universal welcome" that the *Commercial Advertiser* extended to the participants at the 1860 Buffalo *Sängerfest*. As the *Advertiser*'s musings shed light on the complimentary public image of German-speaking migrants, they deserve quotation:

> We are destined to become a mixed nationality and it is of the highest moment that the mixing should be done *secondaem artem*. There are crosses of humanity that are vile and worthless. Two fair originals can be spoiled by intermixture. The mulatto is a hybrid. Amalgamation of colors is only another name for annihilation of races.
>
> And even with many European natives the Anglo-Saxon blood mingles unwillingly. The fair-haired Saxon intermarries with the swarthy Celt, but the two bloods combine like oil and water. In a few generations the original type is restored and among children of one family we may have the white-faced Englishman as the brother of the black-mazzled Celt. They are thus brought back to first conditions; there is no true crossing of the breed.
>
> In this dilemma the Teuton comes in to furnish a strong and predominant element. Whatever our ideas of English ethnology, we all come back to a belief in the practical identity of the leading tribes of Briton with those of Germany. They blend, run in together, fuse, and out of the fusion comes as perfect a type of manhood as the world has yet produced.[95]

The language of racial differentiation that permeates this editorial reminds us that the Irish were not necessarily considered "white" in antebellum America. It thus reflects a "hardening" of the popular Irish stereotype that Dale Knobel observed for the mid-nineteenth century. In the 1840s, Knobel notes, negative commentaries on "Celticism" became linked to physical appearance, and the rationale for ethnic difference was located in "nature" rather than "nurture." It was, in other words, no longer the Old World experience of poverty and oppression that rendered Irish migrants a distinct people (a condition which could be overcome with conscious effort), but the immutable character of race which placed the Irish "outside the pale of 'true' Americanism."[96]

The public perception of the Germans, on the other hand, minimized the distance between "Anglo-Saxons" and "Teutons." Since the early seventeenth century, English philosophers had portrayed "Anglo-Saxons as a vigorous branch of the sturdy Germanic tree," relying heavily on Tacitus's description of the Germanic tribes as a pure, noble, and freedom-loving people.[97] Similarly, across the Atlantic, adherents of the emergent polygenetic "sciences" identified "the ancient German" as "the parent stock from which the highest modern civilization has sprung."[98] The perceived racial kinship, which found expression in the family metaphors of "our Teutonic cousins" and "German brethren," helps explain the benign treatment of German-speaking migrants in antebellum America.[99] Notwithstanding the fact that "Germans, too, were frequently Roman Catholic, had been raised under monarchical institutions, could sometimes be tarred with the brush of political radicalism, and spoke a foreign tongue besides," as Dale Knobel puts it, their "Teutonic" roots catapulted them to the top of the new racial hierarchy.[100]

In sharp contrast to the "swarthy Celt," physical characteristics were rarely attributed to Buffalo's "Teutonic race."[101] More pronounced was the emphasis on innate German qualities such as industry, order, and respectability. American observers at the singers' festival painted a flattering image of German citizens who were "successful in business," exhibited "energy and stability of character," presented "a strong conservative element," respected "law and order," and had "wedded themselves to our institutions by that strongest of ties, the ownership of land."[102] Waxing eloquent about "the breadth and geniality of the German character," the *Daily Republic* left little doubt that a fusion of the German and Anglo-American elements seemed both possible and desirable.[103]

Looking into the German mirror, commentators glimpsed a reflection of Americans as money-making realists who showed appreciation for neither the arts nor sociability. The German singers, they remarked wonderingly, were attuned to "those hidden chords within us, which rouse so mysteriously to the concord of sweet sounds and respond to the utterances of poetry." Their "conservatism and comtemplativeness" enabled them to appreciate "the depth of life."[104] Being "more soul-full" and of "emotional nature," they demonstrated "a youth and joyousness of spirit—a heartiness of enthusiasm" that Americans strongly admired, but scarcely understood.[105] Americans, by contrast, chased "the Almighty Dollar" and embraced "the idea of American progress."[106] As was fitting for practical businessmen, their festivals had "a money-making turn. A surplus of receipts over expenditures is with us the index of success." Not surprisingly, they marvelled at the curious sight of "thousands of strangers gathered from abroad, from East, West, and South" for the sole purpose of "arous[ing] the soul of music."[107] The "Musical Carnival," one commentator suggested, might inspire the American "to divest himself of his cares" and "to enjoy even for a day the actual liberty which only an absolute release from business can yield."[108] The *Commercial Advertiser* went further still; by blending "the fair-haired Saxon" and "the Teuton," a new race would arise, ideally suited to American soil:

> Out of the union of the two—the hard faced and resolute American and the more soul-full German—should come a glorious nationality; at once practical and poetic, utile and dulce, mingling the soft amenities of social life with the stern realities of a work-day world.[109]

If we take seriously the sentiment expressed here, the Buffalo *Sängerfest* (and, by extension, German festive culture) not only provided a forum where Germans and Americans could mingle; it also awakened in American festival-goers a desire for the fine arts and the innocuous pleasures of recreation that could be incorporated (guilt-free) into their own lives. Equally important, it indicated a readiness to broaden the American mainstream by making room for German culture. Rather than being swallowed by the turbulent currents of mainstream culture, German migrants were encouraged to cultivate their ethnic differences and to change "the fair-headed Saxon," just as they were changed by him.

In an elegantly construed argument, David Gerber suggests that something had to be "*lacking* among Americans that led them to lessen their resistance to German things and to seek foreign alternatives to the world they themselves were then creating during the formative era of American modernization." Antebellum Americans, he holds, were disenchanted with Buffalo's bleak cultural life that offered little opportunity for either "aesthetic transcendence" or "ordinary recreation." At the same time, their moral culture imposed strict restraints on the type of leisure that was deemed respectable. It had to refrain from "excessive stimulation" and shield women and children from "public scenes of scandal and embarrassment."[110] The *Sängerfest* admirably fulfilled both requirements. In saturating the city with music—indeed, making American commentators regret "the impracticability of bottling it up, in some fashion, for future use"—the festival brought to Buffalo the grand choral oeuvres of German composers and enveloped the commercial hub in "a whirlwind of sweet sounds."[111] But never did the musical carnival stray across the boundaries of respectable behaviour. On the contrary, notwithstanding the vast crowd assembled" at the picnic, "we heard of no accident or even brawl," noted the *Commercial Advertiser*. Much like on the previous days, the "scene was one of unmixed enjoyment, uproar without riot; jollity without excess. It came fully up to our highest idea of German enjoyment and left us more than ever convinced that the Germans have reached perfection in the art of social intercourse."

The festival, in short, was a memorable event that could teach Americans "a profitable lesson," namely, how to indulge in rational recreation without descending into excess.[112] Rather than suspending societal hierarchies and rules of conduct, the *Sängerfest* represented a festive time that allowed for novel cultural exchanges while simultaneously reinforcing middle-class values of order, respectability, and self-control.[113]

TUNES OF COMMUNITY

It is less evident what German festival-goers themselves thought of the singers' festival. Unfamiliar with the German language, Buffalo's English-language press reported neither on the reception speech in which conductor Carl Adam welcomed the visiting singers, nor on the transactions at the business meeting of the North American Sängerbund.[114] The Buffalo *Demokrat*, in turn, remained mute on the content of German-language speeches, focusing its coverage instead on musical and social events at which German ethnicity was enacted in sound and sociability. Throughout the 1850s, the *Demokrat* had endorsed the refining influence of the fine arts and sought "to foster the German character and German customs."[115] In July 1860, however, the paper was more preoccupied with capturing the spirit of the festivities than reflecting at length on the festival's significance. It chronicled what seemed noteworthy—such as the generous praise the festival garnered in the English-language press—but otherwise enjoyed the mirth of the moment. The prize concert on the festival's third day, for instance, was described in a scant three paragraphs in order to allow "our printers, our journalists, and the entire group down to the newsboys" to rush the paper's production and join the mass picnic in Moffat's Grove that concluded the festivities.[116]

It was left to Buffalo's English-language press to describe the musical contest in St. James Hall that attracted the city's social and economic elite. In a "battle of sweet sounds," eleven visiting singing associations competed for a silver cup.[117] Their performances exhibited a nuance and poise which the male mass chorus had found difficult to master the previous day. Still, after the "grandeur" of the "stupendous concert" on Tuesday evening, as the Buffalo *Express* admitted, the prize concert seemed comparatively "ordinary."[118] Somewhat unexpectedly, however, Anglo-American journalists found themselves captivated by the banquet of the North American Sängerbund at the end of the evening. Seated at eight long tables that extended over the entire length of St. James Hall, the singers celebrated the success of their performances over "cold meats, bread, pickles, onions," and "a double line of Rheinwein bottles, which bristled from end to end of each of the tables." No longer constrained by the formality of the concert stage (or by the presence of female attendees, who had been banned to the galleries), they burst spontaneously into song, their "snatch of a chorus" quickly "taken up by a hundred pairs of lungs."[119] Their wine-fuelled, musical conversations epitomized German *Gemütlichkeit*—that amalgam of conviviality, social harmony, casual socializing, exuberance, and group feeling that is impossible to translate and yet represents a key element of German chorus culture.

Until the 1960s, German male choirs in North America would gather after rehearsals to break into four-part harmony around the beer table. In lengthy singing sessions that could last into the early hours of the morning, they affirmed their social bonds. Their casual conversation and friendly barter were punctuated by the singing of German folk songs in which one singer's tune was taken up by the others and a rousing finale applauded by the other patrons of the pub.[120] German was the language of such musical frolicking and folk songs the idiom of conversation, much as the *Daily Republic* had observed in Buffalo a century earlier:

> One association would rise in their seats, and with their glasses of Rhine wine waved on high, would break forth in some glorious music, ending with three cheers, which would be answered back in harmonious notes from some other quarter, taken up and repeated in every direction, until all the air seemed filled with enthusiastic music.[121]

Playful, spontaneous, and quick, these musical conversations depended as much on the singers' command of the German language as on their knowledge of German folk music. Without fluency in either idiom, the easy flow of the music would have faltered, as it did, in fact, in later decades when the use of the German language became increasingly limited to the concert stage.[122]

Familiar only with the "gauntlet of public dinners and suppers and festivals of the Anglo-American stamp," Anglo-American observers at the Buffalo's singers festival were unprepared for the "glory of song and wine" at the banquet.[123] And yet, it was precisely these "elements of the carnivalesque" that allowed them to cross over from the role of observer to that of festive participant.[124] Surrendering himself willingly to the alcohol-fuelled merriment at the singers' banquet, one reporter captured the social whirlwind in equally fluid prose. Instead of orderly syntax, sentence fragments prevail, with the writer professing

a very confused recollection of Rhine wine; ... a distant collection of some-
body singing—in fact everybody singing all at once; of an attempt to com-
prehend German by one vast mental effort; a general embracing of everybody; a moisture of twenty pairs of *male* German lips on our hitherto irre-
proachable labials; and a universal merging of everything into a happy, misty,
indistinctiveness.[125]

The informal sociability of the banquet allowed this observer to join a German
festive tradition and feel, for a moment, as part of the group. The singers' festival,
which organizers had envisioned as a "festival of fraternization of the participating
singing associations," was thus transformed into a platform for cultural exchanges
between German-American and Anglo-American celebrants.[126]

On the festival's closing day, the singers created a festive space that was open to
German Americans and Anglo-Americans alike, only this time, women and children too were invited to participate. Around twelve noon, "the streets began filling
up with gaily dressed women and children, and Main Street, from the centre of
the city far away to the hill, was one mass of moving multitude" making its way to
the picnic grounds in Moffat's Grove. "The horse cars swarmed with passengers,"
the Buffalo *Daily Republic* reported. "On the platforms, inside, on top, they were
black with people. At every crossing stood crowds waiting for a chance to ride,
who piled on every possible place, and although the car ran every three minutes, not
one-fourth of those desiring to attend the pic-nic had an opportunity of riding." In
more orderly fashion, the singers' procession marched to the picnic grounds from
the city's centre, led by four Fest Marshals on horseback and two standard bearers
who carried "American and German colors." Local dignitaries in carriages followed,
as did, in no particular order, four marching bands, the visiting singing societies,
the Buffalo Liedertafel, the Buffalo Sängerbund, and several wagons "decorated with
flags and entirely filled with ladies."[127] "American commentators," Kathleen Neils
Conzen observes, "constantly remarked upon the presence of seemingly respectable German families in public places where no genteel Anglo-American woman
would venture."[128] On this brisk summer day in Buffalo, however, American families
mingled with German families in an entertainment that the press called wholesome
and pleasant and that evoked memories of the folk festival of St. John's Day which
the German Young Men's Association had instigated in 1851.

The *Sängerfest*'s broad public appeal delighted the organizing committee,
which from the outset had sought to make the Fest as inclusive as possible.[129] Over

12,000 men, women, and children picnicked under shady trees, rode the swings erected for the occasion, ate "heaps of pretzels, sausages, Limburger cheese," and drank generous amounts of the lager beer that was sold at wooden shanties across the grounds. Each singing society settled in different corners of the grove, where they entertained audiences with their festive antics. At three o'clock in the afternoon, the singers of the New York Arion appeared, "dressed in the most outlandish costumes that can be imagined, some as devils, imps, Japanese, pirates, Yankees, corpulent Germans." Other singing societies marched across the grounds, piping on self-made flutes and carrying "huge drinking horns, or large cups of silver, bronze or wood, from which they poured libations of the inevitable Lager Beer on all who approached." And everywhere, marvelled the Buffalo *Commercial Advertiser*, there was music, as the grove resonated with "rich snatches of song, caught up or re-echoed by others, until the air was as alive with music as the earth was saturated with lager."[130]

Seemingly effortlessly, music adapted to a wide range of social occasions. Voiced in the German tongue but representing a universal language, it was equally at home in the concert hall, at the beer table, or beneath the majestic trees of Moffat's Grove, all the while alerting Americans to the fact that "these 'Foreigners' were really quite sociable people," as a local German chronicle would muse thirty-eight years later.[131] Music allowed the German singers to perform their ethnicity in public, just as it encouraged Anglo-American audiences to step across an ethnic boundary that had loomed large in earlier decades.[132] The popular appeal of the "Musical Carnival" lured Anglo-American attendees *en masse* to the picnic in Moffat's Grove where they sank, quite literally, into "the embraces of German brothers, the lips meeting in contact, below black, sandy and bushy moustaches."[133] In the embrace of the clean-shaven American and the moustache-wearing German, the singers' festival reached its symbolic conclusion, its tunes of community encompassing not only the German singers but also their Anglo-American hosts.

We have to be wary not to mistake the exuberant rhetoric of Buffalo's local press for the festive experiences of the celebrants. While some social barriers might have tumbled in the whirlwind of the singers' festival, others remained. The singers from Columbus, Ohio, for instance, offered a very different reading of the musical gathering in Buffalo. While complimenting their hosts on the "greatness" of the *Fest* and their generous hospitality, they found the singers' festival lacking in the most important festive ingredient—*Gemütlichkeit*. The singers had remained strangers, with each association keeping its own company. What was missing, the Columbus singers felt, was the "tone of heartiness and *Gemütlichkeit*" that represented the "true attraction" of singers' festivals, partly perhaps because of the size of Buffalo.[134] Between events, the visitors "were scattered about the city," touring its principal sights in groups of families and friends rather than getting to know singers from other cities.[135] In conveying the singers' criticisms, the *Columbus Weltbote* boosted its own cause. The next meeting of the North American Sängerbund was to take place at Columbus—a "small, Western town" in which "acquaintances are forged quickly" and "true *Gemütlichkeit* and sociability" reigned. The paper did not foresee that the sound of battle would soon drown out the sound of music. During the years of the Civil War, the singers' festivals were suspended. Still, the *Westbote* article is revealing for its suggestion that the most important bonds forged at the singers' festival in Buffalo were those between Buffalo's "German and American population" rather than those among German singers.[136]

News about the singers' festival in Buffalo travelled quickly within German America and crossed the border into Canada. In their accounts, most German-language papers relied on the tales that singers brought home from the festival or copied reports published in the Buffalo *Demokrat*.[137] A few papers sent their own correspondents, who arrived from Rochester, Syracuse, Albany, Pittsburgh, and New York City to listen to this festival of song.[138] In an article published in the *New Yorker Staatszeitung* and subsequently reprinted in the Buffalo *Demokrat*, Oswald Ottendorfer lauded "the ennobling influences of the German song in the formation of the American national character."[139] For this "Forty-Eighter" who had fought in the revolutionary battles at Vienna, Dresden, and Prague, and fled to New York in 1850, music was intimately intertwined with national aspirations.[140] If German nationalists had wielded song as a weapon for national unity, German Americans could wield it to suffuse American materialism with "the blissful power of music."[141]

Ottendorfer's article mirrors the musings of other German-American intellectuals who, since the 1850s, had debated how German culture could best be preserved in American society.[142] Writing in the prestigious *Atlantis*, immigrant commentator Christian Esselen, for example, had suggested in 1856 that participation in singers' festivals constituted "a duty towards societal conditions here, which definitely demand humanizing through German art and sociability."[143] In mediating between the ethnic group and the American mainstream, Ottendorfer and Esselen tried to instill an ethnic consciousness into their fellow Germans that would awaken them to the higher values of their culture and to their duty to "humanize" American society.[144] By 1883, when the North American Sängerbund again convened in Buffalo, the critique of the barren cultural American landscape which German immigrants had transformed through the gifts of their culture and conviviality had become commonplace, and music had donned its new gown as a symbol of German culture that sought to transform the American mainstream.[145]

In 1860, however, German singers and local commentators in Buffalo were less concerned with translating music's appeal into political or ideological gains and more so with fostering community and *Gemütlichkeit* among the singers. Indeed, the Buffalo festival resembled more a festive hymn to German song, sound, and sociability than an ode to cultural nationalism. The grand concert at the railroad depot featured more classical music than folksy tunes.[146] Even at the prize concert of the singing societies, where the charmingly rendered "On the Neckar, on the Rhine" stirred "the *amour patrie* in every German bosom," two songs were markedly absent. At no point did the singers burst into Ernst Moritz Arndt's "Was ist des Deutschen Vaterland?" (1813) or Hoffmann von Fallersleben's "Deutschlands-Lied" (1841)—two patriotic tunes that had encapsulated the longing for German unity and liberty and had dominated many singers' festivals in Germany in the 1840s.[147] Also absent was the rhetorical pledge to the pervasive powers of German folk song which the philosopher Johann Gottfried von Herder had identified as a repository of the national spirit.[148] If the organizers of the *Fest* did possess any missionary zeal, it was channelled into propagating the "cheerful German nature" and revelling in "our talent to enjoy life wholeheartedly."[149]

Conclusion

At a time when the United States was hurtling toward civil war and sectional conflict divided the country as never before, the festival in Buffalo conjured a world of ethnic and musical harmony. In its conspicuous silence on sectional dissonance—which, as Mark Smith tells us, came to infuse aural images of the North and the South in the pre-Civil War decades—the 1860 festival revealed an almost wistful desire for musical enchantment and carnivalesque oblivion.[150] As Anglo-American observers listened to the strains of vocal music in the German choral tradition, they perceived neither alien tunes nor threatening rhythms. Instead, they heard a strangely appealing chorus that told of leisure without excess and festive exuberance within the bounds of order and morality. Although the music to which they listened was readily identifiable as German, they could enjoy it without any formal knowledge of the German language. Music's universal language created a flexible social space that Anglo-American audiences felt comfortable entering: as patrons of Buffalo's German singing societies at the grand concert at the railroad depot; as members of Buffalo's social and economic elite at the prize concert in St. James Hall; and as revellers in the picnic grounds at Moffat Grove. The unequivocally positive coverage in Buffalo's English-language press lent further respectability to the public performances of German ethnicity.

For the German festival-goers, the solemn rendering of mass choruses, the toasts at the banquet, the merriment at the beer garden, and the courteous invitations to upcoming *Sängerfeste* helped build social networks that drew their members deeper into American life, while at the same time their music "continued to sound German," to borrow Philip V. Bohlman's memorable phrase.[151] To be sure, in the largest of the pre–Civil War festivals of song, some participants missed the intimacy of earlier singers' festivals, but with five hundred singers in attendance the Buffalo Fest was still small enough to allow for face-to-face encounters on the concert stage, picnic grounds, and at the "gentlemen's banquet." The German-language press then carried tales from the singers' festival throughout German North America, where audiences listened vicariously to the keynotes of a German ethnicity that rang with song and sociability, community and *Gemütlichkeit*, but did not yet self-consciously intend to alter the soundtrack of American culture itself.

5.

Germania in Amerika
Nation and Ethnicity at the German Peace Jubilees, 1871

"Today was a public holiday as there was a great peace-jubilee in town," Louis Breithaupt scribbled into his diary on 2 May 1871. In a few broad strokes, the sixteen-year-old resident of Berlin, Ontario, captured the festive air of the celebration that marked Germany's military victory over France in the Franco-Prussian War. The jubilee was ushered in by a salute of twenty-one cannon shots, followed by divine service "in all the German churches of Berlin & Waterloo."[1] Later, a procession wound its way to the courthouse where orators celebrated Germany's "righteous" triumph over France. As exuberant as the speeches were the ten thousand celebrants who clapped enthusiastically when an oak was planted "as a truly German symbol." In the evening, a torchlight procession marched down King Street, which was "ablaze with illuminations, every house, workshop, factory, hotel and building being gracefully hung with Chinese lanterns, colored illuminations, devices in glass, and transparencies of every kind."[2] With revellers singing German songs and loudly cheering at portraits of Emperor Wilhelm I, the celebration

Portrait of Louis Breithaupt. As a chronicler of matters both private and public, Louis Breithaupt left a rich description of the 1871 German Peace Jubilee in Waterloo County. COURTESY OF UNIVERSITY OF WATERLOO SPECIAL COLLECTIONS, DORIS LEWIS RARE BOOK ROOM, BREITHAUPT HEWETSON CLARK COLLECTION, BHC 43.

culminated in a fireworks display and the unveiling of an oil painting of *Germania* that symbolized Germany's newly attained national unity.

For three days, this town of less than three thousand residents became a focal point of German festivity, attracting festival-goers from Toronto, Hamilton, London, Guelph, New Hamburg, and a host of other villages and hamlets in southern Ontario.[3] The influx of visitors led organizer Otto Klotz to exclaim that the jubilee represented a "truly ... national festival ... considering that they had among them representatives from many other German associations, from the Province of Quebec, and also from the United States." To Klotz, the presence of American revellers from Buffalo, New York, and Ann Arbor, Michigan, seemed a living symbol of national unity.[4] Little did it seem to matter that Germany itself was still in the process of becoming.[5] Viewed from a transatlantic distance, the newly created political entity had, almost instantaneously, donned the mantle of national greatness.

In paying tribute to Germany's newly attained national unity, the celebrants in Waterloo County were not alone. Across the United States, German communities staged elaborate festivals to honour Germany's ascent to the "leading European people."[6] No fewer than seventy-two communities from New York to San Francisco celebrated jubilee celebrations, described in vivid detail in the pages of the *Berliner Journal*, Waterloo County's foremost German-language weekly.[7] Learning about celebrations in other North American towns and cities, the county's residents quickly concluded that they too had an obligation to organize a peace jubilee.[8] In May 1871, they added their own tune to the celebration of the nation and, shortly thereafter, snapped up the 300 evening extras which the *Journal* had published on the jubilee to mail accounts of "their" festival to family and friends in Germany. As the postmaster of Berlin reported, never before had he sent so many newspapers to Europe.[9] The fluid back and forth between the local and the (trans)national supports David Waldstreicher's assertion that "celebrants of the nation took their cues from printed sources. They improvised upon events they read about and then publicized their own interventions in public life."[10] Listening to stories of ethnicity and nation—and then enacting their own in the public street theatre that was the jubilee festival—celebrants became familiar with the idiom of a festive German culture that prided itself in unity, both the ethnic unity of German migrants in North America and newly attained national unity of the German homelands across the Atlantic.

In telling stories about themselves in the public venues of streets and market squares, immigrants affirmed their folk culture and national heritage—two national constructs which, as historians have taken care to point out, were carefully crafted by an ethnic middle class that sought to harness the festive enthusiasm of the moment in order to overcome internal ethnic divisions and establish its own leadership in the community.[11] Organizers also aimed at weaving their stories so tightly into the national storyline of their host countries that the latter would come to concede the validity of cultural pluralism and dual loyalties.[12] Although they usually harboured these hopes in vain (for mainstream America, as Orm Øverland observes, did not care to listen), the plots and themes of the stories that immigrants crafted at ethnic celebrations, rallies, banquets, and picnics shared "so many characteristics" as to constitute a genre of ethnic storytelling that was peculiar to North America.[13]

This chapter turns to the symbolic universe in which the peace jubilees of 1871 unfolded by probing narratives of nation, the rhetorical tropes of unity and diversity, and the world of myth into which the jubilee celebrations tapped. As we shall see, the jubilees represented powerful forms of communication that projected messages about historical memory, national myths, and cultural identity both in non-literate, visual tableaux and in overtly didactic oratory. The jubilees also brought to the fore the intersections between print and performance, ethnicity and nation. On the one hand, they lifted participants into a transnational space in which German-Canadian revellers took their festive cues from their "German brethren" south of the border, while German migrants in both Canada and the United States looked across the Atlantic for the national imagery and festive symbols out of which to compose their own jubilee celebrations. On the other hand, the celebrations reaffirmed national boundaries, for when it came to inserting their stories of German grandeur and glory into the national narratives of Canada and the United States, rhetorical strategies began to diverge.

NARRATIVES OF NATION

It was the medium of print that allowed the jubilee celebration to collapse boundaries of time and space. In creating "fields of exchange and communication," as anthropologist Benedict Anderson suggests, newspapers furnished both a festive vocabulary and a repertoire of national symbols that could be appropriated and adapted by readers in different national contexts.[14] With avid interest, Waterloo County residents had followed the growing tensions in Europe that erupted in the Franco-Prussian war of 1870–71. So curious, in fact, were many subscribers of the *Berliner Journal* about the outcome of the latest battles that they travelled "many miles on foot, or by vehicle, to procure their copy of the Journal at the press."[15] Devoting its columns to accounts from German newspapers, the county's press chronicled the homeland's military triumphs and later its jubilant celebrations of "peace," thereby inserting its readers into a festive space that transcended national boundaries, for the very rituals celebrated by the "German brethren" in the Fatherland could be re-enacted by German migrants in North America.[16]

News of the Franco-Prussian War reached North America in July 1870 and, almost immediately, galvanized the representatives of organized *Deutschthum* into action.[17] In the United States, "patriotic relief associations" (*patriotische Hülfsvereine*) formed to collect donations for the wounded, the widows, and orphans of the war. Young men flooded the associations with requests to have their fares paid to Europe so they could fight on Germany's side. Fearful that those acts might be construed as unpatriotic by Americans, ethnic leaders routinely denied such requests. Humanitarian missions, by contrast, did not provoke the same misgivings. New York relief societies sent forty-two physicians to Germany, where they worked in makeshift hospitals.[18] In Waterloo County, German spokesmen like John Motz, the editor of the *Berliner Journal*, and Hugo Kranz, who would be elected to the House of Commons in 1878 as its first German member, spearheaded the founding of a "German patriotic relief organization" that raised one thousand dollars for "the wounded and widows and orphans of the German armies," while Toronto's German community contributed two thousand dollars "for the relief of the widows and orphans of the Fatherland."[19] On both sides of the border, ethnic spokespersons were careful to highlight the humanitarian character of their donations, lest they be accused of disloyalty. Indeed, so concerned were some members of the New York City jubilee committee that a grand jubilee procession might arouse the ire of "our American and Irish fellow citizens" that they initially recommended avoiding any public demonstrations of national pride.[20]

The "dear Fatherland" and the "one Germany," as it was described in the peace jubilee celebrations, evoked a feeling of belonging that transcended both time and space. "What could it be that reunited us—we who for years long have lived thousands of miles away from the old Fatherland or know the same only from our parents' accounts?" the *Canadisches Volksblatt* asked rhetorically. The answer, it stated, was the realization of a long-cherished dream, "the unity and power of the country of our descent."[21] Across the border, in Buffalo, orator Edward Storck recalled the eternal ties that bound German migrants to the Fatherland. "Upon such an occasion as this," he said, "we cannot forget that we are Germans; born perhaps in a different province of our country, but still bound by every tie of consanguinity to the Fatherland."[22] What is striking about these descriptions of the imagined homeland, Germany, is the attempt to naturalize the bonds of nationality by likening them to family and kinship ties. The land of their fathers, orators held, was built upon ties of blood (the ties of "consanguinity") and its memory kept alive by immigrants who faithfully handed down stories of the homeland to their children and grandchildren. As another commentator suggested, the grand celebrations of Germany's victory provided ample proof that German Americans represented "a genuine branch of the magnificent trunk whose roots rest in the heart of Europe and whose strong branches reach further, year for year." [23] Germany was represented not as a historical construction, but as an organic entity whose branches reached as far as Germans had travelled to foreign lands.

As in other celebrations of immigrant communities in North America, the organizers constructed a narrative of German ethnicity that was meant to reassure Anglo-American and Anglo-Canadian audiences of the compatibility of their jubilee with mainstream cultural values. The middle-class organizers of the festival in Buffalo pointed out that they were assembling "to sing praises to the Shrine of Freedom." In the words of festival president Dr. Storck, the city's leading German Republican who had migrated to the United States after the failed 1848–49 revolutions and established a popular medical practice, "we meet as the votaries of peace, to celebrate the return of that happy state to our native Germany." Storck's speech was listened to attentively by the members of Buffalo's Common Council who had assembled in the Council Chamber before joining the peace jubilee procession. [24] In Berlin Otto Klotz, a justice of the peace and the county's longest-serving school trustee, addressed a crowd of several thousand in front of the courthouse, reminding them that they were celebrating "one of the noblest of public festivals—a peace festival." It was not to revel in the downfall of Paris but to express their "joy and gratitude that at last an end had been put to the late terrible sacrifice of life and destruction of property" that the Germans of Ontario had assembled. [25] The conciliatory air of the festivities certainly impressed English-language observers, who noted that the celebrants "did not gloat over the sufferings of the French nor do anything by word or deed that could have pained the hearts of the most sensitive Frenchmen." [26] Yet although the festivities were ostensibly peace jubilees, the rhetoric that permeated speeches and addresses served to subvert official tributes to the "return of bounteous peace and the ending of a cruel and devastating war." [27]

It was the laurel of the glorious victor, not the humble olive branch, that fired the imagination of orators in both Buffalo and Berlin. Ethnic group feeling, much like nationalism, depends "on one group's defining itself *against* another (or others)," as Matthew Frye Jacobson remarks. [28] In the case of the peace jubilees, this "other" was France. Not, to be sure, the tiny minority of French-origin migrants who lived in Waterloo County and who represented 4 percent of the county's population, or Buffalo's 2,232 residents who had been born in France and constituted a mere 2 percent of the city's population, but the nation of France that had so arrogantly "medd[led] in the domestic affairs of the Fatherland."[29] In spite of official attempts to devise a festive script that was devoid of martial or nationalist overtones, orators tended to draw upon a historical narrative that pitted the noble nation of Germany against its jealous and frivolous "old hereditary enemy."[30] Since Napoleon's occupation of Germany and his subsequent defeat in the battle at Leipzig in 1813, the notion of France as the "traditional enemy" of Germany had figured prominently at German national festivals.[31] When recounting the history of the war, immigrant orators, too, squarely placed the blame on the shoulders of France. Its "jealousy ... at seeing Germany becoming one and united," James Young, the Member of Parliament for South Waterloo County, said amidst cheers, had triggered "the triumphant but bloody march from Berlin to Paris."[32] Indeed, orator Francis Brunck in Buffalo concurred, the war had been wholly unprovoked on Germany's part.[33] Given that her "most sacred rights had been violated," even Anglo-American observers concluded that "the quarrel out of which she [Germany] came so gloriously was forced upon her. The power that was the first to draw the sword has perished by the sword."[34]

The orators did not stop at assigning blame. Their speeches also served a hefty dose of ethnic chauvinism that conjured the superiority of Germany over France. The war, Dr. Brunck announced in Buffalo, was "a victory of justice over injustice," while Mr. Schunck in Berlin pitted Germany's "noble, prudent, and brave conduct of war" against "the revengeful, helpless, and cowardly behaviour of the French."[35] Unjust, jealous, frivolous, presumptuous, arrogant, insolent, barbaric, and criminal—this was the arsenal of adjectives that orators used to describe the beaten foe.[36] Little wonder, then, that they finished their speeches with literary flourish. "In less than three months," Dr. Brunck concluded his address, "proud France lay helpless under the foot of despised Germany, and had to beg for peace."[37] These, clearly, were not words of conciliation but of triumph and righteousness that stood in marked contrast to the organizers' official agenda of holding a festival of peace.

In representing the nations of Germany and France to festive audiences in Berlin and Buffalo, orators and reporters drew upon gendered images. They celebrated the "militarized masculinity" of Germany, while reprimanding "beautiful" France for its vanity and self-indulgence. "The wickedness of her beautiful capital," charged the Buffalo *Commercial Advertiser,* "has culminated in an attempt at self-destruction. The fair city, like so many of those gay and guilty women of whom she is the prototype, has sought a suicide's grave."[38] By intertwining conceptions of gender and nationality, immigrant commentators reinforced the notion that France itself was to blame for its humiliating defeat. Once renowned for its "ideas, habits, and diplomacy," the country had become entrenched in "luxuries and pleasures." "Self-indulgence had become the law of the Parisian mind," the Buffalo *Christian Advocate* wrote; "there was no sense of duty to the family or the country ... The population were willing to forget their manhood."[39] The thin veneer of civilization, a Berlin speaker suggested, only disguised a rotten core, for a country that ridiculed the sacred bonds of family was undermining its very own foundation.[40] Given the decadence and depravation of France, the *Christian Advocate* suggested, the Germans had acted merely as an "instrument of punishment" and restored morality to European affairs:

> Whatever were the faults of the law, they were especially free from the vices of their Celtic neighbors. They peculiarly represent to the world a pure family life, a profound reverence for law, self-control under the sense duty ... Henceforth the thorough schooltraining of Prussia, the universal service of the nation, and her close discipline and drill, will be the model towards which other countries will aspire.[41]

Cast in gender terms, the Franco-Prussian War of 1870–71 appeared not as a battle for power and territory but as a moral struggle in which "feminine" France had been rightfully chastised by "masculine" Germany. Political unity, of course, did not guarantee cultural unity, either within Germany or abroad. It remained to be seen whether the festive union of German-origin migrants, symbolized in the elaborate jubilee processions in Berlin and Buffalo, would translate into an ethnic identity that could transcend divisions of class, nationality, religion, and gender.

UNITY AND DIVERSITY

The spirit of community that suffused the festivities was perceptible to insiders and outsiders alike. "We question very much," the Toronto *Daily Telegraph* wrote, "whether the Berlin of the Fatherland will exhibit more enthusiasm when the Kaiser and his men make their formal entry into the capital, than was exhibited by the Berlin of Canada today." In fact, the writer could not conceal his surprise over the intensity of feeling he observed in Berlin, for "it is a hard thing to become enthusiastic over a matter that happened three thousand miles away."[42] In a similar vein, the Buffalo Express held that "the spirit of nationality was rife and the sons and daughters of the Fatherland joined heart and soul in celebrating the return of peace to Germany."[43] To these contemporary observers, the imagined bond with Germany and the more tangible community of fellow revellers merged in a whirl-wind of enthusiasm.

The notion of ethnic unity was, indeed, central to the peace celebrations that were staged across North America. Typically, middle-class orators began their speeches by recalling the disgrace of the German people in the era before unifica-tion in 1871. The wretched provincialism, Georg Baltz declared in Buffalo, had allowed foreign armies to devastate the country. Its disunity, Otto Klotz in Berlin chimed in, bode poorly for the Franco-Prussian struggle of 1870–71. Yet as if to defy the boundaries of German principalities and kingdoms, the German people rose as one man to defend the country's integrity. "The Prussian did not look with disdain on the Hessian or the Swabian," Otto Klotz enthused. "Every one appeared in his place, from the sandbanks of the North Sea to the feet of the Alps. The whole people were united, and sacrificed willingly even more than they were asked to do." Young and old, artisans and scholars, sons of day labourers and million-aires, Prussians and Mecklenburgers, Swabians and Bavarians, republicans and monarchists all joined hands to fight against the arrogant neighbour to the west.[44] Out of their courage and unity, the nation was born. Hitherto, the editor of the *Canadisches Volksblatt* reflected, Germany had signified a geographical territory only. Now it stood for a nation. At long last, he wrote, "our dear, old Fatherland" occupied the position which it duly deserved.[45]

From the triumphant cry, "They were all Germans," it was a short step to exclaim that "We, too, are all Germans."[46] Basking in the glory of the newly created German nation-state, the unity of German migrants in Canada and the United States seemed a tangible goal. "Germans, who now look with pride and joy upon united Germany," Dr. Storck in Buffalo exclaimed, "let us here, in this country, be united as our brethren beyond the ocean."[47] Nowhere did the identification with the German Fatherland find a more public expression than in the massive peace jubilee celebrations that were read by many as a visible sign of German unity.[48] Importantly, the pervasive rhetoric of unity that permeated the festivities repre-sented less a description of what was and more a prescription of what ought to be. As the anthropologist Victor Turner notes, in ritual celebrations a social group celebrates not merely an event but rather "celebrates itself." It celebrates, Turner argues, "what it conceives to be its essential life."[49] The very repetitiveness of newspaper accounts that conjured German unity should be read not as an objective description of the celebrants' intentions but as a rhetorical strategy designed to write into existence what presumably already existed.[50]

Evidently, the celebrations in Berlin and Buffalo took place on a very different scale. To an American observer, the peace jubilee in the neighbouring towns of Berlin and Waterloo on 2 May 1871 must have appeared charming in its simplicity. The procession that marched from the railway depot to the Berlin courthouse included—in no particular order—delegations from Hamilton, Toronto, and a host of other towns and villages, "urged into quick time by several excellent brass bands" and headed by twenty-four adjutants on horseback.[51] Its one distinguished feature was two wagons from Preston, carrying girls in white and decorated with wreaths and garlands. Yet another wagon displayed a "beautiful fair-headed girl," Germania, surrounded by thirty-four others, representing the German states.[52] With Berlin decked in "holiday attire" and over eight thousand visitors cramming "sidewalks, balconies, windows, and houses," the procession passed the arches on King Street and broke into enthusiastic cheers once it reached the portraits of Emperor William and Bismarck, "as though they were anxious that they should be heard by the grim Chancellor all the way to the Fatherland."[53]

In Buffalo as well, "the enthusiasm generally expressed was as genuine as it was unrestrained."[54] But the celebration had little of the ad-hoc quality that characterized its Canadian counterpart. For weeks, the festival committee had elicited the participation of German associations, eighty-five of which marched in the three-mile-long parade ("more than anyone knew even existed," historian Andrew P. Yox quips).[55] Festival marshal Richard Flach, a veteran of the Civil War, travelled to New York and Philadelphia to learn first-hand of the work entailed in organizing a peace jubilee. On 29 May 1871, Flach was instrumental in dividing the multitude of organizations into seven divisions, each of which was headed by an assistant marshal. Unlike Waterloo County's three humble wagons, the Buffalo parade showcased float after float. The city's fraternal associations had engaged in a veritable competition as to who would assemble the most memorable display, while local German industries seized the opportunity to demonstrate their patriotism—and, the sceptic may add, benefit from free advertising.[56] Indeed, as historian Heike Bungert has observed in her study of German-American festivals in Milwaukee, the eagerness of participants at the peace jubilee to use their floats to commercial ends "seems to have surpassed even the often derided 'Yankee materialism.'"[57]

With animated floats reminiscent of guild processions in early modern Germany and Labour Day parades in nineteenth-century North America, German workmen proudly put their skills on display.[58] As thousands of admiring Buffalo spectators looked on, the blacksmiths of Reiter's and Eager busily swung their hammers at a steam boiler, while the float of the Buffalo *Telegraph* featured a printing press "in full operation", the printers tossing news sheets gratis into the crowd. "A bakery on wheels threw out hot rolls among the boys without regard to cost," while local butchers headed the seventh division, whose notable feature was a "sausage factory."[59] These displays could be read as admirable signs of German industriousness that took pride in its contributions to building America or, alternately, as tributes to a "mythical world of craftsmen and farmers," evoking a productive, orderly "German" past.[60] At the same time, the floats conveyed a message of social harmony and industrial paternalism as workers displayed their craft on wagons bearing their employers' names.

The cosy feeling of unity that permeated the festivities could not distract from the tensions that surfaced during the course of the jubilees. In Waterloo County, the beginning of the Franco-Prussian War had pitted German-origin migrants from Alsace-Lorraine—then part of France—against migrants from the German core areas. These latent hostilities sometimes erupted into altercations and even fist fights, as the *Berliner Journal* reported in August 1870. One is left to wonder how those "German-French," as the newspaper called them, reacted to Otto Klotz's endorsement of a policy of assimilation that would bring the provinces back into the fold of "German nationality," or how they viewed the ubiquitous banners that celebrated the return of Alsace and Lorraine to the "Fatherland."[61]

Religion also constituted a dividing line at the peace jubilees. In both Buffalo and Berlin, the organizers invited all German churches, regardless of their denomination, to offer divine services on the morning of the jubilee.[62] Such requests, as historian April Schultz suggests in her analysis of the 1925 Norse-American Centennial, may have been motivated by the desire to add "a sacred dimension" to a secular event. "An insistence on religious devotion," Schultz writes, set participants apart from "foreign radicalism" and proved them "worthy Americans" who demonstrated "an abstract sense of religion and spirituality."[63] But in the case of the German peace jubilees, this abstract spirituality never translated into a central role for German churches, which remained marginal to the festivities. In Buffalo, evangelical church groups joined the parade, as did members of Catholic associations; the latter, however, took pains to point out that they marched not as religious representatives but as "friends of the German cause." The Catholic German-language weekly, *Die Aurora,* failed to even mention the grand celebration.[64] The outbursts of patriotism in 1871 did not resonate with a Catholic Church that presided over a community of believers, not national groups. The prominent renditions of "Nun danket alle Gott" ("Let Us Praise Thee Lord") also held little appeal for the Catholic hierarchy. Composed by Martin Luther, the father of the Reformation, the hymn brought to the fore the secular Protestantism that underlay much of the festivities, thus emphasizing that the Catholic Church was central neither to the creation of imperial Germany, a country dominated by Protestant Prussia, nor to the peace jubilees in North America.[65]

One group, finally, was so effectively denied a voice at the celebrations that its presence is easily overlooked. In the historical narrative of the jubilee celebrations, women were relegated to the roles of either cultural guardians or national icons.[66] While "our brethren beyond the ocean" had valiantly fought against the French foe, Dr. Brunck said in Buffalo, the country's women had fed and clothed the German "warriors."[67] The work of political struggle was left to men, while women found fulfillment in their roles as caretakers. At the peace jubilees, women had to be content to decorate towns and market squares or, as in New York, organize "lady fairs" in support of the widows and orphans of the Franco-Prussian War.[68] If they entered the public sphere it was as spectators, not as actors; as icons, not as citizens. Embodying abstract principles such as the ubiquitous Germania, they were effectively excluded from the "*politics* of nationalism," as Matthew Frey Jacobson notes in his dissection of gender roles in immigrant parades.[69] The unity constructed during the course of the peace jubilees was thus a tenuous one. While no contemporary observer could deny the enthusiasm of the revellers who celebrated their Germanness on a scale never before witnessed on the continent, divisions of class, nationality, religion, and gender persisted, only to be temporarily obscured in the exuberance of the celebration.

MYTH

It was in the world of myth that jubilee organizers searched for the symbols and imagery with which to bind together German immigrants. These myths were suffused with ideas of romantic nationalism as they had been developed by the

German philosopher Johann Gottfried von Herder, who had located the "nation's soul" (*Volksgeist*) not in the high culture of the elites but in the multitude of folk traditions. His was a nation defined not by political boundaries but by a shared ethnic descent and culture, intimately shaped by the natural environment.[70] At the 1871 peace jubilees, the special closeness of the German people to their natural environment was evoked in two powerful symbolic gestures—the planting of an oak tree in Waterloo County and the odes to the river Rhine as the mythical source of German identity.

By planting an oak tree in front of the courthouse, the Berlin festival committee drew upon a symbol that had formed part of the repertoire of German celebrations ever since the first German national festival of 1814, in which celebrants had adorned houses and streets with oak leaves, branches, and wreaths to commemorate the liberation of Germany from Napoleon at the Battle of Nations in 1813. The oak —"an incarnation of fertility, steadfastness, and strength"—thereby transformed into a metaphor of the German nation itself.[71] Over half a century later and a continent away, jubilee president Otto Klotz saw in the young oak, which had been imported from Germany for the occasion, a symbol of historical continuity. "The old Germanic tribes," he said, "regarded the oak as the forest's foremost tree; in oak groves they preferred to assemble to make decisions on war and peace, to hold court and divine service; for the old Teutons honoured god not in temples but ... in the grand temple of sacred nature."[72] Reminiscent of Tacitus's *Germania*, which had contrasted German authenticity with Roman decadence, Otto Klotz's speech projected onto the German tribes an image of noble savages whose inner strength and forthright morals were as admirable then as now.[73] The oak not only reached far into Germany's past—back to its ancient roots, so to speak—but also served as a reminder for future generations. "May this oak," the orator's voice urged the audience, "always remind us and our descendants of the great German accomplishments; be it a memorial of the virtues of the old Teutons."[74] Although the oak failed to prosper in later years, its meagre growth a poor testimony to German greatness, its memory would be carved in stone over a quarter of a century later.[75]

If the oak symbolized the inner qualities of the German nation, it was the Rhine that demarcated its outer boundaries. A "myth of spatial origins" is, of course, central to nationalist narratives.[76] In the case of the German Fatherland, the Rhine symbolized the nation's "natural" boundary to the west. For centuries, the Rhine had inspired poets and historians who perceived its majestic stream—

lined by "authentic" German villages and "ancient" castles like Ehrenbreitstein, Stolzenfels, Sonneck, and Rheinstein—to be an embodiment of the nation's past. In more recent historical memory, the Rhine had captured the national imagination as the pivotal symbol of the Franco-Prussian War. "As soon as Germany resounded with the war trumpet," Georg Baltz proclaimed in Buffalo, "a whole nation arose in arms to guard the old and sacred watch of the Rhine, and with might and main to ward off the frivolous and wanton war with all its terrors from the fields of the Fatherland."[77] So powerful was the image of the Rhine that it was thought to constitute the particular property of Europe's "Germanic" tribes, a term broad enough to encompass both the Dutch and the Swiss.

If the jubilees portrayed Germany as an organic, immutable entity, embodied in nature itself, they also offered personifications of the German nation in both Hermann the Cheruscan and the allegorical figure of Germania who presided over a newly unified nation.[78] In topical floats—grand in Buffalo and modest in Berlin—these figures told a tale of German history whose very timelessness framed the experience of migration in terms of historical continuity. The irony that the German nation was depicted as a woman—"a member of the group most completely excluded from the nation as a political community" —was replicated at the peace jubilees in Berlin and Buffalo, where women represented the German nation but were otherwise refused a public voice at the celebrations. Dressed in white, a symbol of moral purity, thirty-four "young ladies" at the Berlin parade personified the German states, with "Miss E. Hoffman, a flaxen haired Saxon lass of fifteen years of age, representing Germania."[79] Observers readily agreed that only the solemn unveiling of the oil painting *Germania* in the evening, accompanied by the tune "Die Wacht am Rhein," could rival this sweet tribute to German unity.[80]

In Buffalo, too, Germania was celebrated but in far more extravagant fashion. A display that had dazzled Manhattan spectators at the New York *Friedensfest* in early April 1871 was brought to Buffalo by the central committee. "Drawn by six horses, each led by a footman arranged in costume of the olden time," the float left Buffalo festival-goers visibly impressed.[81] "The central tableau was illustrative of the 'Watch on the Rhine,'" the Buffalo *Express* reported,

> Germania seated upon a massive rock, about the base of which the famed
> and lovely river was pictured in its winding course. At different points old
> castles might be seen rearing their towers ... and there was everything to

complete the scene and make perfect the allegory. There were other figures also, arranged and costumed in harmony to represent the arts, the sciences, and the avocations of peace. This feature of the procession was truly superb, and was a center of great admiration.[82]

Markedly absent from the display were any references to the defeated foe. Instead, Germania surrounded herself with symbols of a romanticized Germany whose greatness lay not in its martial triumphs but in its cultural accomplishments. By vaguely alluding to a grand cultural heritage, the tableau reflected the pervasive influence of romantic nationalism, which believed nations to be defined by their language, customs, and cultural attributes, a message reiterated in the speeches at the peace jubilee.[83] Germania personified Germany's newly attained national unity while anchoring it in a nebulous past where myth and history merged at the shores of the Rhine.[84]

If Germania presided serenely over a unified nation, another float at the Buffalo *Friedensfest* delved deeply into collective historical memory. It commemorated a battle between the Romans and Teutons in 9 AD that saw Hermann (Arminius) the Cheruscan defeating a Roman army in the Teutoburg Forest.[85] As a popular historical myth, memorialized in stone in the *Hermannsdenkmal* near Detmold, Germany, in 1875, the Cheruscan prince admirably suited the larger narrative of the peace jubilee, for Germany's victory in the Franco-Prussian War mirrored the military founding act of the Germanic tribes.[86] In addition, the dramatic contrast between the "audacious ... and energetic" Teutons and the "lethargic, cynical, and weak" Romans—a plot first devised by Tacitus—found its parallel in the alleged differences between the pure and noble German nation and the decadence of France.[87]

To suggest that the Hermann float at the Buffalo peace jubilee was embedded in a mythical German context is not to say that this myth was consciously evoked by the organizers of the festival. Indeed, it is doubtful whether Friedrich Erstling, upon whom had fallen the honour of representing Hermann, paid much attention to the creation myth as he balanced uneasily on a giant globe, always in danger of stumbling unceremoniously as the float hit one pothole after another.[88] Rather, this is to suggest that the peace jubilee in Buffalo drew upon national myths that had evolved historically in Germany and travelled to North America as part of the popular culture of German-speaking migrants, memories of which were rekindled in the elaborate printed accounts of peace jubilees published in the spring of 1871.

Yet even if Buffalo spectators were only dimly aware of the mythical subtext underlying the display, they would have been hard pressed to miss the float's principal message. Connected to "Hermann" with golden chains "sat eleven young ladies dressed in white representing Prussia, Bavaria, Saxony, Baden, Wurtemberg [sic], Mecklenburg, Hesse, Brunswick, Bremen, Hamburgh [sic], Alsace and Lorraine," who together symbolized "the union of the German States in one great Teutonic Empire," as the Buffalo *Commercial Advertiser* put it.[89]

Although the organizers of peace jubilee celebrations made use of a festive vocabulary that had been developed at national celebrations in Germany, they did add symbols of their own that corresponded to their experience of migration.[90] The globe upon which Hermann struggled precariously for his balance bore two clasped hands, "indicating the union of Germans in Germany and America and the countries themselves through them," as one observer noted. Even the most German of displays thus paid tribute to the migrants' adopted homeland. The image projected by this gesture of friendship and mutual respect was one of dual identity. To be German in 1871 Buffalo, it implied, was not mutually exclusive with being American; on the contrary, the feelings of fidelity and loyalty displayed at the peace jubilee revealed a measure of character that befit any American citizen. Even the Buffalo *Commercial Advertiser,* a paper prone to nativist overtones in the 1850s and 1860s, readily recognized that in "Herman [sic], standing upon the globe and overlooking all, was symbolized that, as Germans when in distant countries still look back to the Fatherland, so does it look on them with pride."[91] It was a realization that did not trouble the *Commercial Advertiser.* Like other English-language papers in the city, it published lengthy reports on the jubilee that cast Germany's victory in the Franco-Prussia war as beneficial both for "the nations of Europe" and the world at large.[92]

Judging from the coverage of the jubilee celebrations, the symbols of dual loyalty that permeated the festivities were as ubiquitous as they were persuasive. As the Buffalo *Express* observed appreciatively, the Germania float featured "trappings of crimson and gold, medallions with coat of arms, and the colors of Germany and America interwoven in all directions."[93] From buildings fluttered the German tricolour in red, black, and white, alongside "the glorious stars and stripes."[94] If the celebrants intoned Luther's hymn "Nun danket alle Gott" and burst into enthusiastic renditions of "Die Wacht am Rhein" ("The Watch on the Rhine"), they ended their ceremony with "The Star Spangled Banner."[95] Similarly, across the border, the Union Jack was as prominent as the German tricolour.[96] Just as in Buffalo, Berlin revellers bowed their heads to their adopted homeland; only upon the rendition of "God Save the Queen" did the crowds disperse and the public celebration end.[97]

ETHNICITY AND NATION

The vivid historical tableaux that the peace jubilees carried onto the streets of Berlin and Buffalo were "read" not only by the thousands of onlookers and participants, but also by the audiences of German- and English-language newspapers. As the one and only peace jubilee in Canada, the Berlin celebration attracted much attention in the province's English-language press. On 18 May 1871, the local *Berliner Journal* reprinted, with evident pride, excerpts from eighteen newspapers that had reported on this "splendid celebration" and praised "the biggest and most successful demonstration which has ever taken place in Canada."[98]

Clearly, the elevation of Waterloo County to Ontario's German heartland did not go unnoticed in the English-speaking press whose reports, in turn, reinforced the association of "Waterloo County" with "German." Ethnicity, of course, is always constructed in a dialogue between immigrants and the host society. Yet the conversations about ethnicity and national belonging did not always garner such publicity as they did during the peace jubilee celebrations of 1871, when organizers self-consciously addressed Anglo-American and Anglo-Canadian audiences.

Celebrants at the 1871 German Peace Jubilee told stories about German unity in both sight and sound. COURTESY OF UNIVERSITY OF WATERLOO SPECIAL COLLECTIONS, DORIS LEWIS RARE BOOK ROOM, BREITHAUPT HEWETSON CLARK COLLECTION, BHC 43.

Once orators began to situate their ethnicity in a specifically national context, the stories of Berlin and Buffalo began to diverge.

In the United States, the "Forty-Eighters," who had long dreamed of a unified Germany that would grant civil liberties to its people, viewed the country's unification initially with mixed emotions. As immigrants who had brought to the United States the German liberal tradition of the revolutions of 1848, the Forty-Eighters were "deeply concerned over the rapid rise of Prussia into a powerful military state," Carl Wittke points out in his classic study of the German-language press in America. These misgivings gave way to mounting pride as the German-American press chronicled Prussia's victories against France and even sent "special correspondents abroad to cover the news."[99] Although Germany's victory over France fuelled the fires of national pride in the German-American press, it soon became apparent that Chancellor Bismarck had no intention of granting responsible government, nor freedom of speech and assembly.

Could the former radicals, many of whom had carved out a comfortable niche in American middle-class society, rejoice in unity without liberty? Most of them did. To be sure, a radical New York paper, *Die Arbeiter-Union* (The Workingmen's Union) folded after its circulation declined, an unmistakable reproof of the paper's critical stance toward Bismarck. There were also those Forty-Eighters, like Karl Heinzen and Friedrich Hecker, who criticized the absence of civil liberties in the newly created German nation-state.[100] More typical, however, was a feeling of fraternal unity that engulfed both "Grays" and "Greens." In Buffalo, for instance, Francis Brunck and Edward Storck, prominent representatives of the city's pre- and post-1848 migration waves respectively, shared the speakers' podium at the peace jubilee. Together, they conjured the "thrill of patriotic gladness" that welled in every German's heart after national unity had been attained.[101] Ironically, it was Buffalo's most radical German society, the gymnasts (*Turner*), that marched proudly in the parade's first division.[102]

If freedom was mentioned at all, it was as an afterthought, coyly hidden in a stream of patriotic declarations. Perhaps, speculated Francis Brunck, the democratic form of government was suited only for those people who had slowly grown accustomed to it. Rather than demanding the immediate introduction of civil liberties in Germany, he encouraged German migrants "to preserve, with all our might, the Republic in North America."[103] Even the city's German Republican paper, the *Freie Presse*, only once hinted at Bismarck's moral obligation to pay the German people in the currency they so duly deserved, freedom and civil liberties.[104] It was not freedom that dominated the German-American discourse on the Franco-Prussian War, but a curious mixture of pride and defensiveness. Finally, ethnic spokesmen concurred, Americans had become aware of the sizeable German element in their midst. Just as importantly, Americans had publicly recognized German diligence and dignity, industry and intelligence—in short, the German gifts to America.[105] But while the orators at peace jubilees basked in the overt admiration, they noted with dismay that some nativists persisted in questioning German loyalty.[106] "They maintain," Dr. Brunck said in Buffalo, "that these demonstrations are not in accordance with our duties as citizens of the republic; that we cannot at the same time bear love and fidelity to our native land and this republic." To refute this "very narrow minded idea," Brunck evoked a popular metaphor that would run as the proverbial red thread through the proclamations of ethnic intellectuals in future years. "If a young man chooses a wife and leaves his father's house, does he cease to be faithful to mother and father because he ardently loves his wife and is faithful to her? We have chosen this republic as our bride, but love not less our native land."[107] A cultural allegiance to Germany, the mother, did not interfere with political loyalty to America, the bride. This was a message reiterated in the following decades whenever calls for the assimilation of all foreigners gathered force.

In Waterloo County, where German-speaking migrants represented the majority of the local population, neither newspapers nor orators dared to question the loyalty of "the Germans of Canada."[108] Instead, speaker after speaker lauded "the German character—naturally quiet and unobtrusive, obedient to the laws, patient under extreme suffering, possessed of dauntless bravery," as Charles Magill, the Member of Parliament for Hamilton, put it.[109] The very presence of dignitaries, who included members of the House of Commons and the Ontario Legislature, the County Court Judge, the bar of the county, the town council, and neighbouring county officials, indicated that the jubilee was a celebration of Waterloo County's cultural mainstream which enjoyed the support of local establishment. The *eminence grise* of the jubilee, Otto Klotz, sought to translate the festive exuberance into political claims. "We Germans, here in Ontario," he said, "should occupy in this country the position to which we are entitled as sons of the grand, enlightened Germany." Then Klotz proceeded to map out both the entitlements and obligations of Canada's German citizens: the preservation of German customs, the cultivation of excellent schools, the promotion of commerce, arts, and science.[110] His tone of confidence was palpable. Evidently, Waterloo County's collective memory did not harbour stories of nativist attacks or even native resentment. As local charter group, German-speaking settlers had cut the forest and cultivated the land. As pioneers, they claimed a place in the nation's narrative that was at its centre, not its margins.

In what was one of the most remarkable characteristics of the peace jubilee, this place was readily conceded to them. Members of the House of Commons who climbed the speaker's platform in Waterloo County emphasized the close ties between the German and the British peoples, who were united "by the bonds of sympathy between the German and British Empires."[111] Here, one is reminded of Matthew Frye Jacobson's assertion that "assimilation is world politics ... insofar as it requires the reconciliation or integration of competing national mythologies."[112] In a very real sense, the perceived closeness of the German and British Empires shaped the discursive universe in which the peace jubilees unfolded. By emphasizing the ties of kinship that bound together Great Britain and Germany, the expressions of German patriotism could be cast as unthreatening. "While the German people took natural pride in the success of the Fatherland," said James Young, MP for South Waterloo, "they loved the Queen of England, and the glorious constitution under which they lived."[113] Nowhere was this image of an essential union between the German and British peoples more powerfully captured than in an address by local English-speaking citizens to the organizers of the jubilee:

> You can hardly fail to remember that the bond of union between your Fatherland and our Motherland is one that has been cemented by relationships the most tender and sacred possible, that in the hatred of oppression and aspirations after true liberty, the genius of our fellow-countrymen in both lands is the same; and that in reverence for truth, morality and religion, the observance of law and order, and respect for constituted authority, as well as in the cultivation of all the graces of every day national life, the people of Germany and Britain have long been in mutual accord.[114]

It was in the Dominion of Canada, the address continued, that German and British citizens had joined forces to build a "Great Canadian nationality." In the New World, these two great peoples were merging "as Canadians and Colonists relying upon the same rights, civic and political, animated by the same principles and aims." In fact, so similar were their character and mission that the "English Residents of Berlin" were proud to assert that "we are so much one with you in everything as it is possible for any two peoples to be."[115] A more public endorsement of the centrality of German migrants to the project of Canadian nation building is hard to imagine.

As early as 1871, the German ethnicity which the peace jubilees brought to the fore had thus acquired distinct American and Canadian tinges. German migrants in the United States framed their identity in the language of republicanism. Keenly aware that Bismarck's German *Reich* refused to grant civil liberties, yet smitten by Germany's unification and its newly achieved national greatness, Forty-Eighters toned down their calls for German democracy and instead expressed their appreciation for the freedoms available in the great American republic. Drawing upon the "doctrine of immigrant gifts," a notion first developed during a wave of anti-Catholic nativism in the mid-nineteenth century, they emphasized German contributions to the project of nation building but never quite succeeded in shedding their defensive air.[116] While revelling in the public tributes to German character and culture, as published in the English-language press, one critical comment seemed enough to evoke the spectre of nativism that had haunted German migrants in the 1850s. In Canada, by contrast, a self-confidence permeated the speeches of German orators. Living in a heartland of German-origin migrants where the cultural norm was German, not British, speakers celebrated the entitlements of German-Canadian citizens without betraying the slightest fear that changing political circumstances might affect their position. English-speaking dignitaries, in turn, confirmed the privileged role that German migrants held in Canadian society by pointing to the close ties between the German and British Empires. When Louis Breithaupt told the Ontario Legislature many a decade later that "German Canadians are devoted to the British crown and, therefore, nobody will blame them for preserving, in their hearts, a strong affection for the old Fatherland," he reflected the customs of a local charter culture that celebrated the birthday of Queen Victoria alongside the birthday of Kaiser Wilhelm I.[117] In reconciling competing national mythologies, Waterloo County's German residents skilfully highlighted the perceived closeness of the German and British Empires, whereas their "German brethren" across the border expressed sentiments of both pride and defensiveness.

As historian Thomas Bender argues, to reimagine the history of the nation and rethink national narratives means to explore "a spectrum of social scales, both larger and smaller than the nation and not excluding the nation; social worlds interacting with one another and thus providing multiple contexts for lives, institutions, and ideas."[118] The German peace jubilees of 1871 provide an example of one such social world that was firmly embedded in the national contexts of Canada and the United States—and indeed, aspired to rewrite the national narratives of both nations by highlighting the seminal contributions of the ethnic group—while simultaneously transcending national boundaries in a new festive space infused with German myth and ritual and steeped in the rhetoric of romantic national- ism. In the medium of print, Waterloo County's German middle class carved out a space that encompassed no fewer than three nation-states, affirmed social and symbolic ties with fellow Germans in both the United States and Germany, and introduced German migrants to the language of nationalism in which they would frame grievances and celebrate achievements in the years to come. Pressures to conform to a national norm appeared greater in the United States, where cultural difference was viewed with suspicion. In Canada, by contrast, German migrants did not seem to feel threatened by the cult of Anglo-Saxon superiority; for did not ties of family and history connect the German and British Empires?[119]

The peace jubilees of 1871, with their joint celebration of nation and ethnic- ity, added a new layer of identity to both the self-image and the public image of German migrants in North America. This is not to argue that the language of nationalism became the central or even the sole idiom, in which migrants expressed their identity, their hopes, and their anguish, nor is this to deny the special appeal that cultural nationalism held for the ethnic middle class as it vied for cultural and political power within both the ethnic group and the nation-state it now called home.[120] Rather, this is to suggest that immigrants became increas- ingly well versed in the language of nationalism, and that the festive spark pro- vided by the peace jubilees was able to ignite an ethnic tradition of remarkable longevity. In Waterloo County, the peace jubilee of 1871 provided the catalyst for the first German-Canadian singers' festival of 1874. Buoyed by the success of the peace jubilee in Berlin, German choral societies in Berlin, Waterloo, Preston, Toronto, and Hamilton founded the Deutsch-Canadischer Sängerbund (German- Canadian Choir Federation) in 1873, an organization dedicated to the cultiva- tion of "German nationality in language, customs, and traditions." Although the federation would fade in and out of existence in the decades to come, the tra- dition thus invented carried over into the twentieth century. Between 1874 and 1912, the German residents of Waterloo County celebrated eight singers' festivals which drew upon a rich local tradition of music-making and carried on a (musi- cal) conversation about what it meant to be German in Canada. The dialogue between migrants and host society, which had assumed such a public dimension in the peace jubilee of 1871, would thus continue to unfold along much the same historical trajectory. Cloaked in the language of tradition, this dialogue pursued an inherently modern rationale by affirming the place of German migrants at the very centre of the Canadian nation.[121]

6.

Soundscapes of Identity
Singing Ethnicity in the Great Lakes Region, 1874–1912

$\mathcal{S}$now still covered the ground when the singers of the Waterloo Liedertafel jumped from the sled that had brought them to the neighbouring village of Preston in the spring of 1874. In the local tavern, they met the Preston Liederkranz who had arrived "man for man," as had several members of Hamilton's singing society, Germania. Also present was the Preston brass band, whose tunes filled the tavern—alongside songs, toasts, and the inevitable speeches that seemed to grace every German gathering. H.A. Zöllner, the conductor of the upcoming singers' festival in Waterloo Village, praised the "true German spirit" of the Preston hosts and called upon the singers to work "tirelessly" for the grand musical gathering in early September, his voice tinged with the warmth that would make singers three decades hence affectionately refer to him as "the father of German song in Canada."[1]

The easy back and forth with which singing societies and town bands—those two pillars of musical life in Waterloo County, Ontario—visited each other for an evening of socializing reflects the rhythms of a local musical culture that had thrived in the county since the early 1850s, although it was not until the 1860s that the county's main German-language weekly, the *Berliner Journal,* began to record the many facets of music-making in a more systematic fashion. In Berlin, still a village of barely 2,000 residents when it was selected county seat in January 1853, a small band and a singing circle had played at social gatherings as early as 1845. In the 1850s, an array of musical associations offered regular performances.[2] The sounds of brass music accompanied the visitors from Berlin who travelled to Toronto in 1856 on the first of many such excursion trains.[3] Annual benefit concerts for Berlin's Mechanics' Institute provided a stage for local musicians.[4] Singers and musicians from both Waterloo Village and Berlin joined forces at concerts in St. Nicholas Hall, where they performed German and English songs in four-part harmony.[5] The county's residents also overheard the sounds of spontaneous serenades and enjoyed weekly brass concerts at market squares during the summer months, courtesy of village and town councils that engaged private bands to provide musical entertainment.[6]

Waterloo Musical Society Band, c. 1867. COURTESY OF
WATERLOO PUBLIC LIBRARY, PHOTOGRAPH J-1-9.

A lively musical soundtrack was woven into the very fabric of sociability in Waterloo County, the heartland of German settlement in nineteenth-century Ontario. No festival of the German gymnasts (*Turner*) in Toronto, Preston, and Waterloo would have been complete without musical accompaniment, and when the *Turner*'s appeal began to wane in the late 1860s, mutual visits between German choral societies from Waterloo County, Hamilton, and Toronto took their place.[7] These informal gatherings paled in comparison with the grand singers' festivals in the United States that the *Berliner Journal* described in lavish detail in its columns, but they did nurture informal social networks out of which a German-Canadian singers' movement could grow.[8]

In her study of immigrant culture and music-making in Sauk Valley, Minnesota, whose rural character mirrored that of Waterloo County, historian Kathleen Neils Conzen has suggested that music in the Sauk "never seemed to take on a strong ethnic coding, and like its urban counterpart it became a significant bridge to a broader, non-ethnic cultural world."[9] In Waterloo County, music similarly reached out beyond the ethnic group, both to the county's English-speaking citizens who earned praise for their supportive presence and to Anglo-Canadians in Ontario who learned about the singers' festivals from effusive articles in the Toronto *Globe*.[10] But as a whole, the festivals did not seem overly concerned with the reactions of Anglo-Canadian onlookers and audiences who, in any case, had nothing but praise for the music-loving, orderly German celebrants. Never did the Germans of Waterloo County seem to feel pressured to make German ethnicity appear "safe" or push it into the cultural mainstream—a concern so clearly felt by orators at German-American singers' festivals in urban centres. In this proud German enclave, the currents of local culture were German, not English, while the soundscapes of German identity fitted melodiously into a racialized environment that lauded the kindred spirit of the "Anglo-Saxon and Teutonic races" and celebrated the bonds of consanguinity between the German and British imperial families.[11] If the festivals reached out to a broader, non-local world, the bridges thus built remained ones of ethnicity that bound together German singers in the Great Lakes region on both sides of the Canadian-American border.

The very "ephemerality of sound," which might linger for a moment only to quickly disappear, allowed both listeners and readers to imbue it with different meanings.[12] If we turn to the reports in German- and English-language newspapers, supplemented by rare personal reminiscences and fragments of material culture, we can discern, quite clearly, four keynotes that were woven into the aural fabric of the singers' festivals in Waterloo County. First, there were the lovers of classical music who saw in the festivals a stepping stone to performing the choral works of the great masters. Professor Theodor Zöllner, who took over the baton from his father H.A. Zöllner, liked to divest the festivals of their folksy appeal by staging Haydn's *The Creation* in 1886 and cultivating the voices of Berlin's Philharmonic Society for the "noble" performance of classical selections in 1898. In the festivals' second keynote, it was ethnicity that constituted the unmistakable leitmotif. Celebrating the twenty-fifth anniversary of the peace jubilee of 1871, the president of Berlin's Concordia singing society, Karl Müller, spearheaded a successful campaign to erect a memorial to Emperor Wilhelm I. Unveiled at the singers' festival of 1897, the memorial represented a German twist on the cult of the empire that enveloped British Ontario in the closing decades of the nineteenth century and provided orators with an opportunity to reflect self-consciously about the historical roots, the ethnic characteristics, and the civic obligations of the county's German Canadians. The romantic nationalism that imbued the official script of some singers' festivals was tempered with an intense localism—the festivals' third keynote—that looked inward rather than outward. By 1898, even the county's English-language press adopted the singers' festivals as their own, as the well-publicized gatherings represented an excellent advertisement of Berlin's progress and prosperity. The musical and social experiences of the celebrants suggest that the ethnic coding of the official program left a rather fleeting impression on singers and audiences, who revelled in sociability rather than the more lofty aims of ethnic unity and national grandeur. A transnational soundscape—cast in a continental, not transatlantic mould—was the fourth keynote of the singers' festivals. Although the festivals cultivated a German "national sound," as reflected in the repertoire of folk songs, participants looked less toward the German Empire and more toward the bordering American states, where many friends and relatives resided, who used the musical gatherings as an occasion to renew old friendships and tighten family bonds.

Setting the Stage

It was the peace jubilee of 1871 that provided the spark for the eight singers' festivals that Waterloo County residents celebrated between 1874 and 1912, not counting the festivals in Toronto and Hamilton or the many informal festivals of song and music that German-Canadian singers and musicians organized in the late nineteenth and early twentieth centuries across southern Ontario.[13] Inspired by the success of the 1871 *Friedensfest*, singers from Toronto, Hamilton, Berlin, Waterloo Village, and Preston met in Hamilton in November 1873 to found the German-Canadian Choir Federation (Deutsch-Canadischer Sängerbund). Vying for the honour of hosting the inaugural German-Canadian Singers' Festival were the village of Waterloo and the county seat, Berlin. The delegates sided with Waterloo's bid, as it had been the enthusiasm of Waterloo's music master H.A. Zöllner's that had drawn them to plan the event.[14] As a German-American correspondent marvelled, the inaugural German-Canadian singers' festival thus took place "in a tiny Canadian rural town that does not even have its own railway link."[15] Deemed the natural choice for the festival's musical conductor, Zöllner also penned the federation's constitution that in its final draft echoed the nationalist rhetoric of the peace jubilee. The federation vowed to promote German song, bind closer together the Germans of Canada and cultivate "German nationality in language, customs, and traditions" so as to "contribute to the refinement of the German character in Canada."[16]

Unlike conductors in later years who cut a striking presence on the concert stage but never climbed the speaker's podium, Zöllner seized the opportunity in 1874 to welcome the "German singing brethren of our great neighbouring republic ... May you be happy in our midst; may this gathering help to strengthen our natural bonds, not only as Germans, but also as singing brethren." Zöllner was keenly aware that his singers' festival paled in both scale and musical proficiency by comparison with the elaborate singers' festivals in the United States, and that visiting singers might be surprised, perhaps even dismayed, at the modest size of "little Waterloo." By way of an explanation, Zöllner ventured that "Canada's Germans are yet too isolated and too poorly represented in the big cities" to organize singers' festivals in large urban centres, whereas Waterloo County provided a congenial concert stage. Still, he admitted, "our musical ability cannot possibly compare with our singing brethren from the United States or our old Fatherland. This is only a small beginning."[17]

Given the tendency of nineteenth-century commentators to record their observations in flowery prose, it is difficult to gauge exactly how well singers and musicians performed at the festivals. Only in retrospect—and from the slyly triumphant perspective of Berlin, which hosted the singers' festival in 1875—could it be admitted that the participating societies in 1874 had been rather inexperienced.[18] Much less circumspect in their criticism were the singers of the Buffalo

Interior of the concert pavilion at the first German-Canadian singers' festival in Waterloo, Ontario, 1874. *Canadian Illustrated News*, September 1874. COURTESY OF LIBRARY AND ARCHIVES CANADA, C-061437.

Sängerbund who attended the festivals in both 1874 and 1875. Marching through heat and dust to the concert hall, they had to consume "a significant quantity of lager" to rejuvenate their voices, and still the performance was marred by "dusty tones." It did not help that the united mass chorus offered a poor rendition of Abt's "Morning Song," while the Hamilton brass band overtaxed itself in tackling the difficult setting of "Bohemian Girl."[19] Overall, however, the Buffalo singers deemed the festival "quite satisfying," particularly since "one could not expect too much from our neighbours in Canada, who had just begun to elevate *Deutschthum* to its proper heights."[20]

In these comments resonated the superiority the city felt over the countryside, and the benevolent condescension was not restricted to music-making alone.[21] The influx of festival attendees into Waterloo Village and Berlin threatened to overwhelm local hotel and tavern owners. Visitors complained about uncomfortable accommodation, and "guests at the hotels had in several instances to wait a couple of hours for a meal."[22] The Berlin beer, the Buffalo singers declared in 1874, was a miserable potion and the Waterloo "stuff" only slightly more palpable. Not to be outdone by local musicians, the Buffalo Sängerbund formed its own impromptu band by purchasing brass instruments at a Waterloo store, thereby revealing the "decisive character of the 'Yankees'" who sought to excel in everything, as the *Berliner Journal* commented tongue-in-cheek.[23]

And yet, according to the tales the Buffalo singers brought home, we can hear how German-Canadian and German-American celebrants forged friendships over liberal amounts of lager that made voices sound hoarse but spirits soar high. In its quarters, the Buffalo Sängerbund organized a singers' banquet in 1874 "after Buffalo fashion," where singers from Buffalo, Waterloo Village, and elsewhere found themselves united in "the true conviviality [*Gemüthlichkeit*] of singing brethren." More than one Buffalo singer stumbled into the night and fell asleep beneath the stars, only to be rudely awakened by a shower of rain the next morning.[24] The Buffalo singers revelled in their reputation of being the "best singers at the Fest" but expressed genuine affection for the festival's conductor, H.A. Zöllner, whom they praised as "the heart and soul of the singers' festival; every singer loves him, for he knows how to make friends with everybody at the very first meeting."[25] These feelings of sympathy were only enhanced when Zöllner seized Carl Braun, the conductor of the Buffalo Sängerbund, in an embrace at the main concert in 1874, exclaiming with tears in his eyes: "Now, I have listened to a male chorus once again; I have not heard anything like it since I left Germany fourteen years ago."[26] When the Buffalo singers returned to Waterloo County in 1875, they made sure to visit their friends in Waterloo Village and also paid a visit to Hamilton's Germania society. After meals and refreshments, they toured the city in eight carriages and bade a "hearty farewell" to the Hamilton singers before boarding the train to Buffalo.[27] This, then, was the counterpoint to the earlier condescension: lively praise for the true "old German hospitality" offered by "our Canadian singing brethren." The Waterloo Liedertafel, in turn, visited the Buffalo singers in a travelling party of sixty "gentlemen and ladies and several babies" in 1877 in what likely constituted one of many informal visits across the border.[28]

At the singers' festivals of 1874 and 1875, organizers, orators, and observers alike evoked memories of the Franco-Prussian War and placed the festivals in the proud festive tradition of the 1871 jubilee.[29] To festival orators in Waterloo County, national pride in Germany's accomplishments and ethnic pride in the awakening of a group consciousness seemed indelibly interwoven. Just as "national airs" had "poured fourth" in the Fatherland as "our brave soldiers went into action," undaunted by the sounds of "the infuriating and revolutionary 'Marseillaise,'" so too would the "sweet and invigorating strains of a national air sung" now bring together "singers in a more friendly contest," festival president Wilhelm Oelschläger declared in 1875. In Waterloo County, he continued, music "draws us Canadians like a magnet to the musical gatherings in the United States, and brings the Americans as welcome guests to us on this occasion," thus fostering "social improvement and friendly intercourse."[30]

Anglo-Canadian observers, as well, viewed the aural and visual spectacle of the first German-Canadian singers' festival of 1874 through the lens of the recent Franco-Prussian War. As he watched "bodies of young men" parading the village streets in "military array, singing German songs," the editor of the Toronto Globe felt transported across time and space: "so hearty were the notes," he wrote, "that it almost seemed as if the flags of the German Empire fluttered through the night in the storm of song."[31] Audiences inevitably greeted these tributes to German greatness with "hearty cheers" and "loud applause." Only when orators tried to leave the realm of myth and legend and translate festive exuberance into specific political claims did resistance stir. When Otto Klotz demanded in 1874 that the Canadian government change its naturalization laws to afford naturalized German Canadians the protection of the British Empire, members of the audience vocally objected to this violation of a festival script that more typically would dwell on the innate love of Germans for music, song, and culture (which in itself seemed a mark of ethnic excellence), voice pride in the accomplishments of the German Empire, and emphasize the unwavering loyalty of German-Canadian citizens to their adopted homeland, Canada.[32]

Toronto and Montreal newspapers published lengthy accounts of the festivals, while the Canadian Illustrated News brought detailed engravings of performances and concert pavilions to a nationwide audience in 1874 and 1875.[33] The Toronto Globe, which accorded the inaugural singers' festival prominent coverage on its front page, seemed baffled that a mere village could stage a mass concert of 350 singers that drew thousands of attendees to Waterloo County.[34] In adopting the ironic, light-hearted tone of a cultural explorer, the reporter took his readers into a strange and foreign territory whose residents spoke English with a heavy German accent, "ate German sausages and drank lager beer," and joined the spirit of the festivities with such "enthusiasm" as if to dispel any notion that "the Teuton is a staid, quiet, unexcitable creature." Good-naturedly, this urban dweller conceded that he liked what he heard and saw: the sounds of industry (even if they were pro-duced, somewhat prosaically, by a "sleep-robbing pump factory") and the "largest tannery in Canada, and several small tanneries, a brewery and distillery, and the

Dominion Button Factory," all of which graced the county seat, Berlin.[35] In an age of industrialization and urbanization in which newsboys, habitual truants, and orphans roamed the streets of Toronto, the writer was pleased to find youthful dignity and innocence in Waterloo County, where "pretty little girls, with deep blue eyes, are playing around everywhere, and here and there one sees a group of small people, the boys with great wide-rimmed straw hats, in the midst of tiny fiddlers about their own age."[36] The young girls, their "fair hair plaited and falling in a long stream behind," seemed direct descendants of Gretchen, the archetypical female character in Goethe's celebrated novel *Faust*. Their admirable mothers and fathers, in turn—"the women strong and domestic looking, the men with their rosy faces and light clothing looking as though they had stepped out of one of the pictures of German artists"—displayed all those qualities that made good citizens: respect for order, love of honest toil, and the will to succeed. Stereotypical as these images were, they did not differ in kind or degree from the characterizations found in the county's boosterish publications—only that the latter tended to project these supposedly innate German qualities even further back in time to the early nineteenth-century pioneers of Waterloo County.

But beneath the *Globe*'s folksy representation of Waterloo County's Germans lay a second narrative strand. The writer voiced excitement over the "great German Canadian Musical Jubilee," the "grandest affair of the kind ever held in Canada" that would introduce Canadian audiences to the "magnificent specimen of choral music of the Fatherland."[37] It was not the sounds of ethnicity that would captivate the Toronto *Globe* in future years but the tantalizing possibility of a home-grown musical culture that would bring the art of music, "which is said to be so characteristic of the Germans in Germany," to Canada.[38] In harbouring this hope, the *Globe* reporter was not alone.

MAKING MUSIC

The core feature of the eight singers' festivals that took place in Waterloo County between 1874 and 1912 was the individual performances of the male singing societies and the singing of the male mass chorus. While the organizers of the first singers' festival of 1874 had expressly rejected the idea of a singing competition, since it "all too often causes jealousy and resentment," this became a mainstay in later years. In 1875, the Anglo-American Orpheus singing society of Detroit won over audiences and judges with its rendition of "Life's a Bumper," edging out its close rival and namesake, the Buffalo Orpheus society.[39] In 1886, Montreal's Teutonia society insisted on a competition at the festival. The Montreal chorus was superior in skill, education, and social status to the younger societies from Waterloo County, as the president of Berlin's Concordia society, Karl Müller, acknowledged, judging the singing abilities of his home-town choristers as rather dubious.[40] But it was a German-American singing society, the Rochester Orpheus, that carried the competition over its fellow societies from Montreal, Toronto, Hamilton, Berlin, Waterloo, and New Hamburg. The greater skill of American singing societies reflected the longer tradition of choral singing in the United States, where singing societies had been meeting since the 1840s in friendly musical rivalry.[41]

Unlike in the United States, where classical selections and ambitious choral works came to dominate singers' festivals in the post–Civil War decades—save, perhaps, for the singing competitions that featured more folksy fare—German choral societies in Canada cultivated folk songs whose style and content varied little over four decades. Singers sang of German forests and mountains, vineyards, balmy nights, love and waltzes in springtime, only occasionally evoking the Fatherland, the river Rhine, or the battles of the Franco-Prussian War.[42] Their songs were sentimental, not political—playful musical variations of the "positive stereotype" of "German culture with its love of wine, women, and song," as historian Berndt Ostendorf writes concerning German-American musicians in these decades.[43] While it was impossible to transplant the German landscape to Canada's shores, an echo could be heard in the soundscapes of the singers' festivals that conjured from the mists of collective memory the snow-capped tips of the German Alps, the majesty of the river Rhine, mysterious German forests and vineyards, and even the cry of the cuckoo or the faint smell of spring blossoms.[44] It was no coincidence that by the early twentieth century, such musical representations of regional landscapes merged into an ode to the German homeland itself. The singers' festival of 1902 was the first to feature three tributes to the German homeland in its official program, including "Homeland" ("Heimath"), "Greetings to the Homeland" ("Grüße an die Heimath") and "Homeward Bound" ("Heimkehr"). In Germany, too, ethnomusicologist Philip Bohlman writes, folk songs began to blend the distinct melodies of many German homelands into a single sound of the nation.[45]

Audiences rewarded singers with a "thunderstorm of applause" and, in the case of particularly compelling performances, warmly congratulated the choristers, easily identified by their society's badges, later on the streets. As the Toronto

Globe noted in 1875, "a more enthusiastic or less critical audience is not often met with."[46] It was not necessarily the quality of singing that left a lasting impression. Newspaper columnists offered carefully measured praise that acknowledged the care and diligence with which singers and conductors had prepared the musical selections to the best of their abilities, each society giving "evidence of having spent many hours in faithful practice."[47] But commentators also frankly observed "that forcing of the voice, which is so unpleasant a characteristic of many of the younger societies." Even the county's main German-language weekly, the *Berliner Journal*, admitted in 1890 that the performances of the singers of Waterloo and Berlin featured "natural singing" rather than "artistic achievement." H.A. Staebler, a participant at the 1898 singers' festival, conceded that "the choral singing was not of a standard that would be considered professional, or even first class amateur." But, he continued, "the nature of the occasion did not demand this. Entertainment was in the ascendant, decorations were colourful, and the whole atmosphere radiated good cheer."[48]

United male mass chorus performing the traditional closing act of the singers' festival in Waterloo, Ontario, as depicted by the *Canadian Illustrated News* in September 1875.
COURTESY OF LIBRARY AND ARCHIVES CANADA, C-062856.

The mass chorus, in which the male choral societies joined forces in the performance of two or three selected songs, attracted similarly mixed praise. Journalists wrote that it was a "pleasure to listen to so large a number of voices singing the beautiful Volkslieder of Germany," but also, and more ambiguously, commended the singers for the absence of "serious hitches" and their "surprising precision and clearness of attack ... considering that only one mass rehearsal was held."[49] Clearly, the mass chorus represented the "grand climax of the festival" less for its polished, artful singing and more for what it symbolized—an audible and visible icon of German unity in North America that blended the voices of both local and visiting singing societies, introduced "the masses" to the "omnipotence of the German folk song," and helped collapse "the many thousands of miles that separate us from the old homeland," as a singer put it in 1902. The music, concurred the Toronto *Globe*, "is of a simple, pleasing nature," but "abounds in good contrast and broad passages." It appealed greatly to the audience that had rushed to their seats, with "every place in the hall ... occupied by 8 o'clock," and loudly demanded an encore, "which, however, was not granted."[50]

Triumphal Arch at the Waterloo Singers' Festival, n.d. COURTESY OF WATERLOO PUBLIC LIBRARY, PHOTOGRAPH A-3-11, COPY J-12-17.

The audience that flocked to the singers' festivals in Waterloo County did not exhibit the qualities of "polite" music lovers who paid tribute to fine art through their punctuality, appreciation and, above all, as historian Michael Kammen puts it, their "quiescence."[51] Theirs was a folk festival that was informal both in its organization and its listening practices. In the inaugural singers' festival in 1874, the concert hall accommodated an audience of two thousand who "panted, perspired, and wilted in that atmosphere of heat and dust" until organizers cut air holes into the canvas to provide relief. Once audience members discovered that the music carried outside the concert pavilion, "the hall was thinned to about two-thirds full, and comfort stole gently in on airy wings."[52] In later years, observers complained in unison that "as usual in such cases, the concert began absurdly late, and the waits between the numbers were unnecessarily long and tiresome."[53] Tired from the summer heat and the lengthy concert programs that comprised up to thirty pieces, men, women, and children left in droves. Midway through the main performance in 1898, one-third of the audience had left the skating rink where the concert was being held; at the concert's end, only half of the listeners remained.[54] Matinee concerts also were attended sparsely, "as the visitors seemed to thoroughly enjoy walking about and inspecting the decorated streets and finely dressed windows of our stores."[55] The musical gatherings in Waterloo County would remain festivals of both song and sociability, with audiences beholden as much to the culture of German *Gemütlichkeit* as they were to musical tributes to the homeland.

Nonetheless, music lovers marvelled at the potential of the singers' festivals to introduce choral culture and classical music to Ontario audiences. The Toronto *Globe* praised the festivals' ambition "to stimulate the cultivation of vocal concerted music" and voiced its hope that English Canadians would, in due time, "take as keen an interest and as active a part in these festivals as the most zealous music loving German could desire." The *Globe*'s comments were rife with the sentiment—shared widely in both Germany and among music critics in late nineteenth-century North America—that music represented the "most German of the arts" and respect for the arts constituted an innate "German" characteristic.[56] But the musical fare the *Globe* reporter enjoyed listening to most was not the folk songs of the "Fatherland" but a classical German repertoire, performed by orchestra and mixed choirs. In an otherwise complimentary concert review in 1875, the writer pointed to the "danger of the German Canadians overlooking the importance of paying special attention to the organization and development of mixed choirs," which were crucial to "producing the choral works of the great

masters." Not only would mixed and female choirs enrich the sound of the singers' festivals—"the voices of the ladies being felt as a relief after the larger number of exclusively male choirs"—but they would also enable German-Canadian
singers to perform complex choral and classical works, thus following the lead of
the Philharmonic Society of Toronto. Thanks to its "large mixed choir," the music
critic wrote, the Philharmonic Society had produced "three oratorios within a
comparatively short space of time" and thus "done more to promote an acquaintance with high class music than twenty male vocal clubs could have done."[57]

It was only under the baton of Theodor Zöllner, son of H.A. Zöllner, that local
mixed choirs would stage the work of the "great choral masters" in the singers'
festivals of 1886 and 1898. Born in Saxony, Germany, the seven-year-old Theodor
had arrived in Berlin, Waterloo County, with his family in 1861. His musical career
bore remarkable resemblance to the life trajectories of the second-generation
German-American musicians Bernd Ostendorf has examined. Like them, Zöllner
grew up in a German cultural milieu that prized music and German song and
offered early musical education in the home. Like the German-American musicians Theodore Thomas and Walter and Frank Damrosch, who made their musical mark in New York and other large urban centres, he sat on the proverbial fence.
On the one hand, he was intimately familiar with the ethnic world of German
singing societies, folk songs, and the exuberant—indeed, sometimes exhaust-
ing—sociability that characterized the singers' festivals. On the other hand, he was
powerfully drawn to "sacralizing" the classics by raising the skill and ambition of
local choristers to a level palpable to professional ears.

Theodor Zöllner was first and foremost a professional musician who found
inspiration in the music of European composers and who, unlike his father, used
the singers' festivals as a vehicle for the performance of classical works and the
education of the musical public.[58] As a young man, he left for Cincinnati, Ohio, "to
obtain both a theoretical and practical musical education." He returned to Berlin
at the age of twenty-six to offer private lessons in vocal and instrumental music.
There he founded the Berlin Philharmonic and Orchestra Society that would
perform Haydn's *Creation* in 1883, Händel's *Messiah* in 1887, and Mendelssohn's
St. Paul in 1896, with the help of specially hired instrumentalists and soloists.
Directing operas, operettas, and musical soirees, serving as the conductor of the
Berlin Sängerbund, the Waterloo Orpheus society, and the Berlin Choral-Union,
establishing the Berlin Music-Academy, and accepting the position of organist-
choirmaster at both St. Peter's Lutheran Church and the Church of the New

Jerusalem, Theodor Zöllner's musical ambitions transcended the ethnic world in which his father had so comfortably made his home.[59] In an evening of song and instrumental music he conducted in December 1882 the young Zöllner included not a single work of German provenance, leading the *Berliner Journal* to offer the criticism that "in a concert, performed by mostly German singers and musicians in front of an almost exclusively German audience, we should not forget about German character and tradition."[60] This, however, was not the aim of Zöllner, who instead sought to bring a classical musical canon to Waterloo County audiences and elevate the musical taste of Berlin's youth through his position as singing master in the public schools and at St. Jerome's College between 1897 and 1922.

As the conductor of the 1886 singers' festival, Zöllner took his cues from the professional musical world, reaching out to Anglo-Canadian soloists and brass bands whose services he engaged and incorporating new musical features such as the children's chorus into the program, whose effect on audiences he had observed at the Toronto music festival only months earlier.[61] In the weeks leading up to the 1886 singers' festival, Zöllner seemed omnipresent. He met with several hundred schoolchildren to practise "their little songs"; initiated the temporary union of the Berlin Philharmonic Society and the Concordia Männerchor, thereby bringing together practitioners of classical music and German folk song; led rehearsals with the individual choral societies in Waterloo County, Hamilton, and Toronto— numbering three hundred voices in total—who would perform Haydn's *Creation* at the festival; hired and worked with an orchestra of sixty musicians who would provide the instrumental accompaniment to the *Creation*; engaged three Anglo-Canadian soloists from Toronto; and prepared himself for conducting the united male mass chorus in three selections: "Laßt schallen deutscher Männerchor," "Die Schildwache," and "Hymne an die Musik."[62]

The press coverage of the festival was unanimously positive. "This is a great day for little Germany," reported the Guelph *Daily Mercury and Advertiser,* whose writer was particularly charmed by the "two excellent children's choruses in one of which the little ones waved their union jacks in time to the chorus of the Red, White, and Blue, creating a tremendous furore among the immense audience." In rhyming off the ingredients that made "Berlin a most noted and popular musical centre," the author pointed to "A chorus that would grace Toronto, an excellent orchestra, a good conductor whose only fault is his indolent time-beat and his satisfaction therewith, first class soloists—Mrs. Caldwell, Mr. Jenkins, and Mr. Warrington," all of which "combined to make an almost perfect performance."[63]

The chorus and the orchestra that performed Haydn's *Creation* were "extremely good," the Toronto *Globe* agreed, impressed "that a comparatively small place like Berlin should be able to make a success of such a large undertaking." With evident pride, the *Berliner Journal* quoted music critics from Toronto, Montreal, Rochester, and Philadelphia, who judged Zöllner's rendition of the *Creation* as amply measuring up to expectations, and splendid, indeed, for "a place like Berlin."[64] In scope and musical ambition, the singers' festival of 1886 had set a standard that subsequent festivals of song would find hard to match.

Only once more, in 1898, did Theodor Zöllner pick up the baton of the singers' festivals, tempted, perhaps, by the opportunity to visit Hamilton, Toronto, Rochester, Buffalo, Detroit, Ann Arbor, and Ypsilanti, where he rehearsed the repertoire for the male mass chorus with local choral societies. At the 1898 festival, the mass chorus let its three hundred voices swell from a soft piano to a formidable fortissimo under the leadership of its conductor.[65] Once again, a children's chorus of five hundred girls and boys, clad in white, with whom Zöllner had practised for weeks in Berlin's skating rink, made its appearance. The *Deutsche Zeitung* of Berlin, while acknowledging the "brilliance" of the children's performance, noted the "strange feeling" produced by the sight of German schoolchildren singing the English national anthem "God Save the Queen" while waving five hundred Union Jacks, thus symbolically casting their future with the British Empire. Less nationalist in its outlook, the *Berliner Journal* did not express similar qualms. Both newspapers, however, reported the "moving" sight of the schoolchildren, who later sang "The Watch on the Rhine" while twirling the black, white, and red flags of Germany and then marched off the stage to the strains of "The Germans onto [sic]Paris."[66] Another musical note that sounded at the singers' festival of 1898 also flowed directly from Zöllner's work with the Berlin Philharmonic Society. The society's mixed chorus, consisting of fifty women and men whose voices had been trained under conductor Zöllner, contributed several classical numbers to the festival's opening concert, including Wagner's "Tannhäuser" chorus, Mendelssohn's "The Nightingale," and Händel's chorus "Oh Great Is the Depth."

The mixed chorus added "nobility" to the program, the *Deutsche Zeitung* wrote appreciatively, although the paper was most impressed by the "mighty, grandiose, roaring" of the male mass chorus.[67] In this, the writer's musical preference mirrored that of audiences at the concerts. As a celebration that had grown out of Waterloo County's local musical scene, the singers' festivals remained remarkably flexible, easily incorporating new features such as Haydn's *Creation* or classical concert numbers. Yet without the express initiative of Theodor Zöllner—who by the turn of the century had established himself as the county's revered music master and had found several outlets for his creative energy—neither the children's chorus nor the mixed choirs that performed complex classical works continued to form part of the festive repertoire. The singers' festivals never transformed into the celebrations of high culture that Theodor Zöllner and the Toronto *Globe* had envisioned. Judging by the audience's reactions, the performances that moved them most were the airs of the male mass chorus, the rendering of German folk songs by individual choral societies, and the singing of female soloists whose "lovely," "marvellous," "clear," and "sweet" voices rang through the concert pavilion or the skating rink and prompted calls for an encore.[68] Unlike the speeches at the singers' festivals that became steeped in nationalist rhetoric around the turn of the century, the concerts remained rooted in a local musical tradition, featuring folk songs that even casual choristers could master comparatively easily, celebrating the sound of the united male mass chorus, and showing off the fine voices of female soloists, especially if the singers themselves heralded from Berlin or Waterloo.

SINGING ETHNICITY

The singers' festivals in Waterloo County remained small-scale enough that an ambitious director could shape them to his liking. If conductor Zöllner had broadened the cosmopolitan appeal of the singers' festivals in 1886 and 1898 by refining the festivals' sound, craftsman Karl Müller transformed the festival of 1897 into a dazzling commemoration of the 1871 peace jubilee. His was a radically different vision of German culture: fiercely protective of German cultural heritage, ideological in its insistence on the superiority of all things German, and overtly nationalistic in its outlook.[69]

The bonds that connected Karl Müller with Germany were many and strong. He had only been fourteen when he followed his older brother, Adolf, to Canada in 1872, where he suffered from homesickness—"this toothache of the heart"— throughout the thirty-four years he spent in Waterloo County. Three extended visits to Germany between 1879 and 1880, 1883 and 1885, and 1907 and 1908 strengthened his inclination "to measure everything in Canada, from brewing beer to church affairs, according to German standards." While in Germany, he worked as an apprentice in a painting shop, thus acquiring the skills for his future craft, but also enjoyed private painting lessons in Munich, visits to the city's galleries, and the carefree life of a student, replete with fencing lessons, card games, and the occasional lecture.[70] Upon returning to Canada, Müller could not help contrasting the prosaic sight of Berlin's King Street with the beauty of German cities. What rankled even more was the "terrible gibberish" spoken by many German immigrants who blended German and English into a language of their own. For this avid reader of German newspapers, such as the "highly conservative *Reichsbote*" that his parents faithfully mailed from Germany, the German language represented a tangible connection to the homeland that was not to be given up lightly.

In his covert courtship with a young woman named Anna, Karl Müller discussed German classics on long evening walks, delighted by his fiancée's "quick grasp, her good judgment ... and her growing love for all things German."[71] His tender tribute to his first wife contrasts with more abrasive comments on Canadian people and customs. Unlike his brother Adolf, eight years his senior, who had a close-knit circle of Anglo-Canadian friends, Müller refused to socialize with his English peers, although he wrote warmly of his long-time friendship with "Mrs. Fennell," who mothered the young German man and welcomed him into her home as a family friend.[72] As a man of strong opinions who considered the "good" German society in Berlin to be relatively small (and the "good" English society to be only slightly larger), Müller did not hesitate to pass judgment: on the poor singing of Berlin's Concordia society, the "silly boredom" of the Canadian Sunday, or the alleged conspiracy against German language lessons at public schools which, he maintained, he had successfully "thwarted."[73]

When the Concordia society was to celebrate the twenty-fifth anniversary of the peace jubilee of 1871, president Müller suggested commemorating the occasion by planting a new oak tree (for the old one had long withered away), adorned with a memorial plaque. Donations poured in so generously that Müller called a special meeting of Concordia, whose members decided to erect a bust of Emperor Wilhelm I in Victoria Park instead. "For weeks, we collected donations from Berlin businesses for several hours each day," Müller recalled. Support from the German Consul in Montreal was also enlisted, as well as from the members of Montreal's affluent Teutonia Club.[74] An organizing committee formed that included local luminaries Reeve Rumpel, editors Motz of the *Berliner Journal* and Sikorski of the *Deutsche Zeitung* and, of course, Müller himself, who kept a low profile but handled the logistics of erecting a monument of the late German Emperor almost single-handedly. It was Müller who ordered the bust, made out of copper, directly from Berlin, Germany; Müller who penned the mail order for the German sheet music that would be distributed among the participating German-Canadian singing societies; Müller who contacted a Hannover flag company in order to obtain a giant German flag "as it waves on the warships of the German navy" to flank the emperor's monument in Victoria Park. The emotional bonds that connected the thirty-nine-year-old with Germany were thus matched by material-iconographic bonds that provided a tangible connection to the German Fatherland.[75]

In Germany itself, Emperor Wilhelm I had long rejected the erection of monuments bearing his likeness. Upon his death in 1888, however, monuments of the late Kaiser began dotting German towns and cities. Among the three to four hundred sites, a selected few—like the "Porta Westfalica" nearby Minden or the "Deutsche Eck" at Koblenz—achieved nationwide significance. While industrial magnates and the educated middle classes led the movement to publicly remember Emperor Wilhelm, it was the petty bourgeoisie who erected monuments in honour of his paladin, Otto von Bismarck, in the mid-1890s. In rejecting the national democratic legacy of the 1848 German revolutions, these monuments celebrated (and unabashedly so) the imperialist ambitions of the German nation-state, embodied in the emperor and his helpers: Prince Bismarck, a fierce opponent of democratic and liberal demands, and General Helmuth von Moltke, who famously upheld the primacy of war over politics.[76]

That Karl Müller and the fellow members of the organizing committee should tap into the political iconography of imperial Germany is hardly surprising. As the cult of empire, with its overt rhetoric of Anglo-Saxon superiority and its tales of imperial glory, enveloped Ontario, the citizens of Berlin celebrated it with a German twist. The editors of the *Deutsche Zeitung* pushed a German cultural agenda, replete with extensive coverage of German festivals and annual tributes to both Emperor Wilhelm and Prince Bismarck.[77] In 1887, the Concordia singing society staged an elaborate celebration of Emperor Wilhelm's ninetieth birthday, donning sashes in black, white, and red and adorning the town's houses with German flags and evergreens. Two years later, the society celebrated the birthday of Prince Bismarck in equally colourful fashion.[78] In 1888, Mayor Louis Breithaupt, who only a decade earlier had visited the palace of Versailles "where Kaiser Wilhelm was crowned" and characterized the French as "restless, even impetuous folk," recorded the emperor's death in his diary. With the consent of the town council, Breithaupt cabled a telegram of condolences to "Her Majesty the Empress of Germany" and requested that Berlin's businesses be closed between 10 AM and noon on March 15 so as "to enable citizens to attend Divine Service in honor of the late beloved

German Kaiser." On the day of the funeral, the town's "German societies i.e. The Landwehr Verein, Concordia Männerverein, German Club, the town council, the high school students & many citizens formed a procession along King St." and then "proceeded to St. Peters Church where the Rev. Mr. Von Pirch delivered an excellent & patriotic sermon in honor of the late Emperor Wilhelm."[79]

It is impossible to know whether the council members felt the connection with the German Empire as deeply as did county residents such as Kurt Müller, Louis Breithaupt, and Reverend Von Pirch, whose nationalist German-language newspaper, the *Freie Presse*, folded in the 1880s because its "militant attitude" failed to resonate with readers.[80] But the county's political and economic elites did pride themselves in the virtues of the German character, the consanguinity of the British and German empires, and the esteem that Canadian government circles extended to this proud German enclave in southern Ontario. To be German in Canada meant to live comfortably in two cultural worlds and intertwine the cultural identities of both loyal British subject and proud German settler. That this self-image was so eloquently endorsed by government representatives helped reinforce it in the public mind.[81] By the early twentieth century, it would become a rhetorical staple, casually deployed in boosterish pamphlets that praised the county's "hardy pioneers" for having combined "the best traditions of both the Teutonic and Anglo-Saxon races."[82] It was in this cultural climate that the singers' festival of 1897 unfolded.

As the most nationalistic singers' festival in the county's history, the 1897 event introduced not so much a new tune as a variation of a familiar melody to which Anglo-Saxon audiences listened indulgently. The Berlin hosts—foremost among them Karl Müller and the Concordia singing society—had vowed to organize a "truly German festival" that would revolve around German song, sociability and, of course, that most German of festive ingredients: *Gemüthlichkeit*.[83] To this end, Müller revived the moribund Canadian Sängerbund and sent formal invitations to the Teutonia (Montreal), Germania (Hamilton), Liederkranz (Toronto), Orpheus (Waterloo), and Harmonie (Waterloo) singing societies.[84] As the first trains arrived in Berlin on 11 August 1897, bearing both singers and visitors, the Montreal delegation attracted particular attention. Dismounting from a Pullman Sleeping Car were twenty-eight "businessmen engaged in the wholesale trade" wearing grey fedoras, formal white vests adorned with badges in the black, white, and red colours of the German Empire, and a "noble singers' ornament" clipped onto their dark coats. Dressed less formally, singers from the neighbouring

Ontario communities greeted each other on the railway platform and "renewed the old friendship with a firm handshake."[85] On the next day, 125 singers, "consisting of vocalists from all the visiting societies," joined voices in a "rousing chorus" that the local *Berlin News Record* called a revelation and whose performance was "all the more creditable," the paper wrote, "when it is considered that the combined voices had only one united practice."[86] As in previous singers' festivals, the music spilled over from the concert stage to the streets and hotels, where singers broke out into "merry song" throughout the day and late into the night.[87]

German attendees from out of town marvelled at the German character of Berlin. One Toronto visitor remarked that "here in Berlin, on the streets and everywhere" only German was spoken, and even small children could carry on a conversation in German. Having witnessed the chat between Torontonian U.L. Steiner and a two-year-old girl, the *Deutsche Zeitung* felt compelled to add a cautionary note: the toddler whose command of German had charmed Mr. Steiner was none other than the daughter of Kurt Müller, and as Berlin locals would have known, few children grew up in such a stridently German household as did little Frieda.[88]

In her father's hands, the singers' festival of 1897 cultivated a self-consciously nationalist tune. As visitors arrived at the station, among them many from the surrounding villages and rural districts, "the band struck up the stirring strains of the German national anthem "Die Wacht am Rhein" ("The Watch on the Rhine") while other visitors were welcomed to the sounds of "Deutschland, Deutschland über alles" ("Germany, Germany above All").[89] The concert itself consisted of a musical fare that blended tributes to archetypical German landscapes with more militaristic melodies such as "Hurrah Germania" and "Das Deutsche Schwert" ("The German Sword").[90] As such, the concert set the mood for the climax of the singers' festival: the unveiling of the larger-than-life bust of Emperor Wilhelm I on 13 August 1897 to the strains of "Germany, Germany above All," "Hail Thee, My Fatherland," and "God Save the Queen."[91]

Although English-speaking observers commented on the curiosity of the occasion—"namely the unveiling of a monument to a foreign monarch"—and noted their inability to follow the lengthy speeches, since "nearly everything said was in German," they gave broad, and mostly sympathetic, coverage to a festival that cast its cultural ambitions not in the fleeting medium of music but instead in copper and granite.[92] The monument, wrote the Hamilton *Spectator*, is "very beautiful." Looking northward over the grounds, the bust sat imposingly on a pedestal of Quebec granite. Modelled in Germany, it was accompanied by two reliefs attached to the columns that pictured former Reichs-Chancellor Otto von Bismarck and General Moltke.[93] The monument's inscription revealed a desire to translate the glory of the German Empire—and more specifically, "the glorious deeds of the German people during the war of 1870–71"—into renewed ethnic pride and self-respect.

It was a theme spelled out in the speech of the elderly John Motz, founder of the *Berliner Journal,* who recalled the local peace jubilee celebration of 1871 as the founding moment for Canada's Germans; for this festival had demonstrated how "Germans can achieve greatness if they only unite."[94] But Motz also reiterated the tune of dual loyalty. While honouring "the land of our birth and its famous Emperor," the celebrants who had gathered today in Victoria Park were "good citizens of Canada and loyal subjects of Queen Victoria" who "did not wish to establish a sectional state in this land; we will remain loyal and true to the land in which we have found a home and a livelihood." Mayor John C. Breithaupt similarly emphasized that "we Germans are proud of the Fatherland, but we are first, last, and always Canadians," while his brother Louis Breithaupt held that "there were no more loyal citizens to Canada and to the British Crown than the German residents of Canada." The latter then stated that he soon hoped to witness the unveiling of "another monument in this beautiful park, one to her Gracious Majesty Queen Victoria—(applause)—thus having memorials of the two greatest personages and Sovereigns of the nineteenth century."[95]

Karl Müller, who had composed so much of the festive script, remained silent. But, then again, his commentary on German ethnicity in Waterloo County fluttered in the wind, for all to see. On the large flagpole in Victoria Park, a giant German flag waved beneath the British ensign, a reminder of the dual nature of civic loyalties. Although the British flag occupied the position of honour, it was dwarfed by the sheer size of the German flag, which made its British companion appear "like a colourful napkin," as Müller wrote decades later in his memoir. His ill-concealed glee stemmed from the satisfaction of having proven wrong a local English minister who had once claimed that a foreign flag would never fly in Berlin's Victoria Park.[96]

English-language observers at the singers' festival did not seem particularly troubled by the unveiling of a monument in honour of the late German emperor. For one thing, the song of German pride was interwoven with expressions of loyalty to Canada and the British Crown. The musical nature of the event also served to blunt its political message. In announcing this "Proud Day For the Citizens of

Berlin," the Toronto *Globe* took care to portray Berlin "one of the most music-loving centres in the Dominion," where visitors could listen to "the strains of the great German masters of music as Germans only can render them." Not even the fact that most speeches in Victoria Park were delivered in the German—with nary a concession to unilingual English speakers—daunted the paper's writer, since "Mr. W.H. Seyler of Toronto, broker and commission merchant in the Board of Trade building, who is Vice-President of the German Benevolent Society of Toronto" was kind enough to take down the speeches in shorthand and translate them "for your correspondent."[97]

Only one paper, the local Berlin *Telegraph*, dared to suggest that the unveiling of the Kaiser's bust amounted to an act of disloyalty—an accusation that was emphatically rejected by its English-language rival, the *Berlin News Record*. "We should not forget," wrote the *Berlin News Record*, "that the German Empire is a great empire, and that a son of the Fatherland may be pardonend for thinking well of it, even if he has chosen to become a Canadian citizen." The county's very prosperity, the editorial continued, depended on the presence of its "industrious, law abiding, thrifty Germans." Instead of denouncing their fondness for the Fatherland, "let us," the paper pleaded, "by the exercise of tolerance and good will, assist in welding the sentiments of all classes of our citizens into a solid, abiding Canadianism," thus following the example of Canadian Prime Minister Wilfrid Laurier, "a Frenchman," who had passed the Kaiser's bust "through the Customs, duty free."[98] To be sure, there were limits to ethnic tolerance, as the writer contended:

> If the monument had borne a bust of Washington, Canadians might well raise
> objections to its appearance on British soil; but here we have a class of citizens
> ... erecting a memorial in commemoration of the peace of 1871 and designed
> ... to act as an incentive to them to acquaint themselves with the richness of
> its literature and traditions, that they may be stirred to become good and use-
> ful citizens in Canada by imitating all that is best in German character.[99]

Anglo-Saxon commentators, by and large, concurred with this assessment. Although they might have regarded the memorial as peculiar and did note the decidedly German-Canadian character of the event (which, unlike earlier singers' festivals, reached out to neither Anglo-Saxon nor German-American musical circles), they did not feel threatened by the occasion. Reassured by the "loyal utterances of all the speakers at the unveiling" and convinced of the civic virtue of the county's German Canadians who justly cherished "their language, their literature and their traditions," they accepted the "Peace Memorial" as an expression of ethnic pride that could be usefully mined for the greater benefit of the Canadian nation.[100]

In the closing event of the 1897 festival, Kurt Müller tried to conduct a spirited German evening at the skating rink, much as he had experienced in the mid-1880s as a student at Munich University. But the rink was too vast, and the singers too animated. Although they joined the renditions of "The Watch on the Rhine" and "Brotherhood," they seemed far more interested in an evening of good fellowship than a re-enactment of German customs.[101] Not for them was the language of nationalism that Kurt Müller, Louis Breithaupt, Reverend von Pirch and the editors of the county's German-language press spoke so reverently. These German-Canadian celebrants would have been surprised to learn how the *New York Staatszeitung* transformed their gathering of song, sound, and sociability into a stately celebration. As the *Staatszeitung* enthused, visitors at the unveiling had arrived "from all the provinces of the Dominion, from Manitoba's northern realms, from British Columbia's far-away coast and Quebec's populous regions." For this hyperbole the *Berliner Journal* had only a chuckle. Wryly, the paper commented on the correspondent's "impressive imagination" that illustrated—if nothing else—the profound ignorance of German-American newspaper editors concerning this German enclave to the north whose Germanness had become deeply embedded into the local mainstream.[102]

SONG, SOUND, AND SOCIABILITY

Sounds of dissonance, however fleeting, were rarely heard at the singers' festivals in Waterloo County and neither were sounds of transgression. As a social phenomenon, festivals always harbour the potential to invert the established social order and transgress rules of hierarchy, often by drawing on elements of the carnivalesque and the topsy-turvy, as Peter Stallybrass and Allon White show.[103] In Waterloo County, however, as at the festivals staged by the German bourgeoisie in the "Fatherland" during these decades, the musical celebrations did "not so much invert the established social order as they parallel[ed] it with different means."[104] Although the festivals represented a "time out of time"—to borrow Alessandro Falassi's phrase—during which daily routines were suspended and many small manufacturers closed their doors, the celebrations remained an orderly affair.[105]

Laudatory comments on the festivals' propriety and respectability run as a leitmotif through four decades of press coverage in both the German- and

Festive decorations adorn Waterloo's Main Street, n.d. COURTESY OF WATERLOO PUBLIC
LIBRARY, PHOTOGRAPH A-3-11, COPY J-12-17.

English-language press. Despite the amounts of lager that singers and festival-
goers consumed, "order and calm" always reigned, as the Galt *Dumfries Reporter*
admiringly wrote in 1875.[106] Two decades later, Mayor Georg Rumpel admitted to
the appreciative laughter of his audience that Berlin had only a single policeman—
and even he suffered from lack of work in this peaceful and orderly town.[107] The
only transgression recorded in over four decades occurred in 1898, when three-
quarters of the celebrants avoided paying the entrance fee to the singers' picnic,
sneaking instead into Victoria Park through side entrances or climbing across the
fence. Even the *Berliner Journal* found it difficult to criticize their actions since it
deemed the entrance fee of twenty-five cents excessive.[108] In seeking to make sense
of an "orderly" cultural event in which alcohol represented a key festive ingredient,
Anglo-Canadian observers seized upon the innate German character that knew
how to indulge in respectable amusement. "Not a drunken man could be seen in
the park," marvelled the Guelph *Daily Mercury and Advertiser* in 1890. "Such is
life amongst the good Germans."[109] The *Berlin News Record*, as well, credited the
festivals' propriety to the fine character of the celebrants. Music and mirth ruled

Spectators at the Waterloo Saengerfest, n.d. COURTESY OF WATERLOO PUBLIC LIBRARY, PHOTOGRAPH A-3-11, COPY J-12-17.

the day—"heaps of amusements" in fact, the paper wrote—"and not a single harsh word or untoward act observed during the afternoon."[110]

It was an explanation that accorded nicely with the self-image of Waterloo County's Germans. When city boosters revelled in Berlin's urban progress and growth, both of which had been achieved by a town without any natural advantages, they pointed to the character of the county's residents, whose "passionate fondness ... for music" was matched by the "habits of thrift and industry, so characteristic of their ancestors in the old lands."[111] In the county's pioneering days, when the civilizing sounds of music were seldom heard over "the howling of the wolf, the cry of the owl, and the battle cry of the red warrior," it had been the "predominating traits of the German character" that transformed a dark and lonely "wilderness" into a rural and manufacturing idyll.[112] Indeed, declared a publication in 1912, the "universally acknowledged" German character traits provided the key to understanding the county's prosperity, namely "honesty, industry, deep religious spirit, close application to the needs of the soil, and many noble traits."[113] Authorized by the same tight-knit group of ethnic cultural leaders who wrote the official script of the festivals, such pamphlets—much like the speeches given at the singers' festivals—reveal just how deeply German values had become embedded into the local culture of Waterloo County. These values, of course, appeared in the same static and stereotypical garb that characterized the filiopietistic writings of immigrant leaders who celebrated group achievement and forged their very own "myths of ethnic descent." And yet, these myths should be taken seriously for what they tell us about the yearning of immigrants to make a "home" out of the land of immigration.[114] "The aim," writes British anthropologist Anthony Smith, "is to recreate the heroic spirit (and the heroes) that animated 'our ancestors' in some golden age; and descent is traced, not through family pedigree, but through the persistence of certain kinds of 'virtue' or other distinctive cultural qualities."[115]

When the *Berlin News Record* defended the right of Berlin's Germans to honour Emperor Wilhelm I with a memorial in Victoria Park in 1897, the English-language paper did so partly in deference to a class of immigrants it called exceptional, as more "moderate, energetic and loyal citizens cannot be found in the Dominion."[116] But notably, the praise that the *Berlin News Record* lavished on the German festival celebrants was infused with a hefty dose of self-interest. By bringing thousands of visitors to Berlin and Waterloo, the singers' festivals served as a colourful advertisement of the county's industrial promise:[117]

> While Berlin possesses the distinction of being the German city, its renown as a manufacturing [centre] is still greater. It possesses thirty-five industries, whose output is large and varied in character. Berlin is pre-eminently a leather, furniture, shirt and collar, button and boot and shoe centre, and its manufacturers in these lines are either leaders of the trade in the Dominion or in the very first ranks.[118]

Such promotional language was characteristic of the age and deployed in communities across southern Ontario.[119] In a somewhat unusual twist, however, Anglo-Canadians in Waterloo County made a German festive tradition their own by declaring participation in the singers' festivals a civic duty.

Local entrepreneurs seized upon the opportunity to sing the tune of local industry which the *Berlin News Record* had intoned in its columns. In order to celebrate Berlin's economic growth and prosperity, local businesses put together a "Grand Trades' Procession" in 1886, whose elaborate floats showcased the "principal mercantile and manufacturing interests of the rising town of Berlin" in the form of a "gigantic shirt," a "rustic house on wheels," and an "artistic display of

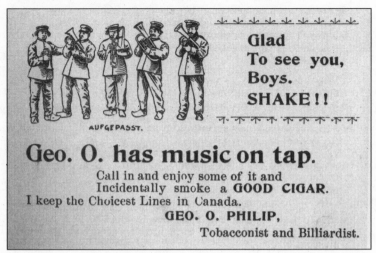

Advertisement in the official program of the thirteenth Peninsular Singers' Festival in Berlin, Ontario, August 1898. COURTESY OF KITCHENER PUBLIC LIBRARY, WATERLOO HISTORICAL SOCIETY, MANUSCRIPT COLLECTION 15.9.C., WILLIAM H.E. SCHMALZ COLLECTION.

barrels."[120] Four years later, the singers' festival offered an incentive to extend electric lightning from the county seat, Berlin, to the host town of Waterloo, thus neatly intertwining the themes of music and local progress.[121] In 1898, the *Berlin News Record* reminded its readers to "show your loyalty to your town; show your sympathy with the Saengerfest Movement. Advertise while you have the opportunity."[122] The county's business owners gladly followed suit. At the turn of the century, *Sängerfest* souvenirs featured advertisements for shirts and shoes, bread and cigars, hardware and hotels.[123]

The organization of the festivals reflected the same sense of acute business acumen that imbued Berlin's Board of Trade when it embraced the singers' festivals for the business they brought into town. Contributions by the town's leading citizens to a guarantee fund prior to the festivals provided a financial cushion that was hardly ever needed. Unlike the Hamilton's festival of 1891, which ran up a deficit of $1,529, the festivals in Waterloo County produced small surpluses of several hundred dollars that were donated to charity or used to pay honoraria to the conductors.[124] To allow singers from afar to attend the festivals, the reception committees negotiated special railroad rates that offered round-trip tickets at the price of a single fare.[125] Prominent citizens lent their time to serve on reception and billet committees, while the county's women worked behind the scenes.[126] They

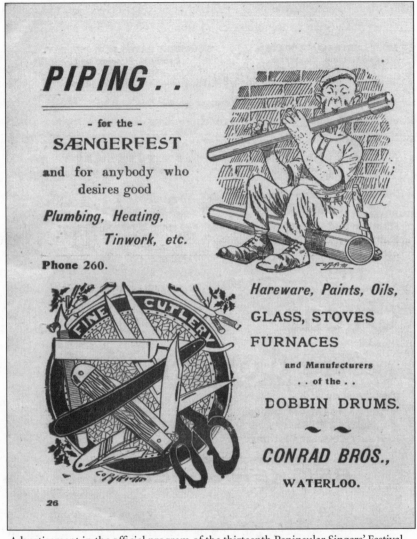

Advertisement in the official program of the thirteenth Peninsular Singers' Festival in Berlin, Ontario, August 1898. COURTESY OF KITCHENER PUBLIC LIBRARY, WATERLOO HISTORICAL SOCIETY, MANUSCRIPT COLLECTION 15.9.C., WILLIAM H.E. SCHMALZ COLLECTION.

hosted friends and relatives, served refreshments, prepared picnic baskets, and decorated concert halls.[127] Their role in shaping the festivals was acknowledged, albeit indirectly, in the late nineteenth century when the organizing committee of a music festival "politely requested" that the "town's housewives" serve lunch—the main meal in German households—in punctual fashion so that the concert could begin at 1 PM sharp in the park.[128]

By the early twentieth century, the character of the singers' festivals was changing subtly, its language adapting to a local community that had begun to celebrate its German ethnicity in the English language. Only a year after local dignitaries had unveiled the bust of Emperor Wilhelm in Victoria Park, on which occasion they spoke German almost exclusively, the organizing committee of the 1898 singers' festival decided to print the festival program in English and advertise in the local English-language press. The move dismayed the *Berliner Journal*, bastion of the German language in Waterloo County. Indignantly, the paper wrote that only out of respect for "out-of-town singers and visitors, as well as the businesspeople and citizens of our town," had it committed all its resources to covering the festival.[129] The tensions surrounding language use capture one of the paradoxes of the singers' festivals. The German language remained enshrined on stage, where "the singing with the exception of one solo, was in German, a real treat for the Germans of whom there are so many in the Twin City," as the *Berlin News Record* wrote in 1912. Yet meanwhile, German singers and festival-goers had begun to converse with each other in English or alternate between English and German with such ease as to make superfluous the task of cultural translation that the *Berliner Journal* had assumed in earlier decades.[130]

A historical source as innocuous as the *Sängerfest* ribbons illustrates the changing contours of German ethnicity. At the first Waterloo County singers' festival in 1874, ribbons were printed in the German language only, their foreignness highlighted by the use of Gothic print. By 1890, the script had become modernized, yet continued to feature a German umlaut in *Sängerfest*. Eight years later, the old Gothic print had all but disappeared, a nostalgic remainder preserved only in the word *Mitglied* (member). The German language had also disappeared. *Sängerfest* had become *Saengerfest*, while the numerical style had been changed to suit Canadian sensibilities ("13th" instead of "13."). In 1902, finally, the ribbon had become thoroughly Canadian, with only a faint German trace to be detected in the ornamental print of *Saengerfest*.[131]

In its embrace of the English language, the festival iconography was symptomatic of greater cultural changes. Similar to Canadian Labour Day parades that were losing their original focus by the beginning of the twentieth century—their emphasis on craft unionism giving way to "holiday fun"—the singers' festivals began to

LEFT: Festival Badge, Singers' Festival, Waterloo, 1874. COURTESY OF WATERLOO REGION MUSEUM, WATERLOO, ONTARIO.

RIGHT: Festival Badge, Tenth Peninsular Singers' Festival, Waterloo, 1890. COURTESY OF WATERLOO REGION MUSEUM, WATERLOO, ONTARIO.

LEFT: Festival Badge, Thirteenth Peninsular Singers' Festival, Berlin, 1898. COURTESY OF WATERLOO REGION MUSEUM, WATERLOO, ONTARIO.

RIGHT: Festival Badge, Lake Erie and Canadian Sängerbund Festival, Waterloo, 1902. COURTESY OF WATERLOO REGION MUSEUM, WATERLOO, ONTARIO.

include an ever-broadening range of amusements.[132] Somewhat apologetically, the *Berliner Journal* wrote in 1898 that a "baseball match presented an ill fit for the program of a German *Sängerfest*." But as the festival committee had hoped, the two-hour game brought in over seven hundred dollars and helped finance the festival.[133] Such cultural pragmatism also ruled in subsequent years when social dances, baseball matches, high-wire performances, boat rowing, and sightseeing tours began to rival musical rehearsals.[134] At the Waterloo singers' festival of 1912, the lone concert was overshadowed by a German evening (*Kommers*), a baseball match, a "Grand Promenade Band Concert and Prize Drawing," a social dance, and an "Automobile trip of the Singers to Berlin."[135]

Cultural purists called the dilution of the original purpose of the singers' festivals "disturbing." As the Hamilton *Spectator* noted, these "conservative musicians" objected to the "introduction of baseball matches, athletic sports and other extras" into the festivals' "musical scheme" and complained "that the convivial celebration is assuming greater proportions than the musical functions."[136] One singer aired his grievances in the pages of the *Berliner Journal.* So poorly, he alleged, had the male mass choruses been rehearsed by visiting singing societies that the "powerful demonstration of German folk song"—the traditional highlight of the singers' festivals—had been compromised. This singer, for one, yearned for the inaugural singers' festival of 1874, where celebrants had been "German among Germans," the "pure" and "sweet" sound of German folk songs bridging the "thousands of miles that separated us from the old homeland."[137] In lamenting the loss of a golden age of ethnicity, just out of reach, the writer was not alone.[138] The Hamilton *Spectator* noted, "There are not wanting grumblers, who say that the introduction into the program of conventional Walts numbers, to say nothing of a xylophone solo is not keeping up the standard of traditional German music."[139] Concert audiences, quite evidently, did not share these cultural misgivings. They greeted the xylophone solo by young Oscar Ziegler, followed by a xylophone duet by the Ziegler brothers, with the "most enthusiastic, prolonged and spontaneous applause of the afternoon," caring more about a splendid performance than the preservation of the "distinctively national ... choral compositions of the fatherland."[140]

German attendees at the singers' festivals proved resistant to the cultural ambitions invested in the musical gatherings. Their festival was one of sociability and spontaneous music-making. At the Waterloo gathering of 1890, packed streetcars carried visiting singers to the neighbouring town of Berlin, where they burst into "popular German folk songs" at street corners "here and there."[141] Former residents of Waterloo County used the occasion to visit friends and family, while others attended the celebration for the express purpose of amusing themselves.[142] As in earlier decades, singers congregated "in an informal and spontaneous manner far into the small hours of the morning."[143] Yet by now, the simple procession to the picnic grounds—the closing note of the festivals—had evolved into an elaborate spectacle that featured colourful hats and uniforms as well as a giant umbrella, measuring twenty-five feet, which gave shelter to the singers from Ann Arbor, Michigan.[144] Seven little pipers in knee breeches and green sports jackets walked alongside the Cannstatter band from Detroit, whose members "appeared to weigh 200 pounds each" and who captivated their audience with a performance "even Mozart" would have envied.[145] The parade, the *Deutsche Zeitung* wrote in August 1898, resembled a "glittering, splendid serpent [that] glided through arches, flags, and bunting and was cheerfully greeted by thousands of spectators."[146]

Here was an ethnic spectacle whose appeal lay precisely in its informality. Having performed—more or less successfully—on the concert stage and listened to the obligatory tributes to the German language and German song, singers now were free to sing more loudly than melodiously, don colourful attire, quench their thirst with gulps of "Canadian milk" from their drinking horns and mingle in the picnic grounds.[147] Pubs reported record revenues of five hundred dollars a day as visitors sampled the local lager, while Mr. F. von Neubronn, president of the Berlin Sängerbund, opened his well-stocked wine cellar to both male and female singers in 1898. As the Detroit *Abendpost* wrote, several "gentlemen" who had descended into Neubronn's cellar found it rather more difficult to climb up the flight of stairs again, due to their happily drunken state.[148] Tales of these musical escapades travelled home with the visiting singers, who found themselves bound together as much, if not more so, by the rhythms of song and sociability than by formal tributes to the Fatherland.

A TRANSNATIONAL SOUNDSCAPE

As historian David Thelen suggests, borderlands are "spaces between cultures" where individuals from different cultures explore and negotiate their relationship.[149] Such encounters occur in the metaphorical borderlands within Canadian society, namely in the zones surrounding the boundaries of ethnicity. But the meanings of German identity were also forged in the ongoing conversation with German-American "singing brethren." As early as 1874, German-Canadian festival celebrants had to fashion an identity similar to, yet different from, the brash self-confidence displayed by German-American singers, who were, not incidentally, called "the Yankees."[150] In later years, the musical rivalry between German-Canadian and German-American singers subsided as bonds across the border strengthened and the festivals assumed the air of a reunion. Many celebrants, in fact, who arrived from Detroit and Buffalo to attend the turn-of-the-century singers' festivals in Berlin and Waterloo, were not strangers at all but former residents of the county who longed "to visit old friends and visit their former home."[151] The number of German-American singers peaked in 1890, 1898, and 1902, when choral societies from Michigan, New York State, Ohio, and Pennsylvania visited Waterloo County. At each of these festivals, the combined strength of up to ten visiting associations from Detroit, Jackson, Bay City, Saginaw, Buffalo, Rochester, Cleveland, and Erie overshadowed the number of German-Canadian participants, who were represented by six singing societies at the most.[152]

Just as German-American singers repeatedly crossed the border to participate in the festivals of song in Waterloo County, so too did local singers attend festivals in the United States. In the summer of 1886, the Waterloo Liedertafel, accompanied by the town band, travelled to Ann Arbor, Michigan, to participate in the seventh festival of the Peninsular Singers' Association (Peninsular Sängerbund).[153] Founded in Jackson, Michigan, in July 1877, the Peninsular Sängerbund was regional in scope, its festivals geared toward singers in southern Michigan. Three years later, residents of Waterloo County travelled to the Peninsular Singers' Festival in Detroit, drawn by both the music and the chance to visit friends and family.[154] Although a musical success, the festival resulted in a "financial fiasco" so dismal that "none of the cities of Michigan" dared to step forward to host the tenth Peninsular Singers' Festival of 1890. Fortunately, wrote the Detroit *Abendpost*, "little Waterloo, a small town of not even 3,000 residents—but German through and through—stepped in" and offered to host the upcoming festival.[155]

In the German-Canadian mirror, the correspondent of the Detroit *Abendpost* caught a reflection of a festival whose simplicity seemed to preserve the true spirit of the German folk. At a time when German-American newspapers had begun to criticize the large-scale singers' festivals in the United States that had fallen victim to the "American national vice," namely the "tendency to exaggerate," the modest scale of the singers' festivals in Waterloo County came as relief.[156] Here, wrote the *Abendpost*, was a festival that resembled the "singers' festivals of our fathers." It delighted in German folk music, gave prominence to male chorus singing and refrained from hiring expensive soloists. No "prima donnas" ruined the *Fest* by demanding "hundreds of dollars" for their performances. Instead, audiences could listen to the voices of male singers delivering German folk songs in four-part harmony, with the simple but pleasing arrangements nicely suited to the singers' abilities.[157]

The tribute the Detroit *Abendpost* paid the Canadian singers formed part of a larger cultural critique that had developed in the United States in the early 1880s. At the singers' festivals of Louisville (1877), Cincinnati (1879), and Chicago (1879), the North American Singers' Association had tried to achieve "notable artistic results" by erecting expansive structures for concert performances, hiring expensive soloists and first-class orchestras, and employing "choruses of mixed voices," which, as a German-American critic stated, "are almost an American creation."[158] These were changes that were viewed with deep scepticism by the adherents of the old-style singers' festivals. Beyond the realization that the "reckless extravagance of engaging solo talent at such high figures as $8,000" meant flirting with "financial disaster," observers were concerned that the very essence of the singers' festivals was being sacrificed. In their eyes, the German festivals of song were, first and foremost, people's festivals at which singers cultivated German sociability and cherished the "true festive spirit of singing brethren."[159] To favour classical music over folk songs or to mimic American music festivals by eliminating "all pageantry, popular songs, singing competitions, and the sale of beer during performances" was to allow an erosion of German culture.[160] In an attempt to insulate German culture from contaminating influences, the delegates at the Chicago singers' festivals of 1881 decided to forego the "trinkets and glitter" of American music festivals and "resume the old ways."[161]

All the more delightful, then, wrote the Detroit *Abendpost* in 1890, that "the good Germans of Waterloo" had volunteered to host the upcoming gathering of the Peninsular Singers' Association in a setting ideally suited to a German folk festival. In a collective effort, "little Waterloo" tackled the task of erecting a temporary concert hall, adorning streets and houses, and preparing "a hearty, merry and truly German welcome for their countrymen from Michigan." As the *Abendpost* promised, "the Canadian singers will dazzle their American brethren with their artful and precise rendition of their songs."[162]

The German-American visitors must have liked what they heard, as the Peninsular Sängerbund returned to Canada in subsequent years. It convened in Hamilton in 1891, in Berlin in 1898, and once again in Waterloo in 1902.[163] At the 1898 singers' festival in Berlin, the Peninsular Sängerbund formally disbanded to be reborn as the Lake Erie Sängerbund, its new name reflecting its expanding geographical scope. The membership now included not only singers from southern Michigan (as the original name had implied) but also Ontario and New York State.[164] The festival that the Lake Erie Sängerbund and the Canadian Sängerbund organized jointly in 1902 could not compete with the grandeur of the singers' festivals staged by the North American Singers' Association which, as in Buffalo in 1901, had dazzled audiences with its "beautiful music."[165] But, then again, the festival's appeal lay precisely in its charming simplicity. While it might have appeared "modest" in comparison with the "gigantic gatherings of German singers held in the United States," it displayed the "qualities of the German amateur in vigor, emphasis, accent and dynamic effect."[166] As a German-American correspondent wrote, the festival's organizers were to be complimented for having chosen folksy fare that did not overtax the participating singing societies.[167]

Only once more did German-Canadian and German-American singers join together in a celebration of German song. At the Waterloo Singers' Festival of 1912, the British Union Jack and the American Stars and Stripes fluttered side by side in the skating rink as the Buffalo Sängerbund and the Buffalo Harugari Frohsinn presented the host society with "a handsome gold harp in honor of its golden jubilee."[168] Once again, observers called the festival of German song "one of the best and most delightful ever held in Canada."[169] But gone was the sense of wonder which newspaper correspondents had voiced in earlier decades. It was as if their ears had grown accustomed to the strains of German music, while their eyes could discern little that was new in the festive spectacle, which now featured automobile rides alongside a single concert performance.

What drew German Americans to this proud German enclave in southern Ontario were the bonds of ethnicity, the pleasures of music-making, and a yearning to experience a festival that appeared to be reminiscent of earlier, simpler times. Here at last seemed to be a singers' festival that featured German folk song over classical music and ethnic substance over the "trinkets and glitter" of overpriced soloists. For German-American commentators, the journey across the border came to resemble a journey into the past where "German folk" created a homeland out of song and sound.

While the singers' festivals in Waterloo County offered room for such lofty aspirations, the ambitions of most German-American visitors (and their Canadian hosts, for this matter) appeared to be of a different kind. They sought to outdo local musicians by forming impromptu bands, to visit family and friends residing in the county, to woo audiences with their rendition of "O Liebchen kommt die Rosenzeit," and to sample both the local lager and the delectable bottles in F. von Neubronn's wine cellar.[170] Music had drawn them to Waterloo County, yet once they arrived, musical pursuits blended with others. Where ethnic gatekeepers liked to single out the keynote of ethnicity, most celebrants let themselves be carried away in a musical potpourri where song, sound, and sociability mingled merrily.

"In the ritual world," Roger Abrahams reminds us, "repetition is commonly carried out to intensify. Things done in unison convey the message that community exists and communion is possible. In festival, repetition is as central to the proceedings as it is in ritual, but with a different anticipation and result. Here, having fun is the key to the occasion."[171] In the ritualistic rendering of German folk songs, ethnic gatekeepers located bonds of community that stretched across the Canadian-American border and indeed, as far as Germany itself. Singers and audiences, as well, approved of a festive script that knew little variation, albeit for a different reason. To them, the familiar rhythms of German festive culture offered the promise of having fun.

Conclusion

"As a performed genre," music-ethnologist Philip Bohlman writes, "folk music can live in a community only through repetition or recreation."[172] The singers' festivals provided performers and audiences with precisely the opportunity for the continuous recreation of a genre that lost nothing of its popularity in the closing three decades of the nineteenth century. This is not to say that the meanings of German folk music remained static or that Waterloo County remained a cultural island. Festival organizers routinely invited Anglo-Canadian bands from Toronto and Hamilton to play at the celebrations, just as they invited musical talent from New York, Detroit, Hamilton, and Toronto to grace concerts with their solo performances—both vocal and instrumental—or to augment the ranks of the festival orchestra.[173] Members of the county's singing societies performed classical music that was not ethnically coded with the Berlin Philharmonic Society, while soloist Mrs. Caldwell sang German tunes with such feeling and expression that the *Berliner Journal* adopted her as one of their own and proudly reprinted the accolades published in the Detroit *Abendpost* on Mrs. Caldwell's performance.[174] Even in this most "German" of counties, making music was a trans-ethnic venture in which the hyphen in "German-Canadian" symbolized not an imposing cultural boundary that shielded German folklore from the outside world, but rather a space of cultural interaction.[175]

As a home-grown musical festival—albeit one with explicit transnational connections—the singers' festivals in Waterloo County never rigidly adhered to the notion that German festivals of song should feature the voices of men alone. Female soloists earned some of the most enthusiastic accolades at the festivals, while mixed choirs regularly performed at the festivals. Such cultural pragmatism also informed all other aspects of the programs. As a malleable expression of German ethnicity, the festivals offered room for a multitude of melodies: for an ode to the German *Heimat*, evoked in the folk songs of the mass chorus; for the strains of the "great choral masters" which conductor Theodor Zöllner so painstakingly rehearsed; for the nationalist overtones with which Karl Müller invested the singers' festival of 1897; for the tune of industry sung by local boosters; for the chorus of community intoned by "singing brethren" from the Great Lakes region.

Intimate in scale, the singers' festivals afforded cultural leaders such as Theodor Zöllner and Karl Müller a stage for their ambitions. In carefully orchestrated celebrations, the former performed classical choral works so as to cultivate the art of music in the county, while the latter imbued the singers' festival of 1897 with an overtly nationalist tone. Each, however, had to contend with a counterpoint, namely the vocal desire of the celebrants to enjoy themselves. Without the express initiative of dedicated individuals, the keynotes of ethnicity that resonated most clearly in the festivals were neither pride in a classical musical canon nor devotion to the German Empire, but a more earthy melody that spoke of frolic and fun.

This is not to deny the emotive power of German folk songs that transported many of the audience across time and space to an (imagined) German homeland. The singers' festivals helped transplant a German national sound to North America, where it was intoned by singers from both Canada and the United States in a transnational setting that became ever more continental in its sensibility. As singers from the Great Lakes region fashioned a transnational soundscape, some German-American observers rejoiced at the apparent tribute to the German folk, while other festival-goers relished a communal setting in which to rekindle old friendships, forge new ones, and partake in a musical extravanganza whose aural fabric offered the comfort of familiarity while easily stretching to accommodate new purposes.

7.

Making a Musical Public
Myth, Music, and Modernity, 1883–1901

By the early 1880s, Buffalo's German-American community had come of age. The confidence of German Buffalo manifested itself in buildings that dotted the cityscape. On Main Street, the steeple of St. Louis Catholic Church rose to a height of 245 feet. Inside the Gothic structure that towered over the downtown area, German-Catholic parishioners worshipped and sang in an ornamented space whose columns of polished granite with richly carved stone capitals, stained-glass windows, and large mosaics were more reminiscent of Europe than North America. In an age of nationalism, as historian Andrew Yox notes, the architectural tributes to the Fatherland that "dutifully followed the German pattern with façade towers, belfries, and fanciful Germanic spires" carved into stone the presumed greatness of German culture. "The Germans," Yox writes, "had a *Turnverein Halle*, spelled with an e, the city's Music Hall with a frieze of a Germanic eagle, book stores, a dark stone bank, a hospital, a 'Buffalo Freie Presse' high-rise, and a half dozen fanciful breweries with loud gables and dentils."[1]

Just as the visual landscape of urban German America signalled the wealth and status German immigrants had achieved, so, too, was the sonic landscape of public life infused with German tunes. Since the mid-nineteenth-century, professional musicians of German origin had made it their mission to "elevate" musical taste by bringing the masterpieces of German composers to audiences more rambunctious than reverent. The twenty-five German musicians of the Germania Musical Society, who had arrived in the United States in 1848 and toured the country for six years, travelling as far as Minneapolis and giving close to nine hundred performances, "complained of people arriving and leaving as they pleased and of loud conversation." To educate audiences was a frustrating task, as director Theodore Thomas, who had come with his family to New York City as a ten-year-old boy in 1845, admitted. Drawn to high culture rather than the popular styles of the day, the young man pioneered the Central Park Summer Concerts that mixed light musical fare like waltzes and polkas with a more classical repertoire. Thomas took small orchestras on national tours well into the 1880s, propelled both by economic necessity and the desire to refine musical taste. "Circumstances forced me to prostitute my art and my talents," Thomas later wrote, thinking, no doubt, of audiences that drank, smoke, and chatted in the concert hall—much as they would have in a beer garden.[2]

It would take the better part of three decades to "elevate" music, whether vocal or symphonic, from popular to high culture, a process that historian Lawrence Levine calls the "sacralization" of high culture.[3] By the 1880s, German music had gone mainstream. Permanent symphonic orchestras such as the Boston Symphony, the Chicago Orchestra, and the New York Symphony could count on the generous support of the Anglo-American establishment, while the urban "larger musical scene" did "become more German in both taste and composition."[4] Under the baton of German-American conductors, the New York Philharmonic Orchestra replaced its French and Italian repertoire with a German one, its orchestral ranks dominated by first- and second-generation German musicians, who represented 97 percent of the personnel in 1892.[5]

The march to musical prominence culminated in a series of concerts at the 1889 World's Fair in Paris. American organizers decided on a classical repertoire that featured German masterpieces. But the concert series failed to impress. If the "politics of sound" in the United States celebrated a cultured public that preferred the more exacting music of the German masters to the "superficial" strains of Italian opera, music critics in Paris derided the Americans "as little more than inept imitators of European styles, and worst of all, those of Germany," as Annegret Fauser observes in her study of the 1889 *Exposition Universelle*. As a nationality in the making, the United States had not yet found its distinctive national sound, contemporary critics in Paris alleged. Having come to listen to the "music of the frontier," as popularized in "the highly successful and oversubscribed Wild-West shows of Buffalo Bill," these critics listened with disappointment to a concert modelled on European musical practices instead.[6]

German Americans were oblivious to the caustic criticism "their" music garnered on the international stage. On the contrary, they basked in the praise which Anglo American commentators heaped upon German musical practice and performance. By the 1880s, public recognition of the "gifts" German immigrants had brought to America's shores had become a rhetorical staple in both the German and the English language press.[7] When the North American Sängerbund gathered once more in Buffalo in 1883, organizers stated matter-of-factly that "we German-Americans can claim without ostentation, that we have exercised a benevolent influence upon American culture, not only in helping to build up and enrich this country, but also in teaching our fellow-men, that there is something higher to live for than the strife for the daily bread—the unselfish love of art."[8] It was a claim endorsed by the city's English language press. "Modern instrumental music," declared the Buffalo *Sunday Morning News* in July 1883, was a genuinely German invention and the "rapid strides made by the people in this country in musical taste" would not have been possible without "the German people who have come among us to live." In words that would surely have delighted German-American musical pioneers, the Buffalo *Morning Express* commended the Sängerbund for having "done much to elevate, as well as popularize music in this country. Its singing fests are at once a treat and an education."[9]

Yet despite such high praise, the singers' festivals straddled an uneasy boundary that hardened in the closing decades of the nineteenth century. Credited with elevating musical taste and forging a musical public, ethnic gatekeepers felt torn between the demands of high culture and popular culture. In staging increasingly difficult concerts, they voiced their frustration over German chorus singers who had come not to pay homage to the arts, but to sing and make merry. As the New York *Daily Tribune* mused, "More and more singers forsook the Temple of Apollo for the groves of Bacchus and Gambrinus, and for over twenty-five years the North American Saengerbund has been struggling to find a happy medium between the two tendencies."[10] When the singers once again congregated in Buffalo in 1901, even German-American commentators would ask whether the festivals, with their gigantic mass choruses, had not outlived their purpose, for performances were enthusiastic rather than artistic; moving, perhaps, but hardly refined.[11]

Organizers never quite succeeded in reconciling the popular bent of the festivals with their own musical ambitions or in fusing the multitude of melodies that echoed through the 1901 festival into a single keynote of ethnicity. As the "music-loving public" headed for the official concert venue, the 74th Armory, many singers stole away to the German Village on the Midway of the Pan-American Exhibition, preferring the exhibition's popular attractions to the cerebral atmosphere in the concert hall.[12] Meanwhile, German-American workers patronized the working-class singers' festival (*Arbeiter-Sängerfest*), whose low admission prices and relaxed sociability struck a markedly different tone from the formality of the Armory. Having helped to create a musical public, German-Americans festival celebrants now literally followed their own tune. While the city's English-speaking elites embraced the singers' festival as "ours," fondly calling Buffalo a "Mecca for lovers of fine music," German-American audiences and singers traded the "sacralized" spaces of high culture for impromptu renditions of German folk songs in city streets and the popular amusements of the Pan-American Exhibition. Their sense of ethnicity was enacted not in formal performances, but in spontaneous encounters in public spaces, gatherings in "Alt-Nürnberg" on the Midway, and participation in working-class popular culture.[13]

Instead of lambasting these revellers for giving short shrift to the concert hall, Buffalo's German-language press focussed its attention on the quality of musical performances. The sounds of ethnicity contemporary commentators now yearned to hear were those of artful music, not amateur song. Concerns over musical taste had supplanted the defence of ethnicity as the main leitmotif of the singers' festival.[14]

"THERE IS, THEN, CHAOS"

In seeking to infuse the singers' festivals with a renewed sense of purpose, the North American Sängerbund vowed in the early 1880s to place greater emphasis on sociability and male chorus singing.[15] As the city of Buffalo prepared for an influx of two thousand singers of seventy participating societies in 1883, the official chroniclers of the festival lauded the folk song as "a powerful bond between our old and new homelands. Whenever we hear the noble sound of our earthy folk songs, we are ... transported back into the happy time of our youth."[16] And indeed, the elderly Edward Storck heard in the melodies of the German folk "the sweet mother tongue, German customs and habits" faithfully preserved.[17] Such tributes were reminiscent of the conservative tone of folk music scholarship that held folk music to be "the crystallization of the cultural core" and folk songs the musical incarnation of a people's spirit.[18]

Given its mandate of ethnic renewal, the beginning of the 1883 Buffalo *Sängerfest* was inconspicuous. Not harmony, but discord characterized initial preparations. In keeping with the loose organizational structure of the North American Sängerbund, all local arrangements were left to the singing societies of the host city. Each society was entitled to one delegate for every twelve active members who, together, constituted the festival's central committee.[19] In September 1881, the Buffalo Liedertafel and Sängerbund, the city's two oldest German singing societies, invited their fellow societies for a meeting to discuss the upcoming festival. The invitation irritated the Buffalo Orpheus society, which had been founded in 1869 when nineteen singers had left the Liedertafel.[20] As one of the city's premier singing societies—with sixty active and 540 passive members—the Orpheus felt "it would be derogatory to their position to be placed on a par with societies having neither musical nor financial standing, and who would likely send delegates having no idea of the responsibility to be assumed." With one stroke, the Orpheus had thus dismissed the seven younger and smaller singing societies on Buffalo's East Side, such as the Arion, the Harmonie, and the Ost Buffalo Männerchor.[21] Only if the central committee was dissolved and constituted anew, the society's secretary informed the committee in May 1882, would the Orpheus society lend its support to the festival.[22]

The Liedertafel, as well, withdrew from the central committee. Indignant that its conductor, Joseph Mischka, had not been elected for the prestigious role of festival conductor (he trailed four votes behind the Sängerbund's conductor, Friedrich Federlein), the society offered to sing at the upcoming festival, but refused to help in any other way.[23] While conceding "Mr. Federlein's musical knowledge, they doubted his administrative ability and foresaw in this election only artistic and financial disaster," as the Buffalo *Daily Courier* informed its readers on 15 May 1882.[24] Not only had the "singers' battle" (*Sängerkrieg*) spilled over into the public arena, it also cost the central committee its president. Dismayed that his advice had been rejected, Phillip Becker resigned from his post.[25] Two of Buffalo's most established and influential singing societies had distanced themselves from the

Sängerfest, as had Becker, the city's former mayor.[26] "There is, then, chaos," wrote the *Daily Courier*.[27]

Yet despite predictions that the festival was doomed, the central committee refused to bow to the singers' elite. While trying to lure both the Orpheus and Liedertafel back into the fold, the interim president, artisan Louis Allgewähr, sought to boost morale, with evident success. The remaining societies vowed to support the festival committee "man for man."[28] In early June, a "mass assembly of German and American citizens" similarly voiced its support for the upcoming festival. Swayed by the momentum of the *Sängerfest* movement, Phillip Becker deigned to accept the position of festival president once more, while the Liedertafel and Orpheus quietly joined the central committee in mid-July.[29] Their decision was eased by the fact that the committee had adapted the statutes of the North American Sängerbund to allow for three festival conductors. At the 1883 festival, Friedrich Federlein (Sängerbund), Joseph Mischka (Liedertafel), and Carl Adam (Orpheus) would share the honour of musical director. Natives of Bavaria, Bohemia, and Silesia, respectively, these men seemed to personify an ethnic unity that had eluded Buffalo's German singers in the stormy months of May and June 1882.[30]

In the decades since the Civil War, Buffalo's German population had expanded from a village to a large, complex community in which ethnic institutions vied for leadership. Notwithstanding the folksy image that English-language newspapers conveyed of the "festive German" whose gatherings floated "on a sea of natural good-fellowship," as the Buffalo *Commercial Advertiser* held in July 1883 (an image, to be sure, that German organizers themselves perpetuated), ethnic associations were locked in a struggle about who would lead, and shape, the group.[31] Yet instead of weakening bonds of ethnicity, the conflict served to strengthen it, a phenomenon that historian David A. Gerber has dubbed the "paradox in intra-ethnic conflict: the more members of the emergent group quarreled with one another, the more they became involved in being ethnic and in attempting to determine the destiny of the group."[32] When Louis Allgewähr took over the greatly diminished festival committee in May 1882, he declared that the battle had only helped the cause: "Formerly passive people have become involved and everybody seeks to do his share to spare Buffalo the embarrassment that the Fest will not take place."[33] Allgewähr's words rang true when the newly united festival committee embarked on the task of providing a hall for the *Sängerfest* concerts. Rather than renting a suitable venue, the committee decided to erect a permanent monument for Buffalo's *Deutschthum*, a local music hall.

The city's oldest German society, the German Young Men's Association, which had been founded in 1841, took the lead.[34] It acquired a plot between Main and Franklin Streets upon which "a magnificent building" was to be erected, "which should in the first place be the assembly hall for the 'Saengerfest', and afterwards the centre of all german [sic] social efforts."[35] Buffalo's German elite stood firmly behind the project; influential businessmen such as Phillip Becker, Jacob Schoellkopf, and Albert Ziegele contributed one thousand dollars each to the music hall fund. To help offset the building cost of $235,000, lifetime membership in the society was offered in exchange for a donation of fifty dollars.[36] The ground was broken on 21 November 1882, and the cornerstone laid on 5 March 1883. In the crisp cold of a March afternoon, the singing societies paraded to the building site, where they held an impromptu concert and Mayor Manning complimented the city's German citizens on their generosity. The music hall, he said, would serve as a memorial to the "public spirit of Buffalo's German Americans."[37]

The hall did represent an important public landmark, as the city's English-language newspapers readily conceded. "Not often," held the *Commercial Advertiser*,

> is a festival celebrated from which permanent results of so great a value to our city may be anticipated ... It is a building that is an ornament to the city, that supplies a long-felt want, and that will enable the people of Buffalo to enjoy entertainments and attract important conventions ... Long after the Saengerfest of 1883 has been forgotten the Music Hall will stand, a splendid monument of private enterprise, and a popular place for public enjoyment and edification.[38]

At the Sängerfest of 1860, the singers had taken possession of the city's streets and squares. Twenty-three years later, they proceeded to "shape the stage to their liking," as historian Kathleen Neils Conzen puts it.[39] Unlike the 1860 event, which had left traces in the memories of participants only, the 1883 singers' festival left behind a tangible legacy. The music hall constituted a welcome addition to the cityscape and a physical testimony that Buffalo's *Deutschthum* had come of age.

The hall, an imposing building in French renaissance style, could seat an audience of eight thousand and accommodate two thousand singers on its massive stage. Its elegant design drew admiration from the local English-language press. "This noble edifice," wrote the Buffalo *Evening Telegraph*, "is solid and generous as the liberality that erected it." The Sängerbund singers, in turn, praised the "excellent acoustic properties" of the hall.[40] Who cared that the interior had not been painted yet or that only a few adventurous souls dared to climb to the unfinished third story to listen to the concert's opening numbers, in a hall packed to capacity?[41] What the building might have lacked in finish, it made up with lavish decorations and electric illuminations, "giving it a gala appearance, and showing it off to decided advantage," as visitors and locals alike concurred.[42] As the builders rushed to construct the hall, the central committee turned to the grand logistic undertaking that was the *Sängerfest*.

Although the official festival gazette "naturalized" folk music by likening its "sweet melodies" to the bird that "warbles its song through the air," thereby evoking the timelessness of folk melodies, the festival itself had become a thoroughly modern affair. The determined drive for a guarantee fund, the establishment of a press office for out-of-town correspondents, the negotiation of special railway rates, and the publication of a professional festival gazette made the 1883 singers' festival a far cry from its 1860 predecessor, whose organizers had discussed affairs "leisurely over a glass of beer," as Edward Storck, a now-frail Forty-Eighter, recalled.[43] A committee was established to spearhead a $50,000 guarantee fund subscription. By mid-July 1883, $40,000 had been pledged, thereby reducing the financial risk of hosting the festival.[44] Provisions had to be made to find accommodation for two thousand active singers and one hundred instrumental musicians, who were entitled to free room and board.[45] The standing committee on railways negotiated special rates for singers and visitors, while the music committee engaged the New York Symphony Society under its conductor, Leopold Damrosch, for the duration of the *Fest*.[46] Meanwhile, the festival conductors expended time and energy on preparing local singers for the reception concert.[47]

Much to the dismay of the music committee, attendance at the weekly rehearsals was sporadic at best, rarely exceeding 60 percent of the registered 301 local singers. To shame singers into attendance, the committee decided to publish the meagre figures in the local press. It also warned that singers would forfeit their right to participate in the reception concert if they missed more than three rehearsals.[48] In striving for musical quality, the committee revealed that, despite all declarations to the contrary, the biannual *Sängerfeste* had become much more than social gatherings. No longer was it acceptable for ill-prepared singers to belt out folk songs or, even worse, ignore the concerts altogether, visiting local taverns instead. The "beer bassos," the North American Sängerbund had ruled after the Cleveland fiasco of 1875, did not deserve to perform at the festivals. Henceforth, only those associations would be admitted that sent a minimum of twelve singers, all of whom were to attend a rehearsal with the festival conductor, demonstrating that they had studiously practised the mass choruses on the program.[49]

This practice was adhered to by the Buffalo music committee. In mid-June of 1883, festival conductors Friedrich Federlein and Joseph Mischka left for two-week-long rounds of inspection in the eastern and western districts of the North American Sängerbund.[50] To all accounts, rehearsals were conducted in a jovial manner, whereupon "inspector" and singers retired to the associations' headquarters to consume generous amounts of lager. No singing society failed the exercise. But many were reminded of the work yet to be done, and some were so incensed over an "unjust" verdict that they travelled to Buffalo to demand clarification.[51] These, evidently, were not the standards enforced at American music festivals, but neither were the conductors' visits a mere formality. By 1883, even popular tunes like the "Lorelei" had to conform to higher musical standards.[52]

The Reception Committee Escorting Visiting Societies to the Saengerbund Hall, Buffalo 1883. COURTESY OF BUFFALO AND ERIE COUNTY PUBLIC LIBRARY, RARE BOOK ROOM, *FRANK & LESLIE'S ILLUSTRIERTE ZEITUNG*, 28 JULY 1883, 369.

"WE ARE ALL GERMANS THIS WEEK"

In the twenty-three years that had passed since the last Buffalo singers' festival, the ears of Anglo-American audiences had become accustomed to the sounds of German music, their musical taste and judgement honed in a steady round of concerts and musical entertainments. German migrants had founded musical societies. They provided conductors and musicians for the country's principal orchestras. They organized "musical entertainments in such numbers, variety and excellence as to place them as high in rank for musical taste as that of any city in Europe," the Buffalo *Sunday Morning News* stated.[53] For Albert Krause, who had migrated to the United States in 1861 and described himself as sadly lacking in "American audacity," the 1883 festival solidified the group's public image.[54] "Dear, good Mother!," he wrote to Germany on 22 July 1883,

> The Americans are completely startled and cannot comprehend how so many people, 2,000 visiting singers and almost 40,000 visitors, can amuse themselves without even the slightest discord or quarrel. With regard to artistic merits, the festival has made history as well; the concerts by good soloists, supported by a trained singers' chorus of 2,000 men in our new, grand music hall ... were splendid indeed, the impression on the Americans overwhelming, as their English newspapers candidly admitted. Thanks to this *Fest*, the respect for the local Germans has markedly increased.[55]

Affirmation came from the highest political echelons. State Governor Grover Cleveland delivered a speech in which he rhapsodized how German migrants had "brought to us their music and their song, which have done much to elevate, refine and improve, and to demonstrate that nature's language is as sweet as when the morning stars sang together." The governor then voiced his hope that musical gatherings "like this will tend to make the love and cultivation of music more universal in our land."[56]

Although the local English-language press greeted the "feast of fun," at least one newspaper felt ambivalent about the praise that Governor Cleveland heaped on German migrants.[57] While conceding that "the Germans are unquestionably a music-loving people," the Buffalo *Commercial Advertiser* took pains to point out that "in the musical portion of the entertainment American singers are doing their full share."[58] The newspaper also questioned the wisdom of "classify[ing] citizens of this municipality, state and republic according to their foreign connections." After all, visitors were "being welcomed [not] by Germans as such, but by

Buffalonians and ... in the cordiality of the city's hospitality there is no distinction of nationalities." The *Commercial Advertiser* claimed the *Sängerfest* as a local affair in which all citizens of Buffalo took equal pride.[59] Just as the festival's central committee had invited members of German church choirs to participate in the grand reception concert, it had asked American singers to lend their support.[60] American residents contributed generously to the guarantee fund and rendered "excellent service" in several standing committees.[61]

Music brought together representatives of the German and American middle and upper classes who saw in the festival an opportunity to boost the city's image. Although festival president Phillip Becker continued to profess his loyalty to the larger German-American community, the former (and future) mayor seemed much more interested in the festival's potential to stimulate local trade, business, and industry.[62] English-language newspapers were also keenly aware that Buffalo's "railroads, the hotels, the restaurants and the mercantile establishments" stood to profit from "every stranger attracted to this city."[63] Even more importantly, as the *Commercial Advertiser* pointed out, the singers' festival would advertise the city's natural and commercial resources: "The Saengerfest brings intelligent businessmen to Buffalo from the leading cities of the North and the West. It puts them in communication with the educated and enterprising residents of the city, and gives them a chance to see what Buffalo is, what she is doing, and what she promises to be."[64] In the age of boosterism, the celebration of German song and sound no longer constituted an exclusively ethnic affair. Instead, it was appropriated for local purposes. Their festival had become ours. Or, as the *Commercial Advertiser* put it with characteristic verve: "We are all Germans this week."[65]

A German *Fest* had become a local attraction. When the singers marched into town, the sidewalks were lined with curious spectators. At the closing concert, there was standing room only. And wherever one looked, one was sure to see a festival badge pinned to men's jackets and women's hats. "Some of the banners and emblems today utter the words of hospitality in two languages," wrote the Buffalo *Commercial Advertiser* on the opening day of the festival, "but the greeting comes from citizens of one mind, heart and purpose."[66] It was an exuberance that would last to the closing day of the festivities. In the unanimous verdict of German- and English-speaking celebrants, the 1883 *Sängerfest* had been an unqualified success, even though it had accrued a small deficit of $2,600.[67]

Scene in the Music Hall, Buffalo, July 1883. COURTESY OF BUFFALO AND ERIE COUNTY PUBLIC LIBRARY, RARE BOOK ROOM, *UM DIE WELT*, NO. 21, 28 JULY 1883, 324.

INTERLUDE

On 25 March 1885, a great fire engulfed the Buffalo music hall. Gas, leaking from a pipe, had become ignited and transformed the building into "a fiery sea from front to rear," as the local press breathlessly reported.[68] "Driven northwards by the strong wind," sparks and flames also set fire to the neighbouring St. Louis Catholic Church, which burned to the ground.[69] Within two hours, two symbols of Buffalo's *Deutschthum* had fallen victim to the flames. The German Young Men's Society had lost its headquarters and its 8,000-volume library. Buffalo's premier singing societies—the Liedertafel, Sängerbund, and Orpheus—had lost their entire collection of sheet music, instruments, and memorabilia, alongside their concert hall.[70]

Almost immediately, Phillip Becker—his eyes set on the fall mayoral elections—called a meeting of German businessmen in which he pledged $5,000 for a construction fund, an offer matched by another industrial giant of the community, Jacob Schoellkopf.[71] An assembly of citizens at the local *Turnhalle* (gymnasts' hall), attended by both German Americans and Anglo-Americans, raised $20,000 in subscriptions. By 1 April 1885, the construction fund had increased to $40,000, whereupon the German Young Men's Association appointed a building committee. One year later, the cornerstone for the new music hall was laid. The new building, whose total cost amounted to $246,000, was completed in November 1887, with the generous support of the non-German community that had grown fond of the local temple of music.[72] In order to express their appreciation to the public, two younger members of the German Young Men's Association suggested presenting the building to the city as a place of public, not ethnic, interest. It was a motion heatedly defeated by the German-born members of the association, who "refused to hand these material symbols of their community over to the city," as historian Andrew P. Yox remarks.[73] The imposing hall was to testify to the solidarity of Buffalo's German-origin population, its sturdy brick walls a symbol of ethnic prosperity.

Despite the apparent solidity of the city's local *Deutschthum*, generational and language changes were about to alter the meanings of ethnicity.[74] As early as 1883, singing societies reported difficulties in recruiting new members.[75] As members of the founding generation retired from the ranks of active singers, their American-born children, who "thought" and "felt" in the English language, had to be attracted to the German associations.[76] This was no easy task, as Sängerbund member Ernst Besser realized. Young German America, he observed, showed far greater enthusiasm for the pursuit of national sports than for the beauty of German poetry that was immortalized in the German folk song.[77] Confronted with a growing number of members who spoke German only with difficulty, even the venerable Buffalo Liedertafel opted to make English the language of its business meetings.[78]

As the Liedertafel's conductor, Joseph Mischka, emphasized, the society did not intend to cut loose its "German affiliations." "By the use of English," he stated in 1888, "the Germans would be best able to fulfill their mission in familiarizing Americans with German sociability and customs."[79] Eleven years later, Mischka was again asked to "explain the paradox of a German singing society without German singers." By then, only ten out of fifty Liedertafel singers were proficient in German. According to Mischka, common sense as well as artistic considerations demanded performances in English, for a "correct pronunciation of the umlauts and gutturals of the German language can only be acquired after careful study," while "the obscurity of the sense of the words in a language one does not understand hinders correct musical expression." Mischka's confident assertion that English could peacefully coexist with a respect for "German habits and customs" did not persuade Ernst Besser, who predicted the demise of the Liedertafel.[80]

Indeed, when the North American Sängerbund reconvened in Buffalo in 1901, the Liedertafel was no longer among the six local participating societies.[81]

By then, Joseph Mischka had long abandoned the baton of the Liedertafel. In May 1894, he had been appointed musical director of Buffalo's public school system, supervising the teaching of vocal music in the city's elementary classrooms.[82] The introduction of singing lessons into the public school curriculum reflected the widespread appreciation for music as a civilizing factor.[83] In entering the realm of public schooling, music had shed its ethnic gown. When the Grand Army of the Republic staged an encampment in 1896, Joseph Mischka trained a chorus of four thousand children to perform a selection of "national and patriotic" songs.[84] The children's performance elicited much praise from the local press, which was more enamoured with the display of patriotism than with the "precision, perfect intonation and enunciation" that so pleased Mischka's ear:

> Two thousand fresh young faces, with eyes dancing and shifting with excitement; two thousand joyous children gaily bedecked in the National colors; two thousand voices rising and swelling with the songs that rang in the ears of the soldiers thirty years ago or more; a shield of the Stars and Stripes, moving and palpitating, breathing and animated with all the glorious sentiments of patriotism in hearts young and innocent.[85]

Music now helped craft a narrative of the nation. The children's voices—under the expert guidance of a German music master—embodied the nation in sonic and visual harmony. The story they enacted was an American one, though the medium of music through which this story reached the "ears of the soldiers" was inflected with German-American musical culture.

Silencing the Audience

At the turn of the century, Buffalo's leading entrepreneurs, many of whom were of German ethnic origin, encouraged the North American Sängerbund to hold its thirtieth festival in Buffalo. Propelled by a healthy dose of self-interest, Major Conrad Diehl, himself a member of the Orpheus singing society, extended a personal invitation to the Sängerbund.[86] A driving force in bringing the Pan-American Exposition to Buffalo, Diehl hoped that two such high-profile events would benefit each other. As the New York *Daily Tribune* noted in June 1901, "the Buffalo managers of the Saengerfest had an auspicious eye on the effect the festival would have upon the Pan-American fair from the beginning. Many of them have more substantial interests at stake in the Rainbow City than in the armory at Niagara and Connecticut streets."[87] Local businessmen supported the exposition by subscribing to bonds while also sitting on the exposition's board of directors.[88] The State of New York sweetened the deal by offering a spacious concert hall, the 74th Regiment Armory, free of charge, while the organizers of the Pan-American exhibition granted $7,500 for the erection of a concert stage.[89]

And thus, they came—the "happy, fun-loving, mirth-provoking musical Teutons" descending upon the city.[90] Buffalo's English-language press giddily painted a portrait of singers who had stepped right out of books of German folklore. "Fully 99 per cent of them are German and most of them are the broad, substantial kind with big moustaches and big voices," penned the Buffalo *Commercial Advertiser*, while other papers waxed lyrical about "the good-natured musical Germans" and the "Happy Germans and their world-renowned songs," who were "enjoying themselves to their heart's content" as befit such "a jolly, rollicking, good-natured lot."[91] In a somewhat less complimentary tone, the *Catholic Union and Times* wrote of German singers who "ate their sausages and drank their beer in musical numbers, and the few not too fat even joined in the merry-go-round of the Strauss waltz."[92] Yet the relentless string of characteristics construed to be German had none of the harshness of mid-nineteenth-century nativist attacks; one only needed to look beneath the veneer of the picturesque German folk, the Buffalo *Times* wrote tongue-in-cheek, to glimpse the "modern, musical Teuton" whose "only conquest will be a conquest of song." The rhetorical jests were aimed at members of the family whose "modern" and "musical" nature were never in doubt, despite their amusing demeanour and appearance.[93]

As soon as the formal concerts began, the city's English-language press abandoned its ironic mode for an earnest, appreciative tone. If earlier coverage had been full of playful stereotypes, concert reviews were now almost devoid of ethnic signifiers. In keeping with the popular notion of music as a universal language, newspapers described the women and men who headed to the Armory of the 74th Regiment simply as "lovers of fine music."[94] What distinguished the audience, in the eyes of contemporary reporters, was not their ethnicity but their class. "The audience," wrote the Buffalo *Times*, "was composed largely of the wealthy and fashionable people of Buffalo, though there were many others who do not belong to the 400."[95] Comments on the social profile of audiences are admittedly sparse, but they do suggest middle- and upper-class concertgoers, mostly comprising

Buffalonians (although a few ticket orders by mail from "out-of-town people" arrived) who treated the concerts as much a social as a musical occasion.[96] The admission charges conspired to keep the audience exclusive; visitors at the singers' festival had to pay between one and three dollars for a seat in the armoury. Evening attire was formal.[97]

In a nod to non-German-speaking audiences (which by now included many second- and third-generation German Americans), the festival program provided the texts of folk songs in both German and English, the ornamental Gothic print on the left joined by the English translation to the right. The printed program also offered clues as to how audiences should listen to the musical selections. Eighteen pages of single-spaced annotations provided short biographical sketches of the featured composers, followed by an analysis of the musical themes of the orchestral selections. A primer in art music, the annotations spelled out the meaning and intricacies of the compositions, alerting audiences, for instance, to the strains of a German folk song first introduced by the flutes, bassoons, and horns, but then "interrupted by a new and graceful melody for the clarinet."[98]

The program's emphasis on instrumental music belied the festival's stated purpose of giving prominence to German choral music and, in particular, the performances of the male mass chorus. As the New York *Daily Tribune* observed, local promoters who had invested millions in the Pan-American exposition could not fathom how the earthy folk song alone could satisfy the audience's ears; and so "behind the amiable subterfuge" of heralding choral works, "orchestral attractions" and "solo voices" were given equal prominence. The singers' festivals had been transformed into high culture, concerned far more with the "artistic point of view" than with demonstrations of ethnic harmony as embodied in the voices of the male mass chorus.[99]

The soundscape of German North America also began to fracture along class lines. This, perhaps, was not surprising in a city that had seen violent confrontations between German American employers and workers since the mid-1880s. Organized in the United Trades and Labor Council (UTLC), a loose federation of trade unions, representing skilled workers of German and Irish origins, had fought for union recognition, the eight-hour day and higher wages. They had also lobbied against the importation of cheap labour from eastern and southern Europe, turning the nativist rhetoric of the 1850s against late-nineteenth-century immigrants. In the late 1890s, the UTLC suppressed memories of past struggles, preferring instead to portray the city's skilled workmen as part of the local establishment. It was a self-image nurtured by Buffalo's proliferating work-ing-class associations and union locals, many of which conducted their affairs exclusively in the German language.[100]

In 1901 Buffalo, the internal differentiation of the city's German popula-tion manifested itself in the working-class singers' festival (*Arbeiter-Sängerfest*) that took place just prior to the official festival. Founded in 1897, the working-men's singers' association had first convened in Cleveland in 1898. Three years later, working-class singers from Erie (Pennsylvania), Toledo (Ohio), Detroit (Michigan), Auburn (New York), and Rochester (New York) met in Buffalo for a second gathering, which was hosted by the singing societies Vorwärts Männerchor, Herwegh Männerchor, and Saxonia Männerchor. The sounds of music and sociability softened the festival's political agenda, as did the decision of the local press not to comment on the address by Robert Steiner, the editor of the Buffalo *Arbeiter-Zeitung*.[101] The festive vocabulary evoked that of its bourgeois counter-part, comprising a parade, a people's festival in Teutonia Park and a concert of the united male mass chorus.[102] But no alderman, mayor, or state governor graced the festival with their presence. No local dignitaries marched along Fillmore Avenue to Teutonia Park. Instead, the parade featured working-class singing societies, music bands, local sharpshooters, benevolent associations, and a host of German union locals including the brewers, coopers, beer drivers, printers, carpenters, butchers, millhands, and barbers.[103]

While the Arbeiter-Sängerfest combined music with festive exuberance, much as the earlier singers' festivals had done, the festival of the North American Sängerbund strove to silence popular notes of sociability and boisterous song. In his pioneering work, *The Emergence of Cultural Hierarchy in America*, historian Lawrence Levine elegantly traces how arbiters of culture first established aesthetic canons and then turned to the difficult task of "taming audiences." In the closing decades of the nineteenth century, Levine writes, "concertgoers were increasingly lectured on the elements of proper behavior. In 1892 Edward Baxter Penny told them they had 'no right' to sit through a concert 'stolid and indifferent,' to think about business or domestic affairs, to read the old letters accumulated in their pockets, to trim their finger nails, to crunch peanuts, or even to take a nap.' Silence, he reminded them, 'is to music what light is to painting.'"[104]

In attempting to silence concertgoers, Buffalo commentators, as well, turned to public censure. A "Rambler" writing in the pages of the Catholic *Union and Times* described how he and several hundreds of others [were] disgusted at the antics of a certain Delaware avenue family which poses as leaders of society and fashion … To start with, they came in late and noisily—they always do. They kept up an uninterrupted flow of loud conversation, to the extreme annoyance of everyone near them. When the rest of the audience of six or seven thousand of music-loving people was hanging on to the liquid notes of Mme. Blauvelt, this degenerate gang of society hoodlums chattered and laughed and paid no attention to the singer or the feelings of their neighbors.[105]

What this writer and others sought to enforce was a "cult of etiquette" and "passive politeness" that would turn formerly actively audiences into "mute receptors" who silently listened to the sounds of high culture.[106] If audiences did not yet acquiesce to these prescriptions, it was not for want of rhetorical zest. The Buffalo *Commercial Advertiser* reported that the audience at the festival showed none of the required attentiveness and restraint:

After the first rush, the crowd straggled in, late and noisy. They were still coming at 9 o'clock. The opening of the concert had to be delayed because of their tardiness. It was because of them that two numbers were omitted from the program. It seemed strange that at a festival of music of the proportions and unparalleled beauty of the Saengerfest, some 1,000 men and women could have the nerve to tram into the hall half an hour after the time fixed for the overture.[107]

The writer also complained about the "steady, unending fluttering of fans" in the hands of the female audience. "The perpetual motion of the fans," he wrote, "affected the vision like the flickering of a badly constructed vitascope, and the roar of voices and skirts and shuffling feet became a burden to the mind."[108] What these contemporary critics spelled out were prescriptions for the enjoyment of fine art. The "noisy days of pleasure," which Buffalo singer Ernst Besser so fondly recalled in his memoirs, were to give way to an appreciative silence, the humble armoury momentarily transformed into a temple of music.[109]

The audience, so roundly berated, committed yet another fault; it never showed up in sufficiently impressive numbers. "Many are able to attend who do not. Many who are able to go do not realize what they miss," the Buffalo *Times* stated. Attendance figures at the concerts lagged behind expectations. In the armoury, fitted to seat twelve thousand persons, only eight thousand were present at the opening concert.[110] To make matters worse, the hall's spacious dimension made an audience of eight thousand look "like a paltry gathering of a few hundred." As the Buffalo *Commercial Advertiser* wrote, "There were over 2,000 persons in the balcony, and yet anyone on the floor, in forming an estimate of the attendance, might easily have overlooked them, so far and infinitesimal did they seem to be."[111] The singers' ranks also thinned considerably over the course of the festival. Despite draconian measures—those who skipped rehearsals and concerts had to eat and drink at their own expense—the singers (along with their entourage of family members and friends) heeded the siren call of the Pan-American Exposition. "The exposition did not help, it hurt the festival," concluded the New York *Daily Tribune*. "The drastic measures enforced by the local committee went far to prevent a collapse of the choral features, but there were great gaps in the choir to-night nevertheless." As German- and English-language newspapers noted in unison, a site of popular culture had attracted far greater crowds than "the greatest singing festival of modern times."[112]

MUSICAL ENCOUNTERS AT THE PAN-AMERICAN EXPOSITION

By the turn of the century, Americans had become familiar with world's fairs—those spectacular displays of science and technology, entertainment and modernity—that attracted close to one hundred million visitors between the Philadelphia Centennial International Exhibition of 1876 and World War I. Staged by the country's elites, eager to "win approval for their visions of America's future," the fairs were "read" by fairgoers, who ascribed their own meanings to the blunt ideological messages on display.[113] Once visitors had toured the official exhibition buildings, they gravitated towards the Midway where amusement beckoned of both the bawdy and edifying kind.

On the Midway, American fairgoers sampled the sights, sounds, and tastes of "Tyrolian, Swiss, Dutch, Swedish, Spanish, English, Irish and Belgian 'villages'" which had been sponsored by European nations, listened to the strains of ragtime (a welcome counterpoint "to patriotic airs blaring from bandstands on the main exposition grounds"), and turned their gaze to the villages of "living people." As a blatant exercise in ethnic and racial stereotyping, the displays of "primitive" and "savage" peoples nurtured a sense of "white" superiority and served to justify the nation's recent imperialist ventures.[114] At the Pan-American Exposition in Buffalo in 1901, a sign at the entrance to the Chinese Village invited visitors to learn about the "sly tricks of the 'heathen Chinee,'" while the Philippine Village celebrated the acquisition of a new colonial empire.[115]

Yet not all sonic encounters involved racialized or colonized peoples. The German Empire, which had sponsored and staged the village of Alt-Nürnberg (Old Nürnberg) at the Buffalo fair, sought to strengthen feelings of ethnic and national loyalty among German immigrants in the United States.[116] Modelled after the townscape of medieval Nürnberg, the German Village projected the origins of the German Empire into medieval times. Bavarian military brass bands marched on the village's streets, while folk dancers performed on the village square.[117] In an open-air restaurant, fairgoers rested on long wooden benches to take in the sounds and sights of Alt-Nürnberg—replete with market squares, half-timbered houses, and German taverns—and celebrate friendships, old and new, over "the foaming German beer from the old-fashioned steins."[118] The festive space of the exposition imposed its own set of stereotypes as they had evolved in ethnic villages of world's fairs since the mid-nineteenth century, thereby inflecting a "German" public image with that of a regional Bavarian identity. Then, again, in a city that "had more Bavarians than any other American city," the sounds of Bavarian music must have carried a familiar ring.[119]

Although the Pan-American Exposition has left behind a rich visual legacy, the photographs of grand exhibition buildings in Italian renaissance style or exotic Egyptian belly dancers are mute.[120] We are left to fill in the sounds. At the Buffalo fair, the "Temple of Music," with a seating capacity of two thousand two hundred, and the five bandstands scattered across exhibition grounds provided the major venues for performances of "light classics" and a steady round of band music. On the Midway, fairgoers could listen to Bavarian musicians in the German Village of Alt-Nürnberg, overhear the performances of Mexican musicians on the "Streets of Mexico," or sample the offerings of Italian music in "Little Venice."[121]

Much as local boosters had hoped, the beginning of the singers' festival marked "a glorious time for the Exposition." Gone were the days of poor attendance. "The very atmosphere seemed to have changed last week," enthused the Buffalo *Review*. "Heretofore it was possible in the course of a walk about the grounds to meet many a friend or acquaintance. Yesterday it was a surging sea of strange faces." The singers "invaded every section of the grounds," their presence announced by "the little gold and enamel emblems which they wore on their coats."[122] Just as the Buffalo's East Side was "alive with melodious Germans" who serenaded the Buffalo Press Club (to the appreciative cheers of local newspa-

Alt-Nürnberg on the Mall at the Pan-American Exposition in Buffalo, 1901.
COURTESY OF BRENDA BATTLESON, PERSONAL COLLECTION.

per men), so too did the visiting singers keep the exposition's turnstiles clicking from early morning to nightfall.[123] Alt-Nürnberg on the Mall quickly emerged as the unofficial headquarters of the festival. It was here that singers congregated after concerts. It was here that visiting delegates could be found who preferred the old-world charm of the "ancient German village" to the formality of the armoury.[124] Offered the choice between listening to a mass chorus of 3,500 voices and strolling through the portals of Alt-Nürnberg, many singers chose to do the latter.

It only seemed fitting, then, that the closing ceremony of the singers' festival would be held on exhibition grounds. In a stadium filled to capacity, more than ten thousand men, women, and children watched dancing dervishes and magicians, lions and swordplay. The "melancholical" march of Native Americans, mounted on horseback, disappointed audience members who had been looking forward to stage mock battles and daring feats of riding. As the Buffalo *Demokrat* wrote in a

Alt-Nürnberg on the Mall. COURTESY OF BUFFALO AND ERIE COUNTY PUBLIC LIBRARY, RARE BOOK ROOM, OFFICIAL BOOK: *THIRTIETH SAENGERFEST OF THE NORTH-AMERICAN SAENGERBUND, HELD IN BUFFALO, JUNE 24, 25, 26 AND 27, 1901* (BUFFALO, NY: SAENGERFEST COMPANY, 1901), 130.

caustic review, the temporary escape of the mid-size lion from his wooden box constituted one of the highlights of the evening; two audience members helped catch the "poor animal that shyly circled the arena." The paper also had kind words for the Cuban band whose "excellent xylophone play" met with lout cheers. Except for a brief performance of the folk singers and dancers from southern Germany and two performances of the male mass chorus, this cultural potpourri was devoid of any ethnic signifiers.[125]

In ceding the stage to the Pan-American Exposition, festival organizers handed over the baton to commerce, spectacle, and empire. On the closing day of the festival, singers and celebrants did not meet in a picnic grove but in the commercialized space of the fair where the sounds of popular culture drowned out the music of the German "folk." Instead of showcasing German-American musicians and singers, the program featured professional musicians from the German Empire who produced the sounds and sights of a stylized Germanness (which, in later decades, would become a convenient shorthand for German culture). Not that festival-goers seemed to mind. They carried the serenading, chattering, loud greetings, and impromptu concerts from Buffalo's streets to the fairgrounds. "For the time being," the Buffalo *Enquirer* observed, "the classical numbers of the masters have been discarded. Volksgesang reigns supreme. By this is meant love, pathetic, patriotic, and Bacchanalian selections."[126]

The response of "ethnopolitical entrepreneurs" was surprisingly muted.[127] Some celebrated German folk music ever more fervently as a "mirror of the people's soul."[128] Also new was the vehemence with which some commentators denounced the "foreign" parts of the program, such as the overture to *Mignon* by the French composer Ambroise Thomas or the compositions by Tchaikovsky and Leoncavallo.[129] These musical selections, they suggested, had no place at a German festival whose singers proudly celebrated their "Germanic" roots.[130] In encountering the unsettling rhythms of popular culture and strains of "foreign" music, these commentators seized on the sounds of the German folk that rang with the promise of cultural purity.

Other observers, however, questioned the rationale of the singers' festivals, whose mass choruses, they held, no longer suited the musical sensibility of the day. The Buffalo *Volksfreund* found the performance of the mass chorus wanting in quality, as the time set aside for mass rehearsals had been insufficient. In terms of artistic merit, the Buffalo *Freie Presse* concurred, small festivals were far superior to the immense gatherings of the North American Sängerbund.[131]

In cultivating a new musical taste, German musicians, singers, and celebrants had written a new cultural score. To middle- and upper-class audiences, who had grown fond of the strains of classical music and the playing of professional musicians, the performances at the singers' festivals must have sounded increasingly plain; for neither singers nor other festival attendees abandoned their practice of casual music-making, their insistence on lager as a festive ingredient, or their loud renditions of "Bacchanalian selections." German concert audiences, in turn, responded to attempts to silence them by heading to the grounds of the Pan-American Exposition, where they broke into song as they pleased. German song and sound had dissolved into "high" and "mass" culture, respectively, infusing elite cultural life while easing the transition of German migrants into the chorus of popular culture.[132] Both melodies called into question the very rationale of a festival that marketed itself as German.

Coda

*I*n his wide-ranging examination of the songs and ballads of nineteenth-century immigrants in the United States, Victor Greene notes a curious characteristic of German singing in America. Whereas the music of Polish, Chinese, and Mexican immigrants provided a running commentary on the hardships, joys, and challenges of immigrant life in the United States, German Americans sang of the homeland they had left behind.[1] Their songs commented on neither cultural change nor intercultural exchange. Instead, they evoked farewells between lovers, friends, and families in whose partings resonated the story of the German exodus to North America.[2] In striking contrast to the Mexican-American *corrido*—an "exceptionally flexible musical genre which encouraged adapting composition to new situations and surroundings," as George Sánchez writes—the repertoire of German singers' festivals in North America remained rooted in the German folk song.[3]

Yet to hear the sameness of the songs as an ode to ethnic continuity is to miss the transformative power of the moment of performance. Although the text of German folk songs struck a conservative tone, the *practice* of music making denoted an ethnicity that was fluid and flexible.[4] By the turn of the twentieth century, German singers and celebrants no longer located a homeland in the bond between a place and its people. Instead, they created a homeland in the shared acts of singing and celebrating. Translated into sound, the German homeland of speech and song retained a tangible, sensuous quality. It continued to "sound" German long after it had become firmly continental in its sensibility.

In listening to practices of music making, we encounter the hyphen in "German-Canadian" and "German-American" not as an imposing cultural boundary but as a space of cultural interaction.[5] In the days of merry-making that enveloped Waterloo County and Buffalo in a symphony of German "mirth and song," English-speaking commentators and audiences listened first bemusedly, then with increasing enthusiasm to the strains of German music. By the turn of the century, they had claimed the singers' festivals as "ours."[6] Anglo-Canadian and Anglo-American musicians joined musical performances, while local boosters embraced the festivals as an opportunity to showcase industrial prowess and local sights. Meanwhile, German conductors such as Theodor Zöllner or Louis Allgewähr used the singers' festivals as springboards into life-long careers as public educators. As music masters in the public schools of Berlin, Ontario and Buffalo, New York State, they would help craft a (musical) narrative of the nation.

Even as they were striving for harmony on stage, German Canadians and German Americans could not help but note how different they were beginning to sound by the closing decades of the nineteenth century. German Canadians were finely attuned to the debates that reverberated through German America and reported at length on the festivals of German song and sound celebrated by their "German brethren" south of the border. German-American gatekeepers, by contrast, could not help but sound a condescending note when it came to the singers' festival in Waterloo County, whose inhabitants seemed to be products of an earlier, more innocent age. When the New York Staatszeitung waxed lyrically on how the unveiling of the emperor's bust in 1897 had drawn German migrants "from all the provinces of the Dominion, from Manitoba's northern realms, from British Columbia's far-away coast and Quebec's populous regions," the German-Canadian press wryly noted the hyperbole of the German-American correspondent who had so magically transformed what had been, in essence, a regional gathering of German-Canadian singing societies.

Although the heartland of German settlement in nineteenth-century Ontario was dwarfed by the sheer size and vitality of German America, public debates on race and nation allowed German Canadians a more self-confident rhetorical stance in defining the "destiny" of the ethnic group. In Waterloo County, German migrants celebrated Victoria Day as exuberantly as they did the birthday of the

German emperor, for both belonged to the same imperial family, tied together by bonds of blood. Even when the cult of Anglo-Saxon superiority enveloped Ontario in the closing decades of the nineteenth century, "Canada's Germans" pointed with equanimity to the "Saxon" as the counterpart to the "Anglo" soul. In the United States, by contrast, the public oratory at the singers' festivals remained preoccupied with the group's public image and never shed the tone of cultural defensiveness that had been forged in the virulent nativism of the 1850s and the resurgence of nativist rhetoric in the 1890s. The vocal assertions of German cultural superiority betrayed a craving for recognition, as historian Wolfgang Helbich argues in his sensitive reading of migrants' letters, for German migrants "implicitly admitted a superior position of Anglo-Americans, who were felt to be the authority that could dispense approval."[7]

It was in acts of casual speech and informal music-making that migrants sounded out the meanings of German ethnicity. Whether ethnic leaders wielded the baton at singers' festivals or the proverbial pen in the columns of the German-language press, their actions served as an important counterpoint to the conservative ethos that imbued their writings. Despite their laments for language loss and their bleak warnings of ethnic decline, they were not content to merely defend the ethnic group and preserve the status quo. Instead, they were as interested in introducing German-language instruction into the public school curriculum as they were in reforming the language of pedagogy itself, as committed to staging successful singers' festivals as they were to making a public musical culture. Notwithstanding their rhetoric of conservation, they pioneered innovative modern language curricula, schooled the ears of the "music-loving public" in the intricacies of classical and folk music, and popularized practices of "polite" listening.

Those migrants who were categorized as German—or identified as such—wore ethnicity as a mantle to don when it fit the occasion. They spoke German, but not necessarily the "pure" High German that ethnic gatekeepers liked to hear. Instead, they forged a hybrid tongue out of the German and English languages in which they lived their lives. They participated en masse in the singers' festivals, but refused to be silenced in the concert hall. By the turn of the century, they traded the spaces of "sacralized" high culture for the streets, picnic groves and beer gardens more amenable to impromptu renderings of German folk songs.

So tightly were the sounds of German speech and music-making woven into the aural fabric of public culture that they no longer denoted ethnicity alone. Instead, they echoed with the language of reform pedagogy, civic boosterism, intercultural exchange, cultural refinement, class conflict, popular culture, and national identity. In sound, migrants enacted stories of ethnicity and nation that spoke of cultural creativity and had a distinctly modern ring.[8]

Endnotes

INTRODUCTION

1. University of Waterloo, Doris Lewis Rare Book Room, Breithaupt Hewetson Clark Collection (hereafter UW, DLRBR), diaries of Louis Jacob Breithaupt, 21 March 1867. In my quotations from the Diaries, I follow the transcriptions and translations prepared by the Doris Lewis Rare Book Room.

2. Ibid., 3 February 1868 and 24 December 1867.

3. Ibid., 8 January 1868 ("Bruder Wilhelm bekam heute Schläge in der Schule und er und Johan bekamen auch zu Hause"); and 1 April 1868 ("Es gehen bei 400 Schüler hinn in Berlin").

4. See *Berliner Journal* for William Breithaupt (6 July 1871), Melvina Breithaupt (19 July 1877, 3 January 1878, 2 May 1878, 7 November 1878), Ezra Breithaupt (2 May 1878, 7 November 1878, 24 December 1874); Albert Breithaupt (4 January 1883, 3 January 1884, 20 March 1884); and Katie Louisa Breithaupt (3 January 1884, 12 June 1884, 12 February 1885).

5. Ibid., 3 July 1880. It was only on 3 January 1884 that Louis Breithaupt resumed keeping a diary.

6. Mark Smith, "Listening to the Heard Worlds of Antebellum America," reprinted in *Hearing History: A Reader*, ed. Mark Smith (Athens: University of Georgia Press, 2004), 365–84.

7. Frederick Barth, ed., "Introduction," in *Ethnic Groups and Boundaries: The Social Organization of Cultural Difference* (Boston: Little Brown and Company, 1969); see in particular 9–38.

8. Kathleen Neils Conzen, David A. Gerber, Ewa Morawska, George E. Pozzetta, and Rudolph J. Vecoli, "The Invention of Ethnicity: A Perspective from the U.S.A.," *Journal of American Ethnic History* 12, 1 (1992): 3–40.

9. Kathleen Neils Conzen, "Mainstream and Side Channels: The Localization of Immigrant Cultures," *Journal of American Ethnic History* 11, 1 (1991), 9, and *Making Their Own America: Assimilation Theory and the German Peasant Pioneer* (New York: Berg, 1990), 9. See also Christiane Harzig, "Gender, Transatlantic Space, and the Presence of German-Speaking People in North America," in *Traveling between Worlds: German-American Encounters*, ed. by Thomas Adam and Ruth Gross (Arlington: University of Texas, 2006), 146–82.

10. It is the notion of "practice" that runs through the pages of this book. Examining culture as practice, as opposed to cultural norms and ideals, allows for a "more flexible approach to symbolizing, one that begins with the idea that cultural practices and patterned social practices are indelibly interwoven." See Sonya Rose, "Cultural Analysis and Moral Discourses: Episodes, Continuities, and Transformations," in *Beyond the Cultural Turn: New Directions in the Study of Society and Culture*, ed. Victoria E. Bonnell and Lynn Hunt (Berkeley: University of California Press, 1999), 228.

11. Rogers Brubaker, "Ethnicity without groups," *Archives européennes de sociologie* 43, 2 (November 2002), 167–68. See also the collection of essays by Rogers Brubaker in which he expands on the themes of this article, *Ethnicity without groups* (Cambridge, MA: Harvard University Press, 2004).

12. Ibid. 160, 169–70.

13. My own reading of narratives of migration and cultural encounters has been shaped by the works of David Gerber, *Authors of Their Lives: The Personal Correspondence of British Immigrants to North America in the Nineteenth Century* (New York: New York University Press, 2006); Orm Øverland, *Immigrant Minds, American Identities: Making the United States Home, 1870-1930*

(Urbana and Chicago: University of Illinois Press, 2000); Matthew Frye Jacobson, *Special Sorrows: The Diasporic Imagination of Irish, Polish, and Jewish Immigrants in the United States* (Cambridge, MA: Harvard University Press, 1995); Brent O. Peterson, *Popular Narratives and Ethnic Identity: Literature and Community in* Die Abendschule (Ithaca, NY: Cornell University Press, 1991); and Franca Iacovetta, *Gatekeepers: Reshaping Immigrant Lives in Cold War Canada* (Toronto: Between the Lines, 2006).

14. Brubaker, "Ethnicity without groups," 175.

15. Mark Smith, "Echoes in Print: Method and Causation in Aural History," *Journal of the Historical Society* 2, 3–4 (2002): 318.

16. As quoted in Mark Smith, "Introduction," in *Hearing History*, xi.

17. Buffalo *Daily Courier*, 26 July 1860.

18. Richard Cullen Rath, *How Early America Sounded* (Ithaca, NY: Cornell University Press, 2003), as quoted in Mark Smith, "Introduction," in *Hearing History*, x. See also R. Murray Schafer, *The Tuning of the World: Towards a Theory of Soundscape Design* (Philadelphia: University of Pennsylvania Press, 1980); Jane Kamensky, *Governing the Tongue: The Politics of Speech in Early New England* (New York: Oxford University Press, 1997); Alain Corbin, *Village Bells: Sound and Meaning in the Nineteenth-Century French Countryside* (New York: Columbia University Press, 1998); Bruce Smith, *The Acoustic World of Early Modern England* (Chicago: University of Chicago Press, 1999); Mark Smith, *Listening to Nineteenth-Century America* (Chapel Hill: University of North Carolina Press, 2001); David Garrioch, "Sounds of the City: The Soundscape of Early Modern European Towns," *Urban History* 30, 1 (2003): 5–25; Nora M. Alter and Lutz Koepnick, eds., *Sound Matters: Essays on the Acoustic of Modern German Culture* (New York: Berghahn Books, 2004). For works by historians of music that focus on both social and cultural practices of listening and music-making, see Reinhard Strohm, *Music in Late Medieval Bruges* (Oxford: Clarendon Press, 1985); James H. Johnson, *Listening in Paris: A Cultural History* (Berkeley: University of California Press, 1995); Philip Bohlman, "'Still, They Were All Germans in Town': Music in the Multi-Religious German-American Community," in *Emigration and Settlement Patterns of German Communities in North America*, ed. Eberhard Reichmann, La Vern J. Rippley, and Joerg Nagler (Indianapolis: Indiana University-Purdue University Press, 1995), 276–93; Tim Carter, "The Sounds of Silence: Models for an Urban Musicology," *Urban History* 29, 1 (2002): 8–18; Derek B. Scott, "Music and Social Class in Victorian London," *Urban History* 29, 1 (2002): 60–73; Celia Applegate, *Bach in Berlin: Nation and Culture in Mendelssohn's Revival of the* St. Matthew Passion (Ithaca, NY: Cornell University Press, 2005); Philip Bohlman and Otto Holzapfel, *Land without Nightingales: Music in the Making of German-America* (Madison: University of Wisconsin Press, 2002); Victor Greene, *A Singing Ambivalence: American Immigrants between Old World and New, 1830–1930* (Kent and London: Kent State University Press, 2004); and John Koegel, *Music in German Immigrant Theater: New York City 1840–1940* (Rochester: University of Rochester Press, 2009).

19. For an elegant and evocative tribute to the role of the visual in constructing German identities, see Peter Conolly-Smith, *Translating America: An Immigrant Press Visualizes American Popular Culture, 1895–1918* (Washington, DC: Smithsonian Books, 2004).

20. Buffalo *Daily Courier*, 25 and 26 July 1860; Buffalo *Daily Republic*, 27 July 1860; Toronto *Globe*, 2 September 1874.

21. Doris Sommer, "Choose and Lose," in *Multilingual America: Transnationalism, Ethnicity, and the Languages of American Literature*, ed. Werner Sollors (New York: New York University Press, 1998), 305, and *Berliner Journal*, 1 October 1885.

22. As Karl Deutsch contended more than half a century ago, "The Swiss may speak four different languages and still act as one people, for each of them has enough learned habits, preferences,

symbols, memories, patterns of landholding and social stratification, events in history, and personal associations, all of which together permit him to communicate more effectively with Swiss than with the speaker of his own language who belongs to other people." As long as "communication channels" allowed for a broad range of social and cultural exchanges, people could speak the same language and share a sense of common identity, even if they expressed themselves in different tongues. See Karl Deutsch, *Nationalism and Social Communication: An Inquiry into the Foundations of Nationality* (Cambridge, MA: MIT Press, 1966), 38.

23. It is no coincidence that historians of German migration have resorted to identifying the subject of their inquiries as "German-speaking immigrants." Given the bewildering diversity of German migrants in North America who were divided along lines of class, religion, regions of origin, and dialect, language seemed to be the one symbolic umbrella broad enough to subsume members of the ethnic group. See Stanley Nadel, *Little Germany: Ethnicity, Religion, and Class in New York City, 1845–80* (Urbana and Chicago: University of Illinois Press, 1990), 6–7 and 14, and Dirk Hoerder, "German-speaking Immigrants—Co-Founders or Mosaic? A Research Note on Politics and Statistics in Scholarship," *Zeitschrift für Kanada-Studien* 14 (1994): 53–55.

24. Glenn Jordan and Chris Weedon, *Cultural Politics: Class, Gender, Race and the Postmodern World* (Oxford: Blackwell, 1995), 565.

25. Vicki Spencer, "Towards an Ontology of Holistic Individualism: Herder's Theory of Identity, Culture and Community," *History of European Ideas* 22, 3 (1996): 251.

26. See also Etienne Balibar, "The Nation Form: History and Ideology," in *Becoming National: A Reader*, ed. Geoff Eley and Ronald Grigor Suny (New York: Oxford University Press, 1996), 141.

27. Smith, "Listening to the Heard Worlds of Antebellum America," 366. As Peter Bailey observes in his study of the Victorian English bourgeoisie, sounds were "as much a mark of their nationality as their class." Bailey, *Popular Culture and Performance in the Victorian City* (Cambridge: Cambridge University Press, 1998), quoted in ibid.

28. David Gerber, "'The Germans Take Care of Our Celebrations': Middle-Class Americans Appropriate German Ethnic Culture in Buffalo in the 1850s," in *Hard at Play: Leisure in America, 1840–1940*, ed. Kathryn Grover (Amherst: University of Massachusetts Press, 1992), 39–60.

29. *Berliner Journal*, 10 September 1874. As Mark Smith remarks, "Aurality, precisely because it was clumsy, blunt, and lacking in subtlety and perspective" carried meanings about "self" and "otherness." See Smith, "Echoes in Print," 332.

30. UW, DLRBR, Diaries of Louis Jacob Breithaupt, 23 August 1867; 5 and 23 October 1867; 20 April 1868; 10 September 1868; 14 and 20 October 1868; 16 and 18 April 16 1869; 29 June 1869; 4 September 1869; 30 September 1869; 22 June 1870; 23 August 1870; 19 October 1870; 6 April 1871; 19 December 1871; 27 April 1872; 25 May 1872; 20 August 1872; 26 October 1872; 31 August 1888; 22 April 1892. See also "William Henry Breithaupt," in *Province of Ontario: A History, 1615–1927, vol. 3*, ed. Jesse Edgar Middleton and Fred Landon (Toronto: Dominion, 1927), 133–34, and UW, DLRBR, *Sketch of the Life of Catherine Breithaupt, Her Family and Her Times* (Berlin, 1911), 5.

31. The classic study of cross-border movement in the Canadian-American borderland is Marcus Lee Hansen's *The Mingling of the Canadian and American Peoples* (New Haven, CT: Yale University Press, 1940). For more recent explorations of the Canadian-American borderland see Bruno Ramirez, "Canada and the United States: Perspectives on Migration and Continental History," *Journal of American Ethnic Studies* 20, 3 (2001): 50–70, and John Bukowczyk, Nora Faires, David Smith, and Randy William Widdis, *Permeable Border: The Great Lakes Basin as Transnational Region, 1650–1990* (Pittsburg: University of Pittsburgh Press, 2005).

32. Royden Loewen, *Family, Church, and Market: A Mennonite Community in the Old and New*

Worlds, 1850–1930 (Urbana: University of Illinois Press, 1993), and *Diaspora in the Countryside: Two Mennonite Communities and Mid-Twentieth-Century Rural Disjunctions* (Urbana: University of Illinois Press, 2006); Alexander Freund, *Aufbrüche nach dem Zusammenbruch* (Göttingen: V & R Unipress, 2004).

33. Bruno Ramirez, *On the Move: French-Canadian and Italian Migrants in the North Atlantic Economy* (Toronto: McClelland and Stewart, 1991); Randy William Widdis, *With Scarcely a Ripple: Anglo-Canadian Migration into the United States and Western Canada, 1880–1920* (Montreal: McGill-Queen's University Press, 1998); Bruno Ramirez and Yves Otis, *Crossing the 49th Parallel: Migration from Canada to the United States, 1900–1930* (Ithaca, NY: Cornell University Press, 2001).

34. For a notable exception, see Susan Wiley Hardwick, "The Ties That Bind: Transnational Migrant Networks at the Canadian-U.S. Borderland," *American Review of Canadian Studies* (Winter 2005): 667–82.

35. The phrasing here is borrowed from Mark Smith's article "Listening to the Heard Worlds of Antebellum America."

36. Kevin Kenny, "Diaspora and Comparison: The Global Irish as a Case Study," *Journal of American History* 90, 1 (2003): 134–62, and David Blackbourn and James Retallack, eds., *Localism, Landscape, and the Ambiguities of Place: German-Speaking Central Europe, 1860–1930* (Toronto: University of Toronto Press, 2007).

37. In coining the term "transnationalism," the anthropologists Nina Glick Schiller, Linda Basch, and Christina Blanc-Szanton defined it as "the processes by which immigrants build social fields that link together their country of origin and country of settlement." See Nina Glick Schiller et al., "Transnationalism: A New Analytical Framework for Understanding Migration," in *Towards a Transnational Perspective on Migration: Race, Class, Ethnicity, and Nationalism Reconsidered*, ed. Nina Glick Schiller, Linda Basch, and Christina Blanc-Szanton (New York: New York Academy of Science, 1992), 1.

38. For introductions to historical work in transnationalism, see Peter Kivisto, "Theorizing Transnational Immigration: A Critical Review of Current Efforts," *Ethnic and Racial Studies* 24, 4 (2001): 549–77, and Dirk Hoerder, "Historians and Their Data: The Complex Shift from Nation-State Approaches to the Study of People's Transcultural Lives," *Journal of American Ethnic History* (Summer 2006): 85–96.

39. As Kenneth McLaughlin has suggested, the relationship between Pennsylvania-Germans in Waterloo County and immigrants from the German states was one of mutual interaction rather than cultural separation. McLaughlin, "Waterloo County: A Pennsylvania-German Homeland," in *From Pennsylvania to Waterloo: Pennsylvania-German Folk Culture in Transition*, ed. Susan M. Burke and Matthew H. Hill (Waterloo: Wilfrid Laurier University Press, 1991), 35–45.

40. This label admittedly obscures the local diversity of Pennsylvania Mennonites, Catholics from southern Germany, North German Protestants, Amish, Swiss, and Alsatians. See Hans Lehmann, *The German Canadians, 1750–1937: Immigration, Settlement and Culture* (St. John's, NF: Jesperson Press, 1986), 66–79, and Elizabeth Bloomfield, "City-Building Processes in Berlin/Kitchener and Waterloo, 1870–1930," (PhD diss., University of Guelph, 1981), 42–50. See also the rich local historiography on the history of German immigrants in Waterloo County, including Elizabeth Bloomfield, *Waterloo Township through Two Centuries* (Waterloo: St. Jacobs Printery, 1995); Geoffrey Hayes, *Waterloo County: An Illustrated History* (Region of Waterloo: Waterloo Historical Society, 1997), and Ulrich Frisse, *Berlin, Ontario (1800–1916): Historische Identitäten von "Kanadas Deutscher Hauptstadt"—Ein Beitrag zur Deutsch-Kanadischen Migrations-, Akkulturations- und Perzeptionsgeschichte des 19. und frühen 20. Jahrhunderts* (New Dundee, ON: TransAtlanticPublishing, 2003).

41. Quoted in W. V. Uttley, *A History of Kitchener* (Waterloo: Wilfrid Laurier University Press, 1985 [1937]), 119–20.

42. National Library of Canada, *Census of Canada*, 1871.

43. Conzen, "Mainstream and Side Channels," 6.

44. David Gerber, *The Making of an American Pluralism: Buffalo, New York, 1825–60* (Urbana: University of Illinois Press, 1989).

45. Ibid., 173, and Ismar S. Ellison, "The Germans of Buffalo: An Historical Essay," *Publications of the Buffalo Historical Society*, vol. 2 (Buffalo: Bigelow Brothers, 1880), 123–25.

46. Agnes Bretting, "Halleluja, We're Off to America!: Western, Central and Northern Europe," in *Fame, Fortune and Sweet Liberty: The Great European Immigration*, ed. Dirk Hoerder and Diethelm Knauff (Bremen: Edition Tammen, 1992), 36–40, and Walter Kamphoefner, *The Westfalians: From Germany to Missouri* (Princeton: Princeton University Press, 1987), 17–19 and 27–30.

47. Gerber, *The Making of an American Pluralism*, 18–19 and 170–73, and Ellison, "The Germans of Buffalo," 124.

48. Laurence Glasco, *Ethnicity and Social Structure: Irish, Germans, and Native-Born of Buffalo, N.Y., 1850–1860* (New York: Arno Press, 1980), 15–18.

49. Ibid., 19 and 144–45, and Gerber, *The Making of an American Pluralism*, 172, 175, 191, and 196.

50. Glasco, *Ethnicity and Social Structure*, 63, 84–95, and 123; Gerber, *The Making of an American Pluralism*, 188; Truman C. White, *A Descriptive Work on Erie County, New York*, vol. 1 (Boston History Company, 1898), 610–28; H. Perry Smith, *History of the City of Buffalo and Erie County*, vol. 2 (Syracuse, NY: D. Mason and Co., 1884), 150–61; *Geschichte der Deutschen in Buffalo and Erie County, N.Y., mit Biographien und Illustrationen hervorragender Deutsch-Amerikaner, welche zur Entwicklung der Stadt Buffalo beigetragen haben* (Buffalo: Reinecke and Zesch, 1898), 54–58, 70–77, 90, 101–5, 124–26, 144–49, 150–59, 177–80.

51. As quoted in *Geschichte der Deutschen*, 116.

52. Buffalo *Daily Courier*, 25 July 1860. Already in the years preceding the Buffalo singers' festival of 1860, the city's musical life—orchestrated almost single-handedly by recent German migrants—had brought together Americans and Germans in the shared enjoyment of sacred, choral, and classical music. See David Gerber, "'The Germans Take Care of Our Celebrations,'" 52.

53. In the past decade, literary scholars and historians of migrant writings have increasingly embraced the notion of an "unbounded language" characterized by language experiments. See, in particular, David Gerber, "'You See I Speak Wery Well English': Literacy and the Transformed Self as Reflected in Immigrant Personal Correspondence," *Journal of American Ethnic History* 12, 2 (1993): 56–62; Werner Sollors, ed., *Multilingual America: Transnationalism, Ethnicity, and the Languages of American Literature* (New York: New York University Press, 1998); and Orm Øverland, ed., *Not English Only: Redefining 'American' in American Studies* (Amsterdam: VU University Press, 2001).

54. Toronto *Globe*, 19 August 1875.

55. Bernd Ostendorf, "'The Diluted Second Generation': German-Americans in Music, 1870 to 1920," in *German Workers' Culture in the United States 1850 to 1920*, ed. Hartmut Keil (Washington: Smithsonian Institution Press, 1988), 261–87.

56. Buffalo *Times*, 26 June 1901.

ENDNOTES

CHAPTER ONE

1. Jane Kamensky, *Governing the Tongue: The Politics of Speech in Early New England* (New York: Oxford University Press, 1997), 9–12.

2. In the early twentieth century, the *Berliner Journal* incorporated the *Ontario Glocke* of Walkerton (1904) and then, in quick succession, the *Canadischer Kolonist* of Stratford (1906), the *Canadisches Volksblatt* of New Hamburg (1909), and the *Canadischer Bauernfreund* of Waterloo (1909), in the process swelling to sixteen pages. See also *Berliner Journal*, 6 January 1881.

3. See the role of homemaking myth, as examined in Øverland, *Immigrant Minds, American Identities*; see also *Berliner Journal*, 29 December 1859, 1 January 1863, 2 February 1899, and 13 July 1904; Herbert Karl Kalbfleisch, *The History of the Pioneer German Language Press of Ontario, 1835–1918* (Toronto: University of Toronto Press, 1968), 87 and 103–104. All translations, unless otherwise noted, are mine.

4. For a discussion of letters as a transnational space in their own right, see Gerber, *Authors of Their Lives*, in particular Chapter 4, "Using Postal Systems: Transnational Networks on the Edge of Modernity," 140–61.

5. For an imaginative discussion of the concept and the metaphor of translation, see Conolly-Smith, *Translating America*.

6. Peterson, *Popular Narratives and Ethnic Identity*, 153–54.

7. *Berliner Journal*, 3 August 1904 and 15 December 1909; Kalbfleisch, *History of the Pioneer German Language Press*, 87; Carl Wittke, *The German-Language Press in America* (New York: Haskell House Publishers, 1973 [1957]), 230.

8. *Berliner Journal*, 30 January 1890 and 15 December 1909.

9. The German-American newspapers, which the *Berliner Journal* explicitly credited, included the Allentown *Weltbote* (Pennsylvania), *Maryland Staatszeitung, Syracuse Central-Demokrat, Illinois Staats-Zeitung, Herold des Glaubens* (St. Louis), *Lutheranisches Kirchenblatt* (Philadelphia), *Wächter am Erie, Louisviller Anzeiger, Protestantischer Hausfreund* (Cincinnati), *Buffalo Demokrat, Texas Vorwärts, Indiana Telegraph, Philadelphia Gazette,* and the *St. Josephs-Blatt.*

10. See, for example, Jerzy J. Smolicz, "Minority Languages and Core Values of Ethnic Cultures: A Study of Maintenance and Erosion of Polish, Welsh, and Chinese Languages in Australia," in *Maintenance and Loss of Minority Languages*, ed. Willem Fase, Koen Jaspaert, Sjaak Kroon (Amsterdam and Philadelphia: John Benjamins Publishing Company, 1992), 277–306; Alejandro Portes and Richard Schauffler, "Language and the Second Generation: Bilingualism Yesterday and Today," *International Migration Review* 28, 4 (1994): 640–61; Walter D. Kamphoefner, "German American Bilingualism: cui malo? Mother Tongue and Socioeconomic Status among the Second Generation in 1940," *International Migration Review* 28, 4 (1994): 846–64; Robert Swidinsky and Michael Swidinsky, "The Determinants of Heritage Language Continuity in Canada: Evidence from the 1981 and 1991 Census," *Canadian Ethnic Studies* 29, 1 (1997): 81–98.

11. Joshua Fishman, "The Sociology of Language: An Interdisciplinary Social Science Approach to Language in Society," in *Current Trends in Linguistics*, ed. Thomas A. Sebeok, vol. 12, *Linguistic and Adjacent Arts and Sciences* (The Hague: Mouton, 1984), 1707.

12. For similar findings in socio-linguistic studies, see Prokop, *The German Language in Alberta*, 114, and Jeffrey G. Reitz, "Language and Ethnic Community Survival," in *Ethnicity and Ethnic Relations in Canada*, ed. Rita M. Bienvenue and Jay E. Goldstein (Toronto: Butterworth, 1985), 115.

13. Wittke, *The German-Language Press in America*, 200. In Waterloo County, too, a new German-language paper, the *Deutsche Zeitung*, was founded in 1891 "to set a high literary standard to combat

the decline of the German language." See John English and Kenneth McLaughlin, *Kitchener: An Illustrated History* (Scarborough, ON: Robin Brass Studio, 1996), 89.

14. Sommer, "Choose and Lose," 305. See also Marc Shell, "Hyphens: Between Deitsch and American," in *Multilingual America: Transnationalism, Ethnicity, and the Languages of American Literature*, ed. Werner Sollors (New York: New York University Press, 1998), 258–60, and Gerber, "'You See I Speak Wery Well English,'" 56–62.

15. Fishman, "The Sociology of Language," 1645.

16. Werner Sollors, "How German Is It? Multilingual America Reconsidered," in *Not English Only: Redefining "American" in American Studies*, ed. Orm Øverland (Amsterdam: VU University Press, 2001), 148.

17. Spencer, "Towards an Ontology of Holistic Individualism," 245-60.

18. Vicki Spencer, "Herder and Nationalism: Reclaiming the Principle of Cultural Respect," *Australian Journal of Politics and History* 43, 1 (1997): 4–5, and Elie Kedourie, *Nationalism* (Oxford: Blackwell, 1993), 56.

19. Quoted in Spencer, "Herder and Nationalism," 5.

20. Spencer, "Towards an Ontology of Holistic Individualism," 250, and F.W. Barnard, *Herder's Social and Political Thought: From Enlightenment to Nationalism* (Oxford: Clarendon Press, 1965), 57.

21. Robert Reinhold Ergang, *Herder and the Foundations of German Nationalism* (New York: Columbia University, 1931), 99, and Isaiah Berlin, *Vico and Herder: Two Studies in the History of Ideas* (New York: Viking Press, 1976), 182.

22. Quoted in Kirsten Belgum, *Popularizing the Nation: Audience, Representation, and the Production of Identity in* Die Gartenlaube, *1853–1900* (Lincoln: University of Nebraska Press, 1998), 32, and Johann Gottlieb Fichte, *Addresses to the German Nation* (Westport, CT: Greenwood Press, 1979), 68–69.

23. Belgum, *Popularizing the Nation*, 32. See also Raymond Geuss, "Kultur, Bildung, Geist," *History and Theory* 35, 2 (1996): 155–56.

24. Maike Oergel, "The Redeeming Teuton: Nineteenth-Century Notions of the 'Germanic' in England and Germany," in *Imagining Nations*, ed. Geoffrey Cubitt (Manchester: Manchester University Press, 1998), 80, 86. For a discussion of linguistic nationalism in nineteenth-century Europe, see also Eric Hobsbawm, *Nations and Nationalism since 1790: Programme, Myth, Reality* (Cambridge: Cambridge University Press, 1990).

25. *Berliner Journal*, 3 March 1865, 23 March 1865, and 30 March 1865. These articles had been translated from English. They belonged to a body of scientific writing—replete with a heavily theoretical and abstract prose—that rarely found its way into the pages of the *Berliner Journal*.

26. In 1888, one author casually asserted that the Romance languages possessed neither "the freshness, power, nor universality of the German," nor its "greater richness, flexibility and originality." Such claims, however, remained the exception. See *Berliner Journal*, 14 October, 21 October, and 28 October 1888.

27. Ibid., 2 August 1860.

28. Ibid., 23 December 1869.

29. Katherine Verdery, "Whither 'Nation' and 'Nationalism'?" in *Mapping the Nation*, ed. Gopal Balakrishnan (London and New York: Verso, 1996), 229.

30. This, of course, is yet another variant of the "homemaking myths" examined by Øverland in *Immigrant Minds, American Identities*, 21.

31. *Berliner Journal*, 23 December 1869, 27 October 1870, and 10 June 1886.

32. This poem was reprinted in the *Berliner Journal* on 28 May 1895.

33. For the multitude of meanings that resonated in the term *Heimat*, see Celia Applegate, *A Nation of Provincials: The German Idea of Heimat* (Berkeley: University of California Press, 1990), 3–4, 8–9, 240, and Alon Confino, *The Nation as a Local Metaphor: Württemberg, Imperial Germany, and National Memory, 1871–1918* (Chapel Hill: University of North Carolina Press, 1997), 159, 170, 172, and 184.

34. *Berliner Journal*, 5 April 1888.

35. Ibid., 4 October 1860. I am referring here to Ernst Moritz Arndt's famous poem "What is the German's fatherland" (1813), which called for a Fatherland greater than the German regions: a German homeland formed out of the lands where German was spoken, a German nation united by the bonds of a common language ("Where'er resounds the German tongue / Where'er its hymns to God are sung / That it shall be / That, valiant German, you're your own"). Quoted in Hans Kohn, *Prelude to Nation-State: The French and German Experience, 1789–1815* (Princeton: D. Van Nostrand Company, 1967), 258. See also Belgum, *Popularizing the Nation*, 33 and 46.

36. *Berliner Journal*, 27 May 1869.

37. Ibid., 13 June 1861.

38. Ibid., 17 September 1885.

39. Ibid., 10 June 1886.

40. Ibid., 27 May 1869.

41. Ibid., 4 February 1886, 15 March 1888, 21 August 1890, 9 April 1891, 22 July 1897.

42. Ibid., 21 March 1901.

43. See also ibid., 17 March 1870, "Deutsche Frauen und Amerikanische Ansichten" (German Women and American Views), and 5 June 1890, "Ein Wort an deutsche Eltern" (A Reminder to German Parents).

44. Ibid., 19 September 1872, 10 February 1875, 29 October 1885, 10 December 1885, 4 February 1886, 22 March 1888, 21 August 1890, 20 April 1899, 21 March 1901, 7 September 1904.

45. Fishman, "The Sociology of Language," 1707.

46. Language maintenance is, indeed, more pronounced in families where both parents speak the ethnic mother tongue, as Manfred Prokop notes in his study of the German language in Alberta. If only one parent spoke the mother tongue at home, less than one-fourth of the children "appeared to acquire German as the mother tongue or to learn and use it as the dominant home language." Manfred Prokop, *The German Language in Alberta* (Edmonton: University of Alberta Press, 1990), 114.

47. *Berliner Journal*, 20 April 1899.

48. Smolicz, "Minority Languages and Core Values of Ethnic Cultures," 284 and 286.

49. For a point of comparison, see Smolicz's finding that ethnic youth in late-twentieth-century Australia consistently preferred English over their mother tongue, even if their parents "attached great importance to the use of [the latter] at home," for English represented "the linguistic system that was better developed and more often activated." Ibid., 284.

50. *Berliner Journal*, 24 June 1880.

51. Ibid., 1 February 1872, 21 October 1880, 19 December 1895.

52. Ibid., 23 November 1899.

53. Wittke, *The German-Language Press in America*, 4.

54. Smolicz, "Minority Languages and Core Values of Ethnic Cultures," 284 and 287; Prokop, *The German Language in Alberta*, 114.

55. *Berliner Journal*, 19 September 1872.

56. Ibid., 22 October 1885.

57. Øverland, *Immigrant Minds, American Identities*, 30, 32, and 40.

58. *Berliner Journal*, 10 September 1885.

59. Ibid., 1 October 1885.

60. Glenn G. Gilbert, "English Loan-Words in the German of Fredericksburg, Texas," *American Speech* 40, 2 (1965): 104.

61. Gerber, "'You See I Speak Wery Well English,'" 60–62.

62. *Berliner Journal*, 4 February 1886.

63. Ibid., 1 October 1885; see also 14 March 1867 and 4 April 1888.

64. Throughout the 1880s, newspaper columnists in both Canada and the United States pointed to the high esteem in which Americans of class and culture held the German language. See, for example, *Berliner Journal*, 4 February 1886 and 5 April 1888.

65. Hermann Kurthen, "Gone with the Wind: German Language Retention in North Carolina and the United States in Comparative Perspective," *Yearbook of German-American Studies* 33 (1998): 58, and Jürgen Eichhoff, "German in Wisconsin," in *The German Language in America: A Symposium*, ed. Glenn G. Gilbert (Austin: University of Texas Press, 1971), 55.

66. See, for example, Wolfgang Helbich, "Immigrant Adaptation at the Individual Level: The Evidence of Nineteenth-Century German-American Letters," *Amerikastudien/American Studies* 42, 3 (1997): 415 and 417.

67. "Bleibt deutsch! Ein Liedlein zum Schutz der deutschen Umgangssprache," *Berliner Journal*, 15 March 1888.

68. Marion L. Huffines, "Language-Maintenance Efforts among German Immigrants and Their Descendants in the United States," in *America and the Germans: An Assessment of a Three-Hundred-Years History*, ed. Frank Trommler and Joseph McVeigh, vol. 1, *Immigration, Language, Ethnicity* (Philadelphia: University of Pennsylvania Press, 1985), 247.

69. Gilbert, "English Loan-Words," 106. Again, it is striking to note the similarities in the rhetoric and concerns of cultural leaders across ethnic groups. In the case of New Mexico's Spanish-language press, for example, one editorial suggested that "a new language, Anglicized Spanish, had developed among people who had been educated in English in the public schools." See Doris Meyer, *Speaking for Themselves: Neomexicano Cultural Identity and the Spanish-Language Press, 1880–1920* (Albuquerque: University of New Mexico Press, 1996), 124.

70. Gilbert, "English Loan-Words," 106–7.

71. Brent O. Peterson, "How (and Why) to Read German-American Literature," in *The German-American Encounter: Conflict and Cooperation between Two Cultures, 1800–2000*, ed. Frank Trommler and Elliott Shore (New York: Berghahn Books, 2001), 91; Dirk Hoerder, "German-Speaking Immigrants: Co-Founders or Mosaic? A Research Note on Politics and Statistics in Scholarship," *Zeitschrift für Kanada-Studien* 14, 2 (1994): 53; Reinhard R. Doerries, "Organization and Ethnicity: The German-American Experience," *Amerikastudien/American Studies* 33, 3 (1988): 310.

72. Benedict Anderson, *Imagined Communities: Reflections on the Origin and Spread of Nationalism* (London: Verso, 1991 [1983]).

73. *Berliner Journal*, 20 April 1882.

74. The series was entitled "Wohin wir mit unserem hiesigen Deutschthum treiben?" (In which direction is our local German community drifting?) See ibid., 10 September 1885, 17 September 1885, 1 October 1885, 22 October 1885, 29 October 1885, 10 December 1885, 4 February 1886, 1 April 1886.

75. Ibid., 4 February 1886 and 29 October 1885.

76. Ibid., 22 October 1885. It is ironic that the author misspelled the name of Goethe, the literary German icon.

77. Ibid., 10 January 1889.

78. Ibid., 21 August 1890; see also 7 October 1886. Over six decades later, Carl Wittke also noted the "deterioration" of the German language in the late nineteenth century "into a corrupted and Americanized jargon." See Wittke, *The German-Language Press in America*, 4.

79. *Berliner Journal*, 27 May 1914.

80. Ibid., 3 September 1885.

81. Ibid., 13 April 1876.

82. Ibid., 21 November 1889. For a discussion of Pennsylvania German, see Jürgen Eichhoff, "The German Language in America," in *America and the Germans: An Assessment of a Three-Hundred-Year History,* ed. Frank Trommler and Joseph McVeigh, vol. 1, *Immigration, Language, Ethnicity* (Philadelphia: University of Pennsylvania Press, 1985), 230-31.

83. Quoted in Øverland, *Immigrant Minds, American Identities*, 82.

84. The article from the *Indiana Telegraph* was reprinted in the *Berliner Journal* on 3 June 1890. See also *Berliner Journal*, 22 July 1897.

85. Øverland, ed., *Not English Only*, 3–4.

86. *Berliner Journal*, 18 November 1886.

87. See, for example, ibid., 10 December 1885; 5 April 1888; 5 July 1890; 19 February 1891; 27 May 1914.

88. Ibid., 1 October 1885 and 5 April 1888.

89. Heinz Kloss, "German as an Immigrant, Indigenous, and Second Language in the United States," in *The German Language in America: A Symposium*, ed. Glenn G. Gilbert (Austin: University of Texas Press, 1971), 119.

90. *Berliner Journal*, 4 February 1886.

91. Ibid., 7 March 1906. See also 5 July 1900, 1 December 1909, and 12 June 1912.

92. Conzen, "Phantom Landscapes of Colonization," 7–21.

93. Scholars such as Wolfgang Helbich and Brent O. Peterson have documented the yearning for the "recognition, the respect, the sympathy or at least the envy of the Americans," which German migrants recorded in both their private and public writings as they pondered what it meant to be German in the New World. Helbich, "Die 'Englischen': German Immigrants Describe Nineteenth-Century American Society," *Amerikastudien/American Studies* 36, 4 (1991): 528, and Peterson, "How (and Why) to Read German-American Literature," 88–102.

94. *Berliner Journal*, 21 February 1912.

95. Fishman, "The Sociology of Language," 1645.

96. *Berliner Journal*, 21 February 1912.

97. Stuart Hall, "The Question of Cultural Identity," in *Modernity: An Introduction to Modern Societies*, ed. Stuart Hall et al. (Oxford: Blackwell Publishers, 1997 [1996]), 629.

98. Kivisto, "Theorizing Transnational Immigration," 569.

99. *Ontario Journal*, 9 October 1918. See also the editorial "Past and Future," *Ontario Journal*, 25 December 1918.

100. Quoted in Kivisto, "Theorizing Transnational Immigration," 568.

CHAPTER TWO

1. April Schultz, *Ethnicity on Parade: Inventing the Norwegian American through Celebration* (Amherst: University of Massachusetts Press, 1994), 28–30.

2. Jonathan Zimmerman, "Ethnics against Ethnicity: European Immigrants and Foreign-Language Instruction, 1890–1940," *Journal of American History* 88, 4 (March 2002): 1383–1404; Dag Blanck, "The Role of the Swedish Language in Shaping a Swedish-American Culture," in Orm Øverland ed., *Not English Only: Redefining 'American' in American Studies* (Amsterdam: VU University Press, 2001), 34–47; Meyer, *Speaking for Themselves*, 111–27.

3. Øverland, *Immigrant Minds, American Identities*, 39.

4. Zimmerman, "Ethnics against Ethnicity," 1384–86.

5. In the past two decades, scholars of German-American studies have called into question the alleged "devastating" impact of World War I on German immigrant communities, pointing instead to long-term processes of voluntary assimilation. See, for instance, Bettina Goldberg's assertion that World War I served "as a catalyst, not as a cause for abandoning German," in "The German-English Academy, the National German-American Teachers' Seminary, and the Public School System in Milwaukee, Wisconsin, 1851–1919," in *German Influences on Education in the United States to 1917*, ed. Henry Geitz et al. (New York: Cambridge University Press, 1995), 179, and Peterson, *Popular Narratives and Ethnic Identity*, 9 and 246–47. By contrast, note the more conservative tone of German-Canadian scholarship, as reflected in Arthur Grenke, *The German Community in Winnipeg: 1872–1919* (New York: AMS Press, 1991), and Gerhard Bassler, *The German Canadians, 1750–1937: Immigration, Settlement and Culture* (St. John's, NF: Jesperson Press, 1986).

6. Patricia McKegney, "The German Schools of Waterloo County, 1851–1913," *Waterloo Historical Society* 58 (1970), 61, 67, 58, and 64. McKegney's interpretation was advanced in a prize-winning graduate essay that has been accepted uncritically in the historical literature on Waterloo County—perhaps because of the dearth of studies on German-language schooling in the county. See, for example, English and McLaughlin, *Kitchener: An Illustrated History*, 50 and 90, and Bloomfield, *Waterloo Township through Two Centuries*, 243.

7. Studies framed around the rhetorical trope of "language decline," whose dismay over the cultural loss of America's/Canada's rich German linguistic heritage is palpable, include Heinz Kloss, "German-American Language Maintenance," in *Language Loyalty in the United States: The Maintenance and Perpetuation of Non-English Mother Tongues by American Ethnic and Religious Groups*, ed. Joshua Fishman (London: Moutin and Co., 1966); Eichhoff, "The German Language in America"; Prokop, *The German Language in Alberta*. More recent historical scholarship has pointed to the pragmatic choices immigrant parents and their children made in their practices of language use, which were rarely affected by "the abstract notion of identification with ancestry, ethnic symbols, or cultural habits." See Kurthen, "Gone with the Wind," 59, and Clinton O. White, "Pre–World War I Saskatchewan German Catholic Thought Concerning the Perpetuation of Their Language and Religion," *Canadian Ethnic Studies* 26, 2 (1994): 15–45.

8. Zimmerman, "Ethnics against Ethnicity," 1386.

9. In this context, see also Carol Eastman, "Language, Ethnic Identity, and Change," in *Linguistic*

ENDNOTES

Minorities, Policies, and Pluralism, ed. John Edwards (London: Academic Press, 1984), 239 and 261.

10. Eichhoff, "German in Wisconsin," 53; Anthony W. Stanforth, *Deutsche Einflüsse auf den englischen Wortschatz in Geschichte und Gegenwart, mit einem Beitrag zum Amerikanischen Englisch von Jürgen Eichhoff* (Tübingen: Niemeyer, 1996); Prokop, *The German Language in Alberta*, 104; Zimmerman, "Ethnics against Ethnicity," 1397.

11. Gerber, "'You See I Speak Wery Well English,'" 60. As literary scholars have argued, these linguistic and cultural transactions often resulted in a new language such as "Germerican." See Shell, "Hyphens: Between Deitsch and American," 258–60.

12. Royden Loewen, "'Hold Your Heads High in Your Usual Unassuming Manner': Making a Mennonite Middle Class Ethnicity in Steinbach, Manitoba and Meade, Kansas, 1945–1975," paper presented at the conference "Assimilation—Integration—Acculturation? The German-Canadian Case," University of Winnipeg, August 2004; Klaus Bongert, "Deutsch in Ontario: Deutsche Sprache und Kultur in Kitchener-Waterloo," in Leopold Auburger et al., *Deutsch als Muttersprache in Kanada: Berichte zur Gegenwartslage* (Wiesbaden: Franz Steiner Verlag, 1977), 28; Grit Liebscher and Mathias Schulze, "Language Use and Identity: Analysing Language Behaviour of German-Speaking Immigrants in Kitchener-Waterloo," paper presented at the conference "Assimilation—Integration—Acculturation? The German-Canadian Case," University of Winnipeg, August 2004.

13. Ontario Institute for Studies in Education (hereafter OISE), *Annual Report of the Normal, Model, and Common Schools, in Upper Canada for the Year 1851 by the Chief Superintendent of Schools* (Ottawa: Hunter, Rose and Col, 1852), 102. As the title of the annual reports varied from year to year, they will hereafter be referred to as *Upper Canada Annual Reports*.

14. OISE, *Upper Canada Annual Report for 1854*, 118.

15. Kitchener Public Library, Waterloo Historical Society (hereafter KPL, WHS), MC 71, "Isaac Moyer, Biography and Reminiscence, January 1st, 1915," 12.

16. Ibid., 13.

17. OISE, *Upper Canada Annual Report for 1852*, 111.

18. OISE, *Upper Canada Annual Report for 1854*, 118.

19. "Otto Klotz," in Middleton and Landon, *Province of Ontario: A History, 1615–1927, vol. 3*, 171.

20. Library and Archives Canada, MG 30, B13, vol. 9, "Statistics and History of the Preston School Compiled and Written by Otto Klotz for the Use of his Family," 54, 58, 68, 92–94 (hereafter Klotz, "School History").

21. Alan William Junker, "Otto Klotz and the Implementation of Education Policy in Waterloo County, 1846–1871," (MA thesis, Wilfrid Laurier University, 1987), 67–70.

22. National Library of Canada, *Regulations and Correspondence Relating to French and German schools in the Province of Ontario* (Toronto: Warwick and Sons, 1889), 1.

23. D.A. Lawr and R.D. Gidney, "Who Ran the Schools? Local Influence on Education Policy in Nineteenth-Century Ontario," *Ontario History* 72, 3 (1980): 132.

24. Klotz, "School History," 94.

25. This tacit approval is reflected by the fact that year after year, the Board asked Otto Klotz "to prepare questions in the German Language for Examination." KPL, WHS, WAT C-87, Records of the Board of Examiners for Waterloo County (Berlin: s.n., 1853–1908), 27 June 1865.

26. OISE, *Upper Canada Annual Report for 1861*, 186.

27. Klotz, "School History," 96.

228

28. Ibid. See also City of Cambridge Archives, Minute Book of the Board of Trustees of the Preston School, January 3, 1852, to January 5, 1853.

29. City of Cambridge Archives, Minute Book of the Board of Trustees of the Preston School, August 6, 1858 to August 5, 1863, 1 February 1860 and 6 January 1861. See also Minute Book of the Board of Trustees of the Preston School, October 7, 1863 to 27 July 27, 1869, 16 March 1864, 4 May 1864, 2 November 1864, 30 November 1864, 9 December 1864, 1 February 1865, 3 March 1865, 19 December 1865, 9 October 1867, 21 October 1867, 5 August 1868, 3 September 1868.

30. Neil Sutherland, "The Urban Child," *History of Education Quarterly* 9, 3 (1969): 305. See also Barbara Beatty, "Children in Different and Difficult Times: The History of American Childhood, Part I," *History of Education Quarterly* 40, 1 (Spring 2000): 74.

31. UW, DLRBR, *Sketch of the Life of Catherine Breithaupt*, 5, 7, and 18; "Louis J. Breithaupt, Middleton and Landon, in *Province of Ontario: A History, 1615–1927, vol. 3*, 131–32.

32. The school desk that Louis received for his twelfth birthday suggests that the boy's family took education seriously. A year later, Louis's mother transformed the loft into a workspace "so we could study in the evenings," and in the winter of 1869 equipped the room of her two eldest sons with a table and a small heater.

33. Only once did Louis mention physical punishment: "Brother William got a beating at school today and then he and John got one at home, too." UW, DLRBR, Diaries of Louis Jacob Breithaupt, 8 January 1868. As Mary P. Ryan has observed in her analysis of Victorian childrearing practices, the "sly manipulations of maternal socialization" were intended to implant "the usual array of petit bourgeois traits—honesty, industry, frugality, temperance, and, pre-eminently, self-control." Ryan, *Cradle of the Middle Class: The Family in Oneida County, New York, 1790–1865* (Cambridge: Cambridge University Press, 1984), 161.

34. UW, DLRBR, Diaries of Louis Jacob Breithaupt, 12 August 1867.

35. Ibid., 24 March 1867, 7 April 1867, 14 April 1867, 18 August 1867, 25 August 1867, 13 October 1867 (verses), 21 April 1867, 28 April 1867, 19 May 1867, 26 May 1867, 28 January 1868 (Bible), 11 October 1868 (donation).

36. Ibid., 5 March 1867, 6 March 1867, 19 March 1867, 1 April 1867, 13 May 1867.

37. Ibid., 12 July 1867.

38. Ibid., 17 October 1867, 22 June 1868, 4 September 1868; 7 October 1868; 13 November 1868.

39. Although government policies left no traces in Louis's childhood recollections, schooling did nurture a new conception of time. Almost imperceptibly, the boy's life became structured by the demands of the classroom, which alone among his many duties and diversions demanded strict punctuality. "To be late" was an experience intimately tied to the realm of schooling. See ibid., "We were late to school today" (4 April 1867); "We were late for school yesterday" (24 October 1867); "We were late for school this morning" (30 November 1868); "We were late for school again today" (2 December 1868).

40. "Circular from the Chief Superintendent to the Inspectors of Public Schools in Ontario, 1871," in *Documentary History of Education in Upper Canada, vol. 3, 1836–40*, ed. J. George Hodgins (Toronto: Warwick Bros. 1895), 135–40; National Library of Canada, "Qualifications of Public School Inspectors and County Examiners," *Journal of Education, Province of Ontario* 24, 2 (1871): 22, and "Programme for the Examination and Classification of Teachers of the Public Schools in the Province of Ontario," *Journal of Education, Province of Ontario* 24, 2 (1871): 22–23.

41. *Berliner Journal*, 8 June 1871.

42. Ibid., 15 June 1871.

43. Regional Municipality of Waterloo (Kitchener), *Journal of the Proceedings and By-Laws of the*

Municipal Council of the County of Waterloo, 1870 and 1872. For praise of Pearce, see *Berliner Journal,* 2 February 1865 and 13 July 1865.

44. David Tyack, "Pilgrim's Progress: Toward a Social History of the School Superintendency, 1860–1960," *History of Education Quarterly* 16, 3 (1976): 258, and Bruce Curtis, "Class Culture and Administration: Educational Inspection in Canada West," in *Colonial Leviathan: State Formation in Mid-Nineteenth-Century Canada,* ed. Allan Greer and Ian Radforth (Toronto: University of Toronto Press, 1992), 118.

45. Tyack, "Pilgrim's Progress," 258, and Bruce Curtis, *True Government by Choice Men? Inspection, Education, and State Formation in Canada West* (Toronto: University of Toronto Press, 1992), 7.

46. Thomas Pearce, "School History, Waterloo County and Berlin," *Waterloo Historical Society* 2 (1914): 49. Biographical data on Pearce has been gleaned from the Manuscript Census of Canada, 1901.

47. Ibid., 49.

48. Tyack, "Pilgrim's Progress," 268.

49. KPL, WHS, MC 14.5.a.b.c., Shoemaker Family Collection, "Draft letter, undated, by Elizabeth Shoemaker to her sister 'Han,'" and "Twentieth Annual Report of the Inspector of Public Schools of the County of Waterloo, For the Year ending 31st December, 1891," 15.

50. M.G. Sherk, "Reminiscences of Freeport—Waterloo County from 1867 to 1873," *Waterloo Historical Society* 12 (1924): 102.

51. Pearce, "School History," 46; City of Cambridge Archives, Minute Book of the Board of Trustees of the Preston School, June 13, 1905 to February 6, 1917, 29 November 1907, 7 April 1907, 10 December 1908; Waterloo County Board of Education, Wilmot Township S.S. 2, New Hamburg, School Board Minutes, 1875–1895, 27 December 1879.

52. KPL, WHS, WAT C-87, Manuscript Annual School Reports for the County of Waterloo, "Report on the Public Schools of the County of Waterloo by the County Inspector Thomas Pearce" (Waterloo: 'Chronicle Office', 1875). The schools in question were Waterloo Township, S.S. 25 (Beringer's); Wellesley Township, S.S. 7 (Jansis); Wellesley Township, S.S. 5 (Gless's); and Woolwich Township, S.S. 1 (Conestogo).

53. Although Pearce listed several educational obstacles in New Hamburg and Wilmot Centre, he did not dwell on the fact that both communities offered German-language instruction. KPL, WHS, WAT C-87, Manuscript Annual School Reports for the County of Waterloo, "Report on the Public Schools of the County of Waterloo, for the Year 1875, by the County Inspector Thomas Pearce" (Berlin: "Telegraph" Office, 1876), 6.

54. Ibid., "Report on the Public Schools of the County of Waterloo by the County Inspector Thomas Pearce, Esq. (for 1872)," 5–6 and 8.

55. Ibid.

56. Ibid., "Report on the Public Schools of the County of Waterloo (for 1872)," 5–6 and 8.

57. Archives of Ontario, RG 2–109–130, Misc. School Records, Box 2, *Report on the Public Schools of the County of Waterloo by the County Inspector Thomas Pearce (for 1872)* (Galt: Hutchinson, 1873), 5.

58. Waterloo County Board of Education, Woolwich Township, S.S. 8 (St. Jacobs), Visitors' Book, 1861–1912, 26 March 1880. See also earlier entries concerning reading on 29 April 1875 and 31 August 1875; KPL, WHS, KIT 6, Visitors' Book: Roman Catholic Separate School, 2 June 1876 and 6 February 1878; KPL, WHS, WAT C-87, Manuscript Annual School Reports for the County of Waterloo, "Twenty-Third Annual Report of the Inspector of Public Schools of the County of Waterloo, for the Year ending 31st December, 1894."

59. KPL, WHS, WAT C-87, Manuscript Annual School Reports for the County of Waterloo, "Report on the Public Schools of the County of Waterloo, for the Year 1875," 7.

60. See Steven L. Schlossman, "'Is There an American Tradition of Bilingual Education': German in the Public Elementary Schools, 1840–1919," *American Journal of Education* 91, 2 (1983), 139–86, and Library of Congress, L. Viereck, *Zwei Jahrhunderte Deutschen Unterrichts in den Vereinigten Staaten* (Braunschweig: Friedrich Viereck und Sohn, 1903).

61. "Letter sent by Thomas Pearce to Egerton Ryerson, November 9, 1871," in National Library of Canada, *Regulations and Correspondence*, 8.

62. Pearce, "School History," 33.

63. KPL, WHS, WAT C-87, Manuscript Annual School Reports for the County of Waterloo, "Report on the Public Schools of the County of Waterloo by the County Inspector Thomas Pearce, Esq. (for 1872)" (Galt, Ontario: S. Hutchinson, 1873), 1.

64. Ibid., "Report on the Public Schools of the County of Waterloo, for the Year 1877, by the County Inspector Thomas Pearce" (Berlin: Telegraph Office, 1878), 1.

65. In assigning the labels "German" and "English," the Commission of 1889 collapsed the county's many German groups into one, just as it subsumed Scotch, English, and Irish residents under "English"(-speaking). Lost in between were the 7 percent of the county's residents who belonged to neither cultural group. See National Library of Canada, *Regulations and Correspondence*, 110.

66. These schools served almost exclusively German areas. Only three schools were even attended by English-speaking students. On teaching methods, see KPL, WHS, WAT C-87, Report on the Public Schools of the County of Waterloo, for the year 1877, by the County Inspector Thomas Pearce, 1.

67. National Library of Canada, *Regulations and Correspondence*, 111–14.

68. Ibid., 110.

69. Ibid., 112. Similar levels of bilingualism existed in the French-Canadian settlements of south-western Ontario, where francophones and anglophones regularly interacted in the spheres of economy, transportation, religion, and education. See David Welsh, "Early Franco-Ontarian Schooling as a Reflection and Creator of Community Identity," *Ontario History* 85, 4 (December 1993): 312–47, and Jack Cecillon, "Turbulent Times in the Diocese of London: Bishop Fallon and the French-Language Controversy, 1910–18," *Ontario History* 87, 4 (December 1995): 369–95.

70. National Library of Canada, *Regulations and Correspondence*, 113.

71. *Berliner Journal*, 14 March 1889, 25 April 1889, 2 May 1889, 20 June 1889, 18 July 1889, 24 July 1890. For a concise summary of these debates, see Chad Gaffield, *Language, Schooling, and Cultural Conflict: The Origins of the French-Language Controversy in Ontario* (Kingston and Montreal: McGill-Queen's University Press, 1987), 5–30.

72. Toronto *Globe*, 9 and 12 March 1889; Toronto *Empire*, 9 March 1889; *Report of the Minister of Education for the Year 1887* (Toronto: Warwick and Sons, 1888), lix.

73. *Berliner Journal*, 23 December 1886.

74. Ibid., 20 June 1889. When the Toronto *Mail* railed against the publication of council resolutions in French, the *Journal* responded with biting irony: "Here, such resolutions are printed in both German and English, and German is sometimes spoken at the municipal council. Yet it is utter nonsense to assume that the British Empire will forfeit the Province of Ontario and the Dominion of Canada for this reason." Ibid., 23 December 1886.

75. Ibid., 5 September 1889 and 12 September 1889.

76. Ibid., 16 July 1874.

77. Ibid., 23 December 1873.

78. Ibid., 6 October 1881.

79. Ibid.

80. Ibid.

81. Ibid., 14 December 1876 and 4 January 1877. Between July 1872 and July 1880, the Waterloo County Board of Examiners compiled biographical profiles of candidates at the annual teachers' examinations that included information on birthplace. See KPL, WHS, WAT C-87, Record of Board of Examiners for Waterloo County. Berlin: s.n., 1853–1908.

82. *Berliner Journal*, 24 January 1877, 12 February 1903, 20 December 1905.

83. Ibid., 17 September 1885 and 7 December 1876. See also ibid., 1 October 1885, 29 October 1885, 10 December 1885, 24 December 1885, 10 January 1889.

84. Ibid., 7 December 1876.

85. Ibid., 4 January 1877. See also ibid., 5 April 1888 and 20 April 1899.

86. Waterloo County Board of Education, Minute Book of Berlin Teachers' Association, October 1891 to November 8, 1912, 10 May 1895.

87. See, for example, Bettina Goldberg, "Die Achtundvierziger und das Schulwesen in Amerika: Zur Theorie und Praxis ihrer Reformbestrebungen," *Amerikastudien/American Studies* 32, 4 (1987): 481–91.

88. This discussion draws upon a computer file which I created from the Manuscript Census of Canada, 1901. In keeping with the methodology developed by the *Canadian Families Project*, households, not individuals, constituted the unit of analysis. This approach proved to be invaluable, as it allowed me to examine the language dynamics within families and between generations. The database consisted of a 50 percent random sample of Berlin's population in 1901, encompassing a total of 4,747 individual cases. Note that the English-language skills of Berlin's German-origin residents far exceeded those of francophones in Eastern Ontario. See Gaffield, *Language, Schooling, and Cultural Conflict*, 181.

89. Karl Müller-Grote, "Onkel Karl: Deutschkanadische Lebensbilder," *German-Canadian Yearbook* 15 (1998): 116–20.

90. Manuscript Census of Canada, 1901.

91. Joshua Fishman, "Language Maintenance," in *Harvard Encyclopedia of American Ethnic Groups*, ed. Stephen Thernstrom (Cambridge, MA: Belknap Press, 1980), 629.

92. I should note that the term "mother tongue" denoted an ambiguous—and, frankly, confusing—concept in the 1901 Manuscript Census of Canada. As the census makers declared, "Mother tongue is one's native language, the language of his race, but not necessarily the language in which he thinks, or which he speaks most fluently, or uses chiefly in conversation." Mother tongue, in other words, signified an ethnically and racially defined community, rather than the home language of a given household or the dominant spoken language. At the same time, however, the census stipulated that the mother tongue "should be entered by name in column 33 if the person speaks the language, but not otherwise." See Chad Gaffield, "Linearity, Nonlinearity, and the Competing Constructions of Social Hierarchy in Early Twentieth-Century Canada: The Question of Language in 1901," *Historical Methods*, 33, 2 (Fall 2000): 255–260.

93. *Berlin News Record*, 27 April 1900.

94. Ibid., 4 July 1900.

95. Portes and Schauffler, "Language and the Second Generation," 642.

96. KPL, WHS, WAT C-87, Report on the Public Schools of the County of Waterloo, for the Year 1875, by the County Inspector Thomas Pearce.

97. See Müller's letter to the editors of the *Berliner Journal*, 17 May 1900, and A. Gläser's comments in ibid., 28 June 1900.

98. Ibid., 17 May 1900.

99. Ibid., 18 October 1905.

100. See the announcement published in the *Berlin News Record*, 21 June 1900.

101. *Berliner Journal*, 28 June 1900. In the ensuing debate, this point was elaborated by Reverend Teufel, Reverend Tuerk, Reverend Boese, Sheriff John Motz, and high school teacher J.W. Connor, among others.

102. Ibid., 28 June 28 1900.

103. Data on the association's membership has been compiled from the following sources: Manuscript Census of Canada, 1901; *Ontario Gazeteer and Directory*, 1901–02; *Vernon's Berlin, Waterloo and Bridgeport Directory for the Years 1903 to 1905*; *Ontario Gazeteer and Directory*, 1905–06; *Province of Ontario: Gazeteer and Directory*, 1910–11; *Vernon's City of Berlin and Town of Waterloo and Bridgeport Directory* for the Years 1912–13; Middleton and Landon, *Province of Ontario: A History, 1615–1927, vol.3* (Toronto: Dominion, 1927–28); Alexander Fraser, *History of Ontario: Its Resources and Development* (Toronto: The Canadian History Company, 1927), vol. 2; KPL, WHS, MC 6.21, Elias Weber Bingeman Snider Collection, "Annual Report of the Board of Trade of the Town of Berlin, 1905"; W.V. Uttley, *A History of Kitchener, Ontario* (Waterloo: Wilfrid Laurier Press, 1975 [1937]); Elizabeth Bloomfield, "City-Building Processes in Berlin/Kitchener and Waterloo, 1870–1930" (PhD diss., History, University of Guelph, 1981); *Dictionary of Canadian Biography*, 1911–20, vol.14 (Toronto: University of Toronto Press, 1998).

104. For a point of comparison, see Roger Chickering, "*We Men Who Feel Most German*": *A Cultural Study of the Pan-German League, 1886–1914* (Boston: George Allen and Unwin, 1984), 111.

105. Fifteen percent of the members could not be identified.

106. As compiled by Bloomfield, "City-Building Processes in Berlin/Kitchener and Waterloo," 502.

107. Ibid., 502.

108. The mayors in question were Hugo Kranz (1874–78), John Motz (1880–81), H.G. Lackner (1886–87), Louis Breithaupt (1888–89), Conrad Bitzer (1892), Daniel Hibner (1894–95), J.C. Breithaupt (1896–97), George Rumpel (1898), William H.E. Schmalz (1911–12), and John E. Hett (1915–16).

109. *Berliner Journal*, 28 June 1900.

110. The evidence of association meetings is fragmentary at best, preserved only in the columns of the *Berliner Journal*. But the fact that the paper rarely quoted speeches by working-class members seems to indicate that the latter belonged to the lower ranks of the German School Association.

111. *Berliner Journal*, 18 October 1905. See also Müller-Grote, "Onkel Karl: Deutschkanadische Lebensbilder," 107–255.

112. The following denominations were represented among the eleven clergymen in the German School Association: Lutheran (3), Evangelical Association (2), Baptist (2), Roman Catholic (1), Presbyterian (1), New Jerusalem (1), Unknown (1).

113. As Louis Breithaupt noted in his diary, this shift had begun as early as 1888: "By a vote of 54 to 20, it was to-day decided by our congregation to have English services every 2d. Sabbath evening." See UW, DLRBR, Diaries of Louis Jacob Breithaupt, 18 March 1888. In Berlin's St. Petri Church,

as well, parishioners asked Pastor von Pirch to hold an English service in May 1884. See *Berliner Journal*, 8 May 1884.

114. English and McLaughlin, *Kitchener: An Illustrated History*, 87–88, and Gottlieb Leibbrandt, *Little Paradise: Aus Geschichte und Leben der Deutschkanadier in der County Waterloo, Ontario, 1800–1975* (Kitchener, ON: Allprint Company Limited, 1977), 158–59.

115. Quoted in the *Berlin News Record*, 4 July 1900.

116. *Berliner Journal*, 27 June 1901.

117. Pearce, "School History, Waterloo County and Berlin," 41.

118. Manuscript Census of Canada, 1901, and *Berliner Journal*, 6 May 1880 and 3 June 1884.

119. *Berliner Journal*, 27 June 1901.

120. Ibid., 24 August 1904.

121. Ibid. See also *Berliner Journal*, 15 May 1902, and Waterloo County Board of Education, "Berlin Board Minutes, 1898–1908," 13 May 1902.

122. Ibid.

123. The work of the local German school inspectors is described in their biannual reports that were published in the *Berliner Journal*. See, in particular, *Berliner Journal*, 27 December 1900, 4 January 1905, 5 December 1906, 8 April 1908, 6 January 1909, 28 June 1911.

124. Waterloo County Board of Education, Berlin Board Minutes, 1898–1908, 16 January 1901.

125. Ibid., 27 March 1906, 29 May 1906, 28 December 1909, 20 September 1912.

126. *Berliner Journal*, 25 June 1903.

127. Ibid., and 27 August 1903. See also Waterloo County Board of Education, Berlin Board Minutes, 1898–1908, 1 September 1903.

128. *Berliner Journal*, December 31, 1903.

129. Waterloo County Board of Education, Berlin Board Minutes, 1898–1908, 26 October 1893, 17 January 1894, 6 April 1899, 10 July 1899, 7 December 1899, 18 December 1899, 30 August 1900.

130. Ibid., 31 August 1900.

131. Compared with their male colleagues, Berlin's women teachers remained poorly paid. In 1901, Berlin's two male principals received an annual salary of $875; the town's two male teachers commanded an annual salary of $536; Berlin's lone female principal earned $400 a year; and the two female German-language teachers were paid an annual salary of $388. At the bottom rank of the salary scale were five kindergarten teachers with an annual income of $315 and fourteen additional female teachers, whose income averaged $271 per year. See also *Berliner Journal*, 2 September 1908.

132. Waterloo County Board of Education, Berlin Board Minutes, 1898–1908, 26 June 1906.

133. *Berliner Journal*, 4 April 1906.

134. Waterloo County Board of Education, Berlin Board Minutes, 1898–1908, 27 March 1906, and *Berliner Journal*, 28 March 1906.

135. *Berliner Journal*, 14 February 1906.

136. Ibid. See also *Berliner Journal*, 4 April 1906.

137. Waterloo County Board of Education, Berlin Board Minutes, 1898–1908, 26 June 1906.

138. *Berliner Journal*, 14 February 1906, and Waterloo County Board of Education, Berlin Board Minutes, 1898–1908, 10 July 1906.

139. *Berliner Journal*, 21 June 1905, 5 December 1906.

140. Ibid., 12 February 1903, 25 June 1903, 23 July 1903.

141. Ibid., 24 August 1904, 7 September 1904.

142. Ibid., 11 March 1908.

143. Waterloo County Board of Education, Berlin Board Minutes, 1898–1908, 26 November 1907, 28 January 1908, and 23 June 1908.

144. Ibid., 27 February 1908.

145. *Berliner Journal*, 14 September 1904, 21 June 1905, 5 July 1905, 19 July 1905; Waterloo County Board of Education, Berlin Public School Board, Minutes, 1908–1915, 18 August 1911 and 19 April 1912.

146. Waterloo County Board of Education, Berlin Public School Board, Minutes, 1908–1915, 17 November 1911.

147. Archives of Ontario ,Sir James P. Whitney Papers, F5, MU 3132, "Memo Regarding Teaching of German in Bilingual Schools."

148. This discussion follows Frisse, *Berlin, Ontario (1800–1916)*, 364–65.

149. The controversy is outlined in Patricia P. McKegney's *The Kaiser's Bust: A Study of War-Time Propaganda in Berlin, Ontario, 1914–1918* (Wellesley, ON: Bamberg Heritage Series, 1991).

150. The committee's report was included verbatim in the *Berlin News Record*, 3 March 1915.

151. Indeed, the local culture of Waterloo County was not fundamentally affected by the war years. For the creative ways in which Waterloo County's German-origin residents reinvented their ethnicity in the post-war period by seizing upon the county's Mennonite heritage and downplaying its "Germanic" culture, see Geoffrey Hayes, "From Berlin to the Trek of the Conestoga: A Revisionist Approach to Waterloo County's German Identity," *Ontario History* 91, 2 (1999): 131–49.

152. *Berliner Journal*, 6 January 1915.

153. *Berlin News Record*, 17 March 1915.

154. *Daily Telegraph*, 20 March 1915.

155. *Berlin News Record*, 19 March 1915.

156. Ibid.

157. Ibid.

158. Berlin *Daily Telegraph*, 20 March 1915.

159. *Berlin News Record*, 19 March 1915.

160. Berlin *Daily Telegraph*, 20 March 1915.

161. *Berlin News Record*, 3 March 1915.

162. Trustee Albrecht, quoted in the Berlin *Daily Telegraph*, 19 March 1915.

163. Trustee Charles Ruby, quoted in the *Berlin News Record*, 3 March 1915 and 19 March 1915; Trustee Lang, quoted in the Berlin *Daily Telegraph*, 19 March 1915.

164. *Berliner Journal*, 31 March 1915.

165. *Berlin News Record*, 17 March 1915, and University of Waterloo, Doris Lewis Rare Book Room, Breithaupt Hewetson Clark Collection, Box #8, "Catherine Olive, née Breithaupt (1896–1977)," Letter by Louis Breithaupt, 3 September 1913.

166. For the "cult of heritage" that elevated a mother tongue to a symbol of ethnicity, see also Jeffrey Shandler, "Beyond the Mother Tongue: Learning the Meaning of Yiddish in America," *Jewish Social Studies* 6, 3 (2000): 98.

167. For a point of comparison, see Dirk Hoerder's *Cultures in Contact: World Migrations in the Second Millennium* (Durham, NC: Duke University Press, 2002), particularly xx–xxi.

168. Kalbfleisch, *The History of the Pioneer German Language Press of Ontario, 1835–1918*, 71.

169. For selected works on linguistic nationalism in the late nineteenth century, see Eugen Weber, *Peasants into Frenchmen: The Modernization of Rural France, 1870–1914* (London: Chatto and Windus, 1977), particularly 303–18; John Hutchinson, *The Dynamics of Cultural Nationalism: The Gaelic Revival and the Creation of the Irish Nation State* (London: Allen and Unwin, 1987); and Hobsbawm, *Nations and Nationalism since 1780*.

CHAPTER THREE

1. Library of Congress, "Protokolle des Ersten Deutschen Lehrertages in Louisvile, Ky., am 1., 2., 3. und 4. August, 1870," *Amerikanische Schulzeitung* [hereafter *Schulzeitung*] 1, 1 (1870): 3–18.

2. "Gruß an die Leser," in ibid., 2–3.

3. Ibid. See also "Rede gehalten auf dem ersten deutschen Lehrertag in Louisville, Ky., von Karl Knortz von Oshkosh, Wisc.," *Schulzeitung* 1, 3 (1870): 80–84. For criticism of the reliance on textbooks, see "Rede gehalten auf dem ersten deutsch-amerikanischen Lehrertage von A. Schneck, Lehrer am deutsch-amerikanischen Seminar in Detroit, Michigan," *Schulzeitung* 1, 2 (1870): 51–52, and E. Dapprich, "Die Stellung der öffentlichen und deutsch-amerikanischen Schule zum Deutschthum in den Vereinigten Staaten," *Schulzeitung* 3, 1 (1872): 16.

4. "Protokoll der dritten Hauptsitzung," *Schulzeitung* 1, 1 (1870): 13.

5. Louis Stierlin, "Der bisherige Mangel an Nationalstolz bei den Deutschen und die Ursachen desselben," *Schulzeitung* 1, 2 (1870): 60–62.

6. "Eröffnungs-Rede des Herrn Direktor E. Feldner," *Schulzeitung* 1, 1 (1870): 21–27.

7. William J. Reese, "The Origins of Progressive Education," *History of Education Quarterly* 41, 1 (2001): 2.

8. William J. Reese, *Power and the Promise of School Reform: Grassroot Movements during the Progressive Era* (Boston: Routledge, 1986), xxi. For a summary description of German peace jubilees in the United States, see Library of Congress, *Die Deutschen in Amerika und die deutsch-amerikanischen Friedensfeste im Jahr 1871: Eine Erinnerungs-Schrift für die Deutschen diesseits und jenseits des Oceans* (New York: Verlags-Expedition des deutsch-amerikanischen Conversations-Lexicons, 1871).

9. For a point of comparison see Ann Taylor Allen, "American and German Women in the Kindergarten Movement, 1850–1914," in *German Influences on Education in the United States to 1917*, ed. Henry Geitz et al. (New York: Cambridge University Press, 1995), 86.

10. See Zimmermann, "Ethnics against Ethnicity," 1383–1404, for an innovative interpretation of such clashes. Also of interest is Goldberg, "The German-English Academy," 177–92.

11. Note that the *Amerikanische Schulzeitung* changed its named frequently; it subsequently appeared as *Erziehungs-Blätter für Schule und Haus* [hereafter *Erziehungs-Blätter*], *Pädagogische Monatshefte/Pedagogical Monthly: Zeitschrift für das deutschamerikanische Schulwesen* [*Pädagogische Monatshefte*], and *Monatshefte für deutsche Sprache und Pädagogik* [*Monatshefte*]. The *Schulzeitung*, in its various incarnations, can be consulted at the Library of Congress, Washington, DC.

12. A similar movement toward centralization and professionalization can be observed in the history of the National Education Association (NEA). See Lawrence A. Cremin, *American Education: The Metropolitan Experience, 1876–1980* (New York: Harper and Row, 1988), 229, and David B.

Tyack, *The One Best System: A History of American Urban Education* (Cambridge, MA: Harvard University Press, 1974), 42.

13. Kathleen Neils Conzen, "Immigrants in Nineteenth-Century Agricultural History," in *Agriculture and National Development: Views on the Nineteenth Century*, ed. Lou Ferleger (Ames, Iowa, 1990), 303–42.

14. Ohio, Kentucky, and Indiana sent 37, 24, and 21 delegates respectively. See "Mitgliederliste," *Schulzeitung* 1, 1 (1870): 20.

15. "Eröffnungs-Rede des Herrn Direktor E. Feldner," *Schulzeitung* 1, 1 (1870): 24. For a history of the Forty-Eighters see, among others, Charlotte L. Brancoforte, ed., *The German Forty-Eighters in the United States* (New York: Peter Lang, 1989).

16. Goldberg, "Die Achtundvierziger und das Schulwesen in Amerika," 484–87.

17. "Protokoll der ersten Hauptsitzung," *Schulzeitung* 1, 1 (1870): 12; "Zweite Hauptversammlung," *Schulzeitung* 2, 1 (1871): 9; Hermann Schuricht, *Geschichte der Deutschen Schulbestrebungen in Amerika* (Leipzig: Verlag Friedrich Fleischer, 1884), 109–15.

18. Goldberg, "Die Achtundvierziger und das Schulwesen in Amerika," 482–84.

19. "Protokolle der dritten Hauptsitzung," *Schulzeitung* 1, 1 (1870): 17.

20. Ibid.

21. "Der 3. deutsch-amerikanische Lehrertag," *Schulzeitung* 3, 1 (1872): 44–45.

22. "Protokolle des zweiten Deutsch-Amerikanischen Lehrertages," *Schulzeitung* 2, 1 (1871): 12: "die erst im Werden begriffene amerikanische Nation."

23. See, for instance, ibid., 12–13 and 37; L. Klemm, "Was trennt die deutsche von der amerikanischen Schule and was verbindet Beide," *Schulzeitung* 3, 1 (1872): 12; "Über deutsch-amerikanische Schulen und Lehrer," *Schulzeitung* 1, 3 (1873): 11; "Protokolle des 6. deutsch-amerikanischen Lehrertages zu Toledo, Ohio," *Erziehungs-Blätter* 2, 12 (1875): 2; "Protokolle des 8. deutsch-amerikanischen Lehrertages," *Erziehungs-Blätter* 4, 12 (1877): 2.

24. For an elegant formulation of the "melting pot" theory in German-American thinking, see Kathleen Neils Conzen, "German-Americans and the Invention of Ethnicity," in *America and the Germans: An Assessment of a Three-Hundred-Year History*, ed. Frank Trommler and Joseph McVeigh, vol. 1, *Immigration, Language, and Ethnicity* (Philadelphia: University of Pennsylvania Press, 1985), 138–39, and Conzen, Gerber, Morawska, Pozzetta, and Vecoli, "The Invention of Ethnicity: A Perspective from the U.S.A.," 11.

25. "Bleiben wir uns selbst treu!" *Schulzeitung* 1, 2 (1870): 63: "mit dem Geiste der Sprache geht ein Theil des Geistes der Nation in den Lernenden über."

26. "Rede gehalten auf dem ersten deutschen Lehrertage in Louisville, Ky., von Karl Knortz," *Schulzeitung* 1, 3 (1870): 82–83.

27. "Eröffnungs-Rede des Herrn Direktor E. Feldner," *Schulzeitung* 1, 1 (1870): 23: "Bürger zweier Zungen."

28. "Verfassung des D.-A. Lehrerbundes," *Schulzeitung* 2, 1 (1871): 3.

29. Dapprich, "Die Stellung der öffentlichen und deutsch-amerikanischen Schule," *Schulzeitung* 3, 1 (1872): 16. See also "Rede gehalten auf dem ersten amerikanischen Lehrertag von A. Schneck," *Schulzeitung* 1, 2 (1870): 50–53.

30. "Eröffnungs-Rede des Herrn Direktor E. Feldner," *Schulzeitung* 1, 1 (1870): 22. For a brief history of free-thinking German-American private schools, see Schuricht, *Geschichte der Deutschen Schulbestrebungen in Amerika*, 56–66.

31. W. Müller, "Ist die deutsch-amerikanische Schule überflüssig," *Schulzeitung* 3, 12 (1873): 449, and A. Douai, "Zweisprachiger Unterricht," *Schulzeitung* 1, 1 (1873): 16.

32. Dapprich, "Die Stellung der öffentlichen und deutsch-amerikanischen Schule," *Schulzeitung* 3, 1 (1872):16. See also Goldberg, "Die Achtundvierziger und das Schulwesen in Amerika, 485, and Schuricht, *Geschichte der Deutschen Schulbestrebungen in Amerika*, 105–6.

33. Müller, "Ist die deutsch-amerikanische Schule überflüssig," *Schulzeitung* 3, 12 (1873): 449.

34. Quintus Fixlein, "Aendern wir unsere Taktik!" *Schulzeitung* 2, 8 (1872): 269–70.

35. See Klemm, "Was trennt die deutsche von der amerikanischen Schule," *Schulzeitung* 3, 1 (1872): 9–13 and the ensuing debate, 20–22.

36. Ibid.

37. According to Paul Rudolph Fessler, these cities were St. Louis, Missouri (1864), Chicago, Illinois (1865), Buffalo, New York (1866), Milwaukee, Wisconsin (1870), Cleveland, Ohio (1870), New York, New York (1870), Indianapolis, Indiana (1871), and Baltimore, Maryland (1874). See Fessler, "Speaking in Tongues: German-Americans and the Heritage of Bilingual Education in American Public Schools" (PhD diss., Texas A&M University, 1997), 23.

38. See William J. Akers, *Cleveland Schools in the Nineteenth Century* (Cleveland, Ohio: W.M. Bayne Printing House, 1901); Dimitri Katasreas, "The Public and Private English-German Schools of Baltimore: 1836 to 1904," (PhD diss., Georgetown University, 1994); Library of Congress, Viereck, *Zwei Jahrhunderte Deutschen Unterrichts in den Vereinigten Staaten*; Heinz Kloss, "Die deutsch-amerikanische Schule," *Jahrbuch für Amerikastudien* 7 (1962): 141–75.

39. Schlossman, "'Is There an American Tradition of Bilingual Education?'" 146–47. For German schooling in Cincinnati, see also John B. Shotwell, *A History of the Schools of Cincinnati* (Cincinnati: The School Life Company, 1902) and Carolyn R. Toth, *German-English Bilingual Schools in America: The Cincinnati Tradition in Historical Context* (New York: Peter Lang, 1990).

40. "Dritte Hauptversammlung," *Schulzeitung* 2, 1 (1871): 12–13, and H. Woldmann, "Der gegenwärtige Stand des deutschen Unterrichts in den Ver. Staaten," *Monatshefte* 8, 7–8 (1907), 221–22.

41. According to Kathleen Neils Conzen, Germans represented 37 percent of all immigrants in 1850, a figure that equalled almost a million. See Conzen, "Patterns of German-American History," in *Germans in America: Retrospect and Prospect*, ed. Randall M. Miller (Philadelphia: German Society of Pennsylvania, 1984), 17.

42. David Gerber, "Language Maintenance, Ethnic Group Formation, and Public Schools: Changing Patterns of German Concern, Buffalo, 1837–1874," *Journal of American Ethnic History* 4, 1 (1984): 49.

43. St. Louis School Board Minutes, 1869, 29–30; as quoted in Schlossman, "Is There an American Tradition of Bilingual Education?" 150–55.

44. Schuricht, *Geschichte der Deutschen Schulbestrebungen in Amerika*, 64–66.

45. Ibid., 185.

46. Ibid., 76.

47. For an excellent discussion of this "reform movement," see Susan N. Bayley, "The Direct Method and Modern Language Teaching in England, 1880–1918," *History of Education* 27, 1 (1998): 39.

48. See, for instance, Ortmann, "Der Sprachunterricht in den beiden ersten Schuljahren: Referat für den deutsch-amerikanischen Lehrerverein zu Baltimore," *Schulzeitung* 2, 7 (1872): 236.

49. Bayley, "The Direct Method and Modern Language Teaching in England," 39.

50. Ibid., 39 and 42. See also Teodor Thurm, "Wie kann die deutsche Sprache mit Erfolg in die

Volksschule eingeführt werden?" *Schulzeitung* 3, 2 (1872), 61–62, and L. Klemm, "Deutscher Sprachunterricht für Kinder nicht deutscher Eltern," *Schulzeitung* 2, 6 (1875): 5.

51. "Rede gehalten auf dem ersten deutschen Lehrertag in Louisville, Ky., von Karl Knortz von Oshkosh, Wisc.," *Schulzeitung* 1, 3 (1870): 79–80. See also W.R. Hailmann, "Thesen zu einem Vortrag über das Thema: Mittel und Wege zur direkten Beeinflussung des Anglo-Amerikaner zu Gunsten deutscher Erziehungsmethoden," *Schulzeitung* 1 (1871): 203.

52. "Rede gehalten auf dem ersten deutschen Lehrertag in Louisville, Ky., von Karl Knortz von Oshkosh, Wisc.," *Schulzeitung* 1, 3 (1870): 82.

53. Ibid., 84; Ortmann, "Der Sprachunterricht in den ersten beiden Schuljahren," *Schulzeitung* 2, 6 (1872): 205 and 2, 7 (1872): 239; "Deutscher Unterricht für Anglo-Amerikaner," *Erziehungs-Blätter* 3, 1 (1875): 7. For a point of comparison, see Susan N. Bayley, "'Life Is Too Short to Learn German': Modern Languages in English Elementary Education, 1872–1904," *History of Education* 18, 1 (1989): 62.

54. Ortmann, "Der Sprachunterricht in den ersten beiden Schuljahren," *Schulzeitung* 2, 6 (1872): 205–6.

55. Ibid., 206.

56. Ibid., 205–6.

57. Ibid., 2, 7 (1872), 236.

58. Ibid., 238.

59. Ibid., 238–39.

60. L. Klemm, "Deutscher Sprachunterricht für Kinder nicht deutscher Eltern," *Schulzeitung* 2, 6 (1875): 5.

61. H. Woldmann, "Deutscher Unterricht für Anglo-Amerikaner," *Erziehungs-Blätter* 3, 1 (1875): 7.

62. "Rede gehalten auf dem ersten deutschen Lehrertage in Louisville, Ky., von Karl Knortz von Oshkosh, Wis.," *Schulzeitung* 1, 3 (1870): 79.

63. See, for instance, "Eröffnungs-Rede des Herrn Direktor E. Feldner," *Schulzeitung* 1, 1 (1870): 24.

64 P. Stahl, "Wie läßt sich die entwickelnde Methode in die englische Normal- und Volksschule einführen?" *Schulzeitung* 3, 1 (1872): 8; "Verhandlungen des dritten deutsch-amerikanischen Lehrertages: Dritte Hauptversammlung," *Schulzeitung* 3, 3 (1872): 112.

65. Stahl, "Wie läßt sich die entwickelnde Methode in die englische Normal- und Volksschule einführen?," 8; "Die deutsche Presse New Yorks," *Schulzeitung* 3, 1 (1872): 47.

66. Stahl, "Wie läßt sich die entwickelnde Methode in die englische Normal- und Volksschule einführen?," 9.

67. L. Klemm, "Wie ist der deutsche Unterricht in die öffentlichen Schulen einzuführen an Plätzen, wo er noch nicht besteht?" *Schulzeitung* 2, 1 (1874): 2–3.

68. Ibid., 3.

69. Daniel T. Rodgers, *Atlantic Crossings: Social Politics in a Progressive Age* (Cambridge, MA: Harvard University Press, 1998), 4.

70. Cecilia Elizabeth O'Leary, *To Die For: The Paradox of American Patriotism* (Princeton, NJ: Princeton University Press, 1999), 177 and 292.

71 Stahl, "Wie läßt sich die entwickelnde Methode in die englische Normal- und Volksschule einführen?," 7.

72. Ibid., 8; "Bericht über die Thätigkeit des N.-Amer. Lehrerbundes für den 3. Lehrertag," *Schulzeitung* 3, 1 (1872): 4; "Arbeitsresultate des 3. Lehrertages," *Schulzeitung* 3, 1 (1872): 45.

73. Schuricht, *Geschichte der Deutschen Schulbestrebungen in Amerika*, 71.

74. "Die 12. jährliche Versammlung der National Educational Association," *Schulzeitung* 3, 1 (1872): 46–47. See also "Die Konvention der nationalen Lehrer-Assoziation in Elmira," *Erziehungs-Blätter* 1, 1 (1873): 9.

75. Stahl, "Wie läßt sich die entwickelnde Methode in die englische Normal- und Volksschule einführen?," 7, and Klemm, "Was trennt die deutsche von der amerikanischen Schule und was verbindet Beide?" *Schulzeitung* 3, 1 (1872): 12.

76. "Verhandlungen des dritten deutsch-amerikanischen Lehrertages: Dritte Hauptversammlung," *Schulzeitung* 3, 3 (1872): 109–11.

77. "Protokolle des 5ten Deutsch-Amerikanischen Lehrertages, gehalten in Detroit, Mich., am 4–7 August 1874," *Schulzeitung* 1, 12 (1874): 2–3.

78. "Protokolle des 7. deutsch-amerikanischen Lehrertages zu Cleveland, O.," *Erziehungs-Blätter* 3, 12 (1876): 1.

79. This discussion has been informed by Conzen, "Mainstream and Side Channels," 8.

80. See, for instance, Thurm, "Wie kann die deutsche Sprache mit Erfolg in die Volksschule eingeführt werden?" *Schulzeitung* 3, 2 (1872): 61 and L. Klemm, "Wie ist der deutsche Unterricht in die öffentlichen Schulen einzuführen?" *Schulzeitung* 2, 1 (1874): 2–5.

81. "Die deutsche Sprache in den städtischen Schulen," in *Geschichte der Deutschen*, 80-81, and Ismar S. Ellison, "The Germans of Buffalo: An Historical Essay," in *Publications of the Buffalo Historical Society*, vol. 2 (Buffalo: Bigelow Brothers, 1880), 142–43.

82. BECPL, Special Collection, Minutes No. 28, August 13, 1866, and Minutes No. 29, August 20, 1866, in *Proceedings of the Common Council of the City of Buffalo, 1862* (Buffalo: Joseph Warren and Co., 1863), 435 and 472. See also Buffalo *Daily Courier*, 12 May 1873, and *Geschichte der Deutschen*, 79.

83. The contours of these controversies have been mapped by Gerber, "Language Maintenance, Ethnic Group Formation, and Public Schools." See also Buffalo *Demokrat*, 15 August 1866 and 4 September 1866, 2.

84. Andrew P. Yox, "Decline of the German-American Community in Buffalo, 1855–1925," (PhD diss., University of Chicago, 1983), 91–112.

85. Ibid.

86. Buffalo and Erie County Historical Society (hereafter BECHS), Buffalo Superintendent of Public Schools, *Thirty-Fifth Annual Report of the Superintendent of Education of the City of Buffalo for the year ending December 31, 1872* (Buffalo: Buffalo Printing Company, 1873), 47.

87. Gerber, "Language Maintenance, Ethnic Group Formation, and Public Schools," 47.

88. *Thirty-Fifth Annual Report of the Superintendent of Education*, 45–46, and *Geschichte der Deutschen*, 80.

89. Gerber, "Language Maintenance, Ethnic Group Formation, and Public Schools," 46.

90. *Thirty-Fifth Annual Report of the Superintendent of Education*, 46–47.

91. BECPL, Special Collection, Minutes No. 45, April 14, 1873, in *Proceedings of the Common Council of the City of Buffalo, 1873* (Buffalo: Haas and Kelley, 1874), 251.

92. Gerber, "Language Maintenance, Ethnic Group Formation, and Public Schools," 47.

93. Quoted in the Buffalo *Express*, 15 April 1873.

94. See, for instance, Buffalo *Express*, 18 April 1873; Buffalo *Daily Courier*, 12 May 1873; Buffalo *Freie*

ENDNOTES

Presse, 20 May 1873; Buffalo *Demokrat*, 20 May 1873; BECPL, Special Collection, Minutes No. 24, June 2, 1873, in *Proceedings of the Common Council of the City of Buffalo, 1873*, 399.

95. Buffalo *Express*, 18 April 1873.

96. Gerber, "Language Maintenance, Ethnic Group Formation, and Public Schools," 49.

97. BECPL, Special Collection, Minutes No. 9, March 2, 1874, in *Proceedings of the Common Council of the City of Buffalo, 1874*, 177–79.

98. "Minutes No. 13, March 23, 1874," in Ibid., 235–36.

99. Ibid., 236.

100. *Union*, Evansville (Indiana), as quoted in the Buffalo *Freie Presse*, 10 May 1873.

101. *Seebote*, Milwaukee (Wisconsin), as quoted in the Buffalo *Freie Presse*, 6 May 1873.

102. *Union*, Evansville (Indiana), as quoted in the Buffalo *Freie Presse*, 10 May 1873; *Illinois Staatszeitung*, Chicago, and New Yorker *Demokrat*, as quoted in the Buffalo *Freie Presse*, 6 May 1873.

103. Yox, "Decline of the German-American Community in Buffalo," 142.

104. Conzen, "German-Americans and the Invention of Ethnicity," 139.

105. Buffalo *Freie Presse*, 25 March 1874.

106. "31. Jahresversammlung in Indianapolis, Ind.," *Pädagogische Monatshefte* 2, 7 (1901): 291.

107. M.D. Learned, "When Should German Instruction Begin in the Public Schools?" *Pädagogische Monatshefte* 3, 3 (1902): 88.

108. *Annual Report of the Superintendent of Education of the City of Buffalo, 1910–1911* (Buffalo: 1912), 41.

109. The percentage of Buffalo's German population was likely to be even higher, as Andrew P. Yox's estimate is calculated not for the year 1910 but for 1915. See Library of Congress, *Census of the United States, 1910*, and Yox, "Decline of the German-American Community in Buffalo," 385.

110. *Annual Report of the Superintendent of Education of the City of Buffalo, 1910–1911*, 41.

111. For endorsements of Superintendent Henry P. Emerson by local German teachers, see Bertha Raab, "Buffalo," *Pädagogische Monatshefte* 1, 7 (1900): 37, and J. Lübben, "Buffalo," *Monatshefte* 13, 1 (1912): 17–18.

112. *Thirty-Fifth Annual Report of the Superintendent of Education of the City of Buffalo*, 33–34.

113. Schuricht, *Geschichte der Deutschen Schulbestrebungen in Amerika*, 89–91. See also "Das Schulwesen in der Stadt Buffalo, N.Y.," *Erziehungs-Blätter* 4, 3 (1876): 4–5.

114. Ibid. See also BECPL, Special Collection, Minutes No. 27, July 3, 1882, and Special Session, Friday, July 7, 1882, in *Proceedings of the Common Council of Buffalo for 1882* (Buffalo: The Courier Company, 1883), 677 and 701.

115. *Annual Report of the Superintendent of Education of the City of Buffalo, 1882* (Buffalo: Henry Nauert, 1883), 49. See also BECPL, Special Collection, J. Henry Wood, ed., *Schools of Buffalo* (Buffalo: Mrs. Ida C. Wood, 1899), 10.

116. *Annual Report of the Superintendent of Education, 1888–9 of the City of Buffalo* (Buffalo: Times Printing House, 1890), 32.

117. Original emphasis. See *Annual Report of the Superintendent of Education of the City of Buffalo, 1889–90* (Buffalo: Haas and Klein, 1891), 31.

118. *Annual Report of the Superintendent of Education of the City of Buffalo, 1893–94* (Buffalo: Baker, Johnes and Co., 1894), 65.

119. *Annual Report of the Superintendent of Education of the City of Buffalo, 1894–1895* (Buffalo: C.E. Northrop, 1895), 83.

120. *Annual Report of the Superintendent of Education of the City of Buffalo, 1897–1898* (Buffalo: The Wenborne-Sumner Co., 1899), 61; *Annual Report of the Superintendent of Education of the City of Buffalo, 1894–1895*, 85; *Annual Report of the Superintendent of Education of the City of Buffalo, 1896–97* (Buffalo: The Wenborne-Sumner Co., 1897), 85. See also the article by Johannes L. Lübben, teacher of German at the Masten Park High School in Buffalo, "Die Direkte Methode in der amerikanischen Schule: Das Brauchbare an derselben für uns," *Monatshefte* 14, 7 (September 1913): 251.

121. *Annual Report of the Superintendent of Education of the City of Buffalo, 1894–1895*, 84, and Lübben, "Die Direkte Methode in der amerikanischen Schule," 251.

122. *Annual Report of the Superintendent of Education of the City of Buffalo, 1894–1895*, 81.

123. Yox, "Decline of the German-American Community," 221–24.

124. *Annual Report of the Superintendent of Education of the City of Buffalo, 1894–1895*, 92.

125. Ibid., 91–92.

126. Ibid., 91, and *Annual Report of the Superintendent of Education of the City of Buffalo, 1897–1898*, 90–91.

127. *Annual Report of the Superintendent of Education of the City of Buffalo, 1887–8* (Buffalo: 1889), 28–31.

128. *Annual Report of the Superintendent of Education of the City of Buffalo, 1894–1895*, 91–92, 123–24, and 161.

129. See, in particular, the articles by Prof. M.D. Learned, "The 'Lehrerbund' and the Teachers of German in America," *Pädagogische Monatshefte* 1, 1 (1899): 10–16; "Deutsch gegen Englisch, oder Deutsch neben Englisch," *Pädagogische Monatshefte* 2, 8 (1901): 290–93; "When Should German Instruction Begin in the Public Schools?" *Pädagogische Monatshefte* 3, 3 (1902), 86–89.

130. Leo Stern, "Vergangenheit und Zukunft des Lehrerbundes," *Monatshefte* 8, 7–8 (1907), 208–9. Here, one is reminded of the "organizational revolution" that characterized American schooling at the end of the nineteenth century. As David B. Tyack argues, "in the governance of education, lay community control gave way to the corporate-bureaucratic model under the guise of 'taking the school out of politics.'" See Tyack, *The One Best System*, 6.

131. See Reese, "The Origins of Progressive Education."

132. Lawrence A. Cremin, *The Transformation of the Schools: Progressivism in American Education, 1876–1957* (New York: Vintage Books, 1961), and Daniel Fallon, "German Influences on American Education," in *The German-American Encounter: Conflict and Cooperation between Two Cultures, 1800–2000*, ed. Frank Trommler and Elliott Shore (New York: Berghahn Books, 2001), 83.

133. "Bericht des Komitees zur Pflege des Deutschen," *Pädagogische Monatshefte* 1, 1 (1899): 21.

134. See the report of the committee of ten to the National Educational Association in 1894, quoted in Library of Congress, L. Viereck, "Chapter XIVL German Instruction in American Schools," in United States Bureau of Education, *Report of the Commissioner of Education for the Year 1900–1901*, vol. 1 (Washington: Government Printing Office, 1902), 639.

135. Ibid., 583–85. See also "Protokoll der 31. Jahresversammlung des Nationalen Deutsch-amerikanischen Lehrerbundes," *Pädagogische Monatshefte* 2, 9 (1901): 314.

136. *Annual Report of the Superintendent of Education of the City of Buffalo, 1894–1895*, 91.

137. Library of Congress, Education Department of the State of New York, *Examination of the Public School System of the City of Buffalo* (Albany: The University of the State of New York, 1916), 109.

138. *Annual Report of the Superintendent of Education of the City of Buffalo, 1893–4*, 64–65.

139. *Annual Report of the Superintendent of Education of the City of Buffalo, 1899–1900* (Buffalo: The Wenborne-Sumner Co., 1901), 67.

140. A similar "massive undercalculation" has been observed for the U.S. aggregate census. See Nadel, *Little Germany: Ethnicity, Religion, and Class in New York City*, 41.

141. Library of Congress, Education Department of the State of New York, *Examination of the Public School System of the City of Buffalo*, 108.

142. *Annual Report of the Superintendent of Education of the City of Buffalo, 1893–4*, 63, and *Annual Report of the Superintendent of Education of the City of Buffalo, 1896–97*, 83. See also Yox, "Decline of the German-American Community in Buffalo," 247.

143. As much is suggested by the names of the German teachers listed in BECHS, *Annual Reports of the Superintendent of Education in the City of Buffalo*. See also Library of Congress, Education Department of the State of New York, *Examination of the Public School System of the City of Buffalo*, 106.

144. Library of Congress, Education Department of the State of New York, *Examination of the Public School System of the City of Buffalo*, 106.

145. Ibid., 108.

146. Ibid., 107.

147. Ibid., 106–8.

148. Cremin, *American Education: The Metropolitan Experience*, 239.

149. Reese, "The Origins of Progressive Education," 4 and 22. See also Larry Cuban, *How Teachers Taught: Constancy and Change in American Classrooms, 1890–1980* (New York: Longman, 1984), 31–32.

150. As Bettina Goldberg, among others, has forcefully argued, World War I served "as a catalyst, not as a cause for abandoning German." See "The German-English Academy," 179. Also of interest are Frederick C. Luebke, "Legal Restrictions on Foreign Languages in the Great Plains States, 1917–1923," in *Languages in Conflict: Linguistic Acculturation on the Great Plains*, ed. Paul Schach (Lincoln: University of Nebraska Press, 1980), 1–19, and La Vern J. Rippley, "Conflict in the Classroom: Anti-Germanism in Minnesota Schools, 1917–19," *Minnesota History* 47, 5 (1981): 170–83. For an innovative re-assessment of the impact of the war years on German-language teaching see Zimmermann, "Ethnics against Ethnicity."

CHAPTER FOUR

1. The number of singers has been calculated from the Buffalo *Demokrat*, 24 July 1860; Buffalo *Commercial Advertiser*, 24 July 1860; BECHS, Vertical File, "Music—Organizations, Soc., Clubs: Buffalo Liedertafel/Buffalo Saengerbund," File, "Constitution, History," "History of the Buffalo Liedertafel with a list of its members" (Buffalo: Gies and Co., n.d.), 4.

2. Buffalo *Commercial Advertiser*, 25 July 1860.

3. Buffalo *Daily Courier*, 25 July 1860.

4. Gerber, "'The Germans Take Care of Our Celebrations,'" 45–46.

5. Among the twenty-two visiting singing societies, most had travelled to Buffalo from Ohio (eight), followed by New York State (six), Pennsylvania (four), Massachusetts (one), New Jersey (one), and Michigan (one). The lone Canadian singing society at the singers' festival hailed from Waterloo County, Ontario.

6. Buffalo *Commercial Advertiser*, 23 July 1860, and Buffalo *Daily Courier*, 24 July 1860.

7. Gerber, *The Making of an American Pluralism*, 371–409.

8. Buffalo *Commercial Advertiser*, 25 July 1860, and Buffalo *Daily Courier*, 26 July 1860.

9. Buffalo *Daily Courier*, 24 July 1860, and Buffalo *Express*, 24 July 1860.

10. Buffalo *Daily Courier*, 25 and 26 July 1860.

11. Buffalo *Express*, 25 July 1860; Buffalo *Commercial Advertiser*, 26 July 1860; Buffalo *Daily Courier*, 26 July 1860.

12. Buffalo *Daily Republic*, 26 July 1860, and Buffalo *Commercial Advertiser*, 26 July 1860.

13. Buffalo *Daily Republic*, 27 July 1860.

14. Buffalo *Daily Courier*, 25 July 1860.

15. Laura Mason, *Singing the French Revolution: Popular Culture and Politics, 1787–1799* (Ithaca, NY: Cornell University Press, 1996), 3; Buffalo *Daily Republic*, 25 July 1860; Buffalo *Commercial Advertiser*, 27 July 1860.

16. Philip V. Bohlman, "On the Unremarkable in Music," *19ᵗʰ-Century Music* 16, 2 (1991): 214. See also Roger Chartier, *Cultural History: Between Practices and Representations* (Ithaca, NY: Cornell University Press, 1988), 40–41.

17. Letter from the singing society Eintracht (Newark) to the organizers of the 1860 Buffalo *Sängerfest*, reprinted in the Buffalo *Demokrat*, 1 August 1860. See also Buffalo *Demokrat*, 4 August 1860 and 7 August 1860.

18. Simon Frith, "Music and Identity," in *Questions of Cultural Identity*, ed. Stuart Hall and Paul du Gay (London: Sage Publications, 1996), 109.

19. Benedict Anderson, quoted in Philip V. Bohlman, *The Music of European Nationalism: Cultural Identity and Modern History* (Oxford: ABC Clio, 2004), 35.

20. Ibid., 48.

21. Celia Applegate, "How German Is It? Nationalism and the Idea of Serious Music in the Early Nineteenth Century," *19ᵗʰ-Century Music* 21, 3 (1998), 287–88. See also Peter Uwe Hohendahl, *Building a National Literature: The Case of Germany, 1830–1870* (Ithaca, NY: Cornell University Press, 1989).

22. James Sheehan, as quoted in Celia Applegate and Pamela Potter, "Germans as the 'People of Music': Genealogy of an Identity," in *Music and German National Identity*, ed. Celia Applegate and Pamela Potter (Chicago: University of Chicago Press, 2002), 3.

23. See the Liedertafel's Constitution, as quoted in Dieter Düding, *Organisierter gesellschaftlicher Nationalismus in Deutschland, 1808–1847: Bedeutung und Funktion der Turner- und Sängervereine für die deutsche Nationalbewegung* (Munich: R. Oldenburg Verlag, 1984), 46.

24. George L. Mosse, *The Nationalization of the Masses: Political Symbolism and Mass Movements in Germany from the Napoleonic Wars through the Third Reich* (Ithaca, NY: Cornell University Press, 1975), 137; Applegate and Potter, "Germans as the 'People of Music,'" in *Music and German National Identity*, 12; Applegate, "How German Is It?" 294–95; Düding, *Organisierter gesellschaftlicher Nationalismus*, 45–47, 161–63.

25. Bohlman, *The Music of European Nationalism*, 48; Applegate and Potter, "Germans as the 'People of Music,'" in *Music and German National Identity*, 13.

26. Applegate, "How German Is It?" 293; Dietmar Klenke, "Bürgerlicher Männergesang und Politik in Deutschland," *Geschichte in Wissenschaft und Unterricht* 40, 8 (1989): 466.

27. Quoted in Mosse, *The Nationalization of the Masses*, 138.

ENDNOTES

28. Düding, *Organisierter gesellschaftlicher Nationalismus*, 162–74.

29. Ibid., 145–46.

30. Dieter Düding, "Einleitung: Politische Öffentlichkeit—politisches Fest—politische Kultur," in *Öffentliche Festkulture: Politische Feste in Deutschland von der Aufklärung bis zum ersten Weltkrieg*, ed. Dieter Düding, Peter Friedemann, and Paul Münch (Hamburg: Rowohlt Taschenbuch Verlag, 1988), 12–13.

31. Düding, *Organisierter gesellschaftlicher Nationalismus*, 174–89.

32. As Jolanta Pekacz observes, the class-levelling role of choirs in Western Europe did not necessarily extend to Eastern Europe. In nineteenth-century Galicia, "fear of social mixing" led to profession-ally based choirs of academics, teachers, craftsmen, and printers. Pekacz, *Music in the Culture of Polish Galicia, 1772–1914* (Rochester, NY: University of Rochester Press, 2002), 145–46.

33. Düding, *Organisierter gesellschaftlicher Nationalismus*, 190–204, 253–57, 259–89.

34. Ibid., 180.

35. Quoted in Applegate and Potter, "Germans as the 'People' of Music," in *Music and German National Identity*, 18. See also Düding, *Organisierter gesellschaftlicher Nationalismus*, 312, and Dietmar Klenke, "Nationalkriegerisches Gemeinschaftsideal als politische Religion: Zum Vereinsnationalismus der Sänger, Schützen und Turner am Vorabend der Einigungskriege," *Historische Zeitschrift* 260, 2 (1995): 404–5.

36. *Geschichte der Deutschen*, 102; Gerber, *The Making of an American Pluralism*, 196 and 229.

37. Gerber, *The Making of an American Pluralism*, 170; Carl Wittke, *Refugees of the Revolution: The German Forty-Eighters in America* (Westport, CN: Greenwood Press, 1952), 3, 341–42.

38. For a discussion of the "diasporic imagination," see Jacobson, *Special Sorrows*, 1–10.

39. Gerber, *The Making of an American Pluralism*, 225–29; Wittke, *Refugees of the Revolution*, 73–74; *Geschichte der Deutschen*, 91, 100–109.

40. Gerber, "'The Germans Take Care of Our Celebrations,'" 52 and 54. See also *Geschichte der Deutschen*, 103–5.

41. BECPL, Rare Book Room, "Zur Erinnerung an das 50-jährige Jubiläum des Buffalo Sängerbundes den 19., 20. und 21. April 1903, 1853–1903," 4. See also Gerber, *The Making of an American Pluralism*, 167; *Geschichte der Deutschen*, 65–67; Kathleen Neils Conzen, "Ethnicity as Festive Culture: Nineteenth-Century German America on Parade," in *The Invention of Ethnicity*, ed. Werner Sollors (New York: Oxford University Press, 1989), 48; Wittke, *Refugees of the Revolution*, 58–59, 181.

42. BECHS, Vertical File "Music—Organizations, Soc., Clubs, Buffalo Liedertafel/Buffalo Saengerbund," "Constitution und Nebengesetze des Gesangvereins Buffalo Liedertafel, Buffalo, N.Y., Organisirt [sic] den 9ten Mai 1848" (Buffalo: Grant Bros., 1880); "History of the Buffalo Liedertafel with a list of its members. Published on occasion of the Fair, held February 13–18, 1882" (Buffalo: Gies and Co., n.d.), 3; "Buffalo Liedertafel, 1848–1898," 14. See also *Geschichte der Deutschen*, 121.

43. *Geschichte der Deutschen*, 123; Buffalo *Commercial Advertiser*, 21 July 1860.

44. BECHS, Manuscript Collection MSS 25 VH B93b, "J.W. Ernst Besser. Historical Sketch and Printed Notes of the German Singing Society Deutscher Sängerbund of Buffalo, N.Y., May 1887"; *Geschichte der Deutschen*, 141–44; Gerber, *The Making of an American Pluralism*, 197–99, 233, 243–74.

45. *Geschichte der Deutschen*, 160.

46. Gerber, "'The Germans Take Care of Our Celebrations,'" 52–55.

47. BECPL, Rare Book Room, *Frank & Leslie's Illustrierte Zeitung*, 28 July 1883, 82, and *Fest-Zeitung für das 23ste Nord-Amerikanische Sängerfest*, No. 20, Buffalo, den 13ten August, 1883, 82.

48. BECPL, Rare Book Room, *Frank & Leslie's Illustrierte Zeitung*, 28 July 1883, 82; see also *Geschichte der Deutschen*, 124; Suzanne Gail Snyder, "The *Männerchor* Tradition in the United States: An Historical Analysis of Its Contribution to American Musical Culture" (PhD diss., University of Iowa, 1991), 141; Mary Jane Corry, "The Role of German Singing Societies in Nineteenth-Century America," in *Germans in America: Aspects of German-American Relations in the Nineteenth Century*, ed. E. Allen McCormick (New York: Columbia University, 1983), 164–65.

49. BECHS, Manuscript Collection MSS 25 VH B93b, "J. W. Ernst Besser: Historical Sketch and Printed Notices of the German Singing Society Deutscher Sängerbund of Buffalo, N.Y., May 1887," 26–27; *Geschichte der Deutschen*, 124.

50. Buffalo *Express*, 25 July 1860.

51. Buffalo *Demokrat*, 19 January 1860.

52. See, for instance, Buffalo *Demokrat*, 17 February 1860.

53. Buffalo *Demokrat*, 24 April 1860.

54. *Rochester Union and Advertiser*, 23 July 1860.

55. Buffalo *Daily Courier*, 24 July 1860; Buffalo *Commercial Advertiser*, 24 July 1860; Buffalo *Demokrat*, 24 July 1860.

56. Buffalo *Express*, 2 July 1860, and Buffalo *Daily Courier*, 25 July 1860.

57. Buffalo *Daily Republic*, 25 July 1860.

58. Buffalo *Express*, 25 July 1860.

59. See, for example, Buffalo *Daily Republic*, 23 July 1860; Buffalo *Commercial Advertiser*, 21 and 23 July 1860; Buffalo *Express*, 24 July 1860.

60. Buffalo *Daily Courier*, 24 July 1860.

61. Buffalo *Commercial Advertiser*, 24 July 1860. See also Buffalo *Daily Courier*, 24 July 1860.

62. Klenke, "Bürgerlicher Männergesang und Politik in Deutschland," 460, and Friedhelm Brusniak, "Männerchorwesen und Konfession von 1800 bis in den Vormärz," in *"Heil deutschem Wort und Sang!" Nationalidentität und Gesangskultur in der deutschen Geschichte—Tagungsbericht Feuchtwangen, 1994*, ed. Friedhelm Brusniak and Dietmar Klenke (Augsburg: Bernd Wissner, 1995), 123.

63. For a point of comparison, see Bohlman, "'Still, They Were All Germans in Town,'" 319.

64. BECPL, Rare Book Room, "Zur Erinnerung an das 50-jaehrige Jubilaeum des Buffalo Saengerbund, den 19., 20. und 21. April, 1903, 1853–1901," 9.

65. BECPL, Rare Book Room, *Official Book: Thirtieth Saengerfest of the North-American Saengerbund, held in Buffalo, June 24, 25, 26, and 27, 1901* (Buffalo, NY: Buffalo Saengerfest Company, 1901), 17; BECPL, Rare Book Room, "Zur Erinnerung an das 50-jährige Jubiläum des Buffalo Sängerbundes, 1853–1903," 9; BECPL, Rare Book Room, *Fest-Zeitung für das 23ste Nord-Amerikanische Sängerfest*, No. 2, 1sten Februar 1883, 5.

66. Buffalo *Daily Courier*, 25 July 1860.

67. Buffalo *Commercial Advertiser*, 25 July 1860.

68. Ibid.

69. BECPL, Rare Book Room, *Fest-Zeitung für das 23ste Nord-Amerikanische Sängerfest*, No. 2, 1sten Februar 1883, 5.

70. Buffalo *Demokrat*, 25 July 1860, and Buffalo *Daily Republic*, 25 July 1860.

71. Buffalo *Daily Courier*, 25 July 1860. The Buffalo *Express* and the Buffalo *Commercial Advertiser* commented in similarly enthusiastic fashion.

72. Smith, *Listening to Nineteenth-Century America*, 263 and 8.

73. Buffalo *Demokrat*, 25 July 1860. Alone among the city's English-language papers, the Buffalo *Daily Republic* offered a critic of the concert that mirrored many of the *Demokrat*'s suggestions and criticisms.

74. Leon Botstein, "Listening through Reading: Musical Literacy and the Concert Audience," *19th-Century Music* 16, 2 (1992): 130.

75. Buffalo *Daily Courier*, 25 July 1860.

76. Botstein, "Listening through Reading," 130.

77. Buffalo *Commercial Advertiser*, 25 July 1860.

78. Buffalo *Daily Republic*, 25 July 1860; Buffalo *Daily Courier*, 25 July 1860.

79. Buffalo *Daily Courier*, 25 July 1860.

80. Buffalo *Daily Courier*, 26 July 1860.

81. Quoted in Kathleen Neils Conzen, "Ethnicity and Musical Culture among the German Catholics of the Sauk, 1840–1920," in *Land without Nightingales: Music in the Making of German-America*, ed. Philip V. Bohlman and Otto Holzapfel (Madison: University of Wisconsin-Madison, 2002), 37.

82. Ibid.

83. BECPL, Rare Book Room, "Zur Erinnerung an das 50-jährige Jubiläum des Buffalo Sängerbund," 9.

84. Buffalo *Commercial Advertiser*, 24 and 25 July 1860; Laurence A. Glasco, *Ethnicity and Social Structure*, 301–14.

85. Quoted in Glasco, *Ethnicity and Social Structure*, 313.

86. Gerber, *The Making of an American Pluralism*, 375, 395, 399–404. See also Yox, "Decline of the German-American Community in Buffalo," 84–90.

87. Glasco, *Ethnicity and Social Structure*, 290–91, 295.

88. Theodore W. Allen, *The Invention of the White Republic*, vol. 1, *Racial Oppression and Social Control* (London: Verso, 1994); Alexander Saxton, *The Rise and Fall of the White Republic: Class Politics and Mass Culture in Nineteenth-Century America* (London and New York: Verso, 1990), 10; Matthew Frye Jacobson, *Whiteness of a Different Color: European Immigrants and the Alchemy of Race* (Cambridge, MA: Harvard University Press, 1998), 40. For a pioneering work on the "construction of identity through otherness," see David R. Roediger, *The Wages of Whiteness: Race and the Making of the American Working Class* (London and New York: Verso, 1999 [1991]), 13–14.

89. Bruce Levine, *The Spirit of 1848: German Immigrants, Labor Conflict, and the Coming of the Civil War* (Urbana and Chicago: University of Illinois Press, 1992), 2. As Levine points out, over four million migrants arrived in the United States between 1840 and 1860, a number equal to 30 per-cent of the nation's free population.

90. Jacobson, *Whiteness of a Different Color*, 41–45.

91. Reginald Horsman, *Race and Manifest Destiny: The Origins of American Racial Anglo-Saxonism* (Cambridge, MA: Harvard University Press, 1981), 135–37; Dale T. Knobel, *Paddy and the Republic: Ethnicity and Nationality in Antebellum America* (Middletown, CT: Wesleyan University Press, 1986), 88–89.

92. *Buffalo Medical Journal* 8 (1854): 152, as quoted in Mark Goldman, *High Hopes: The Rise and Decline of Buffalo, New York* (Albany: SUNY Press, 1983), 102, 300.

93. Glasco, *Ethnicity and Social Structure*, 315–16, and Gerber, *The Making of an American Pluralism*, 375.

94. Jacobson, *Special Sorrows*, 7.

95. Buffalo *Commercial Advertiser*, 24 July 1860.

96. Knobel, *Paddy and the Republic*, 12, 42, 56, 69–70, 88–89, 98–99.

97. Horsman, *Race and Manifest Destiny*, 11–19. See also John Higham, *Strangers in the Land: Patterns of American Nativism, 1860–1925* (New York: Atheneum, 1963 [1955]), 9–11.

98. Josiah Nott (1840s), as quoted in Horsman, *Race and Manifest Destiny*, 131.

99. Buffalo *Express*, 24 July 1860; Buffalo *Commercial Advertiser*, 24 and 25 July 1860; Buffalo *Daily Courier*, 25 July 1860.

100. Knobel, *Paddy and the Republic*, 99.

101. Implied, of course, was the contrasting image of the tall, thin, and clean-shaven American. See Buffalo *Daily Courier*, 25 and 26 July 1860; Buffalo *Daily Republic*, 27 July 1860.

102. Buffalo *Commercial Advertiser*, 24 July 1860. See also Knobel, *Paddy and the Republic*, 31–33 and 89.

103. Buffalo *Daily Republic*, 26 July 1860.

104. Buffalo *Commercial Advertiser*, 24 July 1860; Buffalo *Daily Republic*, 26 July 1860.

105. Ibid.; Buffalo *Daily Courier*, 25 July 1860.

106. Buffalo *Commercial Advertiser*, 24 July 1860, and Buffalo *Daily Republic*, 26 July 1860.

107. Buffalo *Commercial Advertiser*, 24 July 1860.

108. Buffalo *Daily Republic*, 26 July 1860.

109. Buffalo *Commercial Advertiser*, 24 July 1860.

110. Gerber, "'The Germans Take Care of Our Celebrations,'" 42 and 48.

111. Buffalo *Daily Courier*, 25 July 1860; Buffalo *Daily Republic*, 25 July 1860; Buffalo *Commercial Advertiser*, 24 July 1860; Buffalo *Daily Courier*, 24 July 1860; Buffalo *Daily Republic*, 25 July 1860.

112. Buffalo *Commercial Advertiser*, 26 and 27 July 26 1860.

113. For a point of comparison, see Manfred Hettling and Paul Nolte, "Bürgerliche Feste als symbolische Politik im 19. Jahrhundert," in *Bürgerliche Feste: Symbolische Formen politischen Handelns im 19. Jahrhundert,* ed. Manfred Hettling and Paul Nolte (Göttingen: Vandenhoeck & Ruprecht, 1993), 8, 16; Susan G. Davis, *Parades and Power: Street Theatre in Nineteenth-Century Philadelphia* (Philadelphia: Temple University Press, 1986), 20, 159, and 167; Robert Lewis, "Street Culture," *Journal of American Studies* 23 (1989): 86–88.

114. See the comments to this effect in the Buffalo *Commercial Advertiser*, 24 July 1860, the Buffalo *Daily Republic*, 25 July 1860, and the Buffalo *Express*, 25 July 1860.

115. Buffalo *Weltbürger*, 28 June 1851, as quoted in Gerber, *The Making of an American Pluralism*, 225.

116. Buffalo *Demokrat*, 26 July 1860.

117. Buffalo *Commercial Advertiser*, 26 July 1860; Buffalo *Daily Courier*, 26 July 1860.

118. Buffalo *Commercial Advertiser*, 26 July 1860, and Buffalo *Express*, 25 July 1860.

119. Buffalo *Daily Courier*, 26 July 1860; Buffalo *Express*, 25 July 1860.

120. Alan R. Burdette, "'Ein Prosit der Gemütlichkeit': The Traditionalization Process in a German-American Singing Society," in *Land without Nightingales: Music in the Making of German-America*, ed. Philip V. Bohlman and Otto Holzapfel (Madison: University of Wisconsin-Madison, 2002), 233–57, and Barbara Lorenzkowski, "Making Music, Building Bridges: German-Canadian Identities in the Nation's Capital, 1958–1999," in *Construire une capitale—Ottawa—Making of a Capital*, ed. Jeff Keshen and Nicole St.-Onge (Ottawa: University of Ottawa Press, 2001), 307–30.

121. Buffalo *Daily Republic*, 26 July 1860.

122. See the nostalgic reminiscences of Edward Storck, on occasion of the 23rd Singers' Festival of the North American Sängerbund in Buffalo in 1883 in BECPL, Rare Book Room, *Fest-Zeitung für das 23ste Nord-Amerikanische Sängerfest*, No. 20, Buffalo, den 13ten August, 1883, 1.

123. Buffalo *Daily Courier*, 26 July 1860.

124. Peter Stallybrass and Allon White, *The Politics and Poetics of Transgression* (London: Methuen, 1986), 177.

125. Buffalo *Daily Republic*, 26 July 1860.

126. Buffalo *Demokrat*, 13 April 1860.

127. Buffalo *Daily Republic*, 27 July 1860, and Buffalo *Commercial Advertiser*, 27 July 1860.

128. Conzen, "Ethnicity as Festive Culture," 53.

129. Buffalo *Demokrat*, 13 April 1860, and 25 July 1860.

130. The quotes can be found in the Buffalo *Commercial Advertiser*, 27 July 1860. Information on the picnic in Moffat's Grove has also been gleaned from the Buffalo *Daily Republic*, 27 July 1860, and the Buffalo *Demokrat*, 6 August 1860.

131. *Geschichte der Deutschen*, 116.

132. For a point of comparison, see Rudolf Pietsch, "Burgenland-American Music and the 'Ethnic Mainstream,'" in *Land Without Nightingales*, ed. Bohlman and Holzapfel, 287–88.

133. Buffalo *Daily Republic*, 26 July 1860.

134. *Columbus Westbote*, quoted in the Buffalo *Demokrat*, 6 August 1860.

135. Buffalo *Express*, 25 July 1860.

136. *Columbus Westbote*, quoted in the Buffalo *Demokrat*, 6 August 1860.

137. The *Berliner Journal* in Waterloo County, Ontario, for instance, relied in its coverage on the Buffalo *Demokrat*. See *Berliner Journal*, 26 July 1860, and 2 August 1860.

138. These newspapers included the New York *Demokrat*, the New York *Staatszeitung*, the Rochester *Beobachter*, the Syracuse *Demokrat*, the Albany *Freie Blätter*, the Pittsburgh *Chronik* and the Pittsburgh *Courier*. See Buffalo *Daily Republic*, 25 July 1860.

139. Buffalo *Demokrat*, 2 August 1860.

140. A.E. Zucker, *The Forty-Eighters: Political Refugees of the German Revolution of 1848* (New York: Russell and Russell, 1967 [1950]), 324–25. See also Carl Dahlhaus, *Nineteenth-Century Music* (Berkeley and Los Angeles: University of California Press, 1989), 38–40.

141. Buffalo *Demokrat*, 2 August 1860.

142. Conzen, "German-Americans and the Invention of Ethnicity," 131–47.

143. Quoted in Conzen, "Ethnicity and Musical Culture," 37.

144. As Victor Greene has argued in his study on American immigrant leaders, the "awareness of a

new ethnic American identity was chiefly the result of the thinking of some of the group elite." See Greene, *American Immigrant Leaders, 1800–1910* (Baltimore, 1987), 141.

145. See Chapter 7.

146. Buffalo *Demokrat*, 25 July 1860.

147. Düding, *Organisierter gesellschaftlicher Nationalismus in Deutschland*, 270–76.

148. Philip V. Bohlman, *The Study of Folk Music in the Modern World* (Bloomington: Indiana University Press, 1988), xviii–xix, 6–12.

149. Buffalo *Demokrat*, 1 January 1860.

150. Smith, *Listening to Nineteenth-Century America*, 3–16.

151. Bohlman, "'Still, They Were All Germans in Town,'" 276.

CHAPTER FIVE

1.   UW, DLRBR, Diaries of Louis Jacob Breithaupt, 2 May 1871.

2.   Toronto *Daily Telegraph*, 3 May 1871; *Canadisches Volksblatt*, 10 May 1871; *Berliner Journal*, 4 and 11 May 1871.

3.   Toronto *Daily Telegraph*, 3 May 1871; *Berliner Journal*, 18 May 1871.

4.   *Berliner Journal*, 11 May 1871; *Canadisches Volksblatt*, 10 May 1871; Buffalo *Demokrat*, 30 May 1871.

5.   Confino, *The Nation as a Local Metaphor*, 212.

6.   See the reports on the Buffalo peace jubilee in the Buffalo *Christian Advocate*, 27 April 1871 and Buffalo *Daily Courier*, 30 May 1871.

7.   For a summary description of German peace jubilees in the United States, see Library of Congress, *Die Deutschen in Amerika* .

8.   *Berliner Journal*, 9 March 1871; *Canadisches Volksblatt*, 26 April 1871.

9.   *Berliner Journal*, 18 May 1871.

10. David Waldstreicher, *In the Midst of Perpetual Fetes: The Making of American Nationalism, 1776–1820* (Chapel Hill: University of North Carolina Press, 1997), 11. See also David Waldstreicher, "Rites of Rebellion, Rites of Assent: Celebrations, Print Culture, and the Origins of American Nationalism," *Journal of American History* 82, 1 (1995): 37–61.

11. Ellen M. Litwicki, "'Our Hearts Burn with Ardent Love for Two Countries': Ethnicity and Assimilation at Chicago Holiday Celebrations, 1876–1918," *Journal of American Ethnic History* 19, 3 (2000): 3–34; Bungert, "Demonstrating the Value of 'Gemüthlichkeit' and 'Cultur,'" 175–214; Øverland, *Immigrant Minds, American Identities*, 175 and 193; Schultz, *Ethnicity on Parade*. See also the influential cultural-anthropological accounts on the role of national imagery by Benedict Anderson, *Imagined Communities*; Eric Hobsbawm, "Introduction," in *The Invention of Tradition*, ed. Eric Hobsbawm and Terence Ranger (Cambridge: Cambridge University Press), 1–14; and more recently, Belgum, *Popularizing the Nation*.

12. Schultz, "'The Pride of the Race Had Been Touched': The 1925 Norse-American Immigration Centennial and Ethnic Identity," *Journal of American History* 77, 4 (1991): 1280–83 and 1292; Øverland, *Immigrant Minds, American Identities*, 2–4 and 20; Geneviève Fabre and Jürgen Heideking, "Introduction," in *Celebrating Ethnicity and Nation: American Festive Culture from the Revolution to the Early Twentieth Century*, ed. Geneviève Fabre and Jürgen Heideking (New York: Berghahn Books, 2001), 13; Litwicki, "'Our Hearts Burn with Ardent Love for Two Countries,'" 6.

13. Øverland, *Immigrant Minds, American Identities*, 192 and 8–9.

14. Anderson, *Imagined Communities*, 44.

15. Kalbfleisch, *The History of the Pioneer German Language Press of Ontario*, 89.

16. *Berliner Journal*, 17 March 1867, 21 July 1867, 12 July 1870, 28 July 1870, 2 February 1871. See also *Canadisches Volksblatt*, 12 April 1871, 19 April 1871, and 17 May 1871.

17. France had declared war on Germany on 19 July 1870. The war ended with the capitulation of Paris on 28 January 1871.

18. Library of Congress, *Die Deutschen in Amerika*, 3–4.

19. *Berliner Journal*, 25 August 1870, 15 September 1870, 20 October 1870, 27 October 1870, 17 November 1870, 1 December 1870; Buffalo *Daily Telegraph*, 3 May 1871.

20. Library of Congress, *Die Deutschen in Amerika*, 29 and 23.

21. *Berliner Journal*, 16 April 1896, and *Canadisches Volksblatt*, 10 May 1871.

22. Buffalo *Express*, 30 May 1871.

23. Library of Congress, *Die Deutschen in Amerika*, 1–3 and 23.

24. Buffalo *Express*, 30 May 1871; Gerber, *The Making of an American Pluralism*, 230–31.

25. Toronto *Globe*, 3 May 1871.

26. Toronto *Daily Telegraph*, 3 May 1871. See also Hamilton *Daily Spectator*, 4 May 1871; Toronto *Globe*, 3 May 1871; Buffalo *Daily Courier*, 30 May 1871; Buffalo *Express*, 27 and 30 May 1871; Buffalo *Commercial Advertiser*, 29 May 1871.

27. Buffalo *Express*, 27 May 1871.

28. Jacobson, *Special Sorrows*, 18.

29. Buffalo *Daily Courier*, 30 May 1871.

30. Ibid. See also Bungert, "Demonstrating the Values of 'Gemüthlichkeit' und 'Cultur,'" 178.

31. Dieter Düding, "Das deutsche Nationalfest von 1814: Matrix der deutschen Nationalfeste im 19. Jahrhundert," in *Öffentliche Festkultur*, ed. Düding et al.

32. Toronto *Daily Telegraph*, 3 May 1871.

33. Buffalo *Demokrat*, 30 May 1871.

34. Library of Congress, *Die Deutschen in Amerika*, 1; Buffalo *Commercial Advertiser*, 29 May 1871.

35. Buffalo *Demokrat*, 30 May 1871, and *Berliner Journal*, 4 May 1871.

36. See, for instance, Toronto *Daily Telegraph*, 3 May 1871; Toronto *Globe*, 3 May 1871; Buffalo *Christian Advocate*, 1 June 1871; Buffalo *Daily Courier*, 30 May 1871; Buffalo *Commercial Advertiser*, 29 May 1871; Library of Congress, *Die Deutschen in Amerika*, 1–2 and 11–12.

37. Buffalo *Daily Courier*, 30 May 1871.

38. Buffalo *Commercial Advertiser*, 29 May 1871.

39. Buffalo *Christian Advocate*, 27 April 1871.

40. *Berliner Journal*, 11 May 1871.

41. Buffalo *Christian Advocate*, 27 April 1871.

42. Toronto *Daily Telegraph*, 3 May 1871.

43. Buffalo *Express*, 30 May 1871.

44. See the speeches by Georg Baltz and Otto Klotz, quoted in the Buffalo *Demokrat*, 30 May 1871,

and the *Berliner Journal*, 11 May 1871. See also Library of Congress, *Die Deutschen in Amerika*, 1.

45. *Canadisches Volksblatt*, 10 May 1871.

46. Otto Klotz, as quoted in the Toronto *Globe*, 3 May 1871, and the *Berliner Journal*, 11 May 1871.

47. Buffalo *Daily Courier*, 30 May 1871.

48. Library of Congress, *Die Deutschen in Amerika*, 1 and 22–23.

49. As quoted in April Schultz, "'The Pride of the Race Had Been Touched,'" 1282. For a point of comparison, see Hettling and Nolte, "Bürgerliche Feste als symbolische Politik im 19. Jahrhundert," 18.

50. In making this connection, I am indebted to David Waldstreicher's study "Rites of Rebellion, Rites of Assent," 49–51. See also Fabre and Heideking, "Introduction," in *Celebrating Ethnicity and Nation*, 14, and Roger D. Abrahams, "An American Vocabulary of Celebration," in *Time out of Time: Essays on the Festival*, ed. Alessandro Falassi (Albuquerque: University of New Mexico Press, 1987), 180.

51. Toronto *Daily Telegraph*, 3 May 1871, and Toronto *Globe*, 3 May 1871.

52. *Berliner Journal*, 4 May 1871.

53. Toronto *Daily Telegraph*, 3 May 1871.

54. Buffalo *Express*, 30 May 1871.

55. Buffalo *Christian Advocate*, 1 June 1871, and Yox, "Decline of the German-American Community in Buffalo," 129.

56. Buffalo *Demokrat*, 4 May 1871. In this context, see also Library of Congress, *Die Deutschen in Amerika*, 42, and Schultz, *Ethnicity on Parade*, 71–72.

57. As quoted in Fabre and Heideking, "Introduction," in *Celebrating Ethnicity and Nation*, 19.

58. Bungert, "Demonstrating the Values of 'Gemüthlichkeit' und 'Cultur,'" 177; Craig Heron and Steve Penfold, "The Craftmen's Spectacle: Labour Day Parades in Canada, the Early Years," *Histoire sociale/Social History* 29, 58 (1996): 371–73.

59. Buffalo *Christian Advocate*, 1 June 1871; Buffalo *Express*, 30 May 1871; Buffalo *Demokrat*, 30 May 1871.

60. This interpretation was advanced in the souvenir booklet of the peace jubilees in the United States, Library of Congress, *Die Deutschen in Amerika*, 23. See also Peterson, *Popular Narratives and Ethnic Identity*, 224.

61. *Berliner Journal*, 25 August 1870, and 11 May 1871. See also Toronto *Globe*, 3 May 1871.

62. Toronto *Daily Telegraph*, 3 May 1871, and Buffalo *Freie Presse*, 27 May 1871.

63. Schultz, *Ethnicity on Parade*, 82–83.

64. Yox, "Decline of the German-American Community in Buffalo," 131, and Buffalo *Freie Presse*, 13 May 1871.

65. Buffalo *Demokrat*, 2 May 1871, and Toronto *Daily Telegraph*, 3 May 1871. See also Andreas Dörner, "Der Mythos der nationalen Einheit: Symbolpolitik und Deutungskämpfe bei der Einweihung des Hermannsdenkmals im Jahre 1875," *Archiv für Kulturgeschichte* 79, 2 (1997): 401.

66. For a point of comparison, see Bungert, "Demonstrating the Values of 'Gemüthlichkeit' und Cultur,'" 177.

67. Buffalo *Demokrat*, 30 May 1871.

68. Buffalo *Demokrat*, 13 May 1871, and Library of Congress, *Die Deutschen in Amerika*, 67.

69. See Jacobson, *Special Sorrows*, 80.

70. Vicki Spencer, "Herder and Nationalism," 1.

71. Düding, "Das deutsche Nationalfest von 1814," 76 and 68.

72. *Berliner Journal*, 11 May 1871.

73. Simon Schama, *Landscape and Memory* (London: Harper Collins, 1995), 87 and 96–97.

74. *Berliner Journal*, 11 May 1871.

75. Müller-Grote, "Onkel Karl," 226–29; *Berliner Journal*, 16 July 1896, and 19 August 1897; *Hamilton Spectator*, 14 August 1897.

76. Anthony D. Smith, "National Identity and Myths of Ethnic Descent," *Research in Social Movements, Conflict and Change* 7 (1984): 101.

77. Buffalo *Daily Courier*, 30 May 1871.

78. As early as the 1850s, Germania had made her appearance in Germany in "increasingly belligerent portrayals," in which she wielded her sword aggressively, her feet caressed by the waters of the Rhine, her eyes watchfully turned to the west. In 1871, this metaphor for the German people underwent yet another change by representing the German Empire as a political entity, just as she had previously projected a longing for national unity. See Patricia Mazón, "Germania Triumphant: The Niederwald National Monument and the Liberal Movement in Imperial Germany," *German History* 18, 2 (2000): 169–71.

79. Toronto *Daily Telegraph*, 3 May 1871, and Toronto *Globe*, 3 May 1871. See also Jonathan Sperber, "Festivals of National Unity in the German Revolution of 1848–1849," *Past and Present* 136 (1992): 119.

80. *Berliner Journal*, 4 May 1871.

81. Buffalo *Express*, 30 May 1871; *Geschichte der Deutschen*, 40; Buffalo *Commercial Advertiser*, 29 May 1871.

82. Buffalo *Express*, 30 May 1871.

83. Toronto *Globe*, 3 May 1871; Buffalo *Express*, 30 May 1871; Buffalo *Demokrat*, 30 May 1871; and Buffalo *Daily Courier*, 30 May 1871.

84. For the role of myths in creating community see Smith, "National Identity and Myths of Ethnic Descent," 95, and Pierre Nora, "The Era of Commemoration," in *Realms of Memory: The Construction of the French Past*, Vol. III: Symbols, edited by Pierre Nora (New York: Columbia University Press, 1998), 632–33.

85. Dörner, "Der Mythos der nationalen Einheit," 395.

86. Ibid., 397.

87. Schama, *Landscape and Memory*, 102.

88. Buffalo *Demokrat*, 30 May 1871.

89. Buffalo *Commercial Advertiser*, 29 May 1871.

90. See Dieter Düding's discussion of the "matrix of German national holidays" in "Das deutsche Nationalfest von 1814," 67–88.

91. Buffalo *Commercial Advertiser*, 29 May 1871.

92. Buffalo *Daily Courier*, 30 May 1871. The headlines in Buffalo's English-language press announced, for example, "The Great German Peace Jubilee—A Memorable Day in Buffalo—One of the Grandest Demonstrations Ever Witnessed in the City" (Buffalo *Daily Courier*, 30 May 1871) or advertised, in big, bold print, "The Jubilee—Grand Peace Demonstration Yesterday—The

Germans Out in Full Force—Splendid Procession and Interesting Exercises" (Buffalo *Express*, 30 May 1871).

93. Buffalo *Express*, 30 May 1871.

94. Buffalo *Evening Post*, 30 May 1871.

95. Buffalo *Demokrat*, 26 May 1871.

96. Toronto *Globe*, 3 May 1871.

97. *Berliner Journal*, 4 May 1881.

98. London *Advertiser* and Galt *Reformer*, as quoted in the *Berliner Journal*, 18 May 1871.

99. Carl Wittke, *The German-Language Press in America*, 164.

100. Carl Wittke, *Refugees of the Revolution*, 345–52.

101. Buffalo *Express*, 30 May 1871, and Buffalo *Daily Courier*, 30 May 1871.

102. Buffalo *Demokrat*, 27 May and 30 May 1871.

103. Buffalo *Daily Courier*, 30 May 1871.

104. Buffalo *Freie Presse*, 29 April 1871.

105. Library of Congress, *Die Deutschen in Amerika*, 2–5 and 25–26. See also Buffalo *Daily Courier*, 30 May 1871; Buffalo *Express*, 30 May 1871; Buffalo *Commercial Advertiser*, 29 May 1871; and Buffalo *Evening Post*, 30 May 1871.

106. Library of Congress, *Die Deutschen in Amerika*, 9.

107. Buffalo *Daily Courier*, 30 May 1871.

108. Toronto *Globe*, 3 May 1871.

109. Hamilton *Daily Spectator*, 5 May 1871.

110. *Berliner Journal*, 11 May 1871.

111. Hamilton *Daily Spectator*, 5 May 1871.

112. Jacobson, *Special Sorrows*, 216.

113. Toronto *Daily Telegraph*, 3 May 1871.

114. (KPL, WHS) MC 15.1.c, "Address of the English Deputation to the Managing Committee of the German Peace Festival, 1871, Berlin," Tuesday, 2 May 1871.

115. Ibid.

116. Conzen, Gerber, Morawska, Pozzetta, and Vecoli, "The Invention of Ethnicity: A Perspective from the U.S.A.," 13. The defensive tone of the jubilee celebration in Buffalo is even more noteworthy if we consider the "colonizing vision" that imbued German-American ethnic leaders who aspired to transplant culture and sophistication to a presumably culturally barren American landscape. See Conzen, "Phantom Landscapes of Colonization," 11.

117. See, for example, *Berliner Journal*, 26 May 1887, 15 March 1888, 10 May 1888, 31 May 1888, 28 June 1888, 1 May 1890, 29 May 1890, and 2 April 1891.

118. Thomas Bender, "Historians, the Nation, and the Plenitude of Narratives," in *Rethinking American History in a Global Age*, ed. Thomas Bender (Berkeley: University of California Press, 2002), 8.

119. For the cult of empire see Carl Berger, *The Sense of Power: Studies in the Ideas of Canadian Imperialism, 1867–1914* (Toronto: University of Toronto Press, 1970).

120. Litwicki, "'Our Hearts Burn with Ardent Love for Two Countries,'" 11. For more cautious appraisals of the long-term impact of ethnic celebrations see Conzen, "Ethnicity as Festive Culture," 71.

121. On the "affinities of ethnicity and modernity," see Werner Sollors, *Beyond Ethnicity: Consent and*

Descent in American Culture (New York: Oxford University Press, 1986), 240–45, and Gerber, "Forming a Transnational Narrative," 61–77.

CHAPTER SIX

1. *Der Deutsche in Canada* 3, 13 (April 1874). All translations, unless otherwise noted, are mine. For tributes to the elderly H.A. Zöllner who attended the Waterloo singers' festival in 1902 at over eighty years of age, see the Buffalo *Freie Presse*, 15 August 1902, and the Toronto *Globe*, 14 August 1902. Anglo-Canadian guests of honour often showed themselves bemused by the preponderance of speeches at German social gatherings, as they did during the 1899 banquet in honour of John Motz, the long-time editor of the *Berliner Journal*, who was celebrated in no fewer than fourteen speeches and then delivered a lengthy oratory himself. See Gottlieb Leibbrandt, "100 Jahre Concordia," *German-Canadian Yearbook* 6 (1981): 270.

2. National Library of Canada, *Census of Canada, 1860–61*, vol. 1: *Personal Census* (Mountain Hill, Quebec: S.B. Foote, 1863), 74–75; and Hayes, *Waterloo County: An Illustrated History*, 29–30; English and McLaughlin, *Kitchener: An Illustrated History*, 62–63; and KPL, WHS, MC 15.9.c., William H.E. Schmalz Collection, "Official Souvenir: Berlin To-day: Centennial Number in Celebration of the Old Boys' and Girls' Reunion, August 6th, 7th, 8th, 1906" (Berlin: News Record, 1906), and Historical Sketch, "The Berlin Band."

3. English and McLaughlin, *Kitchener: An Illustrated History*, 62. The appeal of these excursions has been nicely captured by Hayes, *Waterloo County: An Illustrated History*, 38.

4. *Berliner Journal*, 3 April 1862, and 28 February 1867. A benefit concert for families in East Prussia in May 1868 similarly brought together county singers and musicians. See *Berliner Journal*, 14 May 1868.

5. See, for example, ibid., 20 December 1866, and 6 June 1867.

6. When Berlin's Professor John A. Zinger returned from his honeymoon in October 1874, the young couple was welcomed, in quick succession, by the tunes of the Berlin Brass Band, the singers of Waterloo's Liedertafel and Berlin's very own Concordia society, all of whom were invited into the newlyweds' home for a convivial evening. *Berliner Journal*, 29 October 1874. Another example of a serenade can be found in ibid., 1 November 1883. For the formal engagements of town bands, see Kenneth McLaughlin, *Waterloo: An Illustrated History* (Canada: Windsor Publications, 1990), 40, and *Berliner Journal*, 31 October 1881.

7. For the festive gatherings of German-Canadian gymnasts in Ontario, see *Berliner Journal*, 3 May 1860, 27 September 1860, 19 September 1861, 27 August 1863, 18 August 1864; and Hayes, *Waterloo County: An Illustrated History*, 48–49. For informal bonds between German singers' association in Ontario, see for example *Berliner Journal*, 6 February 1868, 30 April 1885, and 20 August 1885.

8. Prior to the first German-Canadian singers' festival in 1874, the *Berliner Journal* provided detailed accounts of the singers' festival in Buffalo (26 July 1860 and 2 August 1860), Nürnberg, Germany (29 August 1861), New York (3 August 1865), Philadelphia (25 July 1867), Chicago (23 July 1868), Baltimore (29 July 1869), and New York (29 June 1871). In the wake of the successful singers' picnic in Hamilton in August 1868 that had been celebrated by singing societies from Waterloo County, Toronto, Hamilton, Buffalo, Erie, Cincinnati, and Detroit, the Toronto German Men's Choir attempted to organize a singers' festival for "the Germans of Canada," but soon concluded, somewhat chagrined, that it was "impossible" to stage such an ambitious festival "in Canada, among such few Germans." For the singers' festival in Hamilton in August 1868, see *Berliner Journal*, 27 August 1868, and Leibbrandt, "100 Jahre Concordia," 268. For efforts of Toronto's

"Male German Choir" to organize a German-Canadian singers' festival see *Berliner Journal*, 22 October 1868, and 24 December 1868.

9. Kathleen Neils Conzen, "Ethnicity and Musical Culture," 41.

10. See, for example, *Berliner Journal*, 4 June 1874, 10 September 1874, 28 January 1875, and 18 August 1875; Toronto *Globe*, 18 August 1875 and 14 August 1897.

11. See KPL, WHS, MC 15.9.c., William H.E. Schmalz Collection, Manuscript "Berlin: Celebration of Cityhood, 1912"; and the speech given by the Governor General, the Marquis of Lorne, in Berlin on 13 October 1879 in Library of the City of Kitchener, Berlin City Council Minutes, 13 October 1879. See also English and McLaughlin, *Kitchener: An Illustrated History*, 46 and 86.

12. Smith, *Listening to Nineteenth-Century America*, 263.

13. On the occasion of the singers' festival of 1902, the *Berliner Journal* published a chronicle of past singers' festivals that included the festivals of 1874, 1875, 1886, 1890, 1896, 1897 (*Berliner Journal*, 14 August 1902). To this I have added the festival of 1912, which the German-Canadian Choir Federation and the Lake Erie Singers' Association jointly hosted. Not included in my account are the federation's festivals in Hamilton in 1891 and Toronto in 1895 (*Berliner Journal*, 27 August 1891; 29 October 1891; 2 May 1895). Singers' festivals and picnics that were more local in scope took place in Berlin in 1879, in Waterloo in 1884, in Port Elgin in 1888, in Berlin in 1893, and in Hamilton in 1899 (*Berliner Journal*, 8 May 1879, 5 June 1879, and 19 June 1879; 19 June 1884 and 3 July 1884; 9 August 1888; 17 and 31 August 1893; 22 June 1899 and 6 July 1899). Music festivals that placed greater emphasis on instrumental music were celebrated in Toronto in 1886 and in Berlin and Walkerton in 1888 (*Berliner Journal*, 27 May 1886 and 24 June 1886; 12 July 1888; 16 August 1888).

14. *Berliner Journal*, 20 November 1873 and 6 May 1875.

15. Buffalo *Freie Presse*, 5 September 1874. Only Berlin, as the county seat, had been granted a stop in 1856 on the Grand Trunk Railway, which stretched between Sarnia in the province's southwestern corner to Montreal in Quebec.

16. *Berliner Journal*, 27 November 1873.

17. Ibid., 10 September 1874.

18. See the reflections of a "friend of German singing" in ibid., 6 May 1875.

19. Buffalo *Freie Presse*, 19 August 1875.

20. Buffalo *Demokrat*, 21 August 1875.

21. Keith Walden, *Becoming Modern in Toronto: The Industrial Exhibition and the Shaping of a Late Victorian Culture* (Toronto: University of Toronto Press, 1997).

22. Toronto *Globe*, 20 August 1875. At the singers' festival of 1875, these complaints were frequent enough that several newspapers acknowledged them, as did Berlin's Mayor Hugo Kranz when he apologized "that we are not able to give you such accommodation as might be desirable." See Toronto *Globe*, 18 August 1875; Buffalo *Demokrat*, 20 August 1875; and *Berliner Journal*, 2 September 1875.

23. Buffalo *Freie Presse*, 5 September 1874 and *Berliner Journal*, 10 September 1874.

24. Buffalo *Freie Presse*, 2 and 3 September 2 1874.

25. The *Berliner Journal* acknowledged as much on 10 September 1874. For praise for H.A. Zöllner see Buffalo *Freie Presse*, 19 August 1875.

26. Buffalo *Freie Presse*, 5 September 1875. See also BECPL, Rare Book Room, "Zur Erinnerung an das 50-jährige Jubiläum des Buffalo Sängerbundes," 11.

27. Buffalo *Demokrat*, 21 August 1875.

28. Buffalo *Freie Presse*, 18 and 21 August 1875; and *Berliner Journal*, 20 September 1877.

29. Festivals, as anthropologist Alessandro Falassi explains, often revolve around "ritual dramas" such as "a creation myth, a foundation or migratory legend, or a military success particularly relevant in the mythical or historical memory of the community staging the festival. By means of the drama, the community members are reminded of their Golden Age, the trials and tribulations of their founding fathers in reaching the present location of the community." See Falassi, "Festival: Definition and Morphology," in Alessandro Falassi, ed., *Time out of Time: Essays on the Festival* (Albuquerque: University of New Mexico Press, 1987), 5.

30. *Berliner Journal*, 18 August 1875. See also the assertion of F. Gottlieb, secretary of Berlin's *Concordia* singing association that German singers' festivals represented "German national festivals" in the "highest sense of the word," for they served the "fraternization of all German singing associations in Canada." *Berliner Journal*, 30 April 1874.

31. Toronto *Globe*, 3 September 1874.

32. *Berliner Journal*, 10 September 1874.

33. *Canadian Illustrated News* 10, 12 (19 September 1874):188; Hayes, *Waterloo County: An Illustrated History*, 78.

34. On the number of singers see *Berliner Journal*, 3 September 1874.

35. Toronto *Globe*, 2 September 1874.

36. Ibid., 3 September 1874. See also Walden, *Becoming Modern in Toronto*, 200–4; Neil Sutherland, *Children in English-Canadian Society: Framing the Twentieth-Century Consensus* (Toronto: University of Toronto Press, 1976), 97; Susan E. Houston, "The 'Waifs and Strays' of a Late Victorian City: Juvenile Delinquents in Toronto," in *Childhood and Family in Canadian History*, ed. Joy Parr (Toronto: McClelland and Stewart, 1982), 129–42.

37. Toronto *Globe*, 1 and 3 September 1874.

38. Ibid., 19 August 1875.

39. Ibid., 27 November 1873 and 26 August 1875.

40. Ibid., 29 July 1886; and Müller-Grote, "Onkel Karl," 201 and 205.

41. *Berliner Journal*, 19 August 1886. See also Chapter 4.

42. Typical musical fare at the singers' festivals included the songs "Waldandacht," "Der Welt," "Auf den Bergen" (1874), "Die Maiennacht," "Auf der See" (1886), "Gruss an die Nacht," "Es blühet der Wein," "Abendfeier," "Abendständchen," "Frühling und Liebe" (1898), "Frühlingswalzer," and "Nur einmal blüht im Jahr der Mai" (1902). Rarely did choral societies choose more overtly patriotic songs such as "Dem Vaterland" (1874), "Vor der Schlacht" (1886), or "Am Rhein" (1898). Ibid., 10 September 1874, 19 August 1886, 18 August 1898, 21 August 1902.

43. Ostendorf, "'The Diluted Second Generation,'" 274.

44. *Berliner Journal*, 19 August 1886, 12 August 1897, 18 August 1898, and 21 August 1901.

45. Ibid., 21 August 1901; and Philip V. Bohlman, "Landscape—Region—Nation—Reich: German Folk Song in the Nexus of National Identity," in *Music and German National Identity*, ed. Celia Applegate and Pamela Potter (Chicago: University of Chicago Press, 2002), 109–10.

46. Toronto *Globe*, 18 August 1875, and Buffalo *Volksfreund*, 16 August 1902.

47. *Berliner Journal*, 28 August 1890, and *Waterloo County Chronicle*, 21 August 1902.

48. Toronto *Globe*, 20 August 1875; *Berliner Journal*, 28 August 1890; H.L. Staebler, "Random Notes on Music of Nineteenth-Century Berlin, Ontario," *Waterloo Historical Society* 37 (1949): 16.

49. Toronto *Globe*, 12 August 1886, and 15 August 1902.

50. Ibid., 14 August 1902; *Berliner Journal*, 4 September 1902; *Berlin News Record*, 2 August 1912.

51. Michael Kammen, *American Culture, American Taste: Social Change and the 20th Century* (New York: Alfred A. Knopf, 2000), 31.

52. Toronto *Globe*, 3 September 1874, and *Berliner Journal*, 10 September 1874.

53. Toronto *Globe*, 12 August 1886. See also Berlin *Deutsche Zeitung*, 17 August 1898.

54. *Berliner Journal*, 18 August 1898. See also Buffalo *Freie Presse*, 15 August 1902.

55. Guelph *Daily Mercury and Advertiser*, 22 August 1890.

56. Toronto *Globe*, 18 August 1875. See also Pamela M. Potter, *Most German of the Arts: Musicology and Society from the Weimar Republic to the End of Hitler's Reich* (New Haven, CT: Yale University Press, 1998), and Celia Applegate and Pamela Potter, "Germans as the 'People of Music,'" in *Music and German National Identity*, 13 and 17.

57. Toronto *Globe*, 19 August 875.

58. Ostendorf, "'The Diluted Second Generation,'" 261–87.

59. Staebler, "Random Notes on Music," 15; June Countryman, "Theodor Zoellner," *Canadian Encyclopedia*, http://www.thecanadianencyclopedia.com/; Helmut Kallmann, *A History of Music in Canada, 1534–1914* (Toronto: University of Toronto Press, 1987), 149; Leibbrandt, "100 Jahre Concordia," 270; *Berliner Journal*, 11 July 1889; UW, DLRBR, Diaries of Louis Jacob Breithaupt, 22 January 1894.

60. *Berliner Journal*, 21 December 1882.

61. Ibid., 27 May 1886, and 24 June 1886.

62. Toronto *Globe*, 13 August 1886; *Berliner Journal*, 13 May 1886, 17 June 1886, 22 July 1886, 19 August 1886.

63. Guelph *Daily Mercury and Advertiser*, 13 August 1886.

64. Toronto *Globe*, 13 August 1886, and *Berliner Journal*, 19 August 1886.

65. *Berliner Journal*, 14 July 1898, and Berlin *Deutsche Zeitung*, 17 August 1898.

66. Berlin *Deutsche Zeitung*, 17 August 1898; *Berliner Journal*, 14 July 1898 and 18 August 1898; English and McLaughlin, *Kitchener: An Illustrated History*, 88–89.

67. Berlin *Deutsche Zeitung*, 17 August 1898. The mass chorus performed three musical selections, namely "Friedrich Rothbart," "Die drei Augenblicke" (Three Moments in Time), and "Das deutsche Lied" (The German Song).

68. See, for example, the press coverage on soloist "Mrs. Caldwell" from Hamilton at the singers' festivals of 1886 and 1890 in *Berliner Journal*, 19 August 1886, and 28 August 1890; Toronto *Globe*, 12 August 1886; Hamilton *Daily Spectator*, 22 August 1890.

69. Müller-Grote, "Onkel Karl," 107–255. The conservative attitude that permeates Karl Müller's memoirs sprang partly from his bitterness over the name change of Berlin to Kitchener in 1916. But even though his memories of festive culture in Waterloo County were coloured by World War I, his autobiographical account remains one of the rare personal writings by a festival organizer that complements the narrative published in the more public forum of the press.

70. Ibid., 107–9 and 131.

71. Ibid., 150 (Berlin's townscape), 121, 125, 142 and 252 (German-English dialect), 131 (German newspapers), 220 (courtship).

72. Ibid., 157, 165, and 169.

73. Ibid., 150, 153, 145, 205, and 252.

74. Ibid., 227–28. See also Berlin *Deutsche Zeitung,* 18 August 1897.

75. Müller-Grote, "Onkel Karl," 227–28, *Berlin News Record,* 14 August 1897, and *Berliner Journal,* December 31, 1896. See also Friedemann Schmoll, "Individualdenkmal, Sängerbewegung und Nationalbewußtsein in Württemberg: Zum Funktionswandel bürgerlicher Erinnerungskultur zwischen Vormärz und Kaiserreich," in*"Heil deutschem Wort und Sang!": Nationalidentität und Gesangkultur in der deutschen Geschichte—Tagungsbericht Feuchtwangen 1994,* ed. Friedhelm Brusniak and Dietmar Klenke (Augsburg: Bernd Wissner, 1995), 71.

76. Wolfgang Hardtwig,"Bürgertum, Staatssymbolik und Staatsbewußtsein im Deutschen Kaiserreich 1871–1914," *Geschichte und Gesellschaft* 16 (1990): 273 and 276–78.

77. English and McLaughlin, *Kitchener: An Illustrated History,* 88–89.

78. Gottlieb Leibbrandt, "Jubilaeums-Ausgabe/Centennial Issue—Concordia Club," (Concordia Club, Kitchener, Ontario, No. 57, August 1973): 13–14.

79. UW, DLRBR, Diaries of Louis Jacob Breithaupt, 4 July 1878, and 9, 14, and 15 March 1888. Three months later, the County Council expressed its "heartfelt regret" over the untimely death of the new German Emperor Frederick III in a resolution of condolences that was forwarded to the German Consul in Toronto. See Regional Municipality of Waterloo, Kitchener, *Journal of the Proceedings and By-Laws of the Municipal Council of the County of Waterloo,* 21 June 1888.

80. English and McLaughlin, *Kitchener: An Illustrated History,* 88. Throughout the closing decades of the nineteenth century, Louis Breithaupt closely followed political events in imperial Germany, paying particular attention to news regarding Otto von Bismarck and the Royal Family. See UW, DLRBR, Diaries of Louis Jacob Breithaupt, 20 March 1890, 24 November 1892, 9 September 1893, and 14 August 1897.

81. In his vice-regal visit to Waterloo County in 1879, the Marquis of Lorne had praised the county's "good Germans" for showing their "esteem for the Queen," all the while preserving "the love of the old Fatherland." In a German speech that impressed the audience both for its content and fine "pronunciation" (as the town clerk diligently noted), Lorne complimented the assembly on "German fidelity," the "expressive mother tongue," German "thrift" and "diligence," as well as the "womanly virtues of their wives and daughters." The members of the reception committee, in turn, assured His Excellency of "our love for the Noble Queen" and their desire "to live like British subjects, without abandoning our German peculiarities," namely the desire "to make a home for the German language and even the German song in Canada." See Library of the City of Kitchener, Berlin City Council Minutes, 13 October 1879. Young Louis Jacob Breithaupt similarly noted in his diary that the Marquis spoke "the German remarkably well," while his wife, the Princess Louise, "also spoke a fine German," in UW, DLRBR, Diaries of Louis Jacob Breithaupt, 17 September 1879.

82. KPL, WHS, MC 15.9.c., William H.E. Schmalz Collection, "Berlin: Celebration of Cityhood, 1912."

83. Berlin *Deutsche Zeitung,* 18 August 1897, and *Berliner Journal,* 19 August 1897.

84. *Canadisches Volksblatt,* 18 August 1897.

85 *Deutsche Zeitung,* 18 August 1897, and *Berlin News Record,* 12 August 1897.

86. *Berlin News Record,* 14 August 1897.

87. *Berliner Journal,* 19 August 1897.

88. Berlin *Deutsche Zeitung,* 18 August 1897, and Müller-Grote, "Onkel Karl," 109.

89. *Canadisches Volksblatt,* 18 August 1897, and Berlin *Deutsche Zeitung,* 18 August 1897.

90. *Berliner Journal,* 12 August 1897.

91. Berlin *Deutsche Zeitung*, 18 August 1897, and Hamilton *Spectator*, 14 August 1897.

92. Hamilton *Spectator*, 14 August 1897.

93. Ibid.; English and McLaughlin, *Kitchener: An Illustrated History*, 83; Müller-Grote, "Onkel Karl," 228–28; Rych Mills and the Victoria Park 100ᵗʰ Birthday Historical Committee, *Victoria Park: 100 Years of Park and Its People: An Historical and Photographic Essay on Victoria Park* (Kitchener, ON: 1996), 19.

94. Berlin *Deutsche Zeitung*, 18 August 1897.

95. Ibid., and Toronto *Globe*, 14 August 1897.

96. Müller-Grote, "Onkel Karl," 228–29.

97. Toronto *Globe*, 13 and 14 August 1897.

98. *Berlin News Record*, 5 August 1897.

99. Ibid., 14 August 1897.

100. Ibid., 5 and 14 August 1897.

101. Berlin *Deutsche Zeitung*, 18 August 1897.

102. *Berliner Journal*, 19 August 1897.

103. Stallybrass and White, *The Politics and Poetics of Transgression*.

104. Hettling and Nolte, "Bürgerliche Feste als symbolische Politik im 19. Jahrhundert," 8.

105. Falassi, *Time Out of Time,* and *Berliner Journal*, 18 August 1898.

106. Galt *Dumfries Reporter*, quoted in the *Berliner Journal*, 2 September 1875. In a similar vein, see *Canadisches Volksblatt*, 27 August 1890, and *Berliner Journal*, 19 August 1897.

107. Berlin *Deutsche Zeitung*, 18 August 1897. Rumpel's comments are echoed in the *Berlin News Record* in its praise for the visitors' "very orderly manner, not a single disturbance being reported. One policeman was sufficient for all purposes" (14 August 1897).

108. *Berliner Journal*, 18 August 1898.

109. Guelph *Daily Mercury and Advertiser*, 23 August 1890.

110. *Berlin News Record*, 13 August 1898.

111. Bloomfield, "City-Building Processes in Berlin/Kitchener and Waterloo," 12; English and McLaughlin, *Kitchener: An Illustrated History*, 79; KPL, WHS, MC 15.9.c., William H.E. Schmalz Collection, "Twentieth Century Souvenir of Busy Berlin: The Best Town in Canada," 1901.

112. See the speech given by Moses Springer, MPP and Reeve of the Berlin, at the singers' festival of 1874 (*Berliner Journal*, 10 September 1874).

113. KPL, WHS, MC 15.9.c., William H.E. Schmalz Collection, "Berlin: Celebration of Cityhood, 1912. Issued by Authority of the City Berlin, Ontario—Issued in Commemoration of Its Celebration of Cityhood, July 17ᵗʰ, 1912 (Berlin: German Printing and Publishing Co. of Berlin, 1912), "A Tribute to the Pioneers."

114. Øverland, *Immigrant Minds, American Identities*, 21.

115. Smith, "National Identity and Myths of Ethnic Descent," 96.

116. *Berlin News Record*, 10 August 1898. See also *Berlin News Record*, 14 August 1902. On occasion of the Peninsular Singers' Festival in Berlin in 1898, it again lauded German Canadians' "industry, thrift and respect for discipline and law," their well-known "love of music and the company of their fellows" and their willingness to "make their adopted home their country" and embrace the English language.

117. Newspaper correspondents routinely tried to estimate the number of visitors at the singers' fes-

tivals but provided widely varying figures. Estimates range between 6,000 and 12,000 attendees for the 1886 festival and between 8,000 and 15,000 attendees for the 1890 festival. See *Berliner Journal*, 19 August 1886, and 14 August 1890; Toronto *Globe*, 13 August 1886; and Hamilton *Spectator*, 22 August 1890.

118. *Berlin News Record*, 10 August 1898.

119. The county's German- and English-language press used the singers' festivals to publicize local progress and prosperity. See, for example, *Berliner Journal*, 14 August 1902; Berlin *Daily Telegraph*, 9 August 1902; and the *Waterloo County Chronicle*, 31 July 1902. See also English and McLaughlin, *Kitchener: An Illustrated History*, 79–80, and Bloomfield, "City-Building Processes in Berlin/Kitchener and Waterloo," 68–72.

120. Toronto *Globe*, 12 August 1886.

121. *Berliner Journal*, 14 August 1890.

122. *Berlin News Record*, 10 August 1898.

123. KPL, WHS, MC 15.9.c., William H.E. Schmalz Collection, "Official Programme: 13th Peninsular Saengerfest to be held at Berlin, Ontario, August 10, 11, 12, 1898," and "Saengerfest Souvenir. Waterloo, Ont., Aug. 12th, 13th and 14th, 1902."

124. For the Hamilton singers' festival, see *Berliner Journal*, 29 October 1891. For the surpluses earned by the Waterloo County singers' festivals, see ibid., 10 September 1874, 25 November 1886, and 18 August 1898. For reports on the guarantee fund, see ibid., 4 February 1875, 4 March 1875, and 31 July 1902.

125. Ibid., 3 August 1875, and 21 August 1902. See also London *Free Press*, 13 August 1902.

126. *Berliner Journal*, 22 July 1875, and 12 August 1875; UW, DLRBR, Diaries of Louis Jacob Breithaupt, 10 August 1898.

127. In 1874, female ingenuity had come to the Concordia society's rescue when the singing society desired to have a banner of its own for the upcoming festival. A sewing machine was the prize of a lottery whose revenues were topped by donations, collected by the "German matrons and maids of Berlin." *Berliner Journal*, 18 June and 27 August 1874. See also Toronto *Globe*, 18 August 1875: *Berliner Journal*, 22 July 1875; Berlin *Deutsche Zeitung*, 4 August 1897; and *Berlin News Record*, 1 August 1898.

128. *Berliner Journal*, 19 July 1888.

129. Ibid., 18 August 1898.

130. *Berlin News Record*, 2 August 1912. Three decades earlier, by contrast, German attendnees had spoken mostly German, as English-language observers had been quick to note. See Toronto *Globe*, 12 August 1886.

131. The festival ribbons have been preserved in the Regional Municipality of Waterloo, Waterloo Region Museum, *Sängerfest* Ribbons and Badges, 1874–1901 collection.

132. Craig Heron and Steve Penfold, "The Craftmen's Spectacle: Labour Day Parades in Canada, the Early Years," 368 and 385–86.

133. *Berliner Journal*, 18 August 1898.

134. *Berlin News Record*, 8 August 1902, and *Waterloo County Chronicle*, 12 August 1902.

135. Waterloo Public Library, Local History Collection, Vertical File "Saengerfests," "Saengerfest-Souvenir: 1862 Goldenes Jubilaeumsfest 1912. Waterloo, Ont. Thursday and Friday, August 1st and 2nd, 1912."

136. Hamilton *Spectator*, 14 August 1902.

137. *Berliner Journal*, 4 September 1902.

138. Smith, "National Identity and Myths of Ethnic Descent," 96.

139. Hamilton *Spectator*, 14 August 1902.

140. Ibid. See also *Berliner Journal*, 21 August 1902.

141. *Berliner Journal*, 28 August 1890. See also Toronto *Globe*, 22 August 1890.

142. *Berliner Journal*, 18 August 1898.

143. Stratford *Evening Beacon*, 12 August 1902.

144. Berlin *Deutsche Zeitung*, 17 August 1898.

145. *Berliner Journal*, 18 August 1898.

146. Berlin *Deutsche Zeitung*, 17 August 1898.

147. *Berliner Journal*, 21 August 1902.

148. Quoted in ibid., 18 August 1898; Berlin *Deutsche Zeitung*, 17 August 1898.

149. David Thelen, "Of Audiences, Borderlands, and Comparisons: Toward the Internationalization of American History," *Journal of American History* 79, 2 (1992): 444.

150. *Berliner Journal*, 10 September 1874.

151. Ibid., 21 August 1902. See also ibid., 18 August 1898.

152. Detroit sent by far the largest number of singing societies to the festivals in Waterloo County. The list of participating associations reflected the diversity of the city's German community. It included the Canstatter Männerchor (1890, 1898, and 1902), Canstatter Damenchor (1898), Canstatter Gemischter Chor (1902), Frohsinn (1890), Plattdeutscher Männerchor (1890), Veteranen Männerchor (1890), Germania (1890), Liederkranz (1890), Arion Männerchor (1898), and Teutonia (1898).

153. Regional Municipality of Waterloo, Waterloo Region Museum, *Sängerfest* Ribbons and Badges, 1874–1901, "Liedertafel, Waterloo, Canada; 7. Peninsular Sängerfest, Ann Arbor, Michigan, August 1886." See also *Berliner Journal*, 26 August 1886.

154. *Berliner Journal*, 27 June 1889.

155. The article in the Detroit *Abendpost* was reprinted in the *Berliner Journal* on 21 August 1890.

156. See also Indianapolis *Telegraph*, as quoted in the *Berliner Journal*, 26 August 1886.

157. *Berliner Journal*, 21 August 1890.

158. BECHS, Joseph Mischka, Music Clippings, M67, vol. 6, New York *Daily Tribune*, 25 June 1901. See also BECPL, Rare Book Room, *Fest-Zeitung für das 23ste Nord-Amerikanische Sängerfest*, No. 3, 15ten Februar, 1883, 9, and ibid., No. 14, 18ten Juli, 1883, 2.

159. Buffalo *Daily Courier*, 15 May 1882, and New York *Daily Tribune*, 25 June 1901. See also BECPL, Rare Book Room, *Frank & Leslie's Illustrierte Zeitung*, 21 July 1883; *Fest-Zeitung für das 23ste Nord-Amerikanische Sängerfest*, No. 14, 18ten Juli and ibid., No. 1, 15ten Januar 1884, 1.

160. Robert C. Vitz, "Starting a Tradition: The First Cincinnati May Musical Festival," *Cincinnati Historical Society Bulletin* 38, 1 (1985): 33, and BECPL, Rare Book Room, *Fest-Zeitung für das 23ste Nord-Amerikanische Sängerfest*, No. 3., 15ten Februar, 1883, 9.

161. Buffalo *Freie Presse*, 25 May 1882. See also BECPL, Rare Book Room, *Um die Welt, Keppler & Schwarzmann's Illustrierte Zeitung*, New York, 28. Juli 1883, 323.

162. As quoted in the *Berliner Journal*, 21 August 1890.

163. Ibid., 28 August 1890, 18 August 1898, 21 August 1902.

164. Ibid., 18 August 1898.

165. Buffalo *Commercial Advertiser*, 26 June 1901.

166. Hamilton *Spectator*, 14 August 1902.

167. Erie *Tageblatt* (Pennsylvania), as quoted in the *Berliner Journal*, 8 May 1902.

168. *Berlin News Record*, 2 August 1912, and Hamilton *Daily Spectator*, 3 August 1912.

169. Hamilton *Daily Spectator*, 3 August 1912.

170. Buffalo *Freie Presse*, 15 August 1902, and *Täglicher Buffalo Volksfreund*, 16 August 1902.

171. Abrahams, "An American Vocabulary of Celebrations," 179.

172. Bohlman, *The Study of Folk Music in the Modern World*, 53.

173. See, for example, Toronto *Globe*, 19 August 1875, 13 August 1886, and 22 August 1890; *Berliner Journal*, 26 August 1875, 19 August 1886, 28 August 1890, and 18 August 1898.

174. *Berliner Journal*, 19 August 1886 and 28 August 1890. For the dynamic interactions across cultural boundaries, see Bohlman's probing analysis of practices of folk music in the American Midwest in *The Study of Folk Music*, 65.

175 In this context, see also Ostendorf, "'The Diluted Second Generation,'" 283, and Otto Holzapfel and Philip V. Bohlman, "The Musical Culture of German-Americans: Views from Different Sides of the Hyphen," in *Land without Nightingales*, ed. Bohlman and Holzapfel, 1–27.

CHAPTER SEVEN

1. Yox, "The German-American Community as a Nationality, 1880–1940," *Yearbook of German-American Studies* 36 (2001): 181–83. See also Michael A. Riester, "History of St. Louis RC Church," http://stlouisrc.bfn.org/tc.html.

2. Lawrence Levine, *Highbrow/Lowbrow: The Emergence of Cultural Hierarchy in America* (Cambridge, MA: Harvard University Press, 1988), 110–16; Ostendorf, "'The Diluted Second Generation,'" 266–67.

3. Levine, *Highbrow/Lowbrow*, 133.

4. Buffalo *Daily Courier*, 23 June 1901; Ostendorf, "'The Diluted Second Generation,'" 268.

5. Ostendorf, "'The Diluted Second Generation,'" 264 and 270.

6. Annegret Fauser, *Musical Encounters at the 1889 Paris World's Fair* (Rochester, NY: University of Rochester Press, 1995), 9 and 53.

7. Conzen, "Ethnicity and Musical Culture," 39.

8. Buffalo and Erie County Historical Society (hereafter BECHS), Rare Book Room, *Fest-Zeitung für das 23ste Nord-Amerikanische Sängerfest*, No. 1, 15ten Januar, 1883, 2. See also ibid., 15ten Februar 1883, 4 and BECPL, Rare Book Room, *Frank & Leslie's Illustrierte Zeitung*, 28 July 1883, 82.

9. Buffalo *Morning Express*, 25 June 1901 and Buffalo *Sunday Morning News*, 22 July 1883. See also Buffalo *Freie Presse*, 16 July 1883, 23 July 1883; and Buffalo *Demokrat*, 17 July 1883.

10. BECHS, "Joseph Mischka," Music Clippings, M67, vol. 6, New York *Daily Tribune*, 25 June 1901.

11. See, for example, commentaries on the 1901 singers' festival in Buffalo, published in the Buffalo *Volksfreund*, 28 June 1901, and the Buffalo *Freie Presse*, 27 June 1901.

12. Buffalo *Daily Courier*, 23 June 1901.

13. See also Kathleen Neils Conzen, "Ethnicity as Festive Culture," 63.

14. Buffalo *Times*, 22 June 1901.

15. BECPL, Rare Book Room, *Official Book: Thirtieth Sängerfest of the North-American Sängerbund, held in Buffalo, June 24, 25, 26 and 27, 1901* (Buffalo, NY: The Buffalo Sängerfest Company, 1901), 20.

16. BECPL, Rare Book Room, *Fest-Zeitung für das 23ste Nord-Amerikanische Sängerfest*, No. 1, 15ten Januar, 1883, 5.

17. Buffalo *Freie Presse*, 19 July 1883.

18. See Philip Bohlman's pioneering work *The Study of Folk Music in the Modern World* (Bloomington: Indiana University Press, 1988), 6, 15, 17, and 54.

19. Buffalo *Daily Courier*, 15 May 1882.

20. BECHS, Vertical File: Music—Organizations, Soc., Clubs, "Buffalo Orpheus" file: Programs, 1894–1897, "Buffalo Orpheus, 25th Anniversary, Oct. 6th, 7th & 8th." For a history of the association, see *Geschichte der Deutschen*, 169–77.

21. Buffalo *Daily Courier*, 15 May 1882. See also Buffalo *Express*, 17 May 1882. The membership numbers are estimates, based upon Ernst Besser's reminiscences and attendance figures at the rehearsals for the 1883 reception concert. See BECHS, Manuscript Collection MSS 25 VH B93b, "J.W. Ernst Besser. Historical Sketch and Printed Notes of the German Singing Society Deutscher Sängerbund of Buffalo, N.Y., May 1887," and Buffalo *Demokrat*, 25 May, 28 May, 31 May, and 4 June 1883.

22. Buffalo *Demokrat*, 17 May 1882.

23. Buffalo *Freie Presse*, 22 April and 8 May 1882.

24. Buffalo *Daily Courier*, 15 May 1882.

25. For a concise summary of the 1882 *Sängerkrieg*, see Buffalo *Freie Presse*, 16 July 1883 and 22 April 1882.

26. The wholesale grocer Phillip Becker—a Lutheran, Bavarian, and Republican—was the first German-born migrant to ascend to the mayoralty in the fall of 1875. See Yox, "Decline of the German-American Community in Buffalo," 144–47.

27. Buffalo *Daily Courier*, 15 May 1882.

28. Buffalo *Freie Presse*, 25 May 1882. See also Buffalo *Demokrat*, 20 May 1882 and 25 May 1882. For a profile of Louis Allgewähr, see *Frank & Leslie's Illustrierte Zeitung*, 21 July 1883.

29. Buffalo *Freie Presse*, 16 July 1883.

30. BECPL, Rare Book Room, *Official Text-Book and Programme of the Twenty-Third Saengerfest of the North-American Saengerbund Held at Buffalo N.Y., July 16–20, 1883* (Buffalo: N.S. Rosenau, 1883), 92.

31. Buffalo *Commercial Advertiser*, 18 July 1883.

32. Gerber, *The Making of an American Pluralism*, 168 and 119. See also Nadel, *Little Germany: Ethnicity, Religion, and Class in New York City*, 4.

33. Quoted in the Buffalo *Demokrat*, 27 May 1882.

34. *Geschichte der Deutschen*, 95–97.

35. Ibid, 109.

36. Ibid, 109–12; Yox, "Decline of the German-American Community in Buffalo," 177–81. See also Buffalo *Demokrat*, 2 March 1883; BECPL, Rare Book Room, *Die Deutsche Jungmänner Gesellschaft zu Buffalo, N.Y.: Festschrift zur Feier ihres fünzigjährigen Stiftungsfestes am 11. und 12. Mai 1891* (Buffalo, NY: 1891), 37–42.

37. Buffalo *Demokrat*, 6 March 1883.

38. Buffalo *Commercial Advertiser*, 16 July 1883.

39. Conzen, "Ethnicity as Festive Culture," 64. In this context see also Mona Ozouf, *Festivals and the French Revolution* (Cambridge, MA: Harvard University Press, 1988 [1976]), 126–27.

40. New York *Daily Tribune*, 17 June 1883, and Buffalo *Evening Telegraph*, 17 July 1883.

41. Yox, "Decline of the German-American Community in Buffalo," 181, and Buffalo *Evening News*, 19 July 1883.

42. Buffalo *Evening Telegraph*, 17 July 1883 and Buffalo *Freie Presse*, 16 July 1883. See also BECPL, Rare Book Room, *Um die Welt, Keppler & Schwarzmann's Illustrierte Zeitung*, New York, 28. Juli 1883, 323.

43. Quoted in the Buffalo *Freie Presse*, 19 July 1883.

44. See, for instance, Buffalo *Demokrat*, 18 June 1883, and 23 July 1883.

45. Buffalo *Demokrat*, 20 April 1883, and 27 April 1883. See also Buffalo *Freie Presse*, 19 and 28 May 1883.

46. BECPL, Rare Book Room, *Official Text-Book and Programme of the Twenty-Third Saengerfest of the North-American Saengerbund*, 92. See also the *New York Staatszeitung*, as quoted in the Buffalo *Freie Presse*, 23 July 1883.

47. Buffalo *Freie Presse*, 12 and 17 May 1883. See also Buffalo *Demokrat*, 27 March 1883.

48. Buffalo *Freie Presse*, 22 May 1883, and Buffalo *Demokrat*, 25, 28 and 31 May 1883, and 4 June 1883.

49. BECPL, Rare Book Room, *Frank & Leslie's Illustrierte Zeitung*, 28 July 1883, 82, and *Fest-Zeitung für das 23ste Nord-Amerikanische Sängerfest*, No. 1, 15ten Januar, 1883, 1. See also *Official Text-Book and Programme of the Twenty-Third Saengerfest of the North-American Saengerbund*, 6.

50. In the east, Friedrich Federlein conducted rehearsals in Dunkirk, Erie, Cleveland, Tiffin, Columbus, Wheeling, Allegheny, Philadelphia, Newark, New York, Elmira, and Rochester. Meanwhile, Joseph Mischka visited Detroit, Milwaukee, Chicago, St. Louis, Indianapolis, Louisville, and Cincinnati. See Buffalo *Demokrat*, 16 June 1883.

51. Buffalo *Demokrat*, 26 June 1883, and Buffalo *Freie Presse*, 23 June 1883 and 2 July 1883.

52. BECPL, Rare Book Room, *Official Text-Book and Programme of the Twenty-Third Saengerfest of the North-American Saengerbund*, 11 and 13.

53. Ibid. Music journalism, too, had evolved during the years of the Civil War and helped form musical judgement and taste. For a point of comparison see Celia Applegate, *Bach in Berlin*, particularly Chapter 3.

54. Ruhr-University of Bochum, Bochumer Briefsammlung, "Krause-Krause," Buffalo, 27 August 1865, and 31 December 1865. I am indebted to Wolfgang Helbich for bringing this correspondence to my attention and generously providing me with a complete set of transcripts.

55. Ibid., Buffalo, 22 July 1883: "Die Amerikaner sind ganz frappiert und können gar nicht begreifen, wie so viele Leute, 2000 fremde Sänger und ungefähr 40,000 Besucher sich so fröhlich amüsieren können, ohne auch nur den geringsten Streit oder Mißton unter sich aufkommen zu lassen. Aber auch in künstlerischer Beziehung war das Fest epochemachend, die Konzerte von guten Solokräften, unterstützt mit einem geschulten Sängerchor von 2000 Mann in unserer neuen, großartigen Sängerhalle ... waren wirklich großartig, der Eindruck beim Amerikanertum überwältigend, dessen dann ihre englischen Zeitungen auch ohne Rückhalt sich aussprachen. Durch dieses Fest hat die Achtung vor den hiesigen Deutschen auffallend zugenommen."

56. Quoted in the Buffalo *Commercial Advertiser*, 17 July 1883.

57. Buffalo *Weekly Press*, 19 July 1883.

58. Buffalo *Commercial Advertiser*, 17 July 1883.

59. Ibid.

60. Buffalo *Freie Presse*, 29 May 1883.

61. New York *Daily Tribune*, 19 July 1883, and Buffalo *Sunday Morning News*, 22 July 1883.

62. Buffalo *Demokrat*, 17 June 1882, 4. In this context, see also Buffalo *Demokrat*, 22 May 1882, 10 June 1882, 16 July 1883, 21 July 1883.

63. . Buffalo *Daily Courier*, 15 July 1883.

64. Buffalo *Commercial Advertiser*, 16 July 1883.

65. Ibid.

66. Ibid.

67. See, for instance, Buffalo *Weekly Press*, 19 July 1883; Buffalo *Commercial Advertiser*, 18 July 1883; Buffalo *Evening Telegraph*, 16 July 1883; Buffalo *Demokrat*, 31 July 1883; Buffalo *Freie Presse*, 23 July 1883; Buffalo *Demokrat*, 25 July 1883, and 26 July 1883. See also Buffalo *Freie Presse*, 23 July 1883.

68. *Geschichte der Deutschen*, 86.

69. Ibid.

70. Yox, "Decline of the German-American Community," 182, and BECHS, Vertical File: Music— Organizations, Soc., Clubs, "Buffalo Orpheus" file: Programs, 1894–1897, "Buffalo Orpheus, 25th Anniversary, Oct. 6th, 7th. & 8th."

71. Yox, "Decline of the German-American Community," 182. Having arrived in Buffalo in 1843, Jacob Schoellkopf became the founder of a family dynasty that owned both the area's first power plant and a chemical company that specialized in the manufacture of aniline, "a chemical used in the manufacture of explosives." See Goldman, *High Hopes: The Rise and Decline of Buffalo, New York*, 177–78.

72. BECPL, Rare Book Room, *Die Deutsche Jungmänner Gesellschaft zu Buffalo*, 49 and 52; *Geschichte der Deutschen*, 114; Yox, "Decline of the German-American Community," 183.

73 Yox, "Decline of the German-American Community," 184–85.

74. In this context, see also Conzen, "Ethnicity as Festive Culture," 69.

75. Buffalo *Evening Telegraph*, 16 July 1883.

76. BECPL, Rare Book Room, "Zur Erinnerung an das 50-jährige Jubiläum des Buffalo Sängerbund," 19.

77. Ibid. See also BECHS, Manuscript Collection MSS 25 VH B93b, "J.W. Ernst Besser. Historical Sketch and Printed Notes of the German Singing Society Deutscher Sängerbund of Buffalo, N.Y., May 1887."

78. BECHS, Joseph Mischka, Music Clippings, M67, vol. 3, "Buffalo *Courier*," 4 September 1888.

79. Ibid.

80. Ibid., "Buffalo *Express*," 14 December 1899; "Zur Erinnerung an das 50-jährige Jubiläum des Buffalo Sängerbund," 19.

81. BECPL, Rare Book Room, *Official Book: Thirtieth Sängerfest of the North-American Sängerbund, held in Buffalo, June 24, 25, 26 and 27, 1901* (Buffalo, NY: The Buffalo Sängerfest Company, 1901). See also BECHS, Joseph Mischka, Music Clippings, M 67, vol. 1, "The Lyra: Official Organ of the North American Saenger Bund," 5 August 1897 and 25 April 1899.

82. BECHS, Joseph Mischka, Music Clippings, M 67, vol. 1, "The Lyra: Official Organ of the North American Saenger Bund," 5 August 1897 and 25 April 1899.

83. BECHS, *Annual Report of the Superintendent of Education of the City of Buffalo, 1896–97* (Buffalo: The Wenborne-Sumner Co., 1897), 87–91, and *Annual Report of the Superintendent of Education of the City of Buffalo, 1899–1900* (Buffalo: The Wenborne-Sumner Co., 1901), 69–71.

84. The nation-building functions of these encampments are discussed in O'Leary, *To Die For: The Paradox of American Patriotism*, 55–56.

85. Buffalo *Times*, quoted in BECHS, *Annual Report of the Superintendent of Education of the City of Buffalo, 1896–97*, 88.

86. BECPL, Rare Book Room, *Official Book: Thirtieth Sängerfest of the North-American Sängerbund*, 20-21.

87. New York *Daily Tribune*, 26 June 1901.

88. Robert Rydell, *All the World's a Fair: Visions of Empire at American International Expositions, 1876–1916* (Chicago: University of Chicago Press, 1984), 129.

89. Ibid., and Buffalo *Times*, 27 June 1901.

90. Buffalo *Enquirer*, 25 June 1901.

91. Buffalo *Commercial Advertiser*, 25 June 1901; Buffalo *Daily Courier*, 25 June 1901; Buffalo *Enquirer*, 25 June 1901 and 26 June 1901.

92. *Catholic Union and Times*, 4 July 1901.

93. Buffalo *Times*, 22 June 1901.

94. Buffalo *Daily Courier*, 24 June 1901.

95. Buffalo *Times*, 26 June 1901.

96. Buffalo *Commercial Advertiser*, 19 June 1901.

97. Buffalo *Freie Presse*, 22 June 1901 and 1 July 1901; Buffalo *Times*, 26 June 1901.

98. BECPL, Rare Book Room, *Official Book: Thirtieth Sängerfest of the North-American Sängerbund*, 51.

99. New York *Daily Tribune*, 25 June 1901.

100. Goldman, *High Hopes*, 154–59 and Yox, "Decline of the German-American Community," 192. Compared with New York City's *Little Germany*, intra-ethnic conflict in Buffalo seemed relatively benign. Rarely did labour disputes spill over into industry-wide strikes (with the obvious exception of the 1877 and 1892 railroad strikes). See Nadel, *Little Germany*, Chapters 7 and 8.

101. Buffalo *Demokrat*, 24 June 1901.

102. Buffalo *Freie Presse*, 22 June 1901.

103. Ibid.

104. Levine, *Highbrow/Lowbrow*, 190.

105. *Catholic Union and Times*, 4 July 1901.

106. Levine, *Highbrow/Lowbrow*, 195, 197, and 198.

107. Buffalo *Commercial Advertiser*, 26 June 1901.

108. Ibid.

109. BECHS, Manuscript Collection MSS 25 VH B93b, "J.W. Ernst Besser. Historical Sketch and Printed Notes of the German Singing Society Deutscher Sängerbund of Buffalo, N.Y., May 1887."

On the silencing of concert audiences see also Kammen, *American Culture, American Taste*, 10 and 35, and Johnson, *Listening in Paris*.

110. Buffalo *Times*, 26 June 1901.

111. Buffalo *Commercial Advertiser*, 26 June 1901.

112. New York *Daily Tribune*, 26 June 1901; Buffalo *Times*, 27 June 1901; Buffalo *Volksfreund*, 28 June 1901.

113. Robert Rydell, John Findling, and Kimberly Pelle, *Fair America: World's Fairs in the United States* (Washington: Smithsonian Institution Press, 2000), 1–6.

114. Burton Benedict, "Rituals of Representation: Ethnic Stereotypes and Colonized Peoples at World's Fairs," in *Fair Representations: World's Fairs and the Modern World*, ed. Robert Rydell and Nancy Gwinn (Amsterdam: VU University Press, 1994), 28, 30, and 36, and Rydell, Findling, and Pelle, *Fair America*, 9.

115. Rydell, Findling, and Pelle, *Fair America*, 47 and 49. See also Buffalo *Volksfreund*, 22 June 1901.

116. Christoph Cornelissen, "Die politische und kulturelle Repräsentation des Deutschen Reiches auf den Weltausstellungen des 19. Jahrhunderts," *Geschichte in Wissenschaft und Unterricht*, 52, 3 (2001), 159.

117. Buffalo *Freie Presse*, 26 June 1901.

118. Buffalo *Demokrat*, 28 June 1901 and Buffalo *Review*, 27 June 1901.

119. Gerber, *The Making of an American Pluralism*, 172, 175, 191, and 196.

120. See, in particular, C.D. Arnold, *The Pan-American Exposition* (Buffalo, n.d.: 1901).

121. Fauser, *Musical Encounters*, 8 and 12. The soundscapes, which visitors encountered at the exhibition, were not limited to musical performances alone. As Annegret Fauser writes in her marvelous work on the 1889 world's fair in Paris, "Sound-as-noise," enveloped visitors in "the sounds of the cafes and restaurants, shouts from street vendors, ... machine noises, and snatches from music from various—and often simultaneous—sources." "Sound-as-music," in turn, encompassed the carefully orchestrated musical performances that were invariably "presented within a nationalist framework." See ibid.

122. Buffalo *Review*, 25 June 1901.

123. Ibid. and Buffalo *Enquirer*, 25 June 1901.

124. Buffalo *Freie Presse*, 27 June 1901 and 28 June 1901.

125. Buffalo *Demokrat*, 28 June 1901.

126. Buffalo *Enquirer*, 25 June 1901.

127. Brubaker, "Ethnicity without Groups," 160.

128. Evansville *Demokrat*, as quoted in the Buffalo *Volksfreund*, 27 June 1901. Among the folk songs performed at the Buffalo *Sängerfest* were "Abschied hat der Tag genommen," "Lied eines fahrenden Gesellen," "Hänsel und Gretel," and "Horch die alten Eichen rauschen."

129. Philadelphia *Gazette*, as quoted in the Buffalo *Volksfreund*, 27 June 1901.

130. See the speech by Charles A. Wenborn, chairman of the reception committee, as quoted in the Buffalo *Freie Presse*, 25 June 1901.

131. See Buffalo *Freie Presse*, 27 June 1901; Buffalo *Volksfreund*, 26 and 28 June 1901.

132. See also Levine, *Highbrow/Lowbrow*.

Coda

1. Greene, *A Singing Ambivalence*, 32.

2. In the closing ceremony of the 1901 Buffalo singers' festival, for example, the male mass chorus performed—to "thundering applause"—"Liebchen ade, scheiden tut weh" (Farewell Beloved) and "Weh, dass wir scheiden müssen" (Behold, the Pain of Parting). Buffalo *Demokrat*, 28 June 1901.

3. George Sánchez, *Becoming Mexican American: Ethnicity, Culture and Identity in Chicano Los Angeles, 1900-1945* (New York: Oxford University Press, 1993), 171, 177 and 178.

4. Holzapfel and Bohlman, "The Musical Culture of German-Americans," 7.

5. As Otto Holzapfel and Philip Bohlman note, "Rather than a border between German and American cultural identities, the hyphen comes to represent exchange that flows in several directions." Holzapfel and Bohlman, "The Musical Culture of German-Americans," 15, see also 3.

6. Buffalo *Enquirer*, 25 June 1901.

7. Helbich, "Die 'Englischen,'" 529.

8. For the "affinities of ethnicity and modernity," see Werner Sollors, *Beyond Ethnicity: Consent and Descent in American Culture* (New York: Oxford University Press, 1986), 243.

Bibliography

I.Primary Sources

Canada

City of Cambridge Archives

Minute Book of the Board of Trustees of the Preston School, January 3, 1852, to January 5, 1853.

Minute Book of the Board of Trustees of the Preston School, August 6, 1858, to August 5, 1863.

Minute Book of the Board of Trustees of the Preston School, October 7, 1863, to July 27, 1869.

Minute Book of the Board of Trustees of the Preston School, June 13, 1905, to February 6, 1917.

Waterloo Region Museum

Sängerfest Ribbons and Badges, 1874–1901.

Kitchener Public Library, Grace Schmidt Room of Local History

Waterloo Historical Society (KPL, WHS)

KIT 6. Visitors' Book: Roman Catholic Separate School. 2 June 1876, and 6 February 1878.

MC 6.21. Elias Weber Bingeman Snider Collection.

MC 14.5.a.b.c. Shoemaker Family Collection.

MC 15.1.c. "Address of the English Deputation to the Managing Committee of the German Peace Festival, 1871, Berlin." Tuesday, May 2, 1871

MC 15.9.c. William H.E. Schmalz Collection

MC 53. "Rev. A.B. Sherk."

MC 71. "Isaac Moyer, Biography and Reminiscence, January 1st, 1915."

WAT C-87. Records of the Board of Examiners for Waterloo County. Berlin: s.n., 1853–1908.

WAT C-87. Manuscript Annual School Reports for the County of Waterloo.

Library of the City of Kitchener

Berlin City Council Minutes, 13 October 1879.

Manuscript Census of Canada, 1901

Library and Archives Canada, Ottawa

National Archives

MG 30, B13. Vol. 9. "Statistics and history of the Preston School Compiled and Written by Otto Klotz for the use of his family."

National Library

Annual Reports of Education for the Province of Ontario. 1871–1914.

Census of Canada. 1871–1911.

Debates in the Legislative Assembly of Canada.

Journal of Education, Province of Ontario.

Ontario Gazeteer and Directory.

Province of Ontario: Gazeteer and Directory.

Regulations and Correspondence Relating to French and German Schools in the Province of Ontario. Toronto: Warwick and Sons, 1889.

Vernon's Berlin, Waterloo and Bridgeport Directory.

Archives of Ontario, Toronto

Sir James P. Whitney Papers. F5, MU 3132. "Memo Regarding Teaching of German in Bilingual Schools."

RG 2-109-130. Misc. School Records, Box 2. *Report on the Public Schools of the County of Waterloo by the County Inspector Thomas Pearce* (for 1872). Galt: Hutchinson, 1873.

Ontario Institute for Studies in Education, Toronto (OISE)

Annual Reports of Education for Upper Canada. 1850–1870.

Regional Municipality of Waterloo County, Kitchener

Journal of the Proceedings and By-Laws of the Municipal Council of the County of Waterloo. 1870, 1872 and 1888.

University of Waterloo, Doris Lewis Rare Book Room (UW, DLRBR)

Breithaupt Hewetson Clark Collection

Diaries of Louis Jacob Breithaupt.

"Sketch of the Life of Catherine Breithaupt, Her Family and Her Times." Berlin, 1911.

Waterloo County Board of Education, Kitchener

Berlin Board Minutes. 1898–1908.

Berlin Public School Board, Minutes. 1908–1915.

Minute Book of Berlin Teachers' Association. October 1891 to November 8, 1912.

Wilmot Township S.S. 2, New Hamburg, School Board Minutes. 1875–1895.

Woolwich Township, S.S. 8 (St. Jacobs), Visitors' Book. 1861–1912.

Waterloo Public Library

Local History Collection. Vertical File, "Saengerfests."

Germany

Ruhr-University of Bochum

Bochumer Briefsammlung, "Krause-Krause."

BIBLIOGRAPHY

United States

Buffalo and Erie County Historical Society, Buffalo (BECHS)

Annual Reports of the Superintendent of Education of the City of Buffalo. 1847–1910.

"Joseph Mischka," Music Clippings, M67. Vols. 1, 3 and 6.

Manuscript Collection MSS 25 VH B93b, "J.W. Ernst Besser. Historical Sketch and Printed Notes of the German Singing Society Deutscher Sängerbundof Buffalo, N.Y., May 1887."

Vertical File, "Music—Organizations, Soc., Clubs."

Buffalo and Erie County Public Library, Buffalo (BECPL)

Rare Book Room

Die Deutsche Jungmänner Gesellschaft zu Buffalo, N.Y.: Festschrift zur Feier ihres fünzigjährigen Stiftungsfestes am 11. und 12. Mai 1891. Buffalo, NY, 1891.

Fest-Zeitung für das 23ste Nord-Amerikanische Sängerfest/Official Gazette of the 23rd North American Saengerfest. Nos. 1–20 (January–August), 1883.

Frank & Leslie's Illustrierte Zeitung, 21 July 1883 and 28 July 1883.

Official Text-Book and Programme of the Twenty-Third Saengerfest of the North-American Saengerbund Held at Buffalo N.Y., July 16–20, 1883. Buffalo: N.S. Rosenau, 1883.

Official Book: Thirtieth Saengerfest of the North-American Saengerbund, held in Buffalo, June 24, 25, 26, and 27, 1901. Buffalo, NY: Buffalo Saengerfest Company, 1901.

Um die Welt, Keppler & Schwarzmann's Illustrierte Zeitung. New York, 28. Juli 1883.

Zur Erinnerung an das 50-jährige Jubiläum des Buffalo Sängerbundes den 19., 20. und 21. April 1903, 1853–1903.

Special Collection

Proceedings of the Common Council of the City of Buffalo. 1854–1915.

Wood, J. Henry, ed. Schools of Buffalo. Buffalo: Mrs. Ida C. Wood, 1899.

Library of Congress, Washington, DC

Amerikanische Schulzeitung (hereafter published as Erziehungs-Blätter für Schule und Haus; Pädagogische Monatsheft/Pedagogical Monthly: Zeitschrift für das deutschamerikanische Schulwesen; Monatshefte für deutsche Sprache und Pädagogik). 1870–1914.

Annual Reports of the Superintendent of Education of the State of New York. 1855–1903.

Census of the United States, 1910.

Department of Public Instruction, State of New York. Thirty-Sixth Annual Report of the State Superintendent, 1890, for the School Year Ending July 25, 1889. Albany: James B. Lyon, 1890.

Die Deutschen in Amerika und die deutsch-amerikanischen Friedensfeste im Jahr 1871: Eine Erinnerungs-Schrift für die Deutschen diesseits und jenseits des Oceans. New York: Verlags-Expedition des deutsch-amerikanischen Conversations-Lexikons, 1871.

Education Department of the State of New York. Examination of the Public School System of the City of Buffalo. Albany: The University of the State of New York, 1916.

Viereck, L. "Chapter XIVL German Instruction in American Schools." In United States Bureau of

Education, *Report of the Commissioner of Education for the Year 1900–1901*. Vol. 1, 531-708. Washington, DC: Government Printing Office, 1902.

————. *Zwei Jahrhunderte Deutschen Unterrichts in den Vereinigten Staaten*. Braunschweig: Friedrich Viereck und Sohn, 1903.

II. Newspapers

Canada

Berlin *Daily Telegraph*

Berlin *Deutsche Zeitung*

Berlin News Record

Berliner Journal (later *Ontario Journal*)

Canadian Illustrated News

Canadisches Volksblatt

Der Deutsche in Canada

Guelph *Daily Mercury and Advertiser*

Hamilton *Daily Spectator*

Hamilton *Spectator*

London *Free Press*

Stratford *Evening Beacon*

Toronto *Daily Telegraph*

Toronto *Empire*

Toronto *Globe*

Waterloo County Chronicle

United States

Buffalo *Catholic Union and Times*

Buffalo *Christian Advocate*

Buffalo *Commercial Advertiser*

Buffalo *Daily Courier*

Buffalo *Daily Republic*

Buffalo *Demokrat*

Buffalo *Evening News*

Buffalo *Evening Post*

Buffalo *Evening Telegraph*

Buffalo *Express*

Buffalo *Freie Presse*

Buffalo *Morning Express*

Buffalo *Review*

Buffalo *Sunday Morning News*

Buffalo *Times*

Buffalo *Volksfreund*

Buffalo *Weekly Press*

New York *Daily Tribune*

Rochester Union and Advertiser

Täglicher Buffalo Volksfreund

III. Published Primary Sources

Akers, William J. *Cleveland Schools in the Nineteenth Century.* Cleveland, OH: W.M. Bayne Printing House, 1901.

Arnold, C.D. *The Pan-American Exposition.* Buffalo, n.d.: 1901.

Ellison, Ismar S. "The Germans of Buffalo: An Historical Essay." In *Publications of the Buffalo Historical Society,* 2: 11743. Buffalo: Bigelow Brothers, 1880.

Fichte, Johann Gottlieb. *Addresses to the German Nation.* Westport, CN: Greenwood Press, 1979.

Fraser, Alexander. *History of Ontario: Its Resources and Development.* Toronto: The Canadian History Company, 1927.

Geschichte der Deutschen in Buffalo und Erie County, N.Y., mit Biographien und Illustrationen hervorragender Deutsch-Amerikaner, welche zur Entwicklung der Stadt Buffalo beigetragen haben. Buffalo: Reinecke and Zesch, 1898.

Hodgins, George, ed. *Documentary History of Education in Upper Canada.* Vol. 3, *1836–40.* Toronto: Warwick Bros. and Rutter, 1895.

Middleton, Jesse Edgar, and Fred Landon, eds. *Province of Ontario: A History, 1615–1927.* Vols. 3 and 4. Toronto: Dominion, 1927–28.

Müller-Grote, Karl. "Onkel Karl: Deutschkanadische Lebensbilder." *German-Canadian Yearbook* 15 (1998): 107–255.

Pearce, Thomas. "School History, Waterloo County and Berlin." *Waterloo Historical Society* 2 (1914): 33–50.

Schuricht, Hermann. *Geschichte der Deutschen Schulbestrebungen in Amerika.* Leipzig: Verlag Friedrich Fleischer, 1884.

Sherk, M.G. "Reminiscences of Freeport—Waterloo County from 1867 to 1873." *Waterloo Historical Society* 12 (1924).

Shotwell, John B. *A History of the Schools of Cincinnati.* Cincinnati: The School Life Company, 1902.

Smith, H. Perry. *History of the City of Buffalo and Erie County.* Vol. 2. Syracuse, NY: D. Mason and Co., 1884.

Staebler, H.L. "Random Notes on Music in Nineteenth-Century Berlin, Ontario." *Waterloo Historical Society* 37 (1949).

White, Truman C. *A Descriptive Work on Erie County, New York.* Vol. 1. Boston History Company, 1898.

IV. Secondary Sources

Abrahams, Roger D. "An American Vocabulary of Celebration." In *Time out of Time: Essays on the Festival*, ed. Alessandro Falassi, 173–183. Albuquerque: University of New Mexico Press, 1987.

Allen, Ann Taylor. "American and German Women in the Kindergarten Movement, 1850–1914." In *German Influences on Education in the United States to 1917*, edited by Henry Geitz et al., 85–101. New York: Cambridge University Press, 1995.

Allen, Theodore W. *The Invention of the White Republic*. Vol. 1, *Racial Oppression and Social Control*. London: Verso, 1994.

Anderson, Benedict. *Imagined Communities: Reflections on the Origin and Spread of Nationalism*. New York: Verso, 1991 [1983].

Alter, Nora M., and Lutz Koepnick, eds. *Sound Matters: Essays on the Acoustic of Modern German Culture*. New York: Berghahn Books, 2004.

Applegate, Celia. *Bach in Berlin: Nation and Culture in Mendelssohn's Revival of the* St. Matthew Passion. Ithaca, NY: Cornell University Press, 2005.

———. "How German Is it? Nationalism and the Idea of Serious Music in the Early Nineteenth Century," *19th-Century Music* 21, 3 (Spring 1998): 274-296.

———. *A Nation of Provincials: The German Idea of Heimat*. Berkeley: University of California Press, 1990.

Applegate, Celia and Pamela Potter, eds., *Music and German National Identity*. Chicago: University of Chicago Press, 2002.

Bailey, Peter. *Popular Culture and Performance in the Victorian City*. Cambridge: Cambridge University Press, 1998.

Balakrishnan, Gopal, ed., *Mapping the Nation*. London and New York: Verso, 1996.

Balibar, Etienne. "The Nation Form: History and Ideology." In *Becoming National: A Reader*, edited by Geoff Eley and Ronald Grigor Suny, 132–49. New York: Oxford University Press, 1996.

Barnard, F.W. *Herder's Social and Political Thought: From Enlightenment to Nationalism*. Oxford: Clarendon Press, 1965.

Barth, Frederick, ed. *Ethnic Groups and Boundaries: The Social Organization of Cultural Difference*. Boston: Little Brown and Company, 1969.

Bassler, Gerhard. *The German Canadians, 1750–1937: Immigration, Settlement and Culture*. St. John's, NF: Jesperson Press, 1986.

Bayley, Susan N. "The Direct Method and Modern Language Teaching in England, 1880–1918." *History of Education* 27, 1 (1998): 39-57.

———. "'Life Is Too Short to Learn German': Modern Languages in English Elementary Education, 1872–1904." *History of Education* 18, 1 (1989): 57–70.

Beatty, Barbara. "Children in Different and Difficult Times: The History of American Childhood, Part I." *History of Education Quarterly* 40, 1 (2000): 71–84.

Belgum, Kirsten. *Popularizing the Nation: Audience, Representation, and the Production of Identity in* Die Gartenlaube, *1853–1900*. Lincoln: University of Nebraska Press, 1998.

Bender, Thomas. "Historians, the Nation, and the Plenitude of Narratives." In *Rethinking American History in a Global Age*, edited by Thomas Bender, 1–21. Berkeley: University of California Press, 2002.

Benedict, Burton. "Rituals of Representation: Ethnic Stereotypes and Colonized Peoples at World's Fairs," in *Fair Representations: World's Fairs and the Modern World*, edited by Robert Rydell and Nancy Gwinn, 28-61. Amsterdam: VU University Press, 1994.

Berger, Carl. *The Sense of Power: Studies in the Ideas of Canadian Imperialism, 1867–1914*. Toronto: University of Toronto Press, 1970.

Berlin, Isaiah. *Vico and Herder: Two Studies in the History of Ideas*. New York: Viking Press, 1976.

Blackbourn, David, and James Retallack, eds. *Localism, Landscape, and the Ambiguities of Place: German-Speaking Central Europe, 1860–1930*. Toronto: University of Toronto Press, 2007.

Blanck, Dag. "The Role of the Swedish Language in Shaping a Swedish-American Culture." In *Not English Only: Redefining 'American' in American Studies*, edited by Orm Øverland, 34–47. Amsterdam: VU University Press, 2001.

Bloomfield, Elizabeth. "City-Building Processes in Berlin/Kitchener and Waterloo, 1870–1930." PhD diss., University of Guelph, 1981.

———. *Waterloo Township through Two Centuries*. Waterloo: St. Jacobs Printery, 1995.

Bohlman, Philip V. *The Music of European Nationalism: Cultural Identity and Modern History*. Oxford: ABC Clio, 2004.

———. "Landscape—Region—Nation—Reich: German Folk Song in the Nexus of National Identity." In *Music and German National Identity*, edited by Celia Applegate and Pamela Potter, 105–27. Chicago: University of Chicago Press, 2002.

———. "On the Unremarkable in Music." *19ᵗʰ-Century Music* 16, 2 (1991): 203–21.

———. "'Still, They Were All Germans in Town': Music in the Multi-Religious German-American Community." In *Emigration and Settlement Patterns of German Communities in North America*, edited by Eberhard Reichmann, La Vern J. Rippley, and Joerg Nagler, 276–93. Indianapolis: Indiana University-Purdue University Press, 1995.

———. *The Study of Folk Music in the Modern World*. Bloomington: Indiana University Press, 1988.

Bohleman, Philip V., and Otto Holzapfel, eds. *Land without Nightingales: Music in the Making of German-America*. Madison: University of Wisconsin, 2002.

Bongert, Klaus. "Deutsch in Ontario: Deutsche Sprache und Kultur in Kitchener-Waterloo." In *Deutsch als Muttersprache in Kanada: Berichte zur Gegenwartslage*, edited by Leopold Auburger et al., 25–32. Wiesbaden: Franz Steiner Verlag, 1977.

Bonnell, Victoria E., and Lynn Hunt, eds. *Beyond the Cultural Turn: New Directions in the Study of Society and Culture*. Berkeley: University of California Press, 1999.

Botstein, Leon. "Listening through Reading: Musical Literacy and the Concert Audience." *19ᵗʰ-Century Music* 16, 2 (1992): 129–145.

Brancoforte, Charlotte L., ed. *The German Forty-Eighters in the United States*. New York: Peter Lang, 1989.

Bretting, Agnes. "Halleluja, We're Off to America! Western, Central and Northern Europe." In *Fame, Fortune and Sweet Liberty: The Great European Immigration*, edited by Dirk Hoerder and Diethelm Knauff, 24–47. Bremen: Edition Tammen, 1992.

Brubaker, Rogers. "Ethnicity without groups." *Archives européennes de sociologie* 43, 2 (November 2002): 163-89.

———. *Ethnicity without groups*. Cambridge MA: Harvard University Press, 2004.

Brusniak, Friedhelm. "Männerchorwesen und Konfession von 1800 bis in den Vormärz." In *"Heil deutschem Wort und Sang!" Nationalidentität und Gesangskultur in der deutschen Geschichte—Tagungsbericht Feuchtwangen, 1994,* edited by Friedhelm Brusniak and Dietmar Klenke, 95–108. Augsburg: Bernd Wissner, 1995.

Bukowczyk, John, Nora Faires, David Smith, and Randy William Widdis. *Permeable Border: The Great Lakes Basin as Transnational Region, 1650–1990.* Pittsburg: University of Pittsburgh Press, 2005.

Bungert, Heike. "Demonstrating the Value of 'Gemüthlichkeit' and 'Cultur': The Festivals of German Americans in Milwaukee, 1870–1910." In *Celebrating Ethnicity and Nation: American Festive Culture from the Revolution to the Early Twentieth Century,* edited by Geneviève Fabre and Jürgen Heideking, 175–214. New York: Berghahn Books, 2001.

Burdette, Alan. R. "'Ein Prosit der Gemütlichkeit': The Traditionalization Process in a German-American Singing Society." In *Land without Nightingales: Music in the Making of German-America,* edited by Philip V. Bohlman and Otto Holzapfel, 233–57. Madison: University of Wisconsin-Madison, 2002.

Carter, Tim. "The Sounds of Silence: Models for an Urban Musicology." *Urban History* 29, 1 (2002): 8–18.

Cecillon, Jack. "Turbulent Times in the Diocese of London: Bishop Fallon and the French-Language Controversy, 1910–18." *Ontario History* 87, 4 (1995): 369–95.

Chartier, Roger. *Cultural History: Between Practices and Representations.* Ithaca, NY: Cornell University Press, 1988.

Chickering, Roger. *"We Men Who Feel Most German": A Cultural Study of the Pan-German League, 1886–1914.* Boston: George Allen and Unwin, 1984.

Confino, Alon. *The Nation as a Local Metaphor: Württemberg, Imperial Germany, and National Memory, 1871–1918.* Chapel Hill and London: University of North Carolina Press, 1997.

Conolly-Smith, Peter. *Translating America: An Immigrant Press Visualizes American Popular Culture, 1895–1918.* Washington, DC: Smithsonian Books, 2004.

Conzen, Kathleen Neils. "Ethnicity and Musical Culture among the German Catholics of the Sauk, 1840–1920." In *Land without Nightingales: Music in the Making of German-America,* edited by Philip V. Bohlman and Otto Holzapfel, 31–71. Madison: University of Wisconsin-Madison, 2002.

———. "Ethnicity as Festive Culture: Nineteenth-Century German America on Parade." In *The Invention of Ethnicity,* edited byWerner Sollors, 44–76. New York: Oxford University Press, 1989.

———. "German-Americans and the Invention of Ethnicity." In *America and the Germans: An Assessment of a Three-Hundred-Year History,* edited by Frank Trommler and Joseph McVeigh. Vol. 1, *Immigration, Language, and Ethnicity,* 131–47. Philadelphia: University of Pennsylvania Press, 1985,

———. "Immigrants in Nineteenth-Century Agricultural History." In *Agriculture and National Development: Views on the Nineteenth Century,* edited by Lou Ferleger, 303–42. Ames, IA, 1990.

———. "Mainstream and Side Channels: The Localization of Immigrant Cultures." *Journal of American Ethnic History* 11, 1 (1991): 5–20.

———. *Making Their Own America: Assimilation Theory and the German Peasant Pioneer.* New York: Berg, 1990.

————. "Patterns of German-American History." In *Germans in America: Retrospect and Prospect*, edited by Randall M. Miller, 14–36. Philadelphia: German Society of Pennsylvania, 1984.

————."Phantom Landscapes of Colonization: Germans in the Making of a Pluralistic America." In *The German-American Encounter: Conflict and Cooperation between Two Cultures, 1800–2000* , edited by Frank Trommler and Elliott Shore, 7–21. New York: Berghan Books, 2001.

Conzen, Kathleen Neils, David A. Gerber, Ewa Morawska, George E. Pozzetta, and Rudolph J. Vecoli. "The Invention of Ethnicity: A Perspective from the U.S.A." *Journal of American Ethnic History* 12, 1 (1992): 3–40.

Corbin, Alain. *Village Bells: Sound and Meaning in the Nineteenth-Century French Countryside*. New York: Columbia University Press, 1998.

Cornelissen, Christoph. "Die politische und kulturelle Repräsentation des Deutschen Reiches auf den Weltausstellungen des 19. Jahrhunderts," *Geschichte in Wissenschaft und Unterricht*, 52, 3 (2001): 148-61.

Corry, Mary Jane. "The Role of German Singing Societies in Nineteenth-Century America." In *Germans in America: Aspects of German-American Relations in the Nineteenth Century*, edited by E. Allen McCormick, 155–68. New York: Columbia University, 1983.

Countryman, June. "Theodor Zoellner." *Canadian Encyclopedia*. http://www. thecanadianencyclopedia.com/.

Cremin, Lawrence A. *American Education: The Metropolitan Experience, 1876–1980*. New York: Harper and Row, 1988.

————. *The Transformation of the Schools: Progressivism in American Education, 1876–1957*. New York: Vintage Books, 1961.

Cuban, Larry. *How Teachers Taught: Constancy and Change in American Classrooms, 1890–1980*. New York: Longman, 1984.

Curtis, Bruce. "Class Culture and Administration: Educational Inspection in Canada West." In *Colonial Leviathan: State Formation in Mid-Nineteenth-Century Canada*, edited by Allan Greer and Ian Radforth, 103–33. Toronto: University of Toronto Press, 1992.

————. *True Government by Choice Men? Inspection, Education, and State Formation in Canada West*. Toronto: University of Toronto Press, 1992.

Dahlhaus, Carl. *Nineteenth-Century Music*. Berkeley and Los Angeles: University of California Press, 1989.

Davis, Susan G. *Parades and Power: Street Theatre in Nineteenth-Century Philadelphia*. Philadelphia: Temple University Press, 1986.

Deutsch, Karl. *Nationalism and Social Communication: An Inquiry into the Foundations of Nationality*. Cambridge, MA: M.I.T. Press, 1966.

Dictionary of Canadian Biography. Vol.14, *1911–20*. Toronto: University of Toronto Press, 1998.

Doerries, Reinhard R. "Organization and Ethnicity: The German-American Experience." *Amerikastudien/American Studies* 33, 3 (1988): 309–17.

Dörner, Andreas. "Der Mythos der nationalen Einheit: Symbolpolitik und Deutungskämpfe bei der Einweihung des Hermannsdenkmals im Jahre 1875." *Archiv für Kulturgeschichte* 79, 2 (1997): 389–416.

Düding, Dieter. *Organisierter gesellschaftlicher Nationalismus in Deutschland, 1808–1847: Bedeutung und Funktion der Turner- und Sängervereine für die deutsche Nationalbewegung*. Munich: R. Oldenburg Verlag, 1984.

Düding, Dieter, Peter Friedemann, and Paul Münch, eds. *Öffentliche Festkultur: Politische Feste in Deutschland von der Aufklärung bis zum Ersten Weltkrieg.* Hamburg: Rowohlt Taschenbuch Verlag, 1988.

Eastman, Carol. "Language, Ethnic Identity, and Change." In *Linguistic Minorities, Policies, and Pluralism,* edited by John Edwards, 259–75. London: Academic Press, 1984.

Edwards, John, ed. *Linguistic Minorities, Policies, and Pluralism.* London: Academic Press, 1984.

Eichhoff, Jürgen. "German in Wisconsin." In *The German Language in America: A Symposium,* edited by Glenn G. Gilbert, 43–57. Austin: University of Texas Press, 1971.

———. "The German Language in America." In *America and the Germans: An Assessment of a Three-Hundred-Year History,* edited by Frank Trommler and Joseph McVeigh. Vol. I, *Immigration, Language, Ethnicity,* 223–40. Philadelphia: University of Pennsylvania Press, 1985.

English, John, and Kenneth McLaughlin. *Kitchener: An Illustrated History.* Scarborough, ON: Robin Brass Studio, 1996.

Ergang, Robert Reinhold. *Herder and the Foundations of German Nationalism.* New York: Columbia University, 1931.

Falassi, Alessandro, ed. *Time out of Time: Essays on the Festival.* Albuquerque: University of New Mexico Press, 1987.

Fabre, Genevieve, and Jürgen Heideking, eds. *Celebrating Ethnicity and Nation: American Festive Culture from the Revolution to the Early Twentieth Century.* New York: Berghahn Books, 2001.

Fallon, Daniel. "German Influences on American Education." In *The German-American Encounter: Conflict and Cooperation between Two Cultures, 1800–2000,* edited by Frank Trommler and Elliott Shore, 77–87. New York: Berghahn Books, 2001.

Fauser, Annegret. *Musical Encounters at the 1889 Paris World's Fair.* Rochester, NY: University of Rochester Press, 1995.

Fessler, Paul Rudolph. "Speaking in Tongues: German-Americans and the Heritage of Bilingual Education in American Public Schools." PhD diss., Texas A&M University, 1997.

Fishman, Joshua. "Language Maintenance." In *Harvard Encyclopedia of American Ethnic Groups,* edited by Stephen Thernstrom. Cambridge, MA: Belknap Press, 1980.

———. "The Sociology of Language: An Interdisciplinary Social Science Approach to Language in Society." In *Current Trends in Linguistics,* edited by Thomas A. Sebeok. Vol. 12, *Linguistic and Adjacent Arts and Sciences,* 1629–1784. The Hague: Mouton, 1984.

Freund, Alexander. *Aufbrüche nach dem Zusammenbruch.* V&R Unipress, 2004.

Frisse, Ulrich. *Berlin, Ontario (1800–1916): Historische Identitäten von "Kanadas Deutscher Hauptstadt"—Ein Beitrag zur Deutsch-Kanadischen Migrations-, Akkulturations- und Perzeptionsgeschichte des 19. und frühen 20. Jahrhunderts.* New Dundee, ON: TransAtlanticPublishing, 2003.

Frith, Simon. "Music and Identity." In *Questions of Cultural Identity,* edited by Stuart Hall and Paul du Gay, 108–27. London: Sage Publications, 1996.

Gaffield, Chad. *Language, Schooling, and Cultural Conflict: The Origins of the French-Language Controversy in Ontario.* Kingston and Montreal: McGill-Queen's University Press, 1987.

———. "Linearity, Nonlinearity, and the Competing Constructions of Social Hierarchy in Early Twentieth-Century Canada: The Question of Language in 1901." *Historical Methods* 33, 2 (2000): 255–60.

Garrioch, David. "Sounds of the City: The Soundscape of Early Modern European Towns." *Urban History* 30, 1 (2003): 5–25.

Gerber, David. *Authors of Their Lives: The Personal Correspondence of British Immigrants to North America in the Nineteenth Century*. New York: New York University Press, 2006.

———. "Forming a Transnational Narrative: New Perspective on European Migration to the United States." *The History Teacher* 35, 1 (2001): 61–77.

———. "'The Germans Take Care of Our Celebrations': Middle-Class Americans Appropriate German Ethnic Culture in Buffalo in the 1850s." In *Hard at Play: Leisure in America, 1840–1940*, edited by Kathryn Grover, 39–60. Amherst: University of Massachusetts Press, 1992.

———. "Language Maintenance, Ethnic Group Formation, and Public Schools: Changing Patterns of German Concern, Buffalo, 1837-1874." *Journal of American Ethnic History* 4, 1 (1984): 31–61.

———. *The Making of an American Pluralism: Buffalo, New York, 1825–60*. Urbana: University of Illinois Press, 1989.

———. "'You See I Speak Wery Well English': Literacy and the Transformed Self as Reflected in Immigrant Personal Correspondence." *Journal of American Ethnic History* 12, 2 (1993): 56–62.

Geuss, Raymond. "Kultur, Bildung, Geist." *History and Theory* 35, 2 (1996): 151–64.

Gilbert, Glenn G. "English Loan-Words in the German of Fredericksburg, Texas." *American Speech* 40, 2 (1965): 102–112.

Gilbert, Glenn G., ed. *The German Language in America: A Symposium*. Austin: University of Texas Press, 1971.

Glasco, Laurence. *Ethnicity and Social Structure: Irish, Germans, and Native-Born of Buffalo, N.Y., 1850–1860*. New York: Arno Press, 1980.

Goldberg, Bettina. "Die Achtundvierziger und das Schulwesen in Amerika: Zur Theorie und Praxis ihrer Reformbestrebungen." *Amerikastudien/American Studies* 32, 4 (1987): 481–91.

———. "The German-English Academy, the National German-American Teachers' Seminary, and the Public School System in Milwaukee, Wisconsin, 1851–1919." In *German Influences on Education in the United States to 1917*, edited by Henry Geitz et al., 177–92. New York: Cambridge University Press, 1995.

Goldman, Mark. *High Hopes: The Rise and Decline of Buffalo, New York*. Albany: SUNY Press, 1983.

Greene, Victor. *American Immigrant Leaders, 1800–1910*. Baltimore, 1987.

———. *A Singing Ambivalence: American Immigrants between Old World and New, 1830-1930*. Kent: Kent State University Press, 2004.

Grenke, Arthur. *The German Community in Winnipeg: 1872–1919*. New York: AMS Press, 1991.

Hall, Stuart. "The Question of Cultural Identity." In *Modernity: An Introduction to Modern Societies*, edited by Stuart Hall et al., 595–634. Oxford: Blackwell Publishers, 1997 [1996].

Hansen, Marcus Lee. *The Mingling of the Canadian and American Peoples*. New Haven, CT, 1940.

Hardtwig, Wolfgang. "Bürgertum, Staatssymbolik und Staatsbewußtsein im Deutschen Kaiserreich 1871–1914." *Geschichte und Gesellschaft* 16 (1990): 269–95.

Hardwick, Susan Wiley. "The Ties That Bind: Transnational Migrant Networks at the Canadian-U.S. Borderland." *American Review of Canadian Studies* (Winter 2005): 667–82.

Harzig, Christiane. "Gender, Transatlantic Space, and the Presence of German-Speaking People in North America." In *Traveling between Worlds: German-American Encounters*, edited by Thomas Adam and Ruth Gross, 146–82. Arlington: University of Texas, 2006.

Hayes, Geoffrey. "From Berlin to the Trek of the Conestoga: A Revisionist Approach to Waterloo County's German Identity." *Ontario History* 91, 2 (1999): 131–49.

———. *Waterloo County: An Illustrated History*. Region of Waterloo: Waterloo Historical Society, 1997.

Helbich, Wolfgang. "Die 'Englischen': German Immigrants Describe Nineteenth-Century American Society." *Amerikastudien/American Studies* 36, 4 (1991): 515–30.

———. "Immigrant Adaptation at the Individual Level: The Evidence of Nineteenth-Century German-American Letters." *Amerikastudien/American Studies* 42, 3 (1997): 407–18.

Heron, Craig, and Steve Penfold. "The Craftmen's Spectacle: Labour Day Parades in Canada, the Early Years." *Histoire sociale/Social History* 29, 58 (1996): 357–89.

Hettling, Manfred, and Paul Nolte, eds. *Bürgerliche Feste: Symbolische Formen politischen Handelns im 19. Jahrhundert.* Göttingen: Vandenhoeck & Ruprecht, 1993.

Higham, John. *Strangers in the Land: Patterns of American Nativism, 1860–1925.* New York: Atheneum, 1963 [1955].

Hobsbawm, Eric. "Introduction," in *The Invention of Tradition*, edited by Eric Hobsbawm and Terence Ranger, 1–14. Cambridge: Cambridge University Press, 1983.

———. *Nations and Nationalism since 1790: Programme, Myth, Reality*. Cambridge: Cambridge University Press, 1990.

Hoerder, Dirk. *Cultures in Contact: World Migrations in the Second Millennium*. Durham, NC: Duke University Press, 2002.

———. "German-Speaking Immigrants—Co-Founders or Mosaic? A Research Note on Politics and Statistics in Scholarship." *Zeitschrift für Kanada-Studien* 14 (1994): 51–65.

———. "Historians and Their Data: The Complex Shift from Nation-State Approaches to the Study of People's Transcultural Lives." *Journal of American Ethnic History* 25, 4 (Summer 2006): 85–96.

Hoffenberg, Peter H. *An Empire on Display: English, Indian, and Australian Exhibition from the Crystal Palace to the Great War.* Berkeley: University of California Press, 2001.

Hohendahl, Peter Uwe. *Building a National Literature: The Case of Germany, 1830–1870.* Ithaca, NY: Cornell University Press, 1989.

Holzapfel, Otto, and Philip V. Bohlman. "The Musical Culture of German-Americans: Views from Different Sides of the Hyphen." In *Lands without Nightingales*, edited by Philip V. Bohlman and Otto Holzapfel, 1–27. Madison: University of Wisconson Press, 2002.

Horsman, Reginald. *Race and Manifest Destiny: The Origins of American Racial Anglo-Saxonism.* Cambridge, MA: Harvard University Press, 1981.

Houston, Susan E. "The 'Waifs and Strays' of a Late Victorian City: Juvenile Delinquents in Toronto." In *Childhood and Family in Canadian History*, edited by Joy Parr, 129–42. Toronto: McClelland and Stewart, 1982.

Huffines, Marion. "Language-Maintenance Efforts among German Immigrants and Their Descendants in the United States." In *America and the Germans: An Assessment of a Three-Hundred-Year History*, edited by Frank Trommler and Joseph McVeigh. Vol. 1, *Immigration, Language, Ethnicity.* Philadelphia: University of Pennsylvania Press, 1985.

Hutchinson, John. *The Dynamics of Cultural Nationalism: The Gaelic Revival and the Creation of the Irish Nation State*. London: Allen and Unwin, 1987.

Iacovetta, Franca. *Gatekeepers: Reshaping Immigrant Lives in Cold War Canada*. Toronto: Between the Lines, 2006.

Jacobson, Matthew Frye. *Special Sorrows: The Diasporic Imagination of Irish, Polish, and Jewish Immigrants in the United States*. Cambridge, MA: Harvard University Press, 1995.

———. *Whiteness of a Different Color: European Immigrants and the Alchemy of Race*. Cambridge, MA: Harvard University Press, 1998.

Johnson, James H. *Listening in Paris: A Cultural History*. Berkeley: University of California Press, 1995.

Jordan, Glenn, and Chris Weedon. *Cultural Politics: Class, Gender, Race and the Postmodern World*. Oxford: Blackwell, 1995.

Junker, Alan William. "Otto Klotz and the Implementation of Education Policy in Waterloo County, 1846–1871." MA thesis, Wilfrid Laurier University, 1987.

Kalbfleisch, Herbert Karl. *The History of the Pioneer German Language Press of Ontario, 1835–1918*. Toronto: University of Toronto Press, 1968.

Kallmann, Helmut. *A History of Music in Canada, 1534–1914*. Toronto: University of Toronto Press, 1987.

Kamensky, Jane. *Governing the Tongue: The Politics of Speech in Early New England*. New York: Oxford University Press, 1997.

Kammen, Michael. *American Culture, American Taste: Social Change and the 20th Century*. New York: Alfred A. Knopf, 2000.

Kamphoefner, Walter. "German American Bilingualism: cui malo? Mother Tongue and Socioeconomic Status among the Second Generation in 1940." *International Migration Review* 28, 4 (1994): 846–64.

———. *The Westfalians: From Germany to Missouri*. Princeton, NJ: Princeton University Press, 1987.

Katasreas, Dimitri. "The Public and Private English-German Schools of Baltimore: 1836 to 1904." PhD diss., Georgetown University, 1994.

Kedourie, Elie. *Nationalism*. Oxford: Blackwell, 1993.

Kenny, Kevin. "Diaspora and Comparison: The Global Irish as a Case Study." *Journal of American History* 90, 1 (2003): 134–62.

Kivisto, Peter. "Theorizing Transnational Immigration: A Critical Review of Current Efforts." *Ethnic and Racial Studies* 24, 4 (2001): 549–77.

Klenke, Dietmar. "Bürgerlicher Männergesang und Politik in Deutschland." *Geschichte in Wissenschaft und Unterricht* 40, 8 (1989): 458–85.

———. "Nationalkriegerisches Gemeinschaftsideal als politische Religion: Zum Vereinsnationalismus der Sänger, Schützen und Turner am Vorabend der Einigungskriege." *Historische Zeitschrift* 260, 2 (1995): 395–448.

Kloss, Heinz. "Die deutschamerikanische Schule." *Jahrbuch für Amerikastudien* 7 (1962): 141–75.

———. "German-American Language Maintenance." In *Language Loyalty in the United States: The Maintenance and Perpetuation of Non-English Mother Tongues by American Ethnic and Religious Groups*, edited by Joshua Fishman, 206–52. London: Moutin and Co., 1966.

———. "German as an Immigrant, Indigenous, and Second Language in the United States." In *The German Language in America: A Symposium*, edited by Glenn G. Gilbert, 106–27. Austin: University of Texas Press, 1971.

Knobel, Dale T. *Paddy and the Republic: Ethnicity and Nationality in Antebellum America*. Middletown, CT: Wesleyan University Press, 1986.

Koegel, John. *Music in German Immigrant Theatre: New York City, 1840-1940*. Rochester: University of Rochester Press, 2009.

Kohn, Hans. *Prelude to Nation-State: The French and German Experience, 1789–1815*. Princeton, NJ: D. Van Nostrand Company, 1967.

Kurthen, Hermann. "Gone with the Wind: German Language Retention in North Carolina and the United States in Comparative Perspective." *Yearbook of German-American Studies* 33 (1998): 55–83.

Lawr, D.A., and R.D. Gidney, "Who Ran the Schools? Local Influence on Education Policy in Nineteenth-Century Ontario." *Ontario History* 72, 3 (1980): 131–43.

Lehmann, Hans. *The German Canadians, 1750–1937: Immigration, Settlement and Culture*. St. John's, NF: Jesperson Press, 1986.

Leibbrandt, Gottlieb. "100 Jahre Concordia." *German-Canadian Yearbook* 6 (1981).

———. "Jubilaeums-Ausgabe/Centennial Issue—Concordia Club." Concordia Club, Kitchener, ON, No. 57, August 1973.

———. *Little Paradise: Aus Geschichte und Leben der Deutschkanadier in der County Waterloo, Ontario, 1800–1975*. Kitchener, ON: Allprint Company Limited, 1977.

Lewis, Robert. "Street Culture." *Journal of American Studies* 23 (1989): 85–90.

Levine, Bruce. *The Spirit of 1848: German Immigrants, Labor Conflict, and the Coming of the Civil War*. Urbana and Chicago: University of Illinois Press, 1992.

Levine, Lawrence W. *Highbrow/Lowbrow: The Emergence of Cultural Hierarchy in America*. Cambridge, MA.: Harvard University Press, 1988.

Liebscher, Grit, and Mathias Schulze. "Language Use and Identity: Analysing Language Behaviour of German-Speaking Immigrants in Kitchener-Waterloo. Paper presented at the conference "Assimilation—Integration—Acculturation? The German-Canadian Case," University of Winnipeg, August 2004.

Litwicki, Ellen M. "'Our Hearts Burn with Ardent Love for Two Countries': Ethnicity and Assimilation at Chicago Holiday Celebrations, 1876–1918." *Journal of American Ethnic History* 19, 3 (2000): 3–34.

Loewen, Royden. *Diaspora in the Countryside: Two Mennonite Communities and Mid-Twentieth-Century Rural Disjunctions*. Urbana: University of Illinois Press, 2006.

———. *Family, Church, and Market: A Mennonite Community in the Old and New Worlds, 1850–1930*. Urbana: University of Illinois Press, 1993.

———. "'Hold Your Heads High in Your Usual Unassuming Manner': Making a Mennonite Middle Class Ethnicity in Steinbach, Manitoba and Meade, Kansas, 1945–1975." Paper presented at the conference "Assimilation—Integration—Acculturation? The German-Canadian Case," University of Winnipeg, August 2004.

Lorenzkowski, Barbara. "Making Music, Building Bridges: German-Canadian Identities in the Nation's Capital, 1958–1999." In *Construire une capitale—Ottawa—Making of a Capital*, edited by Jeff Keshen and Nicole St.-Onge, 307–30. Ottawa: University of Ottawa Press, 2001.

Luebke, Frederick C. "Legal Restrictions on Foreign Languages in the Great Plains States, 1917–1923." In *Languages in Conflict: Linguistic Acculturation on the Great Plains*, edited by Paul Schach, 1–19. Lincoln: University of Nebraska Press, 1980.

McKegney, Patricia. "The German Schools of Waterloo County, 1851–1913." *Waterloo Historical Society* 58 (1970): 54–67.

———. *The Kaiser's Bust: A Study of War-Time Propaganda in Berlin, Ontario, 1914–1918*. Wellesley, ON: Bamberg Heritage Series, 1991.

McLaughlin, Kenneth. *Waterloo: An Illustrated History*. Canada: Windsor Publications, 1990.

———. "Waterloo County: A Pennsylvania-German Homeland." In *From Pennsylvania to Waterloo: Pennsylvania-German Folk Culture in Transition*, edited by Susan M. Burke and Matthew H. Hill, 35–45. Waterloo: Wilfrid Laurier University Press, 1991.

Mason, Laura. *Singing the French Revolution: Popular Culture and Politics, 1787–1799*. Ithaca, NY: Cornell University Press, 1996.

Mazón, Patricia. "Germania Triumphant: The Niederwald National Monument and the Liberal Movement in Imperial Germany." *German History* 18, 2 (2000): 162–92.

Meyer, Doris. *Speaking for Themselves: Neomexicano Cultural Identity and the Spanish-Language Press, 1880–1920*. Albuquerque: University of New Mexico Press, 1996.

Mills, Rych, and the Victoria Park 100th Birthday Historical Committee. *Victoria Park: 100 Years of the Park and Its People: An Historical and Photographic Essay on Victoria Park*. Kitchener, ON: 1996.

Mosse, George L. *The Nationalization of the Masses: Political Symbolism and Mass Movements in Germany from the Napoleonic Wars through the Third Reich*. Ithaca, NY: Cornell University Press, 1975.

Mühl, Gunter. "Das Verhältnis der Arbeiter-Sänger zum bürgerlichen Gesangvereinswesen bis 1933." In *Illustrierte Geschichte der Arbeiterchöre*, edited by Rainer Noltenius, 65–71. Münster: Druckwerkstatt, 1992.

Nadel, Stanley. *Little Germany: Ethnicity, Religion, and Class in New York City, 1845–80*. Urbana and Chicago: University of Illinois Press, 1990.

Nora, Pierre. "The Era of Commemoration." In *Realms of Memory: The Construction of the French Past, Vol. III: Symbols*, ed. Pierre Nora, 609–37. New York: Columbia University Press, 1998.

Oergel, Maike. "The Redeeming Teuton: Nineteenth-Century Notions of the 'Germanic' in England and Germany." In *Imagining Nations*, edited by Geoffrey Cubitt, 75–91. Manchester: Manchester University Press, 1998.

O'Leary, Cecilia Elizabeth. *To Die For: The Paradox of American Patriotism*. Princeton, NJ: Princeton University Press, 1999.

Ostendorf, Bernd. "'The Diluted Second Generation': German-Americans in Music, 1870 to 1920." In *German Workers' Culture in the United States 1850 to 1920*, edited by Hartmut Keil, 261–87. Washington, DC: Smithsonian Institution Press, 1988.

Øverland, Orm. *Immigrant Minds, American Identities: Making the United States Home, 1870–1930*. Urbana and Chicago: University of Illinois Press, 2000.

Øverland, Orm, ed. *Not English Only: Redefining 'American' in American Studies*. Amsterdam: VU University Press, 2001.

Ozouf, Mona. *Festivals and the French Revolution*. Cambridge, MA: Harvard University Press, 1988 [1976].

Pekacz, Jolanta. *Music in the Culture of Polish Galicia, 1772–1914*. Rochester, NY: University of Rochester Press, 2002.

Peterson, Brent O. "How (and Why) to Read German-American Literature." In *The German-American Encounter: Conflict and Cooperation between Two Cultures, 1800–2000*, edited by Frank Trommler and Elliott Shore, 88–102. New York: Berghahn Books, 2001.

———. *Popular Narratives and Ethnic Identity: Literature and Community in* Die Abendschule. Ithaca, NY: Cornell University Press, 1991.

Pietsch, Rudolf. "Burgenland-American Music and the 'Ethnic Mainstream.'" In *Land without Nightingales: Music in the Making of German-America*, edited by Philip V. Bohlman and Otto Holzapfel, 258–93. Madison: University of Wisconsin-Madison, 2002.

Portes, Alejandro, and Richard Schauffler, "Language and the Second Generation: Bilingualism Yesterday and Today." *International Migration Review* 28, 4 (1994): 640–61.

Potter, Pamela M. *Most German of the Arts: Musicology and Society from the Weimar Republic to the End of Hitler's Reich*. New Haven, CT: Yale University Press, 1998.

Pratt, Mary Louise. *Imperial Eyes: Travel Writing and Transculturation*. London: Routledge, 1992.

Prokop, Manfred. *The German Language in Alberta*. Edmonton: University of Alberta Press, 1990.

Ramirez, Bruno. "Canada and the United States: Perspectives on Migration and Continental History." *Journal of American Ethnic Studies* 20, 3 (2001): 50–70.

———. *On the Move: French-Canadian and Italian Migrants in the North Atlantic Economy*. Toronto: McClelland and Stewart, 1991.

Ramirez, Bruno, and Yves Otis. *Crossing the 49th Parallel: Migration from Canada to the United States, 1900–1930*. Ithaca, NY: Cornell University Press, 2001.

Rath, Richard Cullen. *How Early America Sounded*. Ithaca, NY: Cornell University Press, 2003.

Reese, William J. "The Origins of Progressive Education," *History of Education Quarterly*, 41, 1 (2001): 1–24.

———. *Power and the Promise of School Reform: Grassroots Movements during the Progressive Era*. Boston: Routledge, 1986.

Reitz, Jeffrey G. "Language and Ethnic Community Survival." In *Ethnicity and Ethnic Relations in Canada*, edited by Rita M. Bienvenue and Jay E. Goldstein, 105–23. Toronto: Butterworths, 1985.

Riester, Michael A. "History of St. Louis RC Church." http://stlouisrc.bfn.org/tc.html.

Rippley, La Vern J. "Conflict in the Classroom: Anti-Germanism in Minnesota Schools, 1917–19." *Minnesota History* 47, 5 (1981): 170–83.

Rodgers, Daniel T. *Atlantic Crossings: Social Politics in a Progressive Age*. Cambridge, MA: Harvard University Press, 1998.

Roediger, David R. *The Wages of Whiteness: Race and the Making of the American Working Class*. London and New York: Verso, 1999 [1991].

Rose, Sonya. "Cultural Analysis and Moral Discourses: Episodes, Continuities, and Transformations." In *Beyond the Cultural Turn: New Directions in the Study of Society and Culture*, ed. Victoria E. Bonnell and Lynn Hunt, 217–38. Berkeley: University of California Press, 1999.

Ryan, Mary P. *Cradle of the Middle Class: The Family in Oneida County, New York, 1790–1865*. Cambridge: Cambridge University Press, 1984.

Rydell, Robert. *All the World's a Fair: Visions of Empire at American International Expositions, 1876–1916*. Chicago: University of Chicago Press, 1984.

Rydell, Robert, and John Findling, and Kimberly Pelle. *Fair America: World's Fairs in the United States* Washington: Smithsonian Institution Press, 2000.

Rydell, Robert, and Nancy Gwinn, eds. *Fair Representations: World's Fairs and the Modern World.* Amsterdam: VU University Press, 1994.

Sánchez, George. *Becoming Mexican American: Ethnicity, Culture and Identity in Chicano Los Angeles, 1900-1945.* New York: Oxford University Press, 1993.

Saxton, Alexander. *The Rise and Fall of the White Republic: Class Politics and Mass Culture in Nineteenth-Century America.* London and New York: Verso, 1990.

Schafer, R. Murray. *The Tuning of the World: Towards a Theory of Soundscape Design.* Philadelphia: University of Pennsylvania Press, 1980.

Schama, Simon. *Landscape and Memory.* London: Harper Collins, 1995.

Schiller, Nina Glick, et al. "Transnationalism: A New Analytical Framework for Understanding Migration." In *Towards a Transnational Perspective on Migration: Race, Class, Ethnicity, and Nationalism Reconsidered,* edited by Nina Glick Schiller, Linda Basch, and Christina Blanc-Szanton, 1–24. New York: New York Academy of Science, 1992.

Schlossman, Steven L. "'Is There an American Tradition of Bilingual Education?' German in the Public Elementary Schools, 1840–1919." *American Journal of Education* 91, 2 (1983): 139–86.

Schmoll, Friedemann. "Individualdenkmal, Sängerbewegung und Nationalbewußtsein in Württemberg: Zum Funktionswandel bürgerlicher Erinnerungskultur zwischen Vormärz und Kaiserreich." In *"Heil deutschem Wort und Sang!" Nationalidentität und Gesangkultur in der deutschen Geschichte—Tagungsbericht Feuchtwangen 1994,* edited by Friedhelm Brusniak and Dietmar Klenke. Augsburg: Bernd Wissner, 1995.

Schultz, April R. *Ethnicity on Parade: Inventing the Norwegian American through Celebration.* Amherst: University of Massachusetts Press, 1994.

———. "'The Pride of the Race Had Been Touched': The 1925 Norse-American Immigration Centennial and Ethnic Identity." *Journal of American History* 77, 4 (1991): 1265–95.

Scott, Derek B. "Music and Social Class in Victorian London." *Urban History* 29, 1 (2002): 60–73.

Shandler, Jeffrey. "Beyond the Mother Tongue: Learning the Meaning of Yiddish in America." *Jewish Social Studies* 6, 3 (2000): 97–123.

Shell, Marc. "Hyphens: Between Deitsch and American." In *Multilingual America: Transnationalism, Ethnicity, and the Languages of American Literature,* edited by Werner Sollors, 258–71. New York: New York University Press, 1998.

Smith, Anthony D. "National Identity and Myths of Ethnic Descent." *Research in Social Movements, Conflict and Change* 7 (1984): 95–130.

Smith, Bruce. *The Acoustic World of Early Modern England.* Chicago: University of Chicago Press, 1999.

Smith, Mark M. "Echoes in Print: Method and Causation in Aural History." *Journal of the Historical Society* 2, 3–4 (2002): 317–36.

Smith, Mark M. *Listening to Nineteenth-Century America.* Chapel Hill: University of North Carolina Press, 2001.

———. "Listening to the Heard Worlds of Antebellum America." *Journal of the Historical Society* 1 (June 2000): 63–97.

Smith, Mark M., ed. *Hearing History: A Reader.* Athens: University of Georgia Press, 2004.

Smolicz, Jerzy J. "Minority Languages and Core Values of Ethnic Cultures: A Study of Maintenance and Erosion of Polish, Welsh, and Chinese Languages in Australia." In *Maintenance and Loss of Minority Languages*, edited by Willem Fase, Koen Jaspaert, Sjaak Kroon, 277–306. Amsterdam and Philadelphia: John Benjamins Publishing Company, 1992.

Snyder, Suzanne Gail. "The *Männerchor* Tradition in the United States: An Historical Analysis of Its Contribution to American Musical Culture." PhD diss., University of Iowa, 1991.

Sollors, Werner. *Beyond Ethnicity: Consent and Descent in American Culture*. New York: Oxford University Press, 1986.

———. "How German Is It? Multilingual America Reconsidered." In *Not English Only: Redefining "American" in American Studies*, edited by Orm Øverland. Amsterdam: VU University Press, 2001.

———. *Multilingual America: Transnationalism, Ethnicity, and the Languages of American Literature*. New York: New York University Press, 1998.

Sommer, Doris. "Choose and Lose." In *Multilingual America: Transnationalism, Ethnicity, and the Languages of American Literature*, ed. Werner Sollors, 297–309. New York: New York University Press, 1998.

Spencer, Vicki. "Herder and Nationalism: Reclaiming the Principle of Cultural Respect." *Australian Journal of Politics and History* 43, 1 (1997): 1-13.

———. "Towards an Ontology of Holistic Individualism: Herder's Theory of Identity, Culture and Community." *History of European Ideas* 22, 3 (1996): 245–60.

Sperber, Jonathan. "Festivals of National Unity in the German Revolution of 1848–1849." *Past and Present* 136 (1992): 114–38.

Stallybrass, Peter, and Allon White. *The Politics and Poetics of Transgression*. London: Methuen, 1986.

Stanforth, Anthony W. *Deutsche Einflüsse auf den englischen Wortschatz in Geschichte und Gegenwart, mit einem Beitrag zum Amerikanischen Englisch von Jürgen Eichhoff*. Tübingen: Niemeyer, 1996.

Strohm, R. *Music in Late Medieval Bruges*. Oxford: Clarendon Press, 1985.

Sutherland, Neil. *Children in English-Canadian Society: Framing the Twentieth-Century Consensus*. Toronto: University of Toronto Press, 1976.

———. "The Urban Child." *History of Education Quarterly* 9, 3 (1969): 305–11.

Swidinsky, Robert, and Michael Swidinsky. "The Determinants of Heritage Language Continuity in Canada: Evidence from the 1981 and 1991 Census." *Canadian Ethnic Studies* 29, 1 (1997): 81–98.

Thelen, David. "Of Audiences, Borderlands, and Comparisons: Toward the Internationalization of American History." *Journal of American History* 79, 2 (1992): 432–62.

Toth, Carolyn R. *German-English Bilingual Schools in America: The Cincinnati Tradition in Historical Context*. New York: Peter Lang, 1990.

Trommler, Frank, and Joseph Mc Veigh, eds., *America and the Germans: An Assessment of a Three-Hundred-Year History*. Vol. 1, *Immigration, Language, Ethnicity*. Philadelphia: University of Pennsylvania Press, 1985.

Tyack, David. *The One Best System: A History of American Urban Education*. Cambridge, MA: Harvard University Press, 1974.

———. "Pilgrim's Progress: Toward a Social History of the School Superintendency, 1860–1960." *History of Education Quarterly* 16, 3 (1976): 257–300.

Uttley, W.V. *A History of Kitchener*. Waterloo: Wilfrid Laurier University Press, 1985 [1937].

Verdery, Katherine. "Whither 'Nation' and 'Nationalism'?" In *Mapping the Nation*, edited by Gopal Balakrishnan, 226–34. London and New York: Verso, 1996.

Vitz, Robert C. "Starting a Tradition: The First Cincinnati May Musical Festival," *Cincinnati Historical Society Bulletin* 38, 1 (1985): 33–50.

Walden, Keith. *Becoming Modern in Toronto: The Industrial Exhibition and the Shaping of a Late Victorian Culture*. Toronto: University of Toronto Press, 1997.

Waldstreicher, David. *In the Midst of Perpetual Fetes: The Making of American Nationalism, 1776–1820*. Chapel Hill: University of North Carolina Press, 1997.

———. "Rites of Rebellion, Rites of Assent: Celebrations, Print Culture, and the Origins of American Nationalism." *Journal of American History* 82, 1 (1995): 37–61.

Weber, Eugen. *Peasants into Frenchmen: The Modernization of Rural France, 1870–1914*. London: Chatto and Windus, 1977.

Welsh, David. "Early Franco-Ontarian Schooling as a Reflection and Creator of Community Identity." *Ontario History* 85, 4 (1993): 312–47.

White, Clinton O. "Pre–World War I Saskatchewan German Catholic Thought Concerning the Perpetuation of their Language and Religion." *Canadian Ethnic Studies* 26, 2 (1994): 15–45.

Widdis, Randy William. *With Scarcely a Ripple: Anglo-Canadian Migration into the United States and Western Canada, 1880–1920*. Montreal: McGill-Queen's University Press, 1998.

Wittke, Carl. *The German-Language Press in America*. New York: Haskell House Publishers, 1973 [1957].

———. *Refugees of the Revolution: The German Forty-Eighters in America*. Westport, CT: Greenwood Press, 1952.

Yox, Andrew. "Decline of the German-American Community in Buffalo, 1855–1925." PhD diss., University of Chicago, 1983.

———. "The German-American Community as a Nationality, 1880–1940." *Yearbook of German-American Studies* 36 (2001): 181–93.

Zimmerman, Jonathan. "Ethnics against Ethnicity: European Immigrants and Foreign-Language Instruction, 1890–1940." *Journal of American History* 88, 4 (2002): 1383–1404.

Zucker, A.E. *The Forty-Eighters: Political Refugees of the German Revolution of 1848*. New York: Russell and Russell, 1967 [1950].

Index